composition paragraph	good sentences	diction	grammar and usage
1a, b Plan purpose & plan	**7a, b SU/Sub** sentence unity; subordination	**10 D/Dict** use of the dictionary	**15** American English
1c Plan/Org organizing	**8a Scoh ‖** sentence coherence: parallelism	**11 D/Use** levels of usage	**16-19** sentence elements; types
2 Org/Outl outline	**8b Scoh/Ref** Reference	**12a-d D/exD** exact diction	**20, 21 Frag/** sentence **CS** fragments; comma splices
3 Log logic	**8c, d Scoh/ Dng/MM** dangling and misplaced modifiers	**12e D/exD/ use of Id** idiom	
4a, c ¶ U paragraph division, and length			**22 Def** definitions of grammatical terms
4b ¶ U/topic S topic sentence	**8e Scoh/Shift** confusing shift	**13a-c D/efD** effective diction	
5 ¶ Coh paragraph coherence	**8f Scoh/Mix** mixed constructions	**13d D/efD/** figures **Fig** and allusions	**23 Agr** agreement
6 ¶ Dev paragraph development	**8g Scoh/ Const** incomplete constructions	**13e D/efD/** awkward **Rep** repetition	**24 Ca** case
			25 Adj/Adv adjectives and adverbs
	9 S/Emp/w emphasis: weak and wordy sentences	**14 Use/gl** glossary of misuse	**26 T** tense and mode of verbs

RHETORIC

HANDBOOK

college
handbook of
composition

SEVENTH EDITION

HEATH'S *college*
handbook
of composition

Langdon Elsbree

Claremont Men's College

Frederick Bracher

Pomona College

D. C. Heath and Company **Boston**

The copyright notices of works used as illustrative material cannot be legibly accommodated here; they appear immediately following the index.

publisher's preface

The Seventh Edition of this *Handbook* presents a new and distinctive treatment of language, logic, and rhetoric within the compact format of a rapid reference guide to practical questions of usage. The newly developed first half of the book combines with material from previous editions to make an entirely rearranged, expanded, and redesigned *Handbook* that strives to take full account of changing views on grammar, usage, and style. At the same time, the *Handbook* retains the basic aim of previous editions: to give plain and unequivocal answers to the problems students actually encounter in their writing.

The new design of this edition has been planned to give students readier access to material of proven value in previous editions, to help simplify the instructor's marking of papers, and to present compactly some new basic material that teachers find helpful in a handbook. Mr. Bracher, author of the Sixth Edition of the *College Handbook of Composition* (Woolley, Scott, and Bracher), has contributed to the Seventh in planning its rearrangement and in writing a comprehensive new unit on the development of English, and Mr. Elsbree has contributed in rewriting and adding material throughout the edition. The resulting *Handbook* is intended to offer the combined advantages of thorough coverage in composition with concise treatment of practical writing problems.

authors'
acknowledgments

In preparing the Seventh Edition of this *Handbook,* the authors have been greatly helped by various colleagues and readers.

The authors owe thanks to W. Nelson Francis of Brown University and Donald Lee of the University of Houston for readings of the chapter on history and development of English; for readings and useful criticism of other chapters they owe thanks to Wayne Harsh of the University of California at Davis; to S. Leonard Rubinstein of Pennsylvania State University; to Woodrow Ohlsen of Pasadena City College; to Hubert M. English of the University of Michigan; Glen A. Love of the University of Oregon; Frank B. Moake of the University of Illinois; Duane C. Nichols of Kansas State University; Mary Purcell of California State College at Long Beach; to Bain T. Stewart of the University of Tennessee.

The authors especially wish to thank Robert Fossum, Hal Painter, and Ladell Payne of Claremont Men's College for advice and examples; George Wickes of Harvey Mudd College for examples; Howard Houston for materials in the library chapter; Gordon Wilson of Miami University, Ohio, for a critical reading of five chapters and for permission to use examples from Miami students; also Virginia McDavid of Chicago Teachers College for criticism of the Sixth Edition; and Devra Kifer of Skidmore College for detailed, careful criticism of the Sixth Edition with planning and suggestions for the Seventh.

Finally, special thanks are given to Allen Workman of D. C. Heath for major editorial help and to Aimee Elsbree, who typed the manuscript and helped revise several chapters.

L.E.

F.B.

contents

rhetoric

THE COMPOSITION AS A WHOLE

1 purpose and plan in writing

2 outlining

3 logic

THE PARAGRAPH

GOOD SENTENCES

RESEARCH AND CORRESPONDENCE

rhetoric

1 *purpose and plan in writing*
a the defining circumstances
b restricting the topic
c organizing the material

2 *outlining*
a uses of the formal outline
b types of formal outlines
c conventions of the topic and the sentence outline

3 *logic: the form and substance of reasoning*
a analysis of an argument's structure
b validity of the argument offered

1

purpose and plan in writing

This handbook is to help you deal with the kinds of writing you will be doing in college and to a great extent afterward. The composition course in many colleges is partly designed, in the terms educators often use, as a "service course," to teach you the techniques of exposition, analysis, and persuasion that are essential in college for writing tests and reports and term papers. At the same time, the basic writing skills and habits you acquire in the composition course should be the ones that set standards useful to you not only in college but in your professional career. However, no composition course, and no Handbook like this one, can by itself "teach" a student simply and automatically how to write well. Both the course and the Handbook make an orderly presentation of the problems and challenges you meet in your college and professional reading and writing, and of some worthwhile ways of dealing with these challenges. It may be helpful to remember that the composition course is not set up like a track meet, merely for forcing you to hurdle a fixed number of themes; rather it is an opportunity for increased mastery of yourself through increased control of the language you use for expressing ideas and feelings. The level and standard of language mastery you can strive to achieve is more fully discussed at the end of chapter 15.

Plan

1
a

This Handbook begins with the most common problem you will face in all your college writing: choosing and limiting your topic.

1 a
the defining circumstances

For all writing that matters, there are certain defining circumstances which, though obvious once we are reminded of them, are fundamental to the choice and restriction of subject. These circumstances are the *intended audience,* the *nature and purpose of the project,* and the *writer's point of view.* They are the context for writing, and they should be fully understood. In many cases, your success with a particular composition, report, or term paper will depend largely upon a full awareness of these circumstances.

1 a-1
the intended audience

The more conscious a writer is of his audience, the more confident he will be in the choice and handling of his topic. Personal letters are one of the clearest examples. If you are writing your parents about a forthcoming party and the money you need for it, you probably know them well enough to figure whether complaints about book and clothing costs, frankness about an inadequate budget, or wheedling about another lonely weekend is the best tack. If you are writing a friend at another college, you mingle your impression of teachers and classmates, your private fears and hopes, and gossip about other friends according to your shared interests and memories, your basis for friendship. If you are writing a "Dear John" letter, you know your audience only too well; your problem is not one of topic but of tact.

What holds for personal letters also holds, in more complicated ways, for college and professional writing: when you have a writing project, determine as exactly as you can the audience for whom it is intended, not in order to appeal to the narrowest prejudices or stock responses you can find (any intelligent reader will spot such appeals, and in any case you can never be sure of knowing your audience better than it knows itself or you), but for a more useful purpose. You need to know *what information and attitudes you can take for granted in your audience and what you cannot.* This is necessary not only to economize your effort and the audience's, by keeping to topics the audience needs or wants to know about, but also to be sure that your approach does not antagonize by placing emphasis on the wrong or unnecessary parts of an argument, or by using a level or style of language that is unfamiliar or unpleasant to your audience.

In a composition class, for example, you should beware of seeing your audience merely as an anonymous reader without personality. You can probably assume that the hypothetical "reader" is not only your instructor but also your classmates, since themes may well be read aloud or passed out in printed form from time to time. Your classmates, having read the same assignments you have, need not be bored with long summaries when evaluation is called for; having the same texts in front of them, they can check the accuracy of your statements.

If you aim your arguments at the kind of scepticism you find in your classmates, and let your preferences make a point to the best intelligence among them, you are likely to find fresh excitement for yourself in the kinds of ideas and topics you present.

1 a-2
the nature of the project

The degree of freedom you have in choosing the topic and developing it is determined by the nature and purpose of the writing project. If the project is a personal letter to get money from parents, you must choose a topic and material that will point convincingly to your unexpected need for funds. Since it is a letter, you will probably not write a formal essay on the high cost of living, and you will probably be careful not to exhaust patience with a tediously long message or sound

Plan

arrogant with a discourteously curt one. If the project is a newspaper assignment to cover a dance of some social importance, you probably will be careful to spend at least as much time commenting on the people attending as on the quality of the music or entertainment.

In your college writing projects, you meet at one extreme the most limiting kind of assignment—test or examination questions, for instance—where you have little if any choice in topic or desirable development. But even in these cases you can broaden your view of the restrictions considerably, and open up the topic in a promising direction by turning the stated assignment into a question. Thus, if you are directed to "Discuss the changes in Huck's friendship with Jim and what these changes signify," you can minimize wandering and point your thinking in a profitable direction by turning the statement into a question: "What changes did develop, and what was their significance?" At this point it will be helpful to take stock of the length and nature of the assignment in order to decide how far the topic should be opened up. As you break down the available material, and arrange it analytically in your mind, you will see a great many directions for expansion (e.g., obviously Huck Finn's friendship with Jim changed at almost every incident), as well as many differences in relative importance among the directions that could be taken. In this process, as you answer the questions of significance, you will find that you are beginning to formulate a main thesis idea for your project (see section 1b-3). If the assignment is quite limited, you will have to meet it exactly in short scope, picking only the very few most significant aspects.

On the other hand, if the assignment is a longer composition, your coverage of the topic may allow you to include more of the material available to you, and to expand the scope of the topic to present a more complex thesis idea. For a composition out of class, you should expect to have time to gain considerable familiarity with the topic, or at least with an aspect of it that interests you, so that you may choose an area for writing that can be honestly and competently covered within the reach of knowledge you can bring to the project.

Plan

Much of your written work in college courses will not be very narrowly restricted, however. The usual college assignment is a short paper or term paper focusing on an important aspect of your reading, or sometimes developing an original argument applying principles discussed in the course. For all college assignments, you can save yourself needless fretting by following two commonplace but often ignored principles:

First, *be certain you understand the instructions*. Too often, students passively listen to an assignment, copy down a few random directions, and then discover the night before the paper is due that they have no clear idea of what is called for. Are you called upon to summarize an author's views, to examine his evidence in detail, or to evaluate and criticize? Most instructors welcome clarifying questions, but if there are none, they can only assume their directions are understood. One useful technique is to restate your understanding of the assignment in your own words. By listening to your version, the teacher can often discover your misunderstandings or the ambiguities in his own instructions.

Second, *regard the suggested length of the paper as an approximate indication, not as a magical number or end in itself*. When your instructor says "A 500-word theme," he is giving an approximate length. He doesn't have the time to count the words and then penalize the student who has 490 or 510. The problem is not really one of words at all; it is rather the challenge of adapting the subject to the space at your disposal. If a preliminary outline shows that you can't treat four points fully in 500 words, limit yourself to three points, or two. If what you have to say takes only 200 words, see if you can expand the topic (see above). *After* you have a usable rough draft, you can begin necessary cutting or expanding.

1 a-3
the writer's point of view

Of all the defining circumstances, the writer's point of view is the most important, and the most difficult to discuss. It is *not*

Plan

simply the gimmick, the "angle" on a subject so often recommended by professional writing magazines. Novelty may be a result of the writer's viewpoint, but when it is an end itself it too often leads to straining for effects—the kind of effects satirized in Thurber's story of the student who skyrocketed into journalism with the lead, "Who has noticed the sores on the tops of the horses in the animal husbandry building?"

Essentially, the writer's point of view refers to *his* particular interest in a general topic, the significance he finds in the material. It means frankness and completeness in thinking about a topic. To write is to act, to behave; to know your viewpoint is to give your writing—your behavior—purpose and direction.

Take, for example, the time-worn assignment of writing on one's reasons for coming to college. Predictably for some students, the writer's point of view here will be identical with a vague "public" point of view, taken second-hand from a college catalogue or an adviser's remarks: they have come to college to better themselves, to prepare for a vocation about which they don't know very much, to make more money, or to spend four pleasant years of social life. All of these reasons may well be "true" enough as far as they go, but they are also likely to be uninteresting and uninformative. None of them explains why a particular student chose a particular college. In reality, it may have been the pressure of parents (gentle or otherwise), the exaggerations of friends and teachers, an habitual expectation or belief that "it's the thing to do," or the mere fact of being accepted that led a given student to a given college. *Your* reason for coming to college, if you examine it concretely, has been influenced by *particular* people, school experiences, or private hopes. Your specific reason, in this case, determines your point of view as writer. Whenever you have some freedom of topic, *you should try to be honest with yourself by looking for an aspect of the general topic that interests you, or at least gives you enough live concern to ask questions about it and seek informative answers*. Even in a limited topic, you can spot a problem somewhere that appeals to you as worth solving. The effort will make your writing

Plan

far more interesting than if you treat the assignment as an exercise in platitudes and conventional sentiments.

SUMMARY

The intended audience, the nature and purpose of the project, and the writer's point of view help determine the choice of subject and its treatment. By knowing as much as you can about these defining circumstances, you can write with greater meaning and pleasure. The following exercises are designed for limbering up. Carry them out in as much detail as will give you satisfactory control of the topic.

EXERCISES

a. For each of the intended audiences listed below, decide what information and attitudes you could take for granted and what you would have to emphasize in writing on the assigned topic.

1. The significance of free speech on campus, written to the Dean of Freshmen.
2. The significance of free speech on campus, written as a report for incoming freshmen.
3. The morality of universal military training, for students in the ROTC program.
4. The morality of universal military training, for a student group of conscientious objectors.
5. The effects of dormitory design on students, for freshman English.
6. The effects of dormitory design on students, for a group of art teachers.
7. The used car market—or racket, for a theme in freshman English.
8. The used car market—or racket, for a satire in a literary annual.
9. The right of college students to protest, for freshman English.
10. The right of college students to protest, for PTA discussion group.

Plan

b. Given the following assignments, decide which are self-explanatory and manageable within the suggested length, and which you would need to ask about before writing. For the ambiguous topics, phrase the clarifying questions you would want to ask.

1. Chinese-American Relationships, 10 pages.
2. Chinese-American Relationships Since 1945, 10 pages.
3. The Pleasure of Singing Folk Songs, 3 pages.
4. The Popularity of Folk Songs, 3 pages.
5. An Impression of a County Fair, 3 pages.
6. Popular Myths about the Small Town, 3 pages.
7. The Scientific Method, 5 pages.
8. The Abuses of the Scientific Method in TV Commercials, 5 pages.
9. The Impact of Automation on America, 10 pages.
10. The Impact of Automation on American Education, 10 pages.
11. The Differences between Comedy and Satire, 3 pages.
12. Dating as a Characteristic American Phenomenon, 3 pages.

c. Examine the following list of general subjects, and for each subject jot down at least two specific subtopics you could include in a paper of 800-1,000 words. Now analyze your choices candidly. Which are stale, safe repetitions of what others have said or everyone knows? About which do you have a distinct, genuine point of view?

1. Racial Prejudice in High School
2. The Desirability of Selective Admissions to State Colleges
3. A Child's View of TV Violence
4. The Grading System as an Obstacle to Education
5. The Treatment of the New Deal in History Texts
6. America's Preoccupation with the Teenager
7. Should Women Have a Different College Curriculum from Men?
8. The Power of Tragedy in the Theatre and in Life
9. Camping in the National Parks and Monuments

Plan

1 b
restricting the topic

As your experience with the preceding exercises may have suggested, no simple, easy formula exists for restricting your topic, still less for the actual writing of the paper. The waste baskets and the diaries of even the most experienced professional writers are proof enough. Nevertheless, you can learn to shape your haphazard ideas and half-remembered evidence into a coherent whole by remembering certain principles of organization—principles which underlie most clear thinking. These principles may strike you as being rather mechanical, as in fact they are. Yet they are valuable precisely because they require you to introduce order into your thinking. The more skilled you become in your writing, the less you will need, consciously, to rely on them; ideally, they will become a habitual part of your approach to writing. These principles concern the restriction of the topic and the organization of the main body of the paper.

While it often helps to be aware of your audience, your assignment's specifications, and your point of view, you may sometimes find your mind does not easily focus on a well-defined topic. The necessary stimulus must come from analysis: pose a problem and then break it down into its parts. For many students, the best start in this process is the *statement of purpose,* a single declarative sentence which states the general intention of the paper.

1 b-1
the statement of purpose

Such sentences as "This paper will discuss the purposes and the organization of the Lewis and Clark expedition," "This paper explains how to resurface a kitchen floor," "This paper

Plan

discusses the value of student government," and "This paper discusses what Riesman means by the paradox of 'The Lonely Crowd'" are all statements of purpose. Statements like these should not be allowed to pass for thesis statements (see section 1b-3), but they serve a very useful function. They may seem simple to formulate—sometimes they may be no more than the instructor's directions—yet they do focus upon the real task, the discovery of the specific topic. Even though the exact content is unspecified by these statements of purpose, at least the writer has fixed his mind upon a problem, a potential question—What are the major steps in resurfacing? the values of student government? (see section 1a-2, "the nature of the project"). He has made himself a promise to find out something. He is ready to begin the second step, an analysis of his statement of purpose.

1 b-2
the analysis

For the short paper of 500–1000 words, a brief series of jotted-down ideas and details may be sufficient. For the research or critical paper of ten or more pages, a formal outline may be necessary (see chapter 2). In either case, *the function of the analysis is to separate ideas completely enough so that the writer can begin to see his main outline*. Like the factoring of a mathematical equation, analysis isolates the parts of the whole and shows the relationships among these parts. Analysis is essential to the short paper because it discriminates between relevant and irrelevant material; it is essential to the long paper because it identifies areas where research is needed and evidence required. We shall postpone until the next chapter the discussion of formal outlining as one kind of analysis.

Let us examine two different statements of purpose and the analysis each might entail. The first of these, not always the easiest, is the autobiographical essay. Suppose that you have been asked to write on why you are going to college, and that you have narrowed the topic and constructed an appropriate statement of purpose, "The intention of this paper is to

Plan

discuss what I expect to get out of college." The trial analysis might run:

Types of Goals	*Specific Objectives*
Vocational	Training for engineering or teaching —not certain since did well in high school science courses (physics and chemistry esp. interesting) and family encourages it, but also have liked working with people (camp jobs, Scouts)—don't know for sure, and don't want to be pushed.
Social	Some fun and new friends—chance to meet people from other parts of the country, keep up old friendships but not be tied to them—be on own in choosing dates, groups, etc.
Intellectual	Balance of liberal arts and job training?—don't know, except that best courses in h. s. were most thorough (physics, American history)— maybe more history (remember Wilcox's lecture on why Puritans thought they had good reason for killing witches and punishing Quakers) and maybe more psychology (had a little in Personal Hygiene course).
Personal	Mainly to be independent in choosing friends, courses, activities, and to find out whether teaching or engineering what I want.

Reviewing this analysis, you begin to see that the first three categories are all subordinate to the fourth, that what is expected from college is personal independence to discover

Plan

friends and profession alike. On further thought, you realize what the writer really expects is freedom—enough distance between himself and well-meaning relatives, between himself and the high school cliques and fashions, between himself and earlier courses and activities, to make his own choices independently. You now see a central idea (*a thesis*) to develop as a basis for choosing certain details and eliminating others; for example, the detail about Wilcox's lecture would be irrelevant to the thesis.

For the second example, suppose you have been asked to model your paper after a reading assignment in which the author examined the main characters in *Lord of the Flies,* concluded they were created to startle the kind of reader who idealizes sportsmanship in boys, and criticized the sentimentality which makes such readers possible. Your choice for discussion might be Steinbeck's *Grapes of Wrath;* your analysis might run:

Types of Characters	*Implied Reader and Criticism*
Joad family—poor "Okie" farmers forced to go to California, mostly victims of events (Tom, grandparents)—try to stick together & keep going (Ma) & see value in group (Tom, Casy). Are better than money-minded who use them.	People unaware of dustbowl poverty & consequences; maybe who think Okies stupid and lazy; readers needing message about value of sticking together & seeing common hardships. Is all of this obvious to us now?

Reviewing this sample analysis, you can now choose. You may decide that Steinbeck's Joad family is not just a collection of period characters, not just created for dramatizing the shocking effects of the dust bowl. They are also intended to show the reader the selflessness of people who suffer together. The question at the end (Is all of this obvious to us now?) may become a thesis—that Steinbeck's intended audience may be those who

Plan

are ignorant or unthinking about poverty and the down-trodden unity of the poor.

Note that the *process of analysis* for this assignment has several distinct parts. They are:

(1) *Break the statement of purpose down into several categories* (Types of Characters; Implied Reader and Criticism). Usually, you won't need more than four or five such categories.

(2) Under these categories, list evidence, illustrations, or arguments. While any of the lists under "Specific Objectives" or "Types of Characters" could be extended, they at least bring concreteness, relationships, and questions to the general headings.

(3) *Review the analysis for dominant impression or idea.* If the analysis has been done with any thought, it ought to imply or reveal a thesis—for example the thesis that Steinbeck's potential audience is readers who are insensitive to poverty and have no concept of the downtrodden unity of the poor. You are now ready to phrase your thesis.

1 b-3
the thesis

The thesis is a single, unambiguous sentence which expresses the central argument or idea the paper is to develop. The statement of purpose declares the writer's general intention (that he will discuss what he expects to get out of college); the thesis states his basic idea (that he wants enough freedom from the past to make his choices independently). Although it may take you a considerable amount of analysis (see the preceding section) and even writing to develop the thesis, the final statement of it is often put in the first paragraph of the composition, where it serves as a useful point of reference for you as writer and a guide for the reader. The insistence by many instructors, almost nagging at times, that you include a clear statement of thesis at the beginning of the paper is for your benefit to help you determine whether a particular fact, idea or paragraph should be included.

Most importantly, it is not vague. Such sentences as,

Plan

"Football is an *exciting* game," "During my summer vacation I had *some very interesting* and *educational experiences*," and "High school plays offer *many excellent opportunities* and *beneficial aspects* to the aspiring actor" are useless as theses. Note that the offending italicized phrases do not commit the writer to anything specific, do not give him any real control over his subject. He still has to decide by analysis what is "exciting" about football (the variety of plays? body contact? the dramatic run? the crowds and cheerleaders?) and to whom (spectators? players? both? always?). Unless he faces the task of thinking analytically toward a thesis, his writing will probably wander from impression to impression as he tries to make up his mind about what he does mean. When you find yourself tempted (very humanly) to bypass the thesis by tossing in a meaningless phrase, go back, re-examine your analysis, and try for the sharply-worded sentence. If you are not an avid football fan, you may end up with something like "For the average football spectator, the long run makes up for all the dull line play" or "Last summer, while visiting several Indian reservations to watch the traditional corn dances, I learned how it feels to be both a welcome guest and an intruder."

A clear thesis often contains within it an implied pattern of development. For example, the thesis "For the average football spectator the long run makes up for all the dull line play" suggests the pattern of comparison and contrast: first the description of the spectator's boredom during a quarter filled with two-yard plunges and shoving linemen, then the description of his excitement during the few seconds he is on his feet to watch the long run. A vague or disunified thesis, however, contains no implied pattern of development. Your thesis, once it is formulated from your analytic thinking or writing, becomes the foundation of your paper. When it is formulated accurately, the rest of the paper becomes easier to plan.

SUMMARY

The suggested sequence for restricting a topic includes the statement of purpose, the trial analysis, and the phrasing of

Plan

the thesis. Particularly important are the trial analysis and the thesis, since they actively engage you in your subject. The following exercises are intended to give you such experience.

EXERCISES

a. Select an essay from a book used in your course or an article from a magazine like *Scientific American, Harper's* or *The New York Times Sunday Magazine* and state what seems to be its thesis. Then see if a trial analysis can be made to determine what kind of categories or distinctions the writer used in planning his article.

b. From the list below, select five subjects. Analyze each subject and by writing a restricted thesis, narrow each of the five to a topic which might be managed in a theme of 500-700 words.

1. How to get a summer job.
2. How to succeed in classes without really trying.
3. How to adjust to a new high school (or in a new community).
4. How to enjoy an art exhibit.
5. How to read an editorial.
6. What is revealed by the trends in popular music?
7. What is the appeal of *Mad Magazine* and its imitators?
8. What are the dangers of censorship?
9. What are the advantages (or disadvantages) of federal health insurance?
10. What is meant by "a fact" in history?

c. The following are typical student theses. Many of them are unclear and lack focus on a well-defined argument. Revise the weak ones so that they could serve as the basis for a 500-700 word paper. Assume that you may be asked to use one of your revisions as the thesis for a paper.

1. During my first week in college, I was very impressed by many things, but the most surprising single factor to me was the variety of students.

Plan

2. In choosing a career, one has to decide what he wants to be.

3. This essay will deal with the advisability of foreign aid and the standards for picking the countries which need it.

4. To get a fundamental understanding of people, you have to study their philosophy, background, and motives.

5. Loyalty oaths are a very controversial subject and have good and bad aspects.

6. Too many Americans count their chickens before they hatch when it comes to the stock market.

7. My uncle is the most colorful and unusual person I know.

8. In my opinion Macbeth is a play which is very difficult to understand.

9. This paper is about some slang terms and the college students who use them, because that is what the instructor assigned.

10. People who don't get along with others have wrong attitudes.

11. To win any kind of election, you have to consider all phases of the situation in order to get popular support.

12. The important factor to a student's success in college is learning how to study the right way.

13. To learn tennis, you have to master the fundamentals of the game.

14. Materialism is a terrible threat to the American way of life, and it comes about because of the movies and TV.

15. There is an old saying that "It takes two to make a fight" and this is true when you apply this saying to us and Russia.

16. The right to choose your religion and the right to vote for your candidate are the same because they depend on the willingness of other people to let you do so, and without the agreement of other people there wouldn't be these rights.

d. Having finished exercise c, pick one of the thesis statements that seems satisfactory (either before or after revision) and, adhering faithfully to it as a thesis, do an analysis and rough outline of the theme it would lead you to write.

1 c
organizing the material

A clear thesis may precede or grow out of the processes of collecting and organizing your material. The sooner your thesis is developed, the easier these processes will be. While there will always be a few students who write well off the tops of their heads, for most students planning is essential. Again, at the risk of seeming mechanical, we can divide these processes of organizing the material into several steps: 1) the gathering and evaluating of material; 2) the grouping of ideas together; 3) the arranging and proportioning of the material.

1 c-1
gathering and evaluating material

If your trial analysis is at all thorough, you should have most of the ideas and details necessary for a short paper and some estimate of what investigation or research will be needed for a long paper. The techniques of formal outlining, note-taking, and bibliography required by the long paper will be discussed in later chapters; for the short paper of 600 words which still lacks materials after your trial analysis, there are several aids. The first of these is a *rough but full list* of ideas, assertions, and illustrations, as full as you can make it within the boundaries set by the thesis. To give a very simple illustration, a project involving a physical process of gathering and organizing, let us take the general topic "how to resurface a kitchen floor." The listing might begin:

1. Must have a smooth surface to work on
2. Plastic tile ideal covering: waterproof and stainproof
3. Wood must continually be painted or varnished
4. Cork absorbs grease too easily, also expensive

Plan

5. Sheet linoleum too stiff to handle
6. Must lay adjacent tiles with pattern at right angles
7. If covering a wooden floor, sand it and coat with sealer
8. Water-proof cement advisable, tiles applied when sticky

And so on until the itemizing is complete. *Whenever you are writing a paper that describes or analyzes a process* ("How To . . ."; lab reports; procedures used for selecting candidates, students, or juries), *you are especially well-advised to list the individual steps and the reasons for them.* Once you have these steps, you can place them in order and eliminate the less important, but you must include them *all* to do so.

At this point, you must reconsider your topic, your audience, and your potential purpose, argument, and thesis. You need to narrow your topic partly on the basis of the character of the readers; it makes a difference whether they are perplexed but concerned house-owners, or perhaps students working at a summer job with minimum concern or effort. Several topics are available from the material, and several theses could be developed from them: The qualifications of a floor refinisher; the kinds of materials a refinisher should choose; three efficient ways of refinishing a floor. Your decision in narrowing the topic, and your formulation of a clear and well-pointed thesis idea, ("Floor refinishing makes an easy kind of summer work if you know how to handle materials efficiently") will determine what you do with the collected items—which you will eliminate and which you will develop in detail.

One way of testing your project, particularly if it is an argument or evaluation of something, is to ask a classmate what seems wrong with your argument. By stating your case aloud, you may notice some unexamined assumptions and unsupported assertions or have them pointed out to you. Perhaps even more important, you may discover the most effective way of building your argument by being forced to defend your position.

1 c-2
grouping ideas

Often the material will determine what order is best and what main headings you should have in your working outline. For example, after reviewing his list on resurfacing a kitchen floor, a writer might note that the items fall naturally under three main headings:

I. Materials
II. Preparations
III. Laying the tile

To take a more complicated example, the writer who expected college to give him freedom to choose might convert his trial analysis into the outline for his paper (see chapter 2):

I. Hope for freedom to make choices
II. Vocational choices
III. Social choices
IV. Intellectual choices
V. Personal choices

But there are other possibilities. As the trial analysis revealed, the other types of choices are subordinated under the personal. If the paper were written from the above outline, the reader would be misled into thinking these types of choices were of equal importance. A more accurate outline—one that spells out his thesis with the intended emphasis—might be:

I. Hope for enough personal freedom from the past to make clear choices
II. Distance from relatives
       To make up mind between engineering and teaching
           Family encourages engineering
           But have worked with people, and liked them, in camp and Scout jobs

Plan

To choose courses without outside pressure
    Have done well in physics and chemistry
    But might like more work in history and psychology
III. Distance from high school groups
    To choose new friends and views
    To keep up old friendships on more relaxed basis
        Escape high school habit of having to go steady
        Look back on group I was in

Remember that the preliminary organizing is temporary and can be changed at any time. Remember, too, that in a short paper you can develop only the most significant aspects of the points listed; probably none of them can be fully developed in a short assignment. Don't take your categories so seriously that they become a strait jacket instead of a support. The actual writing of a composition may suggest new material, or reveal a lack of material, and thus force you to modify your original plan (see chapter 2).

When the material doesn't clearly determine the order of presentation, try what is the standard, safe form: *begin with your conclusion and experiment with several kinds of arrangement, each based on a different method of categorizing.* For full discussion, see section 6a throughout. If you are arguing that grades are an obstacle to education, you might begin by classifying your arguments according to the psychological effects grades can have on students:

Grades become an end in themselves
Direct students into easy courses
Cause cheating in hard exams
Mean concentration only on what is required for tests
Cause anxiety which interferes and disrupts

Then you could try classifying according to the effects on teachers:

Makes teacher a cop, set off against class
Makes teacher a showman to hold attention
Makes teacher into a judge passing on the accused
    and defending verdict

Finally, you might reclassify both these lists according to the effects grades have on the students' attitude towards the teacher, towards the course:

I. Attitude towards teacher
    A. Is expected to be an entertainer and spoon-feed dull, required material
    B. Is thought of as cops and judge defending verdict on tests.
II. Attitude towards course
    A. Makes easy courses attractive and popular, hard and challenging courses unpopular
    B. Means concentration only on what is required for tests
    C. Provokes fear of subjects which have caused anxiety before

By trying various groupings, you visualize the successive points of your paper, the most effective sequence of ideas and proofs supporting your thesis.

1 c-3
arranging and proportioning
the material

In writing the paper, you have at your disposal several methods of paragraph development (see section 6a-5, comparison and contrast; section 5a, chronology; section 6a-3, definition) and ways of sustaining paragraph continuity. The one you select will depend upon the nature of your thesis. There are, however, some general principles about the arranging and proportion of your material worth reviewing.

Plan

1
C-3

1 beginning the paper

Don't waste time looking for a dramatic first sentence. *For the short paper especially, your thesis sentence is a perfectly adequate and direct opening.* Begin the paper with the thesis and develop the paper from there. If, after finishing the rough draft, you are struck by a more felicitous opening, by all means use it; but remember that writing starts when you start. The paper that begins "I want to discuss a topic which interests many people now and has become very controversial," or "Although I may not be a so-called expert on the subject, I think I have good reason for my opinion" has already irritated its reader by the apologies and evasions.

For the long paper, there are several effective ways to begin. One method, used by a student in the following excerpt, is to begin with a sharp contrast and an injection of controversy:

The Voice of America beams radio broadcasts at both Communist and Western nations. To the people of South and Central America, it claims to interpret our way of life; to the captive nations of Europe and Asia, it brings news apparently uncolored by an official party line. In the name of democracy, truth, and free speech it solicits funds for the spread of propaganda.

Another method is to open with a key quotation from the work under discussion, as did the student writer of the following example.

It is the "quick, compact imagery of a single statement, leaving to the hearer the evocation of the picture intended, that forms the basis of Navajo poetry," says Oliver LaFarge. This remark can well be illustrated in LaFarge's own story of Navajo life, *Laughing Boy*, a novel in which things are perceived and identified through "quick, compact imagery." The first image ties the protagonist, Laughing Boy, to his environment: "His new red headband was a bright color among the embers of the sun-struck desert, undulating like a moving graph of the pony's lope"—a simple statement, surely, but nonetheless a "compact image" of the movement of a man on his horse over flat ground.

Still another way is to begin with a short, clear summary or characterization and lead up to a focusing question or statement:

> In 1710 the British Parliament passed the first general copyright statute in history. Called the Statute of Anne, it set forth a time schedule indicating when the ownership of literary compositions passed from private individuals to the public. During this period, the novel also underwent significant development, and critics are now asking why these developments are so strongly parallel.

2 the main body of the paper

Sometimes the main headings in your outline will become the individual paragraphs in the paper, sometimes not (see chapter 4 throughout). *Remember that the more space you give an idea, the more important it may appear to the reader.* Coordinate items in an outline don't always deserve equal weight and space in the composition itself. For example, if the following is part of your outline:

> Reasons for juvenile delinquency
>
> 1. Poverty
> 2. Racial discrimination
> 3. Unhappy family life

and you don't consider points 1 and 2 very significant, dispose of them in a short paragraph and spend your time on point 3. You may try to show briefly that delinquency occurs among the rich as well as the poor and that discrimination accounts for delinquency in only a few parts of the country; then you

Plan

can stress your main point, the connection between unhappy or broken homes and delinquent children.

Similarly, remember that while concrete details are essential to any paper—in fact the paper is probably worthless without them—*their purpose is to illuminate and give precision to your generalities*. Judge your details by their relevance and clarity, not their picturesqueness and abundance. If in discussing poverty and racial discrimination as secondary causes of delinquency the writer gives an extended description of tenement life in New York and Chicago and of gang warfare in Los Angeles, he makes these the subject of his paragraph. He is no longer analyzing the secondary causes of poverty but describing the well-known horrors of urban slum life.

Many writers find that they can concentrate their energies best if they try to write the main body of the paper with as little interruption as possible. It often helps to get your material down first, then revise for proportion and emphasis as well as for sentence structure and word choice.

3 concluding the paper

When you feel you are done, stop. In short papers, an emphatic final sentence in your last full paragraph, or a brief closing restatement of your thesis, is usually the most natural ending. For example, one student concluded a 500-word paper, "Medicine as a Career":

Above all, the physician has the satisfaction of knowing that his service to mankind is widely appreciated and honored.

Another student ended a 700-word theme on Chekhov's play *The Seagull*:

When the curtain falls on *The Seagull* one has the feeling that the story is not at all ended, that the action continues behind the curtain. Reflecting on this, one may find that the secret of Chekhov's effect lies in avoiding the overly dramatic, the play in which everything builds to one climax centered in one character. Chekhov has allowed the themes of love and death, of dreams and reality, to unfold in the random, senseless way that they occur in our lives.

In longer papers, you may want to finish by summarizing briefly the main ideas you have covered and their connections to each other, as did a student in his 1,500-word composition, "The Ascent of Mt. Everest":

The conquest of Everest was a cooperative enterprise. Each expedition made use of the experience of those who had attacked the mountain before them, and the men who waited patiently at the lower camps made possible the advance of their comrades. It is typical that the final victory should have been won by two men, working together.

Beware of the temptation, especially for the short paper, of starting a final paragraph: "Thus, as I hope I have shown throughout my discussion" or "of course there are probably some exceptions," or "This problem will remain with us a long time and take much thinking to solve, perhaps even a change in human nature." These and similar closings, like the self-conscious, windy, or irrelevant beginnings, add nothing. One of the greatest pleasures you can give a reader is a paper which faces its uncertainties straightforwardly, and comes to an emphatic end.

SUMMARY AND REVIEW

This summary is a list of the main steps recommended for planning your theme. If you are unclear about the importance of any of these steps, reread the appropriate section and try some of the exercises again.

1. Familiarize yourself with your intended audience, the nature of your project or assignment, and your own point of view (see section 1a-1).

Plan

2. To restrict your topic, decide on your statement of purpose and divide it into several categories, particularize your ideas and evidence under these categories, and review the trial analysis for a dominant impression or idea (see sections 1 c-1 and 1 c-2).

3. Use this dominant idea to frame your thesis, a clear sentence which expresses the paper's central point (see section 1 c-3).

4. In gathering and evaluating material for the main body of the paper, try a listing, especially if you are describing a process, and try reading your outline aloud, especially if you are making a case (see section 1 d-1).

5. In grouping ideas for your working outline, see if the material itself requires a particular order; if such order isn't immediately apparent, begin with your conclusion and experiment with several kinds of arrangement, each based on a different set of categories (see section 1 d-2).

6. In writing, remember that your opening should point directly to your thesis, that your paragraphs in the main body of the paper should reflect in length and details your intended emphasis, and that your ending should be decisive (see section 1 d-3).

EXERCISES

From the list below, select two subjects. Then analyze each to discover in what areas you would have to do more research for a paper of 10-12 pages. Indicate in a rough outline the main headings you would have, the evidence you can recall to support these headings, and a tentative, restricted thesis.

1. Foreign cars and their effects on the American automobile industry.
2. The main problems faced by my home town (or city) school board.
3. The causes of teen-age gangs.
4. The planning and teaching of a Sunday-school class.
5. The selection and training of an astronaut.
6. The critics and criticisms of evolution.

7. The role of the immigrant in the American labor movement.
8. The rise of the African-Asian bloc in the U.N.
9. The importance of a centralized government in the French and American Revolutions.
10. The development of the printing press and its impact upon religion.
11. The place of fate in Greek or Norse mythology.
12. The treatment of the frontier in the American novel.
13. The significance of the dance in American musical comedy.
14. The designing and engineering of freeways and expressways.

2
outlining

As suggested in chapter 1, outlining is an active analysis to discover a paper's full meaning. This systematic listing of an essay's most important points becomes a visual model of its plan and structure. Even the most experienced writer usually begins with some kind of informal outline, however much he may modify it or deviate from it as he gets into his subject. If you are assigned a formal outline as part of a long written assignment, you are simply being asked to present your plan thoroughly and accurately. If you are assigned a formal outline as an exercise in reading comprehension, you are asked to reconstruct the skeletal structure of someone else's writing. Formal outlines can be very useful to you as reader or writer, but this usefulness depends upon how well you understand and observe their conventions. The uses, types, and conventions of formal outlines are the headings for this chapter. Each applies to outlines when used by either reader or writer.

2 a
uses of the formal outline

The most obvious use of the formal outline—and the reason it is so often required by so many teachers—is *to help the writer (and the reader) anticipate the main divisions of the topic and the connections between ideas and evidence.* Writing about almost any complex topic in economics, history, philosophy, or literature—really, in any field worth writing about—should mean an outline. The student who hurriedly makes one up after writing the paper usually cheats himself more than he does the instructor.

A second use of the formal outline is in the revision of a rough draft or of an unsatisfactory final version. Since instructors seldom have time to write detailed explanations about faulty coherence or organization, you will need to diagnose your own work. Outlining the defective structure of the composition is frequently the best way of finding out what is the matter. You translate the generalized impression that "something's wrong with it" into specific knowledge of how and where the subject needs restriction or development, which paragraphs need transitions or internal coherence. Used diagnostically, the formal outline can reveal the particular failures in plan and structure.

Finally, you can use a formal outline to discover and test another writer's plan and structure. If, for example, you have read three essays on Lincoln's use of power during the Civil War and are to write on the authors' differing assumptions about the Presidency, you can avoid hectic rereading by constructing three accurate outlines. By isolating crucial differences in visual form, you save yourself from skimming over and over the same paragraphs and from snatching at random phrases and details which "sound important." If you are asked to take a stand on, say, right-to-work laws or fair housing legislation, you should first outline your opponent's position. By doing so, you can spot the key issues and his weakest arguments on them. You don't fritter away time and energy elaborately proving the obvious—that rural states are more likely to have right-to-work laws than urban states, or that minority groups are often confined to ghettos. When you outline your reading, you not only discover someone else's intentions but also clarify your own.

2 b
types of formal outlines

There are three types of formal outlines: the paragraph outline, the topic outline, and the sentence outline. Each has its

Org

particular uses and limitations; your instructor will indicate which form he wants submitted with your papers. On your own, you should experiment with each type to learn its advantages and master its form.

2 b-1
the paragraph outline

Paragraph outlines are mainly used in outlining reading, very rarely for planning one's own paper (see 43g, summary).

> Essentially, a paragraph outline is a list of topic or summary *sentences* (one for each paragraph) numbered so that sentence one is the gist of paragraph one, sentence two the gist of paragraph two, and so on.

Such an outline of this chapter so far would read:

Outlining

1. Formal outlines are useful to the writer and to the reader, but their usefulness depends upon how well the writer understands the type chosen and how well he follows it (opening).
2. The first use of the formal outline is to help writer and reader anticipate the main divisions of the topic and the connections between ideas and evidence (2a—uses of . . .).
3. The second use of the formal outline is for diagnosing faulty organization and coherence in rough drafts or in unsatisfactory compositions to be revised.
4. The third use of the formal outline is to discover and test another writer's plan and structure and thereby clarify your own understanding.
5. The three basic types are the paragraph, the topic, and the sentence outline, each having its own advantages which the writer should discover by experimenting (2b—types of . . .).
6. The paragraph outline, used for outlining reading, is a list of summary sentences, one per paragraph, numbered accordingly (2b-1—the paragraph outline).

Since this form summarizes the important content of each paragraph, it serves as a general record and jog to the memory. It enumerates. It helps you recall a loose sequence of ideas. What the paragraph outline *doesn't* show so clearly is the logical relationship of ideas within and between paragraphs and the kinds of evidence and argument the writer employs. Because it is a simple enumeration by paragraph, it gives equal importance to the main point of each. Its usefulness is its brevity. The more qualified and detailed you make each sentence in it, the closer you come to reproducing the complete original—in short to defeating the purpose of an outline. For your own writing and revising, you need a form which shows *both* main ideas *and* their logical relationships and evidence—the topic and sentence outlines.

2 b-2
the topic outline

The topic outline consists of brief phrases or single words, numbered and lettered to show the order and importance of the ideas.

Topic outlines use no complete sentences, except occasionally in the main head which stands at the beginning:

Three-Dimension in the Motion Picture Industry

   I. Revolution in motion picture industry
      A. Need to meet competition of TV
      B. Early box-office success of 3-D
      C. Problems
         1. Fickleness of public interest in fads
         2. Choice of available systems
  II. Methods of producing 3-D illusion
      A. Cinerama
         1. Three-lens camera
         2. Wide, curved screen
         3. No need of glasses for audience

B. Stereoscopic photography
1. Two-lens stereoscopic camera and projector.
2. Polaroid glasses for audience
3. Ordinary screen
III. Evaluation
A. Short-run advantages
1. Looked real to audience
2. Saved money and time in lighting and camera angles
B. Long-run causes of failure
1. Created backlog of standard films
2. Required expensive equipment for exhibitor
3. Failed to develop a standard system
4. Irritated audiences by glasses and goggles

Like the topic outlines in the first chapter, this one is adequate for a short paper of 500–1,000 words and for the relatively simple factual material and conclusions it deals with. It has no thesis at the beginning because it is primarily a straightforward report. For brief papers in class, tests, and short analyses or reports, the topic outline is useful and usually sufficient. Carelessly used or misunderstood, it merely deceives the writer and very often causes vagueness and disorder if he writes from it. Headings like "Introduction," "Main Body," and "Conclusion" and subheadings like "Example," "Reasons," and "Results" delay concrete thinking, reveal nothing. Consider the following typical examples:

VAGUE TOPIC OUTLINE

The Change from School to College
I. Introduction
A. High school ideas
B. Reasons for these ideas
II. What my first impressions were
A. Two examples
B. Results

III. Conclusions
   A. Why I have changed my mind
   B. Advice to high school seniors

In the first example, quite aside from irregularities in form, neither the reader nor, apparently, the writer knows what his "high school ideas" were (misconceptions? partial truths?), why he had whatever "first impressions" he did about college, or the reasons for whatever "advice" he would give to seniors.

OUTLINE DEVOID OF CONTENT

The Mob in the French Revolution
   I. Types during the early days
   A. Leadership
   B. Effects on the course of the Revolution
   II. Types during the Reign of Terror
   A. Leadership
   B. Effects on the course of the Revolution
   III. Types immediately before Napoleon
   A. Leadership
   B. Effects on the course of the Revolution

The second example has an ornamental patina of meaning and may look like a usable outline, but it has no real content and is of doubtful value to the writer. An interesting topic, it is also a complex one, as the writer discovers when he investigates the differences between the mobs in Paris and rioters elsewhere in France. Not all of the possible differences and distinctions would necessarily be relevant to the paper (e.g., are twenty or thirty pillaging peasants a mob?) but the outline does not analyse any distinctive features.

Until the writer uses his outline to explore and analyze important distinctions, he has no focus or depth. He must think through his subject analytically and determine the relative importance of its ideas in order to benefit from the topic outline. The topic outline, then, is helpful so long as it is not too abbreviated or too general.

Org

2 b-3
the sentence outline

The sentence outline has a complete statement, a sentence, for every item in the outline and has a thesis at its beginning.

See section 1b-3 for discussion of the thesis sentence. Note how the following topic outline can be expanded into the sentence outline following it:

USEFUL TOPIC OUTLINE

The Experience of Laughter

I. Single explanation theories of laughter
  A. Social punishment
    1. Mocks differences
    2. Shows feeling of superiority
  B. Defense against social taboos
    1. Relies on dirty jokes
    2. Is relief of tension
  C. Sudden surprise
    1. Stimulated by the unexpected act
    2. Is delight in being startled
II. Complex experience of laughter
  A. Descriptions of feelings
    1. "To have the last laugh"
    2. "To laugh at"
    3. "To laugh off"
  B. Descriptions of vocal expressions
    1. "To chuckle"
    2. "To giggle and titter"
    3. "To snicker"
    4. "To guffaw"
III. Inadequacies of theories of laughter to experience of laughter
  A. Failure to account for description of feelings
    1. No sudden pleasurable surprise in social punishment theory
    2. No sense of superiority in social taboo theory

      3. No self-embarrassment in pleasurable surprise
         theory
  B. Failure to account for sheer joy
      1. No explanation of lovers' spontaneity by any
         theory
      2. No explanation of delight in success by any theory

EXPANSION TO SENTENCE OUTLINE

The Experience of Laughter

Thesis: Though there are several theories of laughter, no single one accounts for the quite distinct emotions which cause it.

I. The theories tend to explain laughter by a single emotion or cause.
  A. Laughter is social punishment inflicted by the majority.
    1. It mocks differences in dress, behavior, and belief.
    2. It is a feeling of superiority and satiric awareness.
  B. Laughter is a defense against social taboos.
    1. It is stimulated by the dirty joke and obscene remark.
    2. It is a safety-valve response relieving tension.
  C. Laughter is the expression of pleasure in the sudden surprise.
    1. It is stimulated by the unexpected physical or verbal act.
      a. The physical is often the sudden fall or thump.
      b. The verbal is usually a witty remark.
    2. It is delight in being startled.

II. The experience of laughter is not a simple one.
  A. Our feelings while laughing vary.
    1. Vindictively we "have the last laugh."
    2. In amusement we "laugh at" something.
    3. In embarrassment we "laugh it away."
  B. The vocal expressions of laughter vary.
    1. We "chuckle" in a low tone when inwardly satisfied.
    2. We "giggle and titter" in rapid, high-pitched sounds when silly.
    3. We "snicker" in sly, half-suppressed tones at another's plight.

4. We "guffaw" in loud tones when heartily enjoying ourselves.

III. The theories are inadequate to the experience of laughter.
  A. No theory accounts for the ways we describe our feelings.
    1. The theory of laughter as social punishment neglects the laugh of sudden pleasurable surprise.
    2. The theory of laughter as a defense against social taboos minimizes the laugh of punishment and mockery.
    3. The theory of laughter as pleasurable surprise slights the laugh of self-embarrassment.
  B. All theories omit the laughter of sheer joy of being and doing.
    1. They do not account for the spontaneous laughter of children, lovers, and parents.
    2. They do not account for the triumphant, delighted laugh of the successful artist or athlete.

In comparing the two outlines, you should notice that the sentence outline contains far more information and reveals a more detailed analysis than the topic outline. The sentence outline has the advantage of compelling you to formulate more explicitly the material you intend to use. It requires a complete thesis, a full assertion for every heading, and an indication of the relationship between the thesis and the headings. For any composition of more than a thousand words, especially if it deals with such complex topics as, say, the activities of UNESCO, Shakespeare's tragic heroes, or the effects of automation on unions, the sentence outline is the best means of really seeing into your subject and organizing it.

> If you have trouble with coherence in papers, you ought to use sentence outlines for your writing whenever possible.

The sentence outline needn't be worshipped—you should feel free to depart from it, if necessary, during the writing of your paper and then to modify the outline accordingly. But since it is the fullest classification and the most complete ranking of ideas and evidence, it is particularly helpful for revising. If you accurately outline the unsatisfactory paper as it is, you should *see* the needless repetition of ideas, the irrelevant material, the breakdown in logical connection and clear transition, the failure to emphasize and develop major points. The topic outline is less satisfactory for such revising, though it is worth trying on the short paper.

2 c
conventions of the topic and sentence outline

Profitable use of topic and sentence outlines depends on understanding and following the conventions common to both. The conventions of the topic and of the sentence outline are few and, once learned, are a real pleasure to work with. These principles apply to the general pattern of the outline and to the logical subdivisions within the outline.

2 c-1
the general pattern of the outline

Both the topic and sentence outline indicate which are the main points and which are the subordinate points by numbering and indentation.

The following system of numbering and lettering is nearly universal:

I.
  A.
  B.
    1.
    2.
      a.
      b.

II.
  A.
    1.
    2.
      a.
      b.
  B.   etc.

Org

Coordinate points—those of equal importance—should be indented the same distance from the left margin. The main heads (I, II, III) are farthest to the left; the subheads (A, B, C) are indented several more spaces to the right; and their subdivisions (1, 2, 3) are moved several more spaces to the right. Rarely will you need to go farther than the third subhead (a, b, c).

For topic outlines, capitalize the first letter of the word beginning the heading but do not punctuate the end of the entry since it is not a sentence:

I. The serve in tennis
   A. The grip
   B. The stance

For sentence outlines, begin with a capital letter and end with a period or other terminal punctuation:

I. The author shows his bias in two striking ways.
   A. He always sneers at non-academic courses.
   B. He never questions the reliability of college test scores.

In both topic and sentence outlines, of course, proper nouns are always capitalized.

2 c-2
the logical subdivisions
within the outline

The headings and subordinate items in the topic and sentence outline should correspond to logical divisions and subdivisions of the material.

The indentation and numbering of items should indicate the parallelism or subordination of ideas. When one sees the pattern

I.   II.
   A.   A.
   B.   1.

he expects to find the two parallel ideas A and B under I, and he expects to find the larger division II parallel in content with I. The writer *misleads himself and his reader* if he divides his material this way:

CONFUSING

I. Advantages of outboard motors
   A. Relatively inexpensive
   B. Attachable to any small boat
II. Easily transportable

"Easily transportable" is logically a subtopic under I, "Advantages of outboard motors." It should be made parallel with A and B:

CLEAR COORDINATION AND SUBORDINATION

I. Advantages of outboard motors
   A. Relatively inexpensive
   B. Attachable to any small boat
   C. Easily transportable
II. Disadvantages of outboard motors
   A. Troublesome to repair on the water
   B. Limited fuel capacity

When one subheading includes material covered in other parallel headings, the subdivisions are said to overlap. Overlapping subdivisions show that you have not analyzed your material fully.

POORLY ANALYZED—OVERLAPPING

I. Organized welfare groups
   A. Early relief organizations
   B. Red Cross
   C. Community Chest
   D. Relief organizations today

Logically, "Relief organizations today" includes the Red Cross and Community Chest. If you are subdividing on a chronological basis, stick to it consistently, and make a subdivision for Red Cross and Community Chest:

Org

CLEARLY SUBDIVIDED
I. Organized welfare groups
   A. History of early relief organizations
   B. Relief organizations today
      1. Red Cross
      2. Community Chest

Similarly, the main headings should indicate equally important divisions of the subject. The following main headings overlap:

NO SUBORDINATION—OVERLAPPING
The Divisions of State Government
   I. The executive branch
  II. Governor's advisors
 III. Bicameral legislature
 IV. The judicial branch
  V. Lower courts

"Governor's advisors" (II) is really part of I; "Lower courts" (V) is part of IV. The following outline shows the proper coordination and subordination of material:

USEFUL SUBORDINATION AND COORDINATION
The Divisions of State Government
  I. The executive
   A. Governor
   B. Advisors
 II. The legislature
   A. Bicameral
      1. House of Representatives
      2. State Senate
   B. Unicameral
III. The judicial
   A. State Supreme Court
   B. Lower courts

Subdivisions which do not, taken together, cover all the material implied by a main heading are logically, though not always practically, an error.

INADEQUATE

I. Literature in the United States
   A. New England
   B. The South

Since New England and the South do not constitute the United States, the main heading needs limiting and, possibly, more subdivisions:

IMPROVED FOR INCLUSIVENESS

I. Literature in the American Colonies   (limitation)
   A. New England
   B. The Middle Colonies   (addition)
   C. The South

The writer's purpose should determine whether the subdivisions are exhaustive or partial. The outline need *not* exhaust every possibility just for the sake of logical consistency. In an essay on Outdoor Recreation, one might have

I. Field sports
   A. Hunting
   B. Fishing

without adding C. Steeplechase riding, D. Bird watching, and E. Other, or Miscellaneous.

One last principle about subdivisions: *it is often stated that each topic that is subdivided must have at least two subheads.* The argument is that dividing something produces at least two parts if it is a genuine division: a lone subtopic is not really a subdivision but rather an amplification or illustration of the point preceding. This is logically sound, and an outline like the following does seem over-elaborate:

UNNECESSARY SUBDIVISION

I. Ancestry
   A. German
II. Birthplace
   A. Farm in Indiana

There are really only two points here, and the subtopics should be combined with them or omitted altogether:

Org

SUFFICIENT FOR BRIEF COVERAGE
I. German ancestry
II. Birthplace (or Birthplace: an Indiana farm)

Occasionally, however, a lone subhead is a useful means of *reminding yourself* of an example, illustration, or reference you don't want to forget:

REMINDER FOR FULL ILLUSTRATION
I. Extension of Mohammedan power under the early caliphs
   A. Eastward and northward
      1. For example, Persian and Greek lands
   B. Westward
      1. For example, Syria, Egypt, and northern Africa

Lone subheads should be eliminated from outlines that are to be turned in, and usually should be revised in your own working outline; free your mind by recording the needed reminder and reclassifying it later.

SUMMARY

Uses and Conventions of Topic and Sentence Outlines
A. Uses
   1. The *topic outline* of brief phrases or single words is usually adequate for the short analysis or report of 500–1,000 words. Be careful, however, to keep main headings and subheadings clear and exact. Avoid headings like "Introduction" and "Conclusion" and subheadings like "Reasons" and "Examples." Such vague labels dangerously weaken the topic outline (see section 2b-2).
   2. The *sentence outline* consists of a thesis supported by complete statements and is the best means of getting into your subject and organizing it. Use it for term papers or any other long composition involving complex analysis and argument. It is also the best means of diagnosing and revising compositions which lack co-

herence since it helps you to see the particular faults (see section 2b-3).

B. Conventions

1. The general pattern for topic and sentence outlines requires consistent numbering and indentation of coordinate headings (1,II; A,B). In topic outlines, capitalize the first word of the heading but do not punctuate the end. In sentence outlines, begin with a capital and end with terminal punctuation (see sections 2c-1 and 2c-2).

2. The headings and subordinate items in topic and sentence outlines should correspond to logical divisions and subdivisions of the material. Revise overlapping headings and subheadings to avoid misleading yourself or your reader. Make your main headings accurately descriptive. Use the lone subtopic as an occasional reminder to yourself (see section 2c-2).

C. Final comment

Try regarding your outline as a guide to your structure and plan, not as a fixed commitment. If, while writing, you discover necessary changes, feel free to make them in the outline and the composition. The outline's purpose is to help you anticipate the number and length of your paragraphs, your topics and the evidence for the paragraphs, and the needed transitions. By experimenting, you can discover which type of outline best suits your habits and needs.

REVIEW EXERCISES

The following exercises are divided into two kinds: those to give you experience with the outline in *planning* your compositions, and those to give you experience in *revising* with it. If you have doubts about the form or uses of a particular kind of outline, refer to the appropriate section.

a. Exercises for planning the composition

1. Pick a machine or a process, either household or industrial. Write a topic outline for a 500-word paper in which you analyze the machine or process by its *struc-*

ture, that is, how it is set up. Your main headings can indicate *what* materials are required and *how* they are assembled or organized.

2. Pick a club to which you have belonged, a business or professional organization you know about, or some other kind of group you are familiar with. Write a topic outline for a 500-word paper analyzing its *function,* that is, how it works. Your main headings can describe *what* it does and evaluate *what* its strengths and weaknesses are.

3. Notice that for analyzing processes and groups you can *combine* structure and function into one complete outline. Now take either the process or group used, or select a new one, and expand it into a sentence outline for a composition of 1,000 words, making your main headings indicate both structure and function.

4. Select some controversial subject about which you have strong convictions—religion in the schools, the civil rights movement, the draft. Prepare a thesis and sentence outline of the position you *oppose.* Then construct a thesis and sentence outline for a 1,000 word composition which answers the most telling arguments of the opposition.

5. Select the same kind of controversial topic assigned in exercise 4. Consult the *Reader's Guide to Periodical Literature* (see chapter 42) for an article which states the opposing view. Make a paragraph outline of it, and construct a topic outline for a 500-word composition in which you answer the writer. Then compare the sentence outlines for exercise 4 with the paragraph and topic outlines. What are the advantages and limitations of each method?

6. Make a tentative topic or sentence outline for a long research project or term paper assigned in another course. Submit it to your English instructor or your course instructor, if either or both are willing. Go over the outline in as much detail as you can with them, particularly noting gaps in evidence and needed reorganization. The

sentence outline will be more helpful to both of you, but it will be hard to construct if you are still in the very preliminary stages of planning and research.

b. Exercises for revising the composition
   1. Occasionally, faulty organization occurs because the particular material is difficult to classify without some overlapping or repetition. Below are two outlines from which poorly organized themes were written. Granted the difficulty of the material, see what improvements you can make in each outline and be prepared to explain your changes. You may need a sentence outline.

Groups Served by Family Counsellors

   I. High school truants
   II. Runaway adolescents
   III. Teenagers
   IV. Married couples
   V. Broken homes
   VI. Separated couples
   VII. Divorced parents

Hardy's Use of Setting in *The Return of the Native*

   I. Hardy's familiarity with the heath
   II. The symbolism of the setting
   III. The relationship of the setting to the theme
   IV. The relationship of the setting to the plot
   V. The effects of the setting on the characters
   VI. The significance of the setting to the reader
   VII. The significance of the setting to Hardy

   2. Take an in-class theme, an essay test, or a short composition you had trouble organizing and make paragraph, topic, and sentence outlines of it *as it was written.* Then construct revised paragraph, topic, and sentence out-

lines for it. Be prepared to write a revised version from one of the new outlines if your instructor should ask you to.

3. Make paragraph, topic, and sentence outlines of the following student themes *as they are written*. Diagnose any faults you find in the organization of the compositions and construct a new topic and sentence outline for a coherent theme. If you find it necessary to omit material from the original theme in your revised outlines, be prepared to explain why.

A Living Pump: The Plant

Since the days of the early Greeks, men have been trying to explain various natural phenomena and find the laws governing them. Sir Francis Bacon pointed out a method which promised to give better results than had been obtained by medieval scholars, who tended to accept and pass on whatever "the authorities" had said.

Bacon urged scientists to examine particular instances instead of arguing over theories. This is called the inductive method and has been used by scientists ever since. Of course they weren't called scientists in Bacon's day.

Many mysteries regarding plant life have baffled scientists for centuries. One of these is the way in which a plant gets water to its topmost branches and leaves.

All plants must have water constantly in order to live and grow. Some plants in the desert need relatively little water, since they have developed ways of storing and conserving water. They are usually prickly to discourage foraging animals, and they often have shiny leaves which check evaporation.

Sequoia redwood trees in California have grown to a height of 264 feet. Some eucalyptus trees are said to have been even taller. Obviously some force is required to get water to the tops of these giants.

Air pressure cannot lift water higher than thirty-four feet. It was once thought that trees might have tiny water pumps built into their structures, but the microscope soon disproved this theory. In reality, plants use forces found within the water itself.

Water is made up of tiny particles called molecules. There is a vast number of these particles in water. It has been said that if a person were to take a cup of water to the Pacific Ocean, pour it in, and then stir the ocean thoroughly, he would have eight or ten of the original molecules in the cup if he filled it again with ocean water.

Each of these molecules has a strong force pulling on the other molecules of water near it, much as the gravity of the Earth holds things to its surface. This force in water is known as molecular cohesion. The strength of cohesion has been measured to be about thirty times the pressure of air. Of course this force is effective at only a very short distance.

Through a complicated process, which is not yet clearly understood, a tree uses this force to send water to its top. If such a process did not exist, the upper parts of a tree would die. As water is used by the leaves to make sugars, each cell, of which there are many in each leaf, draws water from another nearby. This drawing of water by its cohesive forces goes on in chain fashion all the way from the leaves, down through the trunk, on to the roots in the moist ground. It sends water to the top of the tallest tree. This same process goes on in all plants, even ordinary flowers. This can be seen by the fact that if a flower is cut under water, it will last much longer than if it is cut out of water. When the stem is cut under water, the attraction chain is not broken, so the flower will keep on "pumping" water.

Org

Seemingly, water would travel very slowly by this method. Actually, water can rise in a plant at a rate of four feet in an hour.

Pure Wind

In his essay "Politics and the English Language," George Orwell criticizes the use of clichés "for concealing or preventing thought." Although Orwell does not mention it, no better example of this manipulation of clichés can be found than in advertising. The advertisement must convince the public there is a sound basis for the superiority of the product when, very often, there is none. We will take a typical product, Schlitz Beer, and analyze one of its magazine advertisements, recognizing as we do that there are no great differences among American beers and that the Schlitz people must, nevertheless, convince the public of the uniqueness of their product.

The full page Schlitz advertisement is three-fourths covered with a color, close-up photograph of a man drinking beer. We immediately notice certain things. The man's tan face, square features, and crewcut give him a ruggedly handsome look. His left hand, on which there is an emblazoned ring, holds the mug as he drinks. The beer itself is a bright gold with a rich, white head that clings to the glass. The man, dressed in a black tuxedo that blends in with the background, is obviously enjoying himself.

These observations we can make with little more than a casual glance. However, it is not the individual details themselves which are important but the total impression they leave with us. The first and primary impression we receive is that the man is a rugged outdoorsman—the tan face, the athletic-looking crewcut, the square features. We also feel that he is a ladies' man; men who wear rings have that certain intangible sophistication. The tuxedo he is wearing softens his outdoor look, and we can easily believe that he is as much at home at the theatre as he is in the field. In general, he is a man we can admire and trust.

The advertisement, however, would not be a completely effective one for the Schlitz people if we centered our attention on the man alone. It's the beer they are selling, and it's the beer that stands out in the center of the picture. The bright gold beer shines refreshingly against the black tuxedo and background (we notice that it is in a manly mug, not a thin-stemmed glass). Visually, we are led by the clichés to conclude that if this enviable man can enjoy Schlitz, Schlitz must be a good beer.

The clichés in the prose re-enforce this impression. Below the photograph and to the left is the caption, "Jim Cramer worked his way up the hard way. He likes a beer that drinks down the easy way." Neatly printed in black letters, the caption leads us to certain conclusions. First, he is a rough man who made his way up in the tough world—though neither he nor the advertiser are going to offend us by identifying any particular job as being menial or profession or business as cutthroat. Next, he likes his beer—his pleasure—to be softly refreshing in contrast to his hard world. Finally, he is our type of man—his friends call him Jim and we can, too. We then think about the beer he is drinking and wonder if this isn't our type of beer.

We believe in Schlitz because we believe in Jim. We do not ask for any specific details—just what makes up "gusto"?—but accept generalities—"the beer that made Milwaukee famous." We know nothing more than when we started. But we'll remember the name if we go to buy beer. The Schlitz people have given, to use Orwell's words, "an appearance of solidity to pure wind."

3
logic:
the form and substance of reasoning

Any expository writing which is more than a bare chronicle of dates and events involves reasoning: making generalizations, drawing deductions, arriving at conclusions. You may be justifying your actions or beliefs; you may be reporting on a book you find persuasive or unpersuasive; you may be urging a new policy or attitude. In each case, you are trying to convince your reader, and if you credit him with intelligence, you will want to convince him by reason.

As used in this chapter, the term "logic" applies in the broad sense of sound and adequate reasoning. The treatment is necessarily brief, ignoring many technicalities more suitably taken up in a full course in logic.[1] It also postpones discussion of certain *specific* expository techniques which are basic to all

[1] For more detailed treatments of matter discussed in this opening section and throughout the chapter, see Monroe K. Beardsley's *Thinking Straight* (3rd Edition, Prentice-Hall, 1966) and Manuel Bilsky's *Patterns of Argument* (2nd Edition, Holt, Rinehart and Winston, 1963). For a more technical treatment, see Irving M. Copi's *Introduction to Logic* (2nd Edition, Macmillan, 1961).

clear reasoning but which are more properly taken up else-where: the definition and restriction of terms, considered in section 6a-3 (paragraph development by definition);·the means of achieving paragraph coherence, considered in chapter 5; and the means of achieving sentence coherence, considered in chapter 8.

Aside from its brevity, much of this chapter is necessarily negative. It cannot teach you "how to be logical." The chapter can, however, supplement the comments of your teachers, who are often forced to confine themselves to such labels as "logic" or "loose gen" (loose generalization). Since these are only labels, the real challenge you face is the rethinking of your ma-terials, and here the chapter may be helpful. It tries to indicate some of the most common errors in logic and some precautions you can take. The main divisions of this chapter are *the analysis of an argument's structure* and *the validity of the arguments offered*.

3 a
analysis of an argument's structure

Definitions are preliminary to the *argument* (see section 6a-3). Having defined capital punishment as "execution, the death penalty for a crime," you can then argue for or against it. One "argument," or "reason," you might give *for* capital punish-ment is that it deters murder. A "reason," or "argument," *against* it might be that it does not deter murder. Observe that the words "argument" and "reason" are interchangeable and that they imply an identical process of thinking. The process can be diagrammed:

premise or evidence	*inference or immediate conclusion*
Capital punishment deters murder.	It should be continued.
Because it does not deter murder,	capital punishment should be abolished.

Log

3
a

In most discussions of logical analysis, the word *argument* signifies any two statements connected in such a way that one is drawn as a conclusion from the other. Notice that the argument has two parts: a *premise* (or evidence) and an *inference* (or immediate conclusion).

We use arguments constantly in writing and in speaking, and we recognize them by the actual or implied presence of connectives like "because," "so," and "since," and by verbs like "ought," "should," and "must." Moreover, we often intend, though we may not always state explicitly, a final conclusion or *point of the argument:*

premise ⟶ *inference*
It's cold in here. The window must be open.
    ↓ *final conclusion*
    Somebody should shut it.

premise ⟶ *inference*
I'm tired out *because* I've been studying hard.
    ↓ *final conclusion*
    So I'll take a break now.

inference ⟵ *premise*
The window *must be* open *because* it's cold in here.
    ↓ *final conclusion*
    You *ought to* shut it.

final conclusion ⟵ *inference* ⟵ *premise*
She was only kidding. She didn't mean it *since* she was joking about it later.

The structure of an argument, then, is an observed fact or set of facts, or else a generalization presumably based on facts (the premise), leading to a conclusion (the inference). And usually the argument points toward a final conclusion. Notice that the argument stands midway between the *assumption* and the final conclusion.

assumption 1
Academic success and creativity are related.

premise	*inference*
ARGUMENT 1 Hayes has an A— average and an I.Q. of 130. Brookes has a B— average and an I.Q. of 127.	Hayes is more likely to do better work in the restricted creative writing course.

final conclusion
Consequently, he ought to be admitted over Brookes.

assumption 2
Motivation and success in creative work are not necessarily identical with motivation and success in academic work.

premise	*inference*
ARGUMENT 2 I.Q. difference is trivial and Brookes has already talked about writing as a possible career and written several promising poems and stories.	Brookes is more genuinely interested in and likely to benefit personally from the course.

final conclusion
So Brookes should be given an equal chance, if not preference.

> The assumption is a connection, between the premise and the inference, which is taken for granted *before* the argument is advanced; and it is a *presupposed* relationship between the argument and the final conclusion.

That is, unless you *took for granted* that high grades and creativity are related, you couldn't very well argue that Hayes' superior average was proof that he would do better work in creative writing than Brookes and that *therefore* Hayes ought to be given priority. (The importance of sound key assumptions will be discussed later; the assumption that academic success and creativity are related is dubious.) In principle, you could begin a paper with either your assumption or your final conclusion, since either could be made into a thesis. Actually,

Log

you usually begin with your final conclusion and omit your assumptions entirely. But in both simplified examples, regardless of whether you began with your assumption or your conclusion, and supposing you had defined terms like "creativity," your argument would be the core of your paper.

Usually, a final conclusion has several arguments, not simply one, to support it. The relationship among different arguments is more complex than the examples have so far suggested. The inference of one argument may be the premise for the next, and so on in a chainlike pattern to the final conclusion, the clasp:

premise 1 and . . .   *premise 2*
Hayes has an A— average and an   Brookes a B— average and
I.Q. of 130,   an I.Q. of 127.

inference from premises 1 and 2, becomes premise 3
Since Hayes is obviously brighter and more energetic,
inference from premises 3 and 4
he should do better work in a restricted creative writing course.
premise 4
Hayes' past record shows his excellent response to class work.
final conclusion
Consequently, he certainly should be given preference over Brookes.

Several distinct, separate strands of argument may be knotted into the one final conclusion:

final conclusion
There is no clear reason for preferring Hayes over Brookes.
First Argument introduced   *premise 1*
          In the first place, **since** both boys are in the superior I.Q. range

          premise 2
and **since** a three-point difference is statistically trivial,
infer. from premises 1 & 2 →   premise 3   *infer. from prem. 3*
they are equally qualified intellectually.   The standard is
          irrelevant in this
          case.

So far as the *premise 1 in New Argument* different grade point average is concerned,
infer. from premise 1
all it proves is that Hayes has a higher one,
negative inference from premise 1 and inference from premise 2
not that he has the special interest or talent for this course that Brookes has.
premise 2
Brookes has already written several promising stories and poems.

New Argument: premise 1
Moreover, Brookes has talked seriously about becoming a writer,

premise 2, and so on to the end
while Hayes certainly has no such intentions . . . .

Just as a paragraph can develop several arguments to support one conclusion, so several paragraphs can each develop one or more arguments to support a thesis, itself a final conclusion (see section 1 b-3). And just as an outline helps you sort out your arguments for the paragraph, it also helps you sort them out for the paper. But nothing has been said yet about the kind of argument used and its content. So far, we have considered an argument's structure, not its truthfulness. An argument's structure may be quite consistent yet its premises and conclusions unsound.

3 b
validity of the arguments offered

The first part of this chapter has dealt with the nature of inference—the structure of an argument. The second part deals with some of the major problems that arise in making inferences. Two common causes for unsound arguments are the writer's failure to examine his key assumptions and his failure to distinguish between fact and judgment. The writer may fail to question the connections he has taken for granted, or he may fail to recognize that what can be proved and what he approves of are not necessarily identical.

Log

3 b-1
key assumptions

The key assumptions underlying the argument or arguments must be sound before they are built on.

If the underlying assumptions are unwarranted, the writer risks overlooking troublesome details which do not support his assumptions, and he may find unreal evidence which does. For example, if he were to assume that academic success and creativity are related, he would have to overlook the students with mediocre averages who are talented painters or dramatists and the quite intelligent honor students who seem to lack imagination, or at least seldom do more than safe, thorough work. The writer might, moreover, allow himself to find an unreal significance in the difference between an I.Q. of 130 and of 127, and from this trivial difference make a dubious inference.

To take another example, some student themes on short stories narrated by a first person "I" automatically assume there must be a one-to-one correspondence between the narrator and the author in real life. By failing to distinguish between the "I" as a device for telling the story and the author's personal identity, the analysis turns the story into autobiographical self-confession, distorting fact and fiction alike.

One way of detecting your fundamental assumptions is to ask yourself what you have taken for granted in your argument. If the assumptions need defending, defend them; if they need explaining, explain them.

EXERCISES

Each of the following arguments contains one or more key assumptions. Analyze each argument to determine the key assumptions it makes and which of these assumptions, if any, would need to be explained or defended.

1. Novelists like Faulkner and Salinger give an unfair picture of American life because they show mainly its violence and sordidness.
2. An enriched course for able students is a valuable addition to the high school curriculum because it offers them a chance to fulfill college requirements and to begin specializing earlier.
3. Many sororities are hypocritical because they choose members on the basis of family, money, and looks.
4. Some civil rights laws are useless because you can't legislate morality.
5. A politician who takes an unpopular position during an election is foolish because it simply increases his chances of losing.

3 b-2
the differences between fact and judgment

As the preceding exercises may have suggested, what can be *proved* and what one *approves of* do not always coincide.

> The differences between fact and judgment, though not always easy to determine in a given case, are important. A fact may be defined as any statement, any declarative sentence, which can be proved true or false.

The definition says nothing about who does the proving, what his qualifications are, or how he proves it. *It merely stipulates the possibility of verifying the statement,* the central idea intended here. It rules out commands, questions, and ejaculations as provable assertions—no one will try to prove or disprove utterances like "Shut the door!" "How old is he?" or "Great!"

The definition eliminates more than these obvious examples. "Water is wet"; "A yard has three feet"; "New York has

Log

more people than Chicago"; "Shakespeare was born in 1564"—most people would agree that such statements are all "facts." But saying "Water is wet" isn't the same as saying "The paint on the door is wet." The first sentence is either a tautology, a needless repetition of an idea to anyone familiar with the qualities of "waterness," or else instructions to a very young child on *how to identify* the feeling of liquid on his fingers. To say "A yard has three feet" is also to state a truth-by-definition—quite different from saying "The track was only ninety-nine yards long." We can touch the paint and measure the track and thereby answer "Yes, it is" or "No, it isn't" to the assertion. But what point is there in responding "Yes, it is" or "No, it isn't" to statements like "Water is wet" or "A yard has three feet" except to agree with the definition?

Some statements are verifiable facts because they are stated in *quantifiable* terms, that is, in such a way that what is asserted can be weighed, measured, or counted: "Jean weighs eighty pounds," "That last discus throw was 147' long," "There are two blue-books apiece for the thirty-five of you." Even in these cases, of course, you assume that the scales or the tape measure is accurate, that neither has been jiggled, and that your index finger has not missed a cover or pointed at the same head twice. Other facts presuppose greater faith: If you believe "New York has more people than Chicago" and "Shakespeare was born in 1564" are factual statements, you are not simply accepting the authority of an almanac and an encyclopedia. You are trusting the accuracy and conscientiousness of every census taker hired in these cities by the Bureau of the Census in 1960 and the reliability of scholars who have inspected the parish records of baptism in Stratford-on-Avon.

Admittedly, life is too short for anyone to verify personally more than a fraction of the "facts" he learns and many things have to be taken on authority. Still, you ought to cultivate the habit of skeptical analysis in reading and writing. It can help you detect those judgments which are unverifiable and which are often "proved" in writing by heavy underlining and double exclamation marks and in conversation by rising voices and tempers. How, for instance, can one prove (or dis-

Log

prove) such statements as "You can't change human nature" or "Materialism is the greatest threat to our way of life"?

> A judgment is a conclusion expressing some form of approval or disapproval.

Judgments cannot be avoided. The term should not be dismissed because it is taken to connote "mere opinion." There are, after all, reasonable grounds and confirming facts for "good judgment" as well as the arbitrary assumption and disregarded fact in "poor judgment." Sometimes, the judgment is a fairly simple, safe inference from the facts, as in the judgment "Ty Cobb was one of the finest hitters of baseball" which is based on his record of 4,191 hits and 2,244 runs, and on a .367 lifetime average for twenty-four seasons. The phrase "one of the finest" is a judgment of Cobb's record. Sometimes, a judgment is a complicated inference from many facts, none of which are immediately clear. Consider three propositions in which the judgments are italicized:

1) In 1920, there were 6,448,343 farms with a total acreage of 955,844,000 acres in America; by 1959, farms were larger and fewer totaling 3,703,894 in number and accounting for 1,120,157,789 acres, and these figures exclude Alaska and Hawaii.
2) Between 1920 and 1959, the American farm *has become more efficient through improved mechanization and specialization, now able to cultivate more land and feed a larger population with fewer people doing the work.*
3) *Profit-seeking specialization and mechanization are destroying the small, self-sufficient family farm in America and the deep attachment to the land and tradition that are so much a part of the family farm.*

The first statement contains the terms "larger and fewer" which possibly connote a judgment of greater efficiency but which unmistakeably denote a factual inference—that fewer

Log

farms and a greater total acreage mean larger farms. The statement is clearly factual and the inference results from a simple computation. The second sentence, a judgment, not only presupposes the first statement's facts ("now able to cultivate more land . . .") but presupposes others. To prove "improved mechanization and specialization," the writer would need figures showing the increased use of electricity and various kinds of power machinery and the increased percentage of farms that raise only crops, livestock, or dairy goods. The evidence exists, of course, to defend the judgment that "the American farm has become more efficient."

In the third statement, the judgment is far more conspicuous than in the first two, and the facts are less immediately evident. To prove, for example, the existence of "the small, self-sufficient family farm" with its "deep attachment to the land and tradition" would require: detailed information about income, expenses, size of family, acreage worked, period of ownership without tenancy, length of political and religious affiliations, and a study of attitudes towards marriage, education, and the like. Such information, whether in the form of statistics or the extensive observations of qualified observers, would have to include: the New York family raising sheep and a few cows, some acres of wheat, and garden tomatoes; the North Carolina family raising a hillside of tobacco and corn, supplemented by hogs and hunting; the Illinois family running a small dairy and orchard; and the Colorado family raising grain and beef near the foothills of the Rockies. Then the information about all of these families would have to be analyzed to see whether there is such a type as "the small, self-sufficient family farm" with distinct values or whether there are sharply different regional variations.

You can no more help making judgments about human actions and goals than the writer of the third statement could help feeling strongly about the changes taking place in the American farm. In fact, the writer might say that information about income and attitudes towards marriage had little to do with his judgment, that he was talking about qualities which could only be experienced personally. The grounds for his judgment might be his own life on a small Iowa farm or New Mexico ranch; novels like Willa Cather's *O Pioneers!,* Steinbeck's *The Red Pony,* or Harriet Arnow's *The Dollmaker;* or the memoirs of a country doctor. The question would then be what other qualities are slighted. Do the novels and memoirs show only loyalty, belief, the close-knit family, and hard work? What of the fatigue and boredom, the bigotry and narrow vision, the drudgery and failure they reveal? Novels and memoirs are images of possibility, not mathematical probability: they can make us see and feel the intensity and variety of human life in a particular time and place rather than convince us of statistical likelihood. If the writer argues their details and experiences are "factually typical," he *then assumes as true* what only statistics or the extensive testimony of many qualified observers could confirm.

> When you make judgments, then, express your facts clearly and accurately, and show clearly the way in which the facts warrant your judgment; when you don't know the facts, or have reason to suspect their authority, suspend final judgment.

Try to distinguish between those judgments which involve personal preference and are not provable and those which may be supported by evidence and arguments. For your college writing, this advice implies your willingness to do research; to distinguish among facts, statements which may be factual, and judgments; and to tolerate uncertainty. The last is especially hard to do: often the experts in specialized fields are so much at odds that either you are tempted to give the matter up entirely or else arbitrarily decide "one side *must* be right, the other wrong, so I will choose." If, for example, you were to look up the statistics and analyses on capital punishment, you would find no clear-cut agreement among the criminologists, psychologists, and various law officials as to what the figures prove—and no agreement among the statisticians, either. But lives, the victim's, the accused murderer's, and their families', are too important to be forgotten about simply because you

Log

cannot prove conclusively that capital punishment is or is not a deterrent. There are other factual grounds which may help you form a judgment: How many innocent men have been executed, or how many saved at the last minute? Do the poor and the ignorant more frequently receive the death sentence than others convicted of murder? How often are murderers declared insane, later to be released and commit another murder?

As has been pointed out, one cannot verify personally more than a fraction of the "facts" he learns and necessarily he has to take many things on authority. Still, when experts disagree about their facts and their judgments, you do have a few guides for your judgment.

The first guide is to be sure that a man is an authority on the subject. If a famous physicist and chemist differ about disarmament, you may have to suspend judgment so far as their argument about the technical difficulties is concerned, but you don't have to feel that either of them is an expert on Russia and Russian foreign policy. Other writers and scholars have made the study of Russian aims and behavior their life's work, and you should turn to them.

A second guide is to consider a man's announced motives or position in relation to his testimony. A pathologist, regardless of what medical school he attended, who does research for a tobacco company and who testifies that the correlation between smoking and lung cancer is "not yet proven" may be suspected of bias and certainly shouldn't be given the same heed as an independent study by other doctors. An executive for a major car manufacturer who testifies that "in recent years all reasonable safety precautions have been taken" in the designing of automobiles may well not be as reliable an authority as an independent trade magazine or engineering firm.

A third guide is to see whether there is agreement among others in the field on the strengths or weaknesses in a man's research. These guides are easier to recommend as general principles than to apply in specific cases, but they are the best guides you have.

EXERCISES

For each of the following statements, determine which parts are facts and which parts are judgments. For each judgment, decide what kind(s) of facts or evidence, if any, could be cited to support the judgment.

1. Smoke Cigarillos! They last longer and burn cooler than cigarettes. They are cleaner and cheaper than pipes.
2. Julius Caesar, Rome's greatest general and ruler, was assassinated in 44 B.C. by Cassius, Brutus, and other personal enemies.
3. There is no such creature as "the average college freshman": there are only individuals, each with his unique tastes, beliefs, and backgrounds, who happen to begin their college education during the same year.
4. Bill Russell has been one of the finest defensive players of all time in professional basketball.
5. A meter equals 39.37 inches.
6. A kilometer contains 1,000 meters.
7. The average college freshman of today can read with greater understanding, write with fewer spelling and mechanical errors, and speak more intelligently on a wider range of topics than his counterpart of thirty years ago.
8. The early bird catches the worm—but who wants the worm?
9. If one compares Jefferson's wide and varied interests with Jackson's boorish prejudices and manners, one sees how narrow and provincial the American ideal of what a statesman should be had become in a short time.
10. A recent classification of land use in Afghanistan estimates 76% waste lands, 5% meadows and pastures, 1.5% forests and woodland, 14% arable, 3.5% cultivable but unused.
11. More often than not, European journalists and writers who travelled in America during the first half of the nineteenth century were surprised by our belligerent

Log

nationalism and confident optimism, though why they should have expected a young country to be otherwise is a puzzling question.

12. Since language changes, there can be no criterion of what is good or bad usage except what the majority is willing to accept at any given moment.

13. Since language changes, the criteria of what is good or bad usage also change.

14. Spanish is an easier and therefore better language for Americans to learn than French.

15. Real mastery of a foreign language means the ability to think in the language, not simply to translate headlines and signs, word by word.

3 b-3
faulty reasoning

The failure to examine key assumptions and to distinguish between fact and judgments which are unprovable are by no means the only causes for faulty reasoning. Of the other possible causes, hasty generalizing is one of the more common.

1 hasty generalizations

To generalize is to draw conclusions about a whole class or group, or about the relationships between groups, after studying individual groups or members of a group. A hasty generalization is one drawn from improbable odds or from inadequate or non-typical examples.

Suppose, for example, that after meeting several bright and articulate fraternity rush chairmen, you are convinced that the outstanding student is typically a fraternity product. Do you have reason to question this generalization? Yes, because your sampling may be unrepresentative and in any case is quite small. The chairmen may well have been chosen for their jobs because they are so impressive. But granted they may have been chosen for this reason, suppose you are still convinced that the outstanding student is probably a fraternity product. How would you establish such a generalization?

Establishing an effective generalization usually requires several steps. First, you would have to identify the group "outstanding student" by defining it as, say, those on the college's honor roll. Otherwise the generalization is so subjective that it is no more than a vague judgment, without clear meaning or evidence. You would then have to control the group by showing there was a higher percentage of fraternity men on the honor roll than of nonfraternity men. Otherwise, the outstanding student is no more likely to be a fraternity member than he is to be an independent, possibly even less so. And even if there were a higher percentage of fraternity men on the honor roll, you would still have to show that many of these members did not have good records before joining. Otherwise, they would have been able students all along: the fraternity did not "produce" them but simply took them in.

Not all generalizations can be thus established. In cases where all the relevant facts about a limited group are available, one may indeed generalize by simply counting or checking accurately—a parking attendant inspects each car on the lot and generalizes that all headlights are off; a dean reviews all the high school transcripts and generalizes that every freshman has had at least a year of foreign language before entering the college. But much of the time it is not possible to do a complete check. Necessarily, one also generalizes by *induction,* that is, by observing a number of specific examples of the group and then concluding that other examples will *probably* be like those observed. A young child uses induction when, after grabbing at two or three cats, he concludes that all cats scratch. Later on, when he understands what grabbing is and when he has seen more cats, he may generalize that most cats will not scratch unless they are grabbed. Pollsters use induction when they *sample* a representative cross-section of voters to determine how all voters feel or will probably vote. If their cross-section is not representative, as happened in 1948, they will be embarrassed. A consumers' research organization uses induction when it purchases all different brands of a mass-

Log

produced item, tests several samples of each brand carefully, and then generalizes about which brands are likely to be the best buys and in what ways.

Hasty generalizing takes several forms. Hasty generalizations usually occur when a writer does not qualify the probabilities or consider the adequacy and typicality of his examples as fully as he should.

The stereotype is one form of hasty generalizing—the trite, unchanging picture of an ethnic group, a profession, or a social role. "He was the typical Italian father, singing with gusto and crying, 'Mama Mia.'" "He was the typical college student, a dirty-looking beatnik." Other stereotypes include the scheming Jew, the Philistine business man, the dumb athlete, etc. Stereotypes are crude caricatures which deny actual variety and diversity.

Oversimplification is another form of hasty generalizing. Usually, it entails making a question seem easier than it is. Statistics, especially, can lead to oversimplifying. For example, if two groups have a markedly different class average on a reading comprehension test, you could not generalize that every member of the first class was better than every member of the second. Since a few very high scores might have pulled up some mediocre ones in the averaging, you would have to compare all the individual scores to reach such a conclusion. Still less would you be entitled to simplify the results by generalizing that one group was "innately" better than the other. You would have to know a good deal about the income and education of the parents, the reading matter (if any) in the homes, each child's previous training, and other crucial factors before drawing any conclusions.

The unqualified generalization makes a third form of hasty generalizing, the exaggerated claim made from insufficient evidence. On the basis of a peace petition signed by a few thousand college students, a commentator generalizes that all undergraduates are becoming pacifists. His sampling is highly inadequate. He not only ignores those who refused to sign but also those who are being drafted. The unqualified generalization is a rather frequent weakness in college writing—e.g., "All the freshmen think 'Orientation Week' is a waste of time" or "Not one girl in the whole college trusts the Dean." To the literal-minded, "How do you know? Have you talked with *every* freshman or every girl?", the writer usually answers: "Of course not, but I know several [or some] people who feel . . . ." The least the writer can do is to rephrase his generalization more accurately and responsibly by identifying the approximate numbers involved and the source of his real evidence: "Several of us who are freshmen and attended 'Orientation Week' with high hopes have decided that . . . ." or "After the girls on our corridor had met with the Dean, we agreed that . . . ."

In order to generalize effectively, you need to know and follow some criteria of generalizations.

> Since generalizations are made about classes or groups, the first criterion of generalizations is that the evidence be typical of the class or group.

A theme using students in remedial English as the basis for generalizing about the abilities of all the freshman class would obviously be unconvincing, just as would a theme using the Black Muslims to generalize about all Negroes.

Often, though, the untypicality is less crude, more a question of interpretation than of outright error. Are Hemingway's heroes and heroines in *A Farewell to Arms* and *The Sun Also Rises* "typical" of the period in their disillusionment with World War I and its aftermath? Was the fear of "majority faction" by the authors of *The Federalist* "typical" of the Constitution's other proponents? If you read Hemingway's novels or *The Federalist* essays, you will agree on some conclusions: Hemingway's heroes and heroines do distrust "causes" and conventional moralities—they say so and ignore them; Hamilton and Madison often speak of "majority faction" especially in *Federalist 10*. Many of your most interesting writing assignments will be ones like these, or at least ones in which you use complex facts for complex judgments. *When you have to evaluate typicality, define what features you be-*

Log

lieve typical and show how these features are found in the evidence. If you had only read the two Hemingway novels, but none by F. Scott Fitzgerald, John Dos Passos, or Ford Madox Ford about this period, you would want to confine your discussion of typicality to Hemingway's novels.

The second criterion of generalizations is that the evidence be adequate.

The American who spends three days in London or Moscow, the European who spends two weeks in the United States on a lecture tour, or the student who visits Washington, D.C. for a weekend has many superficial impressions, some of them probably accurate as such. But if he generalizes "The English are reserved" or "Americans are friendly but ignorant," he reveals more about himself than about the English or Americans. Other examples of inadequate evidence are the citation in a theme of Dave Beck and Jimmy Hoffa to show that the entire Teamster Union's leadership is corrupt, or an analysis in a term paper of the stormy Scopes trial in 1925 to show that all Americans were either militant agnostics or Protestant fundamentalists. Like typicality, adequacy is sometimes difficult to judge—the anthropologist with only a jaw fragment and a few bones or the archeologist with only a faded temple painting may have to infer what he can and hope for more evidence. *But you can assist yourself and your reader by saying why you think your evidence is adequate and for what, if there is likely to be doubt.* If only one half of the 250 freshmen vote for class officers, you have adequate evidence that "something" is wrong with morale, but you would have to talk with many of the nonvoters to find out what it was.

The third criterion of generalizations is that the evidence be relevant.

Figures showing that all sororities on campus have a "C" average or better would not be proof that sororities produce outstanding students. The figures would be more *pertinent* to the generalization that sororities care enough about their eligibility to satisfy academic requirements. In a different fashion, the fact that an artist or musician was once a communist or fascist is irrelevant evidence to prove his work incompetent, if you define incompetence as a lack of artistic ability or skill. The only way he can be shown to be incompetent is by musical or artistic standards of performance. You might find it personally distasteful to attend his exhibit or recital, but if you condemn his present work because of his past associations, you adopt the propaganda view of art and the illogic used by the Nazis and the communists.

> The fourth criterion of generalizations is that the evidence be accurate.

This standard seems self-evident, yet if you were to read through the long, careful book reviews in such publications as *Scientific American, The American Historical Review,* or *The Journal of American Folklore,* you would find two common criticisms are that the writer has been careless about checking his facts and indiscriminate about his sources. The reviewer's intention isn't necessarily to nag or to counsel perfection, but to set the record straight. In cases of extreme carelessness, the reviewer legitimately questions the author's right to be trusted, regardless of how original his ideas are. Beyond the advice in the chapters 43 ("The Library") and 44 ("The Research Paper"), the most helpful guides you have are the ones for expert testimony: Does the information come from a recognized source? What are the man's announced motives or position in relation to his evidence if it is disputed? What agreement is there among others in the field about the strengths or weaknesses in his research? Like an editor or reviewer, your teacher has greater confidence and pleasure in conclusions based on accurate facts.

2 mistaken causal relationships
Mistaken causal relationships are errors in reasoning about cause-and-effect. Perhaps the two most frequent kinds are the *post hoc, ergo propter hoc* fallacy and the reductive fallacy.

Log

The "post hoc, ergo propter hoc" fallacy is the error of arguing that because B follows A, A is the cause of B. The fact that B follows A is *not* proof that B was caused by A. Sequence is not proof of a causal relationship. Primitive beliefs like a full moon "causing" pregnancy and their modern equivalent in the television commercial connecting marriage with a change in deodorant are easy enough to laugh at. But what about the unqualified generalization which makes the loss of religious belief the cause of crime, membership in a minority group the reason for success or failure, political parties the cause of depressions or wars?

> The first test of causal generalizations is *regularity:* A and B must always be present together; in any instance where one or the other is absent, there cannot be a direct causal relationship.

Crimes have been committed by people who had not lost their faith; not every person who loses his faith commits a crime.

> The second test is *sufficiency:* A alone must be sufficient to produce B before it can be called a cause.

The reductive fallacy occurs when simple or single causes are given for complex effects, creating a generalization based on insufficient evidence. In history when motives and events are enormously complicated and cannot be exactly duplicated, such generalizations as "Athens fell because of mob rule" or "Luther caused the Reformation" are *reductive*. That is, instead of simply specifying the mob or Luther as *one important condition,* these assertions make Luther or the mob *the single agent* of causation. Strictly speaking, the historian rarely uncovers the cause or causes of events. Rather, he tries to decide which were the more important conditions, the more probably necessary circumstances, that preceded an event. In scientific studies when a sequence cannot be directly observed and controlled and the investigator cannot know whether Y is the result of X only, W and X together, or whether XY are both the result of W, he speaks of a *correlation*. In 1964 when the Surgeon General announced a high correlation between cigarette smoking and lung cancer, he indicated there was a high frequency between the two, that one was probably a *contributary cause* of the other. But since not all heavy smokers die of lung cancer and since there is evidence that industrial fumes and car exhaust are injurious, one cannot say that smoking is the *only* cause of lung cancer. Insofar as he cannot directly isolate, identify, and control each factor in a sequence, the scientist, like the historian, usually observes the test of sufficiency: only if *A* alone is sufficient to produce *B* can it be called the cause.

Except for laboratory reports in physics or chemistry and perhaps a research project in psychology or education, you will seldom have space or occasion in college writing to prove strictly a causal relationship. Usually, so far as causal relations are concerned, you will be judging or reporting on research done by others, or else trying to determine what are the *more likely connections* between an effect you have observed or experienced and events preceding it.

> To let your readers judge the sufficiency of your argument, define its conditions and limitations as clearly as you can.

With complex relationships, it is often helpful to know that there is a significant difference between saying "It is due to" and "It has been helped by," just as there is between saying "Luther caused" and "Luther contributed to" or "The reason for the Revolution" and "One reason for the Revolution." The limited statement can be more exact because it is more tentative: it implies that other conditions, other contributing factors, may be as important as the one singled out for discussion. This kind of exact tentativeness requires careful, analytical thinking. When you analyze complex historical events and personalities, complex social issues and complex motives, avoid the reductive fallacy.

Log

3 false analogies

> An analogy is a comparison between two different things or events to show the one or more ways in which they are similar.

To illustrate, for example, how the novelist works, one could draw the analogy between him and the potter: both begin with a rough idea or image, but discover the particular shape of the plot or vase as they work with their materials, often modifying the outlines several times before they are satisfied.

Analogies can vividly illustrate and clarify difficult ideas. They have been fruitful in science because they have suggested new lines of research and testing: Franklin saw an analogy between lightning and electric sparks; mathematicians like John von Neumann, instrumental during the early development of computers, saw an analogy between the way the human nervous system works and the way a relay of vaccuum tubes can be made to work. But in science, an analogy is a hypothesis to be proved or disproved. Though it suggests a possibility, it is *not* proof by itself.

> An analogy can be illustrative or suggestive, but it cannot be conclusive. You do well to suspect any conclusions which are supported only by an analogy.

Sometimes, a false analogy offered as proof is relatively easy to detect. The student who argued that the new African countries should have federated into a United States of Africa to solve their political and economic problems ignored some obvious dissimilarities. The thirteen colonies in America were unified by a common language and foe and had in most cases a long tradition of local self-government. African countries are separated from each other by deep linguistic and cultural differences and in several cases are inwardly divided by tribal rivalries. The analogy also ignores the difficulties we had—the failure of the Articles of Confederation and the opposition to the Constitution. Often, however, a false analogy is more deceiving. Consider the following, a widespread argument by analogy:

Like arsenic, pornographic literature poisons the system. It's not enough just to label it and put it on a shelf. Just as some children can't read the label on the bottle and others want to experiment, some juveniles and adults can't discriminate and others are tempted by the warning. Such books should be locked up in libraries where only scholars with special reasons for using them can get at them, in the same way druggists only sell arsenic from behind the counter by special permission.

Diagrammed, the analogy runs:

	Arsenic	**Pornography**
QUALITIES	Poisons system	Poisons system
VICTIMS	Children who don't read or whom label tempts	Those who don't discriminate or whom publicity tempts
AVAILABILITY	Not on shelves merely labelled "poison"	Openly in stores, libraries, cheaply and unmarked
CONCLUSION	Sold only by druggist from behind counter by special request	Should be locked in libraries where only scholars see by request

The diagram should indicate why such analogies, though they prove nothing, so often sound convincing and are hard to refute: they trap the reader in a closed system of comparisons. Two principles for judging analogies offered as proof will help you cope with arguments like this one:

1) The more concrete similarities there are, and the more instances that can be cited, the higher is the possibility that the conclusion is true.

2) The greater the magnitude of the differences and the more irrelevant the similarities that do exist, the less is the chance the conclusion is true.

If you analyze the argument by these principles, you should see that the analogy is false. In no meaningful way can pornography be said to "poison the system" in the sense that

Log

arsenic does. Arsenic's lethal ingredients are not a matter of opinion. They can be demonstrated to any observer and are known and agreed upon by qualified observers—chemists, doctors, and druggists. Who are the "qualified observers" to decide what is "pornography," and what is their training? Do they usually agree on its "ingredients"? In what meaningful sense can pornography be shown to kill?

False analogies obscure the real issues of and prevent clear thinking about serious and difficult questions, such as: What is pornography? To detect analogies used as proof, examine the argument to see if any evidence is offered other than a comparison between two different things or events.

> In your own writing, if you think an analogy is essential to your argument, rethink your entire case: don't allow yourself to be taken in by shallow or deceiving similarities.

4 avoiding the question

When a writer has failed to give relevant evidence for his argument and failed to draw relevant inferences, he is *avoiding the question.*

Begging the question is one such common failure. A question is begged when the writer uses as a proven argument the very point he is trying to establish. For example, the writer who argues that the poor are lazy and cites families on relief as "evidence" is assuming *without proof* that only lazy opportunists would take relief—the very point *to be* demonstrated.

The ad hominem argument is a second common form, the argument "to the man." The writer attacks the morals, the motives, the friends, or the family of his opponent and diverts attention from the substance of his opponent's argument. The evaluation of expert testimony should not be confused with the *ad hominem* argument: in the former, you *ask* what a man's professional credentials are and the reasons for his position—that is, you attempt to *distinguish between fact and judgment* (see section 3b-2); in the latter, you *insinuate* by sarcasm or similar means that a man's word is untrue or his case unsound because there is something wrong with him personally.

The straw man is another device commonly used for avoiding the question. As the label implies, the technique is to stuff, set up, and knock down a position which is not being contested. If the question is whether or not Shylock deserves his punishment and the writer goes to great lengths to prove that bitterness can make a man lonely, he is erecting a straw man. The issue is whether Shylock is treated too severely, either by his own standards or Christian ones. No one argues the fact that bitterness can isolate people.

5 false deduction

The false "either/or" deduction is a common but easily avoided error. The error lies in assuming that there are only two alternatives and that if one of them is true, the other must be false. If a parent tells his child, "You must be lazy because the only reasons for poor school work are laziness or stupidity, and I know you aren't dumb," the parent commits this error. He ignores other alternatives: the child may be bored with easy work, or he may lack adequate training, or he may be unhappy for a variety of reasons.

> The reliable "either/or" deduction must have two mutually exclusive alternatives which include all possibilities.

For example: "By state law a bond issue needs a two-thirds majority, or else it fails. This bond issue must have failed because it officially received 17,200 votes for it and 9,890 against it."

SUMMARY AND REVIEW

Unsound reasoning is often the result of ignorance rather than intentional deception or unchangeable prejudice: the writer has not known enough, and perhaps not cared enough, about his subject and so he has generalized hastily. Clear and cogent

Log

arguments require clear and cogent evidence. Whenever you have freedom in choosing a topic, pick the one that interests you the most. If the topic is appropriate to the assignment and limited in scope, it is probably your best choice because you are willing to learn more about it.

The review is a checklist of some key points. The exercises which follow the review will give you an opportunity to apply concretely much of what has been said in this chapter.

a. Facts and Judgments
   1. When you make judgments, be clear and accurate about your facts and the way in which the facts warrant your judgments.
   2. When you have to evaluate conflicting judgments of experts, be sure the men are authorities about the subject; consider a man's announced motives or position in relation to his testimony; and determine whether there is agreement among other experts about the quality of his work.

b. Hasty Generalizations
   1. Avoid the stereotype, the trite, unchanging picture of an ethnic group or social role.
   2. Avoid the unqualified generalization by identifying the approximate numbers involved and the source for your real evidence.
   3. When you have to evaluate typicality, define what features you believe typical and show how these features are found in the evidence.
   4. Assist your reader and yourself by saying why you think your evidence is adequate and for what, if there is likely to be any doubt.
   5. Be sure that your evidence is relevant to your generalizations.
   6. Be sure the evidence for your generalizations is accurate.

c. Mistaken Causal Relationships
   1. To avoid the *post hoc, ergo propter hoc* fallacy, be sure that A and B are always present together before looking for a causal connection.

2. To avoid the reductive fallacy, specify as clearly as you know them the important conditions surrounding your argument, and show as clearly as you can how the causes are sufficient to produce the complex effect.

d. False Analogies

1. Use analogies to illustrate and clarify difficult ideas, not as proof of an argument.

2. To test analogies offered as proof, follow two principles:

   a. The more concrete similarities there are and the more instances that can be cited, the higher is the possibility that the conclusion is true.

   b. The greater the magnitude of the differences and the more irrelevant the similarities that do exist, the less is the chance the conclusion is true.

REVIEW EXERCISES

a. Analyze each of the following generalizations by the four criteria suggested in section 3 b-3, part 1. Be prepared to explain which generalizations are defective and in what ways.

1. From a recent "Letters to the Editor": "Christmas is more commercialized and materialistic this year than it has ever been before. Read the business page and notice the record sales reported by every major city in the country. People are spending at an all-time high just to gratify their love for belongings."

2. From a recent college newspaper: "This school has the worst meals of all of the state colleges. Any athlete or debater can tell you the meals you get at other colleges make the ones we get look awful."

3. From a magazine article: "Stereotypes change and clichés become dead. In the 1920's the American college student was pictured as a gin-swilling Yahoo, complete with raccoon-skin coat and a Model-T; in the 1950's, he was pictured

Log

as a status-seeking conformist, complete with Ivy-League suit and attaché case. By the 1960's, however, these images were dead, replaced by a far truer one. He had become a thoughtful, practical idealist, not out to reform the world but to help where he could. No better proof can be found than in the dramatic growth of the Peace Corps, which, according to the *World Almanac*, had planned for 9,970 members by September 1, 1963."

4. From *Guinness Book of World Records:* "The only admissible evidence upon the true height of giants is that of recent date made under impartial medical supervision. Biblical claims, such as that for Og, King of Bashan, at 9 Assyrian cubits (16 feet 2½ inches) are probably due to a confusion of units. Extreme mediaeval data from bone measurements refer invariably to mastodons or other non-human remains. Claims of exhibitionists, normally under contract not to be measured, are usually distorted for the financial considerations of promoters. There is an example of a recent 'World's Tallest Man' of 9 feet 6 inches being in fact an acromegalic of 7 feet 3½ inches."

5. From Daniel Defoe's "The True-Born Englishman":
But grant the best, how came the change to pass;
A *True-Born Englishman* of *Norman* Race?

      .   .   .

These are the heroes who despise the *Dutch*
And rail at the new-come Foreigners so much;
Forgetting that themselves are all derived
From the most Scoundrel Race that ever lived,
A horrid Crowd of Rambling Thieves and Drones,
Who ransacked kingdoms, and dispeopled towns.
The *Pict* and Painted *Britain,* Treach'rous *Scot*
By hunger, theft, and rapine thither brought;
Norwegian Pirates, Buccaneering *Danes,*
Whose Red-hair'd Off-spring every where remains:
Who joined with *Norman-French* compound the Breed
From whence your *True-Born Englishman* proceed.

Log

A *True-Born Englishman's* a Contradiction,
In Speech an Irony, in Fact a Fiction.
A Banter made to be a test of Fools,
Which those that use it justly ridicules.
A Metaphor invented to express
A Man *a-kin* to all the Universe.

6. From Coleridge's *Biographia Literaria,* Chapter XVII:
   "I am convinced that for the human soul to prosper in rustic life a certain vantage ground is prerequisite. It is not every man that is likely to be improved by a country life or by country labors. Education, or original sensibility, or both, must pre-exist, if the changes, forms, and incidents of nature are to prove a sufficient stimulant. And where they are not sufficient, the mind contracts and hardens by want of stimulants; and the man becomes selfish, sensual, gross, and hard-hearted. Let the management of Poor Laws in Liverpool, Manchester, or Bristol be compared with the ordinary dispensation of the poor rates [taxes to be levied to aid the poor] in agricultural villages, where the farmers are the overseers and guardians of the poor. If my own experience have not been particularly unfortunate, as well as that of the many respectable country clergymen with whom I have conversed on the subject, the result would engender more than skepticism concerning the desirable influences of low and rustic life in and for itself."

b. *Analyze each of the following causal relationships by the tests suggested in 3 b-3, part 2. Be prepared to explain which statements are defective and in what ways.*

1. Smog deteriorates rubber.
2. The Puritan ethic of hard work and thrift started the development of capitalism.
3. Every child in that remedial reading class watches at least fifteen hours of television a week. With all that passive sitting, no wonder they can't read!

Log

4. Since 1940, the government has gotten bigger and bigger and taxes have gone higher and higher. The conclusion is obvious.

5. Not one of his classes had less than fifty people in it. I'm not surprised he nearly flunked out.

6. The reason so many college students are now majoring in the natural sciences is that much better-paying jobs in research became available after Sputnik.

7. More than two-thirds of the people in my district voted against the Fair Housing Law. The only explanation is sheer selfishness: they were afraid for their property values.

8. You can't dismiss the value of magic entirely. There are many authenticated cases of remarkable cures and recoveries. In some instances, the medicine man succeeded after the medically trained missionary had failed.

9. There must be a conspiracy. No country as powerful and as wealthy as ours could have suffered the reverses it has for the last twenty years by accident. Things don't just happen that way; someone plans them.

10. The world population explosion has several causes—better diets, better medical care at childbirth and for the aged, greater control of plagues and diseases, and an increased life span. Of these causes, probably the most important is the increased life span; not only are more children born but they will survive and live longer.

c. *Analyze each of the following analogies to determine whether it is used as an illustration, a hypothesis suggesting further investigation, or as proof. If the analogy is used as proof, judge its validity by the criteria suggested in 3 b-3, part 3. Be prepared to explain how the analogy is false or misleading.*

1. From a student theme: "The sight of a monkey pushing through the jungle, leaping from tree to tree, seems 'natural' and, perhaps, graceful. However, when a monkey is placed in a small cage or zoo, his boundings from side to floor to side to ceiling seem antic and 'unnatural.' The satirist employs the same technique of limitation. He confines his subject, as it were, to a small cage, or at least one tree, for

purposes of close observation. The setting in which he moves his object is limited and its barriers are precisely drawn. The satirist, in effect, traps the victim in his most ridiculous positions and does not allow him to wander off or in any way escape an intensely mocking portrayal— Gulliver chained by the Lilliputians.''

2. From a composition handbook: "Many of the rules in this book, making no mention of exceptions or permissible alternatives, *are* dogmatic—purposely so. If a stranger is lost in a maze of city streets and asks for directions, one doesn't give him the several possible routes, with comments and cautions about each. He will simply become more confused and lost. One sends him arbitrarily on one route without mentioning equally good alternative ways. Likewise, the unskilled writer can best be set right by simple, concise, stringent rules.''

3. From a student editorial: "The administration never gets tired of telling us that the state college is part of society as a whole. It harps on student responsibility for 'good taste' in plays and publications, student responsibility to obey state laws about drinking and driving, and student responsibility for property. By the same line of reasoning, then, how can the administration claim it has the final right to approve of campus organizations and their speakers? If the state university is 'part of society as a whole,' it ought to recognize *our* rights as well as our obligations. We aren't asking for the privilege of being subversive; we are asking for the civil rights we have in 'society as a whole'—the rights to hear whom we wish and join the groups we wish.''

4. From a political pamphlet: "Although sincere and personable, my opponent is young and untried. I have twenty years' experience in the Assembly and I have served on major committees. I know the legislative process intimately. When you choose between us, please remember that 'You don't send a boy to do a man's job.' ''

Log

5. From a research psychiatrist's remarks about LSD: "The argument is sometimes made, 'Prohibition failed, and now alcohol is legal—why not LSD.' Well, we have five million problem alcoholics. Would you add five million 'acid heads' [chronic users of LSD] to this social problem that is already a tremendous burden? We might have been far better off if public opinion had permitted closer control of alcohol than we now have. LSD control will work only if public opinion supports it. Otherwise, we'll have Prohibition all over again."

6. From a student theme: "The college has the same obligation to satisfy the student that a store does to satisfy a customer. Students and their parents pay the bills and they ought to have a much freer say about what courses they take. No clerk would think of telling a customer he had to buy several things he didn't want before he could buy the item he came for. And no store would keep as clerks some of the men the college keeps as professors. They can't even sell their product."

7. From a medical journal: "If you place a number of mice together in fairly close quarters and then systematically introduce an increasing variety of distractions—small noises, objects, movements—you increase the probability of neurotic behavior. Cannot something like this process help explain the growth of neurotic behavior in our ever more crowded, complex society? The possibility is worth considering."

d. *Pick one of the following analogies and write a paragraph using the analogy as proof. Then, in a second paragraph, show precisely how the analogy is false or misleading, as you have developed it.*
    1. The family budget and the federal budget.
    2. The referee in boxing and the arbiter in labor disputes.
    3. The captain of a ship and the president of a democracy.
    4. Tastes in art and tastes in food.

Log

5. Eugenics for humans as well as for animals.
6. The authority of a dictionary and the authority of a rule book.
7. The right to publish the news and to televise trials.
8. Packaging the goods well and giving a lecture well.

e. *The following statements contain unsound reasoning. Identify the different kinds of fallacies and specify what change, if any, would improve the argument.*

1. Either you trust a man or you don't. And if you don't trust him, you don't do business with him. The same principle ought to be observed in foreign affairs: you don't do business with countries you can't trust.

2. Anyone with a grain of sense would have known the county didn't need to buy land for a park. But those officials don't learn easily. It wasn't proof enough for them that a majority voted against the purchase in the election. They had to go to the state legislature and get voted down, too.

3. Freshman "Hell-Week" is one of the oldest and dearest traditions of the college. Many of us alumni can remember having our heads shaved and getting up at midnight for roll calls and jogs around the track. Those of us on the Alumni Board oppose the abolition of the custom. We find the arguments for doing away with "Hell-Week" childish and tiresome. We were good enough sports to go along with the sophomores in our time.

4. I don't see why I received such a low grade on this term paper. I put in hours of work on it and did several rough drafts. And I followed the format you asked for. It doesn't seem fair.

5. Public school employees have gotten more than their fair share of the national income, and they exaggerate their financial needs. According to the *World Almanac*, the average salary on the national level for teachers, supervisors,

Log

and principals was $3,010 in 1950. By 1960, it had risen to $5,135, an increase of 70%. In the same period, according to the *World Almanac*, the Consumer Price index rose from 102.8 in 1950 to 126.5 in 1960, an increase of about 25% in the cost of living. Teachers' complaints about being underpaid hardly seem justified. Besides, they only teach ten months of the year and have a long vacation in which to relax or work as they please.

6. Opposition to the new expressway comes only from a small, loud, selfish minority of home owners who are holding out for more money. State engineers say the proposed route is the cheapest and safest to build. State appraisers have made fair offers, which even the owners themselves admit are equal to average market prices. Hence the inescapable conclusion is that these few holdouts are willing to sacrifice the public good for their own private gain.

7. To be an actor, you have to lack self-restraint. That's why people become actors. All you have to do is look at any famous star and you'll see the living proof.

8. "Greatness" in literature is largely the result of national pride and language. If it weren't for the fact that the English once had a great empire and made their language so important, who would ever have heard of Shakespeare? He would have about as much fame as the national poet of Iceland or Korea. After all, Voltaire and Napoleon found many of Shakespeare's plays unreadable and all of them inferior to the plays of great French dramatists.

9. Candy
   Is dandy
   But liquor
   Is quicker—Ogden Nash

f. *The following is a satire, written by a student, of the arbitrary assumptions, unexamined generalizations, and misleading analo-*

gies which all too often are found in print. In analyzing the argument, see how many of these logical errors you can find.

"Why Have Teachers?"

In the early days of America, before the establishment of compulsory schooling, moral standards were high. People were contented with the simpler virtues. Girls learned to sew, cook, and keep house; men, to farm or work at some trade. Marriages were stable and happy; there was no such thing as divorce. Today this happy scene has changed—the morals of modern America are corrupted. Every newspaper carries stories of murder, embezzlement, adultery, and divorce. What has caused this shocking situation? Is it possible to regain the happy state of the early America?

The most influential institution during the formative years of each American is the school, governed and dominated by the teachers. From these teachers children learn the human faults of blind obedience, prejudice, and the betrayal of one's kind in the form of tattling. These early sown seeds bear the bitter fruit of low morality. Clearly, teachers do much to undermine the morality of American children, and through them, that of society.

The obvious solution is to eliminate the teacher as much as possible. The modern child is increasingly capable of educating himself. There are more college students today than ever before, a fact which proves that youth today possesses superior intelligence. By educating themselves, they would not be subjugated to the influence of teachers. They would share their knowledge willingly, each gaining from the other, with no one person dominating the others. As applied to colleges, this would mean that students would gather in pleasant informal surroundings and discuss intelligently matters with a common appeal, as was done in the medieval university. Not only would they enrich

Log

their knowledge, but they would also learn how to compromise and see each other's viewpoint. By obtaining many viewpoints instead of the one our system presents, the students would learn to know their own minds and think objectively instead of receiving opinions on a silver platter.

Cynics will sneer that this system is impractical, that students need guidance and even indoctrination in fundamentals before they can think on their own. Nothing could be further from the truth! One of the most clear-thinking, intelligent men in this nation's history, Abraham Lincoln, was almost entirely self-educated. Think of the effect on our society of an entire generation with the training and characteristics of Lincoln. The present immorality would disappear; a high moral standard would be developed. The group that is undermining morality would be minimized in its influence, and the education of American youth placed where it belongs—in the hands of these same youth.

THE PARAGRAPH

4

the paragraph as a unit

A paragraph is both a unit in itself and part of a larger whole. As subdivisions of a larger whole, your paragraphs help to indicate the structure of your composition. Paragraph divisions are a conventional signal to the reader that one point is completed and that you are going to the next point. Your paragraphs should therefore mark the logical subdivisions of the subject matter of the whole composition, and each paragraph should follow naturally from the one preceding and lead smoothly into the next. At the same time, a paragraph must be complete in itself. Ask these questions of each paragraph: *Is the paragraph unified? Does it hang together and read smoothly? Is the idea of the paragraph adequately developed?*

Unified paragraphs are not magically created by indented openings; often they are signaled only by spaces or headings, notably in letters (see section 44a-4) or books. This text follows a style omitting indentions after a heading or space.

4 a
paragraph division

As a unit in itself, each paragraph should deal with a single topic. It should have a central idea or purpose, and each sentence in the paragraph should aid in developing this central idea and making it clear. But before you test for unity in any single paragraph, you should consider the relationship of that paragraph to the composition as a whole.

¶U

The essential principle in dividing material into paragraphs is making sure that each paragraph will represent a genuine subdivision of your material and that each break will show a significant turn in the thought.

Check back to your outline and make sure that your paragraph breaks come at an important point in the development of your composition (see chapter 2).

Notice how the writer of the following disunified, overlapping paragraphs was led astray by an illogical thesis statement, which in turn was the result of inadequate analysis:

A Traffic Surveyor

1. [THESIS] **To qualify as a traffic surveyor, you must have patience, perseverance, toleration for odd working hours, and the ability to concentrate.** These qualifications are found in many older college students and graduate students who are looking for a part-time job which will not interfere with classes.

2. In a survey to determine traffic conditions for one whole week, your particular shift might be from 11 p.m. to 3 a.m. when the traffic is very light. The long hours with little to do would make the job impossible for someone who lacks patience.

3. These surveys must be accurate. You must have perseverance to do the job faithfully. If you dislike your job, you must still keep at it; for if you decided to stop, it would prove difficult to obtain someone to take your place on such short notice.

4. In a round-the-clock survey, the early morning and late night hours must be covered. These are generally considered poor working hours. The survey might be arranged so that one group of checkers works four hours on the job and takes eight hours off. Your

sleeping habits must be arranged to meet this schedule. If you could not adjust to this schedule, you would not qualify for such a survey.

5. Your ability to concentrate affects the accuracy of the survey. A survey demands high accuracy, so that if you have difficulty concentrating on one thing for a period of hours, you are lacking in the qualifications for a good traffic surveyor.

6. For keeping high accuracy in the survey, all these qualifications must be met by the surveyor. A lack of one of these would detract from the accuracy of the survey.

The thesis statement specified four qualities necessary in a traffic surveyor, and the writer has tried to make a paragraph of each. But three of the qualities he specified—patience, perseverance, and the ability to concentrate—overlap and run together; even though a separate meaning can be distinguished for each, they are not different enough to justify separate subdivisions. Accordingly, the paragraphs in the composition are fragmentary, repetitive, and disunified. If the writer had combined, in his thesis statement and outline, the necessary qualities into two subdivisions—tolerance of odd working hours and patient concentration—he would have improved his chances of writing unified paragraphs. And he might have noted the omission of some important material: What *is* a traffic survey? Does the surveyor count busses and trucks, or only cars? Why, and for whom? A more careful analysis might have produced an outline something like this:

> I. What a traffic surveyor does
>   A._____
>   B._____
>   C._____etc.
> II. Qualifications for a traffic surveyor
>   A. Ability to tolerate odd working hours
>   B. Patient concentration

¶U

The first step in achieving unified paragraphs is a careful analysis of the material and the coverage of the thesis statement.

Notice in this second student theme how the writer's unified paragraphs (in non-indented style, with spacing) reflect his unified, carefully stated thesis and his clear topic sentences:

A Beet Gatherer

A mechanical sugar-beet gatherer, like many other agricultural machines, is far from perfect. Its main imperfection is that it leaves beets behind, either by breaking them off or missing them altogether. Thus, someone is needed to walk behind the machine, pick up all the beets missed, and toss them into the truck. This is not a complex task, admittedly, but **it is one which requires a good deal of stamina for walking, a sharp eye, and the mastery of some special techniques.** [THESIS]

A most important qualification for the job is knowing how to walk rapidly and steadily over ground which has many large clods on it. The machine moves about four miles per hour and leaves behind it a line of plowed-up dirt about four feet in width. The beet gatherer has to walk upon this plowed dirt (which has large clods every few feet) about as fast as the average person can walk, and for periods up to seven hours without any appreciable time for rest, except the lunch break. On certain types of ground, like dry adobe, the machine may leave as many as one hundred beets in a quarter mile of travel. When this occurs, it is impossible for the gatherer to keep up with the machine, and he must either leave some beets behind or stay behind himself, pile the beets in the field, and pick them up later.

The beet gatherer also needs a keen eye. The beets are about the same color as the dirt around them— this is especially true of the light-colored, sandy soils— and it is difficult to see the beets while walking at a rapid rate. To offset this difficulty, he has to familiarize himself with the shapes of beets, their sizes, and roughly where they will be found in the row. He acquires this familiarity by experience, but even so, sometimes he is fooled.

The beet gatherer soon learns certain techniques which help him do his job more efficiently. For instance, his walking step becomes different from the average person's. He picks up his feet more, in much the same manner as a person tramping through deep snow. This step enables him to avoid large clods while he maintains a rapid rate of motion. He also learns how to carry beets (up to fifteen or twenty) in the crook of his arm in a manner similar to that of a football player who is carrying the ball. Even in routine work such as this, one can take pride in a job well done, and it is this pride which in some measure compensates for the physical labor involved.

Here, the writer has specified in his thesis the minimum qualifications of a beet gatherer. He has established an *orderly sequence* of significant ideas and therefore has made the job of paragraphing much easier for himself. Each paragraph discusses only *one* of the different qualifications and fills it out with relevant specific detail. Each paragraph, in short, is unified in itself and is a logical subdivision of the whole composition.

If you have prepared a detailed outline to accompany your thesis, you may have as many as fifteen or twenty subdivisions of what you wish to say. Yet these subdivisions will not necessarily correspond to the number of paragraphs in your paper, since the size and coverage of your assignment may be a very limited one.

In general, the number of your paragraph divisions is determined by the length at which subtopics are discussed.

In a short paper, it may be desirable to treat several subtopics of an outline in a single paragraph. In other cases, a single topic of an outline may need to be divided into several steps or paragraphs. But in any case, the paragraphs must represent coordinate subdivisions of the whole composition. Consider the following part of a student outline:

II. Advantages of the two-party system
    A. Channeling opinion
        1. Disadvantages of giving the voter too many choices
            a. No clear-cut definition of issues
            b. No majority decision likely
        2. Value of limiting the alternatives to two
    B. Making political choices effective in practice
        1. Compromise and unity within the party
        2. Fixing responsibility for political acts

If the writer, planning a short paper, intends to cover this section of the outline in two paragraphs, he should *not* make the division of A come between 1(a) and 1(b). Such a division would distort the logical structure of his paper, and the two paragraphs would not be unified. A division between A and B would produce unified paragraphs and would help indicate the organization of the material.

If, however, this section of the outline should represent a major part of a long paper, a full discussion of A might take several pages. In that case, several paragraphs would be useful to show the subdivisions of A and several more might be necessary for B.

4 b
the topic sentence

You may have noticed that a writer often begins each paragraph with a sentence that summarizes the paragraph's topic, as in the preceding piece, "A Beet Gatherer": "A most important qualification for the job is knowing how to walk rapidly and steadily over ground which has many large clods on it," or "The beet gatherer also needs a keen eye." *These are topic sentences.*

Topic sentences perform the same function for the individual paragraph that the thesis does for the whole paper. *A topic sentence summarizes the central idea of a paragraph.*

It is a valuable aid in securing paragraph unity: in the rough draft, the writer can use it as a guide to the paragraph's content, and in revising he can check to see that everything in a paragraph is related to the topic sentence, cutting out any details which do not contribute to its development.

4 b-1
topic sentence first

A topic sentence is most frequently found at or near the beginning of a paragraph. A topic sentence located at the beginning guides the writer and prepares the reader for what is to come.

A topic sentence, however, may be placed anywhere in the paragraph—in the middle, after some transitional sentences, or at the end, as a conclusion. Note in the following student paragraphs how the topic sentences at the beginning help unify the material of each paragraph.

OPENING WITH TOPIC SENTENCE
Rachel Carson has used simple illustrations to get important information over to the reader without using complex technical terms. Rather than tell her readers that scarps are formed which mark the upper part of a

great fault, along which the crustal block under Valley X moved in relation to the range, she simply mentions that the crust of the earth fell into folds and wrinkles and that valleys were formed. Miss Carson's statement is clearer to the average reader than the technical one, and yet it gets the same point across. Similarly, because most people already know what sponges, jellyfish, worms, and starfish look like, Miss Carson has chosen these to represent her specific examples of early animal life. They give the reader a general idea of all primitive animal life, since each one is representative of a specific phylum.

In this first example, the writer uses the topic sentence at the beginning as a broad generalization which he then illustrates. The key phrases "simple illustrations" and "without using complex technical terms" give the writer a *framework* into which *to fit* his observations. Similarly, in the second example which follows, the student has used the topic sentence as a framework to contain a series of generalizations as well as observations:

OPENING TOPIC SENTENCE
In *Jude the Obscure*, Hardy shows the disappearance of the traditional, isolated rural community and its ways, and the failure of those born into this dying order to find meaning in it. Very early in the novel, we are told by the eleven-year-old Jude that the village of Marygreen is a "small, sleepy place." There is nothing here to hold a young man's interest or allegiance. The thatched cottages are disappearing and the quaint old church has been torn down and replaced by an ugly modern Gothic building. The very bones of Jude's ancestors are unmarked since the iron crosses set up with the new church have rusted away in the rain. Nature herself, the essence of the rural community, has nearly left the pages of this novel. Here there is a mention of sunshine, there of rain or fog. But the earth is no longer

a vital force in men's lives. There are no seasonal cele-
brations—so often found in Hardy's earlier novels—to
recall the eternal cycles of birth, courtship, and death.
Jude becomes a lonely exile who walks on paved
streets and lives in city apartments where the seasons
pass largely unnoticed.

In this next example, the topic sentence at the beginning is
less a framework than a point of departure:

START WITH TOPIC SENTENCE

**My self and my home, the things naturally closest to
me, are my subjects.** To write about a subject, I must
narrow it down to a particular time or place and,
finally, to the mind of a particular person—me. There is
little chance for a universal theme. My best stories are
of a girl and her family (the women, mostly), of a camp
experience, of a young girl's rebelliousness and mood-
iness. My least satisfactory stories are those cast into a
third rather than a first person narrative and concerning people removed from my experience. An old man
standing on a hot street corner behaves in a contradictory way. Sometimes he speaks as an old man would,
but he is then the old man of other stories I have read.
I have only an approximation of how an old man
would feel through what others have written. Suddenly, the old man breaks into a way of speaking particular to me—quick and girlish—and he becomes a
clumsy, inaccurate character sketch. To escape, I
thrust a trick ending onto my story. The old man is not
convincing; I know it. He is not close to me.

In developing her topic sentence, the girl relies on the phrase
"the things naturally closest to me" as her point of departure.
It helps her explain *why* her best stories are about a young
girl and to understand and explain *why* she cannot write convincingly about an old man.

¶U

4 b-2
topic sentence in the middle or at the end

When a topic sentence occurs in the *middle* of a paragraph, it usually refers back to the sentences which precede it and summarizes the material which follows it. When it *concludes* the paragraph, it usually pulls together a long series of details which have been designed to lead up to it.

Notice how the topic sentence functions in each of the following examples.

TOPIC SENTENCE IN THE MIDDLE
Then something unforeseen happened. The waters of the River, shut out from much land, rose higher upon the lands that were left, and so broke over many dikes and again flooded the farms. The white men cursed, thinking that the rains must have been heavier than before; they decided to build levees a little higher and be safe for ever. *In those years that followed, a confusion as of a nightmare fell upon the Valley.* More and more levees were built, and each one made the water rise so that men had to build up the old ones higher still. The white men would not withdraw from the lands, and neither in their peculiar madness would they all work together against the River. Instead, in the dark rainy nights a man might break his neighbor's levee to lower the water-level against his own; so, not with shovels, but with loaded guns, men patrolled the levees, like savages brandishing spears against the river-god.

TOPIC SENTENCE AT THE END
At last, although the white men hated the very sound of the words, they began to talk more and more of "the government" and "regulation." Then finally came engineers who looked shrewdly not at one part of the River, but at the whole. They

measured snow and rain, and the depth of streams. They surveyed; they calculated with many figures how high the levees must be and how wide the channels between. Gradually even the fiercest fighters among the white men came to see that the River (which was always the whole River) was too great for any man or company of men. Only the Whole People could hope to match the Whole River. *So, after many years of disaster the white men began to live in a truce with the river.*

—George R. Stewart

In narrative writing, especially, the topic sentence at the paragraph's end is often a forceful climax to the build-up of details or a means of gaining distance from them. Notice in the following student paragraph how the topic sentence gives perspective:

TOPIC SENTENCE ENDING

I was not sure when I hated onion weeding the most. There were the hot days when I would be covered with powdery muck and the sweat would form in beads on my head and arms and run down in dirty streams from my bare back and chest, and my knees would feel as if I were crawling across the grill over a big charcoal fire. There were also the muggy days after a rain when I would come to work in the morning and the tops of onions would seem to lop over in the middle of the rows so they could smear the water clinging to them off on me, and the earth would seem like an enormous warm sponge oozing black mud that would stick to everything that touched it. **But rain or shine, I was sure that I would rather have gone to school the whole year around than weed onions in the summer heat and humidity.**

Not *every* paragraph you will write will have a topic sentence, though the practice of including a focusing sentence in each paragraph is a useful one. In some cases, the topic sentence may be omitted altogether without violating unity. *But it*

¶U

should always be possible to summarize the central thought in a sentence. For instance, in the following student paragraph, though there is no topic sentence, the central idea might be summarized thus: *The long school day at the medieval University of Paris demanded much from the students.*

TOPIC SENTENCE LEFT IMPLIED

Classes at the medieval University of Paris began at 5 a.m. First on the agenda were the ordinary lectures, which were the regular and more important lectures. After several ordinary lectures and a short, begrudged lunch hour, students attended extraordinary lectures given in the afternoon. These were supplementary to the ordinary lectures and usually given by a less important teacher, who may not have been more than fourteen or fifteen years old. A student would spend ten or twelve hours a day with his teachers, and then following classes in the late afternoon, he had sports events. But after sports, the day was not over. There was homework, which consisted of copying, recopying, and memorizing notes while the light permitted. Nor was there much of a break. Christmas vacation was about three weeks, and summer vacation was only a month.

If your papers are criticized for disunified paragraphs, you should certainly make a conscientious effort to write a clear topic sentence for each of your paragraphs.

Similarly, you can often clarify an assigned reading by locating and underlining the topic sentence for the paragraphs that confuse you. If the paragraphs have no identifiable topic sentences, construct them yourself. Remember that the great value of the topic sentence for the reader and writer alike is its function as an accurate summary of the paragraph's central idea.

4 c
length of paragraph

The principle which governs paragraph length is the convenience of the reader. If each sentence is a separate paragraph, the reader will be unable to see the groupings the writer has in mind. If, on the other hand, there are too many sentences in the paragraph, the reader will be unable to see the subdivisions of the material clearly.

Paragraphs which run *consistently* to more than a page are little better than no paragraphing at all, since the reader is forced to make the subdivisions of the material for himself.

Ordinarily, then, a paragraph should consist of more than one sentence but less than a page. But note that paragraphs vary considerably in length in different kinds of writing. In formal, scientific, or scholarly writing they are sometimes as long as 250 words. In ordinary magazine articles the average length is about 150 words. In newspapers the average is 50 words or less. Good questions to ask yourself are "Should any of my paragraphs be written as two, for clarity?" and "Are there any noticeably short paragraphs so closely related that they should be combined?" If the writer of the first theme which follows had questioned himself about the paragraphing on his opening page, he would have revised it for greater unity. Here is a major part of the first page, followed by the student's revision.

DISUNIFIED: GROUPINGS UNCLEAR

(1.) In **Barchester Towers** Anthony Trollope's most fully developed character is Mr. Slope. Slope is the nearest Trollope comes to a villain.

(2.) He commits the mortal sin of the age—the disrupting of social order. Barchester is a quiet, easygoing Victorian province and Mr. Slope is a pusher who upsets the harmony of this clerical paradise.

(3.) But Slope is not wholly despicable. Although he is an opportunist, he is not a hypocrite.

(4.) Slope believes wholeheartedly in the religion he teaches and dedicates himself realistically and entirely to its furtherance.

(5.) He craves no materialistic benefits but only the power to convey his beliefs.

However, Slope violates the "natural laws" of society by disturbing the social order and he must suffer....

PARAGRAPHS COMBINED FOR UNITY

In **Barchester Towers** Anthony Trollope's most fully developed character is Mr. Slope. Slope is the nearest Trollope comes to a villain; Slope commits the mortal sin of the age—the disrupting of social order. Barchester is a quiet, easygoing Victorian province and Mr. Slope is a pusher who upsets the harmony of this clerical paradise.

Paragraphs #1 and #2 combined (non-indented spaced style).

But Slope is not wholly despicable. Although he is an opportunist, he is not a hypocrite. He believes wholeheartedly in the religion he teaches and dedicates himself realistically and entirely to its furtherance. He craves no materialistic benefits but only the power to convey his beliefs.

Paragraphs #3, #4, and #5 are combined.

Nevertheless, Slope violates the "natural laws" of society by disturbing the social order and he must suffer. . . .

By joining the first two paragraphs together and the second two together, the student achieved greater unity. The reader

can now more easily follow the student's argument that a) Slope commits the mortal sin of disrupting social order, and b) Slope sincerely wants power only to further his religious beliefs. The student might even have joined the first four paragraphs into one unified whole. But as it stands, his revision eliminates the needlessly short paragraphs and groups the ideas more conveniently.

The writer of the following passage did not build it up painfully by adding one paragraph to another; rather, he conceived of the passage as a unified and coherent whole. Consequently, it has movement and continuity. Nevertheless, it is too long to appear as a single paragraph, and the division into three (non-indented opening style), which may well have been made in revision, helps the reader follow the line of thought.

UNITY TO HELP CONTINUITY

An American making his first trip abroad will do well to go first to London and then move on to the cities of the continent. In this way he proceeds gradually from the familiar to the strange and avoids what international travel agencies call cultural shock. England will be enough different from the United States to interest and excite him, but it will not be so totally unfamiliar as to overwhelm and frighten him.

A landing in Genoa or Le Havre may have, on a normally sensitive person, the effect of a blow. The newly arrived visitor is too dazed by the difficulties of a new language, new money, and new customs, to enjoy or even to see clearly what is around him. By the time he has recovered his self-possession, he has lost some precious time. And then he is confronted with some of the greatest art in the world and some of the most colorful people. His appetite for seeing is soon dulled by an excess of riches. Florence and Rome and Paris are too magnificent to be taken in without some preparation and training. Almost certainly the tourist will suffer from a kind of visual indigestion. It will eventually be cured by his developing a protec-

tive immunity: he simply will not see, or even try to see, everything. Overstimulation leads to jaded sensibilities, and by the time he reaches London on his way home, London may strike him as a bit drab and dingy.

This judgment is unfair to London, which although not so exotic to Americans as Naples, is still one of the most interesting and lively cities in Europe. For an American just arriving abroad, London has the special charm of being new and different but not completely strange. He will be able to understand the language at once, and thus he will have a good start toward understanding the people and their culture. The plays he may wish to go to will be intelligible, and he will probably wish to go because London has more new, varied and exciting theatre than any other city in the world. The places and buildings he sees will be memorable because their names and associations are already fixed in his mind. Westminster Abbey, St. Paul's, Buckingham Palace, Downing Street, and Piccadilly—such words represent an existing framework into which he may fit the exciting realities he is now seeing for the first time. And he will be able to really see them, since he will not be dazed by a completely new way of life, nor surfeited with the splendors of St. Peter's and the Pitti Palace and the Champs Élysées.

4 c-1
short paragraphs for transition and for emphasis

To call attention to an important transition or shift in the line of thought, or to emphasize a crucial point, you may occasionally use a very short paragraph.

Sometimes, a short paragraph will serve both these purposes. *In any case, such paragraphs should be used sparingly.* In the following example, the writer could have placed his transitional sentence at the end of the first paragraph or, more gracefully, at the beginning of the second; but he chose instead to emphasize its importance as a transitional sentence by making it into a separate paragraph:

TRANSITION STRESSED

The amount of specialized training required of a physicist or chemist today is enormous. In high school and college he will need to acquire a thorough grounding in mathematics—the essential tool of engineer and scientist alike. As an undergraduate he will take nearly half of all his work in his special field, and this will consist not of general surveys but of highly technical courses aimed at giving him a full knowledge of a few parts of his field and at least an awareness of the areas he has barely touched on. In graduate school he will try to fill in these gaps and at the same time move on in a few areas to more advanced research. Seven years after graduating from high school, he may have his Ph.D. and the feeling that he is competent in at least some areas of his field.

But although this highly specialized study is essential to the making of a competent scientist, something more is needed if we are to produce great scientists.

This first requirement is. . . .

Similarly, in this next example the student could have joined his short paragraph of rhetorical emphasis to the preceding paragraph or to the one following. By making the two sentences into a separate paragraph, he stresses the importance of his early training and the shock he was to receive.

TURNING POINT STRESSED

. . . I know from personal experience that Erich Fromm's criticism that the American male is forced to repress his feelings has truth in it. Our society does tend to suspect emotional outbursts in a man as signs of "abnormality." From childhood onward, I was taught to "control" my emotions. I was told constantly that good little boys don't cry; they act like big strong men. The little boy who fell off his tricycle and got up with a smile was admired and recommended as a model to be emulated by the rest of the tricycle set. Nor were feelings of pain the only emotion I was encouraged to suppress. Anger, hostility, envy, and melancholy were all taboo. I gradually became accustomed to this training. It was almost impossible to resist.

By the age of thirteen, I was a true believer in this Spartan code. It was at this age that I was first startled into doubting it.

My uncle had been ill but had kept this fact secret from. . . .

4 c-2
short paragraphs for dialogue

In a narrative, direct quotation, together with the rest of a sentence of which it is a part, is usually paragraphed separately. The reason for this convention is to make immediately clear to the reader the change of speaker.

For example:

IDENTIFIED SPEAKERS PARAGRAPHED SEPARATELY

"Now lookee here!" said the man. "Where's your mother?"

"There, sir!" said I.

He started, made a short run, and stopped and looked over his shoulder.

"There, sir!" I timidly explained. "Also Georgiana. That's my mother."

"Oh!" said he, coming back. "And is that your father alonger your mother?"

"Yes, sir," said I; "him too; late of the parish."

—Charles Dickens

This same convention is usually observed in cases where the speaker is not named each time.

UNIDENTIFIED SPEAKERS PARAGRAPHED SEPARATELY

"Hello," she said. "Are you awake?"

"Where have you been?"

"I just went out to get a breath of air."

"You did, like hell."

"What do you want me to say, darling?"   —Ernest Hemingway

However, a short quoted speech which is closely united with the context is sometimes included in a paragraph of narration:

SHORT DIALOGUE INCLUDED

Now and then Mr. Bixby called my attention to certain things. Said he, "This is Six-Mile Point." I assented. It was pleasant enough information but I could not see the bearing of it. I was not conscious that it was a matter of any interest to me. Another time he said, "This is Nine-Mile Point." Later he said, "This is Twelve-Mile Point." They were all about level with the water's edge; they all looked alike to me; they were monotonously unpicturesque. . . .   —Mark Twain

SUMMARY AND REVIEW

To assist yourself in writing unified paragraphs, be sure that:

    a. Your thesis is clear and your outline indicates the major steps for your whole analysis.

    b. Your individual paragraphs represent logical divisions of the whole composition.

    c. Your individual paragraphs have topic sentences or can be summarized accurately in a sentence.

To assist your reader's comprehension, be sure that:

    a. Your ordinary paragraphs consist of more than one sentence but less than a full page.

    b. Your paragraphs are not short and choppy and that if one is brief, it marks an important transition or emphasizes a crucial idea.

REVIEW EXERCISES

4

a. The following selection was originally written as six paragraphs. Try outlining it, first. Then indicate where, in your opinion, the divisions should be made and be able to give reasons for your choice. In dividing the section, try to find topic sentences for your paragraphs.

To begin to understand economic development we must have a picture of the problem with which it contends. We must conjure up in our mind's eye what underdevelopment means for the two billion beings for whom it is not a statistic but a living experience of daily life. Unless we can see the Great Ascent from the vantage point of those who must make the climb, we cannot hope to understand the difficulties of the march. It is not easy to make this mental jump. But let us attempt it by imagining how a typical American family, living in a small suburban home on an income of six or seven thousand dollars, could be transformed into an equally typical family of the underdeveloped world. We begin by invading the house of our imaginary American family to strip it of its furniture. Everything goes: beds, chairs, tables, television set, lamps. We will leave the family with a few old blankets, a kitchen table, a wooden chair. Along with the bureaus go the clothes. Each member of the family may keep in his "wardrobe" his oldest suit or dress, a shirt or blouse. We will permit a pair of shoes to the head of the family, but none for the wife or children. We move into the kitchen. The appliances have already been taken out, so we turn to the cupboards and larder. The box of matches may stay, a small bag of flour, some sugar and salt. A few moldy potatoes, already in the garbage can, must hastily be rescued, for they will provide much of tonight's meal. We will leave a handful of onions, and a dish of dried beans. All the rest we take away: the meat, the fresh vegetables, the canned goods, the crackers, the candy. Now we have stripped the house: the bathroom has been dismantled, the running water shut off, the electric wires taken out. Next we take away the house. The family can move to the toolshed. It is crowded, but much better than the situation in Hong Kong, where (a United Nations report tells us) "it is not uncommon for a family of four or more to live in a bedspace, that is, on a bunk bed and the space it occupies—sometimes in two or three tiers —their only privacy provided by curtains." But we have only begun. All the other houses in the neighborhood have also been removed; our suburb has become a shantytown. Still, our family is fortunate to have a shelter; 250,000 people in Calcutta have none at all and simply live in the streets. Our family is now about on a par with the city of Cali in Colombia, where, an official of the World Bank writes, "on one hillside alone, the slum population is estimated at 40,000—without water, sanitation, or electric light. And not all the poor of Cali are as fortunate as that. Others have built their shacks near the city on land which lies beneath the flood mark. To these people the immediate environment is the open sewer of the city, a sewer which flows through their huts when the river rises." —Robert L. Heilbroner

b. *In the following selections find and mark the topic sentence. Be prepared to explain why your choice is the most complete summary or statement of the paragraph's main idea.*

It is easy to idealize Lincoln and to read into him your own views and beliefs until they become his as well. But it is even easier to deflate than to idealize, to set him down as just a shoddy horse-trading politician. He was not that. If ever there was a man in our history who had the difficult stuff of heroism, this was the man. He was no absolutist and no program-builder. But neither was there any cant in him, as we know when we read his ironic letter to the delegation of ministers protesting as Christians against the war. He did a hard job well, with dignity, firmness, and—in the midst of desperate measures—with compassion. Always he had the distinguishing mark of greatness, the ability in any problem to get at the jugular. He saw when he came to office that the crux of adequate Presidential power in an emergency lay in the President's role as commander-in-chief. And although a hard-bitten realist, he could know the meaning and the value of a dream. —M. Lerner

If we would discover the little backstairs door that for any age serves as the secret entranceway to knowledge, we will do well to look for certain unobtrusive words with uncertain meanings that are permitted to slip off the tongue or the pen without fear and without research; words which, having from constant repetition lost their metaphorical significance, are unconsciously taken for objective realities. In the thirteenth century the key words would no doubt be God, sin, grace, salvation, heaven, and the like; in the nineteenth century, matter, fact, matter-of-fact, evolution, progress; in the twentieth century, relativity, process, adjustment, function, complex. In the eighteenth century the words without which no enlightened person could reach a restful conclusion were nature, natural law, first cause, reason, sentiment, humanity, perfectibility (these last three being necessary only for the more tender-minded, perhaps). —Carl L. Becker

Disease from contaminated food or beverages was very common a few generations ago, and nutritional deficiencies were almost the rule. Now laboratories check on the safety of what we eat and drink. Furthermore, the nutritional requirements of man are now well known, and in the Western World, at least, we have the means to satisfy them. But all this theoretical and practical knowledge does not guarantee that nutrition will not present problems in the immediate future, even assuming that economic prosperity continues. On the one hand, modern agriculture and food technology have come to depend more and more on the use of chemicals to control pests and to improve the yields of animal and plant products. The cost of food production would enormously increase without these chemicals, and for this reason their use is justified. Unfortunately, however, and despite all care, several of them eventually reach the human consumer in objectionable concentrations. As more and more substances are introduced in agriculture and food technology every year, it will become practically impossible to test them all with regard to long-range effects on human health, and the possibility of toxic reactions must be accepted as one of the inevitable risks of progress. —René Dubos

I never observed in William James any personal anxiety or enthusiasm for any of these dubious tenets [certain beliefs discussed in James's *The Varieties of Religious Experience*]. His conceptions even of such a thing as free will, which he always ardently defended, remained vague; he avoided defining even what he conceived to be desirable in such matters. But he wished to protect the weak against the strong, and what he hated beyond everything was the *non possumus* [we cannot] of any constituted authority. Philosophy for him had a Polish constitution; so long as a single vote was cast against the majority, nothing could pass. The suspense of judgment, which he had imposed on himself as a duty, became almost a necessity. I think it would have depressed him if he had had to confess that any important question was finally settled. He would still have hoped that something might turn up on the other side, and that just as the scientific hanging was about to dispatch the poor convicted prisoner, an unexpected witness would ride up in hot haste, and prove him innocent. Experience seems to most of us to lead to conclusions, but empiricism has sworn never to draw them.

—George Santayana

c. *In each of the following paragraphs, several sentences have been italicized as possible topic sentences. For each paragraph, choose the sentence which you think is the most complete summary or statement of the paragraph's main idea. Be prepared to justify your choice by showing in detail how it more adequately summarizes the paragraph's contents than the other possible topic sentences do. If none of the alternatives seems acceptable, write your own topic sentence.*

Let us define a plot. We have defined a story as a narrative of events arranged in their time-sequence. *A plot is also a narrative of events, the emphasis falling on causality.* "The king died and then the queen died" is a story. "The king died, and then the queen died of grief" is a plot. The time sequence is preserved, but the sense of causality overshadows it. Or again: "The queen died, no one knew why, until it was discovered that it was through grief at the death of the king." This is a plot with a mystery in it, a form capable of high development. *It suspends the time-sequence, it moves as far away from the story as its*

ℚU

limitations will allow. Consider the death of the queen. If it is in a story we say "and then?" If it is in a plot *we ask "why?" That is the fundamental difference between these two aspects of the novel.* A plot cannot be told to a gaping audience of cave-men or to a tyrannical sultan or to their modern descendant the movie-public. They can only be kept awake by "and then—and then—" They can only supply curiosity. *But a plot demands intelligence and memory also.*   —E. M. Forster

Inside the play-ground an absolute and peculiar order reigns. *Here we come across another, a very positive feature of play: it creates order, is order.* Into a very imperfect world and into the confusion of life it brings a temporary, a limited perfection. *Play demands order absolute and supreme.* The least deviation from it "spoils the game," robs it of its character and makes it worthless. *The profound affinity between play and order is perhaps the reason why play, as we have noted in passing, seems to lie to such a large extent in the field of aesthetics.* Play has a tendency to be beautiful. *It may be that this aesthetic factor is identical with the impulse to create orderly form, which animates play in all its aspects.* The words we use to denote the elements of play belong for the most part to aesthetics, terms with which we try to describe the effects of beauty: tension, poise, balance, contrast, variation, solution, resolution, etc. Play casts a spell over us; it is "enchanting," "captivating." *It is invested with the noblest qualities we are capable of perceiving in things: rhythm and harmony.*   —Johan Huizinga

Thus the differences between the conservative and the radical seem to spring mainly from their attitude toward the future. Fear of the future causes us to lean against and cling to the present, while faith in the future renders us receptive to change. Both the rich and the poor, the strong and the weak, they who have achieved much or little can be afraid of the future. *When the present seems so perfect that the most we can expect is its even continuation in the future, change can only mean deterioration.* Hence men of outstanding achievement and those who live full, happy lives usually set their faces against drastic innovation. The conservatism of invalids and people past middle age stems, too, from fear of the future. They are on the lookout for signs of decay, and feel that any change is more likely to be for the worse than for the better. The abjectly poor also are without faith in the future. The future seems to them a booby trap buried on the road ahead. One must step gingerly. *To change things is to ask for trouble.* —Eric Hoffer

d. *Select any two of the following statements. Use each as the topic sentence for a unified paragraph.*

1. Students often learn more from each other than they do from their classes.
2. Unless he rebels, an adolescent can't grow up.
3. The slogan "Progress is our most important product" is misleading because progress is an attitude towards achievement, not the achievement itself.
4. Curiosity and intelligence are not identical because curiosity is often nothing more than animal inquisitiveness or rude snooping.

for 20 OCT 69
to pg 132

5

paragraph coherence

Within every paragraph the sentences should be arranged and linked in such a manner that the reader can easily follow the thought.

It is not enough for the reader to know what the sentence means; he must also see how each sentence is related to the one which precedes it and how it leads into the one which follows it. The connections may be clear enough to the writer but not at all clear to the reader: incoherence means that the relationships have not been shown, not that they don't exist.

If paragraphs lack unity, they will, of course, lack coherence; but even if paragraphs have unity, they may not be as coherent as they should be. That is, even if a paragraph has a clear central idea, its individual sentences may be arranged in a poor order and they may be poorly connected. The means of securing continuity—paragraph coherence—are, first, the arrangement of sentences in a logical order and, second, the use of special devices such as the repetition of key words to link sentences.

5 a
logical order of ideas

Though a topic sentence will help secure paragraph unity, it will not by itself "write" the paragraph. You need a consistent pattern of organization within the paragraph to help ensure coherence. The particular pattern will depend on the kind of

material which is to go into the paragraph. The four patterns of development to be discussed include chronological order, spatial order, deductive order, and inductive order.

5 a-1
chronological order

The pattern most often used for narrating personal experiences, summarizing steps in a process, and explaining historical events and movements is *chronological* order, arranging events in an orderly time sequence.

If the time sequence of a narrative is unclear or disorderly, for example, incoherence can result:

INCOHERENT

During my first week as a waitress, I could only stumble home after a day's work and fall into bed. My routine is the regular one [PRESENT TENSE]: take orders, carry food, clean up tables, and repeat— eight hours a day, six days a week. By the end of the summer, I had firmly resolved never to take another job unless the work itself was interesting [CONCLUSION BELONGING LAST]. I took the job for purely ulterior motives: I had been attracted by local fables of the generous tips left by tourists and thought I would earn some easy money towards a college wardrobe [CHRONOLOGICALLY, MOTIVES BELONG PRIOR TO ROUTINE]. Even when I had become accustomed to the routine, I never had any trouble distinguishing between the drudgery of that hot, noisy restaurant and the relaxation which came naturally but too briefly with the leisure of a cool evening.

In revising the paragraph for greater coherence, the student placed her motives first and then arranged the rest of the paragraph in an orderly chronological sequence— routine, first week on the job, following weeks on the job,

¶Coh

5
a-1

conclusion at the summer's end about the value of interest-ing work. She also eliminated the confusing shifts in tense.

PATTERNED CHRONOLOGICALLY

Last summer I took a job as a waitress. My motives at the time were purely ulterior: I had been attracted by local fables of the generous tips left by tourists and thought I would earn some easy money towards a col-lege wardrobe. My routine was the regular one: take orders, carry food, clean up the table, and repeat—eight hours a day, six days a week. During that first week, I could only stumble home after a day's work and fall into bed. Even when I had become accus-tomed to the routine, I never had any trouble distin-guishing between the drudgery of that hot, noisy res-taurant and the relaxation which came naturally but too briefly with the leisure of a cool evening. By the end of the summer, I had firmly resolved never to take another job unless the work itself was interesting.

For a more specific use of chronological order, see section 6a-6 on development by cause and effect.

5 a-2
spatial order

An important pattern of organization is *spatial,* useful for many kinds of description. This pattern helps pro-vide coherence by arranging visual details from left to right, right to left, east to west, west to east, from the distant to the near, or the near to the distant.

If the writer moves haphazardly from one place to another, he violates the pattern and produces an incoherent pattern like this one:

INCOHERENT

The night was clear and cool. A biting wind from snowy Taos Mountain made the girls shiver as

they crouched close to the embankment and looked down at the procession passing beneath them. There was only a small crescent moon and the small blue stars, cold and far away. Janet heard loud squeaking and creaking and rose up for a better look. She saw the Carreta del Muerto, the cart of death, passing below. On the top of the cart sat a figure of death, an intricately carved skeleton representing expert craftsmanship and a detailed knowledge of the human body. A bent-over man was pulling the crude wooden cart on large wheels. The skeleton was veiled in a black cloak and held a drawn bow and an arrow nocked for flight. He rode in the middle of the procession, instilling fear into the heart of every man, for the mystery of death is veiled, and no man can tell where he will strike next. The skeleton's eyes were obsidian, glass, or mother-of-pearl, some shiny stone to catch the pale moonlight and show that death was alive, his eyes searching the darkness.

By hopping from the girls to the sky, from the sky to the squeaking and the cart, from the cart to the intricately carved skeleton, from the skeleton to the bent man and large wheels, from the man and the wheels back to the veiled figure carrying a bow, from the veiled figure to the middle of the procession, and from the middle of the procession back to the skeleton's eyes, the writer has blurred her focus. In revising, she began with the sky, moved down to the girls, down from them to the cart and the man, and then concluded with the skeleton. Notice how the increased coherence gives the description a real climax:

SPATIAL PATTERN

The night was clear and cool. There was only a small crescent moon and the small blue stars, cold and far away. A biting wind from snowy Taos Mountain made the girls shiver as they crouched close to the embankment and looked down at the procession passing beneath them. Janet heard loud squeaking and creaking and rose up for a better look. She saw the Carreta del Muerto, the cart of death, passing beneath. A bent-over man was pulling the crude wooden cart on large wheels. On top of the cart sat a figure of death, an intricately carved skeleton representing expert craftsmanship and a detailed knowledge of the human body. The figure was veiled in a black cloak and held a drawn bow and an arrow nocked for flight. The skeleton's eyes were obsidian, glass, or mother-of-pearl, some shiny stone to catch the pale moonlight and show that death was alive, his eyes searching the darkness. He rode in the middle of the procession, instilling fear in the heart of every man, for the mystery of death is veiled, and no man can tell where he will strike next.

5 a-3
deductive order

A paragraph laid out in *deductive* order makes a well-known logical structure. The pattern of organization is one which moves from a general statement to the particular details which support or explain it.

The deductive pattern helps provide coherence by grouping details to show which part of the generalization (usually the topic sentence) they are most relevant to. See section 6a-1 for a discussion of development by specific detail. When the details are scattered throughout the paragraph, however, incoherence results. The reader is left with a blurred memory of miscellaneous information, as in the following example:

SCATTERED

The Roman Empire expanded because the Romans were great organizers as well as fine builders and engineers. A few of their bridges and roads in France and Italy are still used today. The Romans introduced Latin as a common language. They didn't try to change all of the religious beliefs and

social customs of the conquered people. For example, they didn't compel the Egyptians to accept the Roman gods. When the Romans conquered a territory, they systematically tried to make it a willing part of the Empire. They brought Roman law and the promise of Roman citizenship. Sometimes they recruited and trained native men to become Roman soldiers, as in the case of the members of the German tribes who became part of the Praetorian Guard. These were the Emperor's personal soldiers. Roman engineers built excellent roads and bridges. Also, the Romans constructed key cities and highways to consolidate their military and financial power in the colony, as they did when they built London as a military depot and trade center. The roads leading to the city gave the Romans good control over the surrounding countryside.

The paragraph jumps from bridges and roads to language and religion, from language and religion to law and citizenship, from law and citizenship to the training of soldiers, from the training of soldiers back to bridges and roads. To make the paragraph coherent, the student revised it by dividing the paragraph into two parts and grouping his details accordingly:

PATTERNED DEDUCTIVELY

The Roman Empire expanded because the Romans were great organizers as well as fine builders and engineers. **When they conquered a territory, they systematically tried to make it a willing part of the Empire** [FIRST PART]. They brought Roman law and the promise of Roman citizenship and they introduced Latin as a common language. Sometimes they recruited and trained native men to become Roman soldiers, as in the case of the members of the German tribes who became part of the Praetorian Guard, the Emperor's personal soldiers. But they did not try to change all of the religious beliefs and social customs of the conquered people. For example, they did not try to compel the Egyptians to accept the Roman gods. **Moreover, when the Romans conquered a territory, they constructed key cities and highways to consolidate their military and financial power in the colony** [SECOND PART]. London, for instance, was built as a military depot and trade center. The excellent roads and bridges built by Roman engineers to the main administrative city gave the Romans good control over the surrounding countryside. A few of these bridges and roads in France and Italy are still in use today.

In revision, the student located the two main aspects of his topic sentence about the Romans—their systematic efforts to make subject peoples loyal, and their skill in building roads and power centers. By locating these aspects, he was also able to combine or de-emphasize certain particulars. In the original, for example, "These were the Emperor's personal soldiers" is apparently as important an idea as "Sometimes they recruited and trained native men to become Roman soldiers . . . ." In the revision, this particular bit of information about the Praetorian Guard is properly de-emphasized. By grouping his details, the student has made his paragraph more coherent.

5 a-4
inductive order

Another logical pattern for paragraphs is arrangement by *inductive* order. The inductive paragraph is organized with the details at the beginning and in the middle, and with an ending which is a summary or generalization, usually the topic sentence.

The inductive pattern is the complementary counterpart of the deductive; some of the preceding deductively arranged material about the Romans might just as easily have been arranged and more fully developed in this pattern:

INDUCTIVE PATTERN

Roman roads were built on a solid stone base and paved with flat rocks. They were crowned on the top and ditched along the sides for drainage. They were designed to run in almost straight lines and to go over hills, not around them. Roman armies used them as military highways—ten to twenty feet wide—to move legions rapidly and to supply them adequately. These roads led to and from key administrative cities such as London, originally built as a depot and trade center, and gave the Romans good control over the surrounding countryside. In Britain alone, a great series of roads radiated from the southeast to all parts of the island. **Thanks to these superbly designed roads linking cities and ensuring rapid troop movement, the Romans could hold conquered territory and expand the Empire.**

These four patterns of organization—the chronological, spatial, deductive, and inductive—can help make your paragraphs coherent. They do so by following a consistent structure, apparent to the reader. But remember that to be effective, the pattern must be suited to the material which goes into the paragraph, and the pattern must be consistently followed.

5 b
special devices

The other means of providing coherence include the use of transitional words, the use of linking pronouns, the repetition of key words, and the use of parallel structure. Usually, an experienced writer employs *all* these means, and he is not much interested in the label attached to the method he uses. Instead, he is concerned to achieve coherence accurately and gracefully. But here it will be helpful to discuss separately and clearly each technique available to you for improving paragraphs which lack coherence. What happens when the available means are not fully employed can be seen in the following paragraph:

¶Coh

ERRATIC

I was a naive child. My parents sheltered me. All playmates were picked with care. I wasn't allowed to join any of the gangs that roamed the neighborhood so freely, and the TV shows I saw and books I read were carefully picked. When I went to camp, I was on my own. I expected the other campers to "play fair" and abide by the rules. At the dinner table, one camper opened my eyes, as well as making them sting, when he blew pepper into them. He had invited me to see something in his hand. I was surprised the next day when I found another camper reading a comic book called "Tales of the Horror from the Crypt." He lounged on my bunk and dripped a melting candy bar onto my blanket. This was the beginning of my real education. I had to learn how to make my own decisions about people and situations and act on these decisions for myself.

Though it has unity and development, the paragraph generally lacks coherence because the writer too often leaps and jumps erratically from one sentence to the next, as reading aloud will make especially clear. Revised by slight rephrasing and the addition of connecting words, the paragraph becomes easier to follow:

MORE COHERENT

I was a naive child **because** my parents sheltered me. **They picked** my playmates carefully **and** kept me from joining any of the gangs that so freely roamed the neighborhood. **They censored** the TV I watched and the books I read. **Thus, when they sent me** away to camp, I was on my own **for the first time in my life, and as a result of my training,** I exected the other campers to "play fair" and abide by the rules. The **first camper** to open my eyes, as well as make them sting, did so at the dinner table by blowing pepper into them, **after inviting** me to see something in his hand. **Another camper** surprised me the next day when I found him

reading a comic book called "Tales of the Horror from the Crypt" **as** he lounged on my bunk and dripped a melting candy bar onto my blanket. **That summer** at camp was the beginning of my real education. **For the first time** I had to learn how to make my own decisions about people and situations and act on these decisions myself.

In the revised passage, *the writer is no longer thinking in single sentences only.* Instead, he has looked for the continuity among his ideas and for the most accurate means of showing this continuity in each case.

5 b-1
use of transitional words

Transitional words and phrases should be used according to the kind of relationship they indicate.

Here are some helpful classifications for relationships that may be shown by various transitional words:

1. Result or consequence: *hence, consequently, as a result, therefore.*
2. Comparison or contrast: *similarly, likewise, however, on the other hand, yet, still, nevertheless.*
3. Example or illustration: *as an illustration, for example, specifically, for instance.*
4. Additional aspects or evidence: *moreover, furthermore, also, too, next, besides, in the first place, first.*
5. Conclusion or summary: *in conclusion, to sum up, to conclude, in short.*

These logical signals must be clearly and accurately used. If they are not, the reader will be misled. Some transitional words like "however" and "nevertheless" are important indicators of a sharp *turn* in the thought—a qualification or a statement of an opposite point of view. They show unmistakably that the new idea is contrary or adversative rather than supporting or complementary. Notice the careful use of transitional words in the following passage:

RELATIONSHIPS INDICATED

Past and future are two time regions which we commonly separate by a third which we call the present. *But* strictly speaking the present does not exist, *or* is at best no more than an infinitesimal point in time, gone before we can note it as present. *Nevertheless* we must have a present; *and so* we get one by robbing the past, by holding on to the most recent events and pretending that they all belong to our immediate perceptions. If, *for example,* I raise my arm, the total event is a series of occurrences of which the first are past before the last have taken place; *yet* I perceive it as a single movement executed in one instant of time.

5 b-2
use of linking pronouns

Sentences are often linked by the use of pronouns which have antecedents in preceding sentences. *Provided the antecedents are clear,* this technique is an effective way of avoiding needless repetition.

Notice in the following example how Henry James substitutes "it" for "symbolism" and later for "this suggestion" and how he uses the phrase "*this* suggestion" to point back to the entire preceding sentence.

LINKING PRONOUNS

In *The Scarlet Letter* there is a great deal of symbolism; there is, I think, too much. *It* is overdone at times, and becomes mechanical; *it* ceases to be impressive, and grazes triviality. The idea of the mystic A which the young minister finds imprinted upon his breast and eating into his flesh, in sympathy with the embroidered badge that Hester is condemned to wear, appears to me to be a case in point. *This* suggestion should, I think, have just been made and dropped; to insist upon *it,* and return to *it,* is to exaggerate the weak side of the subject. Hawthorne re-

turns to *it* constantly, plays with *it,* and seems charmed by *it;* until at last the reader feels tempted to declare that *his* enjoyment of *it* is puerile. —Henry James.

5 b-3
repetition of key words

Another technique for maintaining paragraph coherence is the repetition of key words which are related to a central idea.

In the following passage, notice the key words *darkness, deep sea,* and *blackness* and the words related to them by contrast such as *sunlight, red rays,* and *surface:*

KEY WORDS REPEATED

Immense pressure, then, is one of the governing conditions of life in the **deep sea; darkness** is another. The unrelieved **darkness** of the **deep waters** has produced weird and incredible modifications of the **abyssal** fauna. It is a **blackness** so divorced from the world of the **sunlight** that probably only the few men who have seen it with their own **eyes** can visualize it. We know that **light fades out rapidly** with **descent below the surface.** The **red rays** are gone at the end of the first 200 or 300 feet, and with them all the **orange and yellow warmth of the sun.** Then the **greens** fade out, and at 1,000 feet only a **deep, dark brilliant blue** is left. In **very clear waters** the **violet rays** of the spectrum may penetrate another thousand feet. Beyond this is only the **blackness** of the **deep sea.**

—Rachel L. Carson, *The Sea Around Us*

5 b-4
use of parallel structure

Parallel structure involves putting elements of like meaning into like constructions. By parallel structure, the writer shows that certain ideas are equally important.

¶Coh

When Macaulay wrote, "We *read the scandal, talk about it* for a day, and *forget it*," he used parallel structure in the phrases italicized. (Parallelism in sentence structure is discussed in section 8a.) In a series of sentences, parallel structure helps maintain coherence by calling attention to similar ideas. Notice in the following passage how Macaulay links his sentences:

PARALLEL STRUCTURE   We cannot . . . .
                      We must . . . .
                      We must . . . .

PARALLEL STRUCTURE   If he has children . . . .
                      If he has a profession . . . .

PARALLEL STRUCTURE   Our anger . . . .
                      Our victim . . . .
                      Our virtue . . . .

We know no spectacle so ridiculous as the British public in one of its periodical fits of morality. In general, elopements, divorces, and family quarrels pass with little notice. We read the scandal, talk about it for a day, and forget it. But once in six or seven years our virtue becomes outrageous. **We cannot suffer the laws** of religion and decency to be violated. **We must make a stand** against vice. **We must teach libertines** that the English people appreciate the importance of domestic ties. Accordingly some unfortunate man, in no respect more depraved than hundreds whose offenses have been treated with lenity, is singled out as an expiatory sacrifice. **If he has children,** they are to be taken from him. **If he has a profession,** he is to be driven from it. He is cut by the higher orders, and hissed by the lower. He is, in truth, a sort of whipping-boy by whose vicarious agonies all the other transgressors of the same class are, it is supposed, sufficiently chastised. We reflect very complacently on our own severity and compare with great pride the high standard of morals established in England with the Parisian laxity. At length, **our anger** is satiated. **Our victim** is ruined and heart-broken. **And our virtue** goes quietly to sleep for seven years more.

—Thomas Babington Macaulay

When the writer has a series of equally important ideas to list, the paragraph with parallel structure can be very helpful.

Parallel coordination of equally important ideas is often useful with introductory or summary paragraphs, though its use is by no means confined to such paragraphs. In the following example, the first paragraph is taken from the beginning of a chapter, the second from near its conclusion.

To "become a pueblo" *meant to adopt* many of the ways and political forms and ambitions of townspeople. *It meant to accept* the tools, leadership, and conceptions of progress which were then being offered to the villagers of Yucatan by the leaders of Mexico's social revolution. *It required* the inhabitants *to give* up some of the isolation which was theirs in the remote and sparsely inhabited lands that lay apart from the goings and comings of city men. In future they would be a part of the political and economic institutions of Yucatan, of Mexico, and— though of course they would not have put it so—of the one world that was then in the making.

. . .

Chan Kom had attained its loftiest political objective. *It had become* the head of its own municipality. *It had made* itself into a pueblo, a community of dwellers—some of them—in masonry houses. *It had* a municipal building, with a stone jail; a school building, also of masonry; a masonry church—and a masonry Protestant chapel. *It had* two gristmills and four stores. *It had* two outdoor theatres and a baseball diamond.

—Robert Redfield

Notice how the parallel structure in the first three sentences of the second paragraph restate what it meant for Chan Kom to achieve its "loftiest political objective." Notice how the parallel structure in the last three sentences of the second paragraph lists equally important features in a "community of dwellers." And notice how the parallel structure of the second paragraph harks back to the parallel structure of the first paragraph— from what Chan Kom "had attained" back to what "it required" to become a pueblo.

¶Coh

Provided that it is not misleading or needless, parallel structure helps maintain coherence within and among paragraphs. See section 8a for further discussion of parallel structure.

5 c
connections between paragraphs

If the paper is to read smoothly, the reader must be able to see the relationships between successive paragraphs as well as the relationships within a paragraph.

Even though a single paragraph is well set up in itself—its main ideas properly emphasized, its sentences varied, its ending conclusive—it may fail to be an integral part of the paper. Indeed, from the reader's viewpoint, it is more important that a paragraph should carry him along from one point to the next than that it should be a little masterpiece in itself. A striking opening sentence may be less valuable than a sentence linking the paragraph to the preceding discussion; a final sentence which points ahead is probably more useful than a rhetorical flourish.

Aside from the short transitional paragraphs discussed in chapter 4, the main devices for providing coherence among paragraphs are the same as those used for providing coherence within a paragraph: the use of transitional words, the use of linking pronouns, the repetition of key words, and the use of parallel structure. Probably more important than any of these devices is the gradually acquired ability to plan the arrangement of material so that a paragraph ends with some reference to the idea that is to be taken up next. Nevertheless, you can test—in part at least—the strengh of the connections between your paragraphs by checking to see whether you have used any of these transitional devices.

The following paragraphs analyze how the American hobo was related to two frontiers. The first was the frontier of open land, disappearing by 1890, which early adventurers staked out and exploited. The second was the frontier of the growing western town and city, populated increasingly by immigrant

¶Coh

laboring families and pretty well settled by 1920. Notice how coherence is achieved within and between paragraphs.

Omitted material concerns the trail blazers who became successes.

. . . These westward waves of people [following the early trail blazers of the first frontier] usually found excitement and adventure *but* seldom wealth. *The great majority worked for others.* *They* worked and wandered, carrying their beds on their backs. *They* were the first hoboes. Their numbers multiplied when the railroad building began and when other types of firm structuring were needed. *They worked in places where no labor supply existed.*

Notice in the first sentence that "but" is a transitional word to "The great majority . . . ."
Pronouns "they" link "The great majority" and "the first hoboes." The last sentence introduces the hobo as a worker who filled in. "In-between worker" makes explicit the idea of the hobo as an interim laborer; it links "the true hobo" with "they" at the end of the first paragraph.

The true hobo was the in-between worker, willing to go anywhere to take a job and equally willing to move on later. His *in-between* role related to the two frontiers. *He* came on the scene after the trail blazer, and *he* was *off the scene as the second frontier was closing.* We can hardly overestimate the importance of his *interim* role. His kind of labor was going out of demand at the time *The Hobo* was written [1923]. *Migratory workers* were still needed, and still are in agriculture, but they have been drawn from other sources of supply. They no longer belong to Hobohemia.

Continuity in the second paragraph is sustained by "he." The hobo is placed between two frontiers, "off the scene as the second frontier was closing"; at the end he is linked to "migratory workers." In the last paragraph, "With the moving of more people to the land" echoes "as the second frontier was closing." "Migrating cowboy" echoes migratory workers."

With the moving of more people to the land, the big ranches began to disappear. The wide empire of the *migrating cowboy* was broken into thousands of fragments. Mining camps depending on a **mobile labor force** have since become mining towns with a **permanent supply of labor** within walking distance. The **same** applies to old-style lumber camps. Certain kinds of **seasonal work,** like ice harvesting, have been eliminated by technological change. The harvesting combine in the grain fields **reduced** the old **rush each summer** to the harvest. Extra workers are still needed to move the crops, but the demands are much less compelling than before.   —Nels Anderson

Most of the paragraph shows why the hobo was displaced from different jobs. Continuity is sustained by repetition of key phrases like "mobile labor" and "seasonal work" and the contrasting phrases like "permanent supply of labor."

SUMMARY AND REVIEW

1. To assist yourself in making each paragraph coherent, use these devices:
   A. A clear and recognizable pattern of organization—chronological, spatial, deductive, inductive—best suited to the material going into the paragraph.
   B. The accurate and graceful use of transitional words, linking pronouns, key words, and parallel structure within the paragraph.
2. To assist yourself in connecting your paragraphs, look for:
   A. An arrangement of the material so that a paragraph ends with some reference to the idea that is to be taken up next.
   B. A transition which is closely related to the main idea of the preceding paragraph, whether this transition is made by transitional words, linking pronouns, repetition of key words, parallel structure, or several of these devices.

REVIEW EXERCISES

a. *The following student paragraphs (presented in non-indented style after spacing) are jerky and incoherent. Rewrite them, putting*

5

*the material into logical order, combining sentences, making con-
nections clear, and supplying traditional devices.*

Dentistry is an attractive profession. It offers money and security
and respect in the community. Many dentists are active in community affairs, such as the local school board and service clubs.
Dentistry offers a chance to work hard and to work with one's
hands. There is relatively little night work, and the dentist is
better off in this respect than the doctor. Working with one's
hands provides a needed change from working with one's head.
A dentist uses his brain, too. A dentist is also independent. He
is his own boss and can set his own hours and pace of work.

In 1826, Froebel published his book *The Education of Man*. It
was a unique and complex book dealing with his theories of
education. He conceived play to be one of the child's first steps
in growth. Froebel believed all children are innately creative.
To further stimulate this creativity, he arranged a series of toys
to be given to some children he had taught and was reporting
on in *The Education of Man*. These were wooden blocks and
various other materials. The blocks came in varying geometrical
shapes to invite the child to construct patterns of his own choosing. The other materials consisted of things like pencils, paper,
beads, clay, and paint to allow the child even more freedom to
develop his own ideas. Out of Froebel's theories and experi-
ments developed the concept of the kindergarten.

Meriwether Lewis belonged to the Virginian aristocracy, and the
Lewises associated with the Randolphs, Jeffersons, and other
well-known families. His friendship with William Clark dates
back to childhood. At an early age, Meriwether learned to assume responsibility, being "the man of the family." His father
had died when Meriwether was quite young. When Meriwether's younger brother, Ruben, was old enough to take the
role of "man of the family," Meriwether joined the Virginia
Militia which had been summoned by President George Washington. Meriwether inherited a Revolutionary War spirit from
his aristocratic parents and grew up as a robust, outdoor type.

¶Coh

He spent most of his time, when he was not working on the family farm, in the woods hunting.

5

b. *For the following paragraphs, identify the pattern of organization and the specific transitional devices used in each.*

It is astonishing to see how many philosophical disputes collapse into insignificance the moment you subject them to this simple test of tracing a concrete consequence. There can be no difference anywhere that doesn't *make* a difference elsewhere—no difference in abstract truth that doesn't express itself in a difference in concrete fact and conduct consequent upon that fact, imposed on somebody, somehow, somewhere, and somewhen. The whole function of philosophy ought to be to find out what definite difference it will make to you and me at definite instants of our life, if this world-formula or that world-formula be the true one.   —William James

Thirty-one miles north-west of Madrid on a platform of the mountains three thousand feet up, stands the royal monastery, palace and burial house of the Escorial, the supreme architectural symbol of Castilian ambition and its tragedy. The eye comes suddenly upon the monotonous prison-like facade, and the first pleasure which the sight of gravity and order give us, as they break the wild mountain scene and the grim wilderness of pine and boulder, quickly gives way to awe and melancholy before the cold statement of military power and the governing will. Built from the bluish granite of these mountains, so that it seems to be a projection of them, and coldly slated, the sombre establishment is one of bare overstatements of Castilian genius. Its thousands of windows stare and blink in the mountain light.
                    —V. S. Pritchett

After my return to England it appeared to me that by following the example of Lyell in Geology, and by collecting all facts which bore in any way on the variations of animals and plants under domestication and nature, some light might be shed on the whole subject. My first note-book was opened in July 1837.

¶Coh

I worked on true Baconian principles, and without any theory collected facts on a wholesale scale, more especially with respect to domesticated productions, by printed inquiries, by conversations with skillful breeders and gardners, and by extensive reading. When I see the list of books of all kinds which I read and abstracted, including whole series of Journals and Transactions, I am surprised at my industry. I soon perceived that selection was the keystone of man's success in making useful races of animals and plants. But how selection could be applied to organisms living in a state of nature remained for some time a mystery to me.   —Charles Darwin

The humanist who looks at science from the viewpoint of his own endeavors is bound to be impressed, first of all, by its startling lack of insight into itself. Scientists seem able to go about their business in a state of indifference to, if not ignorance of, anything but the going, currently acceptable doctrines of their several disciplines. Science maintains no museum for its mistakes. Its body of truth consists at any moment of those findings which have survived; the false starts and the blind alleys are no longer of interest. Its picture of its own history is therefore an arbitrary selection of the successful strikes, the lodes that panned out, a retrospective map made up of nothing but the roadways which led, as though inevitably, to the point where we now stand. This is not history but historicism, the imputation of pattern and purpose to the mere passage of time. The scientist is so committed to the notion of cumulative knowledge that only with the greatest effort can he regard himself as historically equal with his predecessors. It is almost as though he were cut off by temperament and training from any detached perspective on the nature of his own enterprise.

   The one thing the humanist knows about the past is that it didn't *have* to happen as it did. The alternatives are veiled; but the challenge, the labor, and the art for a historian is to unveil them, to blank out all the benefits of his own hindsight, and to live poised on the edge of the problematical immediate moment alongside the long-vanished men and women whose lives he is trying to recreate and share. To some degree, there is a

¶Coh

tide in the affairs of science which makes some of its developments seem next to inevitable; they sit there nesting in the bosom of time, waiting only for the moment when they can take wing and fly, if not this year then next, if not under this man's name then under some other's. The phenomenon of simultaneous discovery, as with Darwin and Alfred Russell Wallace, confirms scientists in their conviction that the order they find in nature is a given, already there, waiting only to be teased forth a fragment at a time.
　　　　　　　　　　　　　　　　　　　　　—Eric Larrabee

The democratic rule that all men are equal is sometimes confused with the quite opposite idea that all men are the same and that any man can be substituted for any other so that his differences make no difference. The two are not at all the same. The democratic rule that all men are equal means that men's being different cannot be made a basis for special privilege or for the invidious advantage of one man over another; equality, under the democratic rule, is the freedom and opportunity of each individual to be fully and completely his different self.
　　　　　　　　　　　　　　　　　　　　　—H. M. Kallen

The village to which our family had come was a scattering of some twenty to thirty houses down the south-east slope of a valley. The valley was narrow, steep and almost entirely cut off; it was also a funnel for winds, a channel for the floods, and a jungly, bird-crammed, insect-hopping sun trap whenever there happened to be any sun. It was not high and open like the Windrush country, but had secret origins, having been gouged from the escarpment by the melting ice caps some time before we got there. The old flood-terraces still showed on the slopes, along which the cows walked sideways. Like an island, it was possessed of curious survivals—rare orchids and Roman snails; and there were chemical qualities in the limestone springs which gave the women pre-Raphaelite goitres. The sides of the valley were rich in pasture and the crests heavily covered in beech woods.

　　Living down there was like living in a bean pod; one could see nothing but the bed one lay in. Our horizon of woods was

the limit of our world. For weeks on end the trees moved in the wind with a dry roaring that seemed a natural utterance of the landscape. In winter they ringed us with frozen spikes, and in summer they oozed over the lips of the hills like layers of thick green lava. Mornings, they steamed with mist or sunshine, and almost every evening threw streamers above us, reflecting sunsets we were too hidden to see.

Water was the most active thing in the valley, arriving in the long rains from Wales. It would drip all day from clouds and trees, from roofs and eaves and noses. It broke open roads, carved its way through gardens, and filled the ditches with sucking noises. Men and horses walked about in wet sacking, birds shook rainbows from sodden branches, and streams ran from holes, and back into holes, like noisy underground trains.

—Laurie Lee

On that hot summer afternoon when the body of Muhammad lay in the arms of Ayesha and the wives were lamenting and the companions were preparing to wash the body and clothe it in a shroud, the ferocious old warrior Umar Ibn-Khattab blundered into the hut. He took one look at Muhammad, so still and calm in death, and refused to believe what he saw. He was heard muttering: "Verily, by the Lord he shall return!" and then he ran off to the nearby mosque and began shouting that Muhammad was not dead, he would return accompanied by his angels, and was even now preparing to take his place in the mosque. He was dead, but in a twinkling of an eye he would arise again. Saying this, Umar unsheathed his sword, prepared to drive it into the heart of the first believer who refused to believe in the immortality of the messenger of God.

—Robert Payne

I went to the woods because I wished to live deliberately, to front only the essential facts of life, and see if I could not learn what it had to teach, and not, when I came to die, discover that I had not lived. I did not wish to live what was not life, living is so dear; nor did I wish to practice resignation, unless it was quite necessary. I wanted to live deep and suck out all the mar-

¶Coh

row of life, to live so sturdily and Spartan-like as to put to rout all that was not life, to cut a broad swath and shave close, to drive life into a corner, and reduce it to its lowest terms, and, if it proved to be mean, why then to get the whole and genuine meanness of it, and publish its meanness to the world; or if it were sublime, to know it by experience, and be able to give a true account of it in my next excursion. For most men, it appears to me, are in a strange uncertainty about it, whether it is of the devil or of God, and have *somewhat hastily* concluded that it is the chief end of man to "glorify God and enjoy him forever."
—Henry David Thoreau

c. *Pick one of the following topics. Then write two separate paragraphs about it in which you try to develop the same idea each time but use a different pattern of organization for each paragraph.*

1. The art of telling stories to children
2. The pleasure of being a good bridge player (or poker player)
3. The most effective way to procrastinate without feeling guilty
4. The most offensive commercial on TV
5. How to make your advisor remember your name
6. How to keep your temper in a traffic jam

d. *Analyze the two paragraphs you have written for exercise three to determine what specific devices you have used most frequently for coherence.*

6

paragraph development

A paragraph may be unified and coherent, yet lack development. Although its central idea may be clear and its sentence transitions effective, the paragraph's content may be brief, general, and dull. Developing a paragraph does not mean padding out a simple statement nor repeating the same idea in different words. It means filling out the bare statement of an idea with specific details.

Developing a paragraph requires that the writer take time to see clearly and say accurately what his generalities signify.

Unless the writer shows how his generalities apply to particular cases, how his conclusions differ from someone else's, or what specifically has led him to his view, the reader remains uninformed and unpersuaded. Consider the following scrawny, undeveloped paragraphs:

UNDEVELOPED

I arrived here at Millberry College on Saturday, September 20. One of the first things I learned of was the dinner the following evening which each freshman was supposed to attend with his faculty advisor. I found my advisor was Mr. Ward.

6

We met in his room in West Hall. We obviously couldn't all eat there, so Mr. Ward had arranged that we eat at Dr. Miller's house.

As we walked to Dr. Miller's, I began to talk with the others of our group of about ten.

Mr. Ward was not what I had expected of a faculty member. He was not over fifty years old. He was not wearing thick glasses. He was, in contrast, about twenty-six, rather athletic looking, and a very interesting conversationalist, not only in his own field, but in every subject we discussed.

My classmates, most of whom I had not met before, were also a surprise. There were no socially backward introverts, interested only in the physical sciences, as I had feared. I found instead some very interesting people with whom I immediately wanted to become friends. Some were interested in sports, some in hobbies, some in card games, and all in women. Each individual had something to offer me.

Mrs. Miller did a marvelous job of preparing the dinner. We did a marvelous job of eating it. However, the real purpose of the dinner was to become acquainted with at least two of our faculty members and about ten of our fellow students. In this endeavor we were also quite successful, for the discussions begun during the meal lasted for a long time after and, as a matter of fact, some of them were continued the next day.

This year's advisor dinner was very rewarding and I believe it should remain a tradition. The students really get to know each other, and a few of the faculty are pleasantly surprised.

A reader might well wonder why the dinner should be continued as a tradition. Nothing the writer says carries real conviction because nothing is developed concretely. These paragraphs raise more questions than they answer: 1) Why should

the writer have expected the faculty to resemble his caricature of them as ancient, near-sighted bores? 2) What was Mr. Ward's "field" and what did he talk about as a "very interesting conversationalist"? 3) What "sports," "hobbies," and "card games" was he so pleased to discover he shared in common with his classmates? 4) If the meal was so memorable, what was it and how many servings did he have? If it wasn't important, why give two vague sentences to it? 5) What was talked about so enthusiastically and "for a long time after" the meal?

The writer has substituted clichés (the trite phrasing "very interesting conversationalist," "socially backward introverts"), vague generalities ("some were interested in sports, some in hobbies, some in card games"), and unexplained events (the dinner discussion) for specific detail. The paragraphs are not developed; they merely repeated the same idea unconvincingly—that the advisor's dinner was a good chance to discover that faculty and students were in some vague way "interesting" and "rewarding," not what the writer "had expected."

Specific detail is achieved partly by specific wording, a topic discussed more fully in chapters 12 and 13. Concrete, exact diction cuts out the dullness and fuzziness and gives a paper sharpness and depth. Consider these sentences: "Mrs. Miller did a marvelous job of preparing the meal. We did a marvelous job of eating it." Do they mean Mrs. Miller barbecued three dozen hamburgers and tossed a spicy bean salad for a delicious buffet meal on paper plates? Or do they mean that she gave a formal dinner, complete with white linen, silver settings and candlelight, and served roast beef, hot rolls, and two vegetables? Either of these alternatives is better than the empty generality of the original. A buffet meal for thirteen people implies a relaxed hostess and guests, students going back for several helpings, and comfortable informality. A formal dinner for thirteen people implies a busy hostess and reserved freshmen, hushed requests for the gravy, and long, earnest discussion as the coffee lingers in the cups and the candles melt. Whatever the case was, specific wording would help the reader *see* the event and prepare him for the writer's conclusions about it.

> To get specific detail by specific wording, the writer has to think in concrete *images*. He has to recall and re-create the taste, touch, sound, and sight as clearly as he can. He is not simply being "vivid"; he is trying *to give his reader as much relevant information about an event* as he can.

In the following two versions of the same paragraph, notice how the student has improved the second by more complete information. Her revision is not much longer than the original, but it tells far more. It is the choice of words, not the number of words, which creates an image. The boldfaced passages indicate the places where she made her major changes.

VAGUE ORIGINAL

Though the air was **uncomfortable,** the sand was **soothing** and warm, and I dug a **hole** into it and piled it up **until it half-covered** me from the air. I sat there, shivering in the **air,** until the sand **began falling away** from me. I tried to **bury my legs** again, but the sand **was dry** and it **would not stay in place. I tried to find** damp sand near me, but in a short time it also dried out and **wouldn't stay in place.** So I rested **for awhile** and watched the sea rise and fall and the various objects it threw onto the beach. **Seaweed** and **other things** were washed up, then carried back in a **regular rhythm.**

REVISION FOR CONCRETENESS

Though the air was **cold,** the sand **felt soft** and warm, and I dug a **damp trough** in it and piled it up around my **legs until I had a body only from the waist up.** I sat there, shivering in the **cool mist,** until the sand began **to crumble down** around me. I tried to **gather it back up** on my legs, but it **had dried** and **kept slithering down** again in little shifting rivers. I dug with my

hands beside me until I came to damp sand which I piled on my legs, but in a short time it too **dried and slipped away.** So I rested **my head on my knees** and watched the sea rise and fall **and rise and fall, bringing with it,** to the beach, something new each time: **a loop of rust-colored** seaweed, **a shell, a rock, a small jelly-fish. And falling away,** it would **often take with it** what it had **just brought.**

In the revision, the writer has helped the reader see and feel the experience far more completely by her changes in diction. As she sits "a body only from the waist up" and "shivering in the cool mist," the reader sees her as a solitary figure, motionless except for a slight quivering of the shoulders, waiting for the sun to burn off the traces of vapor. Notice that the writer has done more than make the diction specific. She has developed her paragraph by adding extra details and tried to re-create the experience. She has recalled her experience more minutely and slowed down the tempo of the narrative. In the original, when she says that "the sand *was dry* and *it would not stay in place*," she is merely summarizing. In the revision, when she says that the sand *"had dried* and *kept slithering down again in little shifting rivers,"* she appeals to the shared experience of any reader who has spent days at the beach. When she says that "seaweed and other things were washed up," she merely leads the reader to ignore the scene, instead of filling it out for him, as in the revision.

> Developing a paragraph requires that a writer give content to his generalities by using relevant details and illustrations.

Specific details may be found in particular actions, sensory impressions, objects, processes. But whatever the subject, the details must be *selected,* not merely inventoried. Details become boring—mere padding—when the writer confuses quantity with quality. If, for example, an American student has

been asked by his Nigerian correspondent what a "drugstore" is, the American should not try to explain it by listing every type of cold tablet, sleeping pill, foot powder, lipstick, face cream, hair remover, shaving lotion, cigarette, stale candy, and garish paperback it sells. But neither should he content himself by saying a drugstore fills prescriptions and sells medical supplies, cosmetics, tobacco, and books. The Nigerian can get this broad definition from a dictionary. The American might begin with such a definition, and then suggest through selected details that "medical supplies" *range* from cough syrups through pink bandages and that cosmetics *range* from green fingernail polish through perfumed hair rinses. Without trying to be exhaustive, he would try to suggest the odd variety and specialization of items covered by the general terms "medical supplies" and "cosmetics."

6 a
methods of paragraph development

There are many ways of developing paragraphs, and each has its own advantages. In actual practice a writer is apt to use a combination of these methods, suited to his immediate ends. A few of the commonest methods are worth illustration and analysis. In most cases, two examples of each method are provided, one written by a student and one by a professional writer.

6 a-1
development by specific detail

In developing a paragraph by specific detail, a writer carefully selects each detail to contribute to the dominant impression or idea, his *topic sentence*.

In the following student paragraph, notice how skillfully the writer has picked his details to show why he remembers an attic which would only seem dirty and uncomfortable to an adult.

DETAILS SUPPORTING THESIS

The attic was the third floor of an old Victorian house, one of those countless look-alike monstrosities of towers and porches and trim. **To the adult eye, the attic was dirty and uncomfortable, but to the boy it was a sanctuary.** The attic always had that sneezy smell of twenty-year-old newspapers just shuffled; and its roof arched clear down to the floor at the four corners so that the boy had to play near the middle of the room. And the floor had a thick layer of—not exactly dust, not exactly dirt—dry, yet slick gray pollen that filters out of old wooden rafters. On the floor the boy had his Lionel trains and build-it-yourself brick houses and farms— but they were merely strategic positions and crucial points of supply which he, as General, and his army defended against the Enemy. The whole floor was occupied with troops marching at the slope or resting in position. Here, all bundled up in a jacket, he used to spend his dark winter evenings directing his men. He sometimes even played up here in the summer, when it was so hot his face would turn prickly red and he had to worry about the hard, black wasps knocking at the window sills. Here, he would set up Gettysburg with some paper-paste mountains he had molded or trap the Enemy on an isthmus, using the rough-finished chimney as a barrier.

In the next example, notice how Constance Rourke characterizes the backwoodsman as a noisy, rhapsodic type by her selection of detail. Notice also that the pattern of organization in her paragraph (and in the paragraph about the attic) is deductive (see section 5a-3). Many paragraphs which are developed by specific detail have this pattern of organization.

SELECTED DETAILS PATTERNED DEDUCTIVELY

Like the Yankee in the Revolution, the backwoodsman had leapt up out of war as a noticeable figure—the War of 1812; in the scattered western country his portrait had taken shape slowly. Once on the national horizon, however, he made up in noise what he had lost in time. *He grew rhapsodic—about himself—and like the Reverend Samuel Peters betrayed a strong leaning toward natural history.* He was not only half horse, half alligator, he was also the sea-horse of the mountain, a flying whale, a bear with a sore head. He had sprung from the Potomac of the world. He was a steamboat, or an earthquake that shook an enemy to pieces, and he could wade the Mississippi. "I'm a regular tornado, tough as hickory and long-winded as a nor'wester. I can strike a blow like a falling tree, and every lick makes a gap in the crowd that lets in an acre of sunshine." He was the most cunning of the creatures of the backwoods, a raccoon, a "ring-tailed roarer." Oddly enough, he was also a flower. "I'm the yaller blossom of the forest!" Heels cracking, he leapt into the air to proclaim his attributes against all comers like an Indian preparing for warfare. As a preliminary to a fight he neighed like a stallion or crowed like a cock. He was "the gamecock of the wilderness" and the "Salt River Roarer." "Down thar you go, war you a buffalo," he chanted in wrestling matches, with hands placed on the shoulder and hip of his opponent. —Constance Rourke

6 a-2
development by extended example

In developing a paragraph by extended example, a writer picks one or two illustrations of his generalization and focuses his reader's attention upon them.

This method is a good way to make a point forcefully, as in the following student paragraph.

ILLUSTRATION SUPPORTING THESIS

The modern advertisement presents the United States as a land of gullible people who are awed by secret formulas and scientific demonstrations. Every product from Bardahl to hair remover has some secret ingredient like XL-712 or Chlorinol. When this kind of claim gets monotonous, just for variety some advertisements

proclaim they do *not* contain some horrible ingredient like acetylsalicylic acid. Take the common example that used to be heard on television almost daily: This toothpaste is best for you because it contains GL-70, that super new ingredient that helps kill mouth odor all day long. It sounds pretty convincing except that every other toothpaste has its secret too and that GL-70 could be anything from water to food coloring. Other advertisements consist of "scientific dramatizations" that prove, "without a shadow of a doubt," that their product is the best. When, for example, a man appears on your television screen, dressed in white, and says, "What do doctors do for the pain of a headache?", everyone must jump to attention in respect for his superior knowledge as a man of science. When he answers his own question and says, "I take Anacin," we must all be grateful for a free diagnosis.

In this next example, Swift attacks two hundred years of European exploration and colonizing with an extended bitter example supporting the irony of his opening and closing statements.

ILLUSTRATION SUPPORTING IRONIC COMMENT
But I had another reason which made me less forward to enlarge his Majesty's dominions by my discoveries. *To say the truth, I had conceived a few scruples with relation to the distributive justice of princes upon those occasions.* For instance, a crew of pirates are driven by a storm they know not whither, at length a boy discovers land from the topmast, they go on shore to rob and plunder, they see an harmless people, are entertained with kindness, they give the country a new name, they take formal possession of it for their King, they set up a rotten plank or stone for a memorial, they murder two or three dozen of the natives, bring away a couple of more by force for a sample, return home, and get their pardon. Here commences a new dominion acquired with a title by *divine right*. Ships are sent out with the first opportunity, the natives driven out or destroyed, their

princes tortured to discover their gold, a free license given to all acts of inhumanity and lust, the earth reeking with the blood of its inhabitants: and this execrable crew of butchers employed in so pious an expedition is a **modern colony** sent to convert and civilize an idolatrous and barbarous people.

—Jonathan Swift

6 a-3
development by definition

In developing a paragraph by definition, a writer limits the range of a term's application.

In this kind of development, he uses a number of sentences to tell the reader what the key term or terms signify. A few words about definitions are in order here.

In formal logic, a term is defined by referring it to a general class (or genus)—i.e., classifying it—and then distinguishing it from others in the general class.

To take a simple example, one might begin by *classifying* a pen as a "writing instrument." But since the class "writing instrument" also includes pencils, one would have to *differentiate* a pen by continuing ". . . writing instrument which makes use of a hard point and a colored fluid."

term		*class*	*differentiation*
Pen	is	a writing instrument	making use of a hard point and a colored fluid.
Pencil	is	a writing instrument	with a core of solid-state material like graphite inside a wooden or plastic case.

A description of the object can include all kinds of details—the pencil has a chewed end, used to cost five cents, peels in bits of yellow paint—but these details are irrelevant to the definition of the term. Similarly, examples do not constitute a definition, although they can certainly help to clarify a definition. To say

that a Dixon Ticonderoga, #2 Soft is an example of a pencil is not the same as specifying what the meaning of the term "pencil" is.

Much of the time a writer can successfully define technical terms or concrete words by using an appositive construction.

DEFINITION BY APPOSITION

The X-ray showed a crack in the *tibia, or shinbone.*

Please analyze the importance of the *denouement—the final unraveling or outcome of the plot*—in Lord Jim.

Tonight the moon will be in *apogee, that is, the point farthest from the earth in its orbit.*

Sometimes, however, especially when dealing with complex or highly abstract terms, a writer will need a fuller definition. He may spend several paragraphs, not just one, in defining the term if the term is crucial to a long essay or research paper. To do so, he should observe several principles.

First, avoid circular definitions. "Democracy is the democratic process" and "An astronomer is one who studies astronomy" are circular definitions. When words are defined in terms of themselves, no one's understanding is improved.

Second, avoid long lists of synonyms if the term to be defined is an abstract one. When a paper begins, "By education, I mean to give knowledge, develop character, improve taste, draw out, train, lead," the reader knows he is in for the shotgun treatment. The writer has indiscriminately blasted all the abstract terms he can at the reader, hoping one will hit.

Third, avoid loaded definitions. Loaded definitions do not restrict key terms to be used but make an immediate appeal for emotional approval. A definition beginning, "By federal aid to education I mean government meddling and thought control" is loaded with pejorative emotional connotation. Conversely, "By federal aid to education I mean one of the great blessings of democratic planning" is loaded with favorable emotional connotation. Such judgments can be vigorous conclusions to a discussion, but they invite argument, not clarification, when offered as definitions.

The following student paragraph illustrates the process of definition. The writer first classifies "democracy" as "a form of government" and then distinguishes it from other forms by pointing out that it provides for free, secret elections and that it is based on the concept of the sovereignty of the people. To further clarify his use of the term, he points out that democracy is a political system, not an economic one.

DEFINITION BY DISTINCTION

Democracy is a form of government in which the people elect their representatives in free, secret elections and in which the will of the people determines the policies by which they shall be ruled. There are several forms of democracy, but generally they are consistent as political systems in that each is founded on equality of legal rights and opportunity. England has a socialist economy in which the government owns important industries, sponsors socialized medicine, and directs the policies of a large communications system. However, the people of England have the right of free, secret elections to select their representatives, are guaranteed equal privileges in industry and society by law, and control the decisions of government through their representatives. Similarly, in the United States the people believe in free elections, group representation, and legal rights, but tend to endorse private enterprise instead of socialism.

Two examples by professional writers will indicate how definitions are formulated, developed, and put to use. In the first, notice that Lionel Trilling begins by contrasting snobbery with class pride and then, having indicated what the term "snobbery" does not signify, goes ahead in the next paragraph to indicate what it does signify. He *restricts the term's application*.

DEFINITION BY RESTRICTION

Snobbery is not the same thing as pride of class. Pride of class may not please us but we must at least grant that it reflects a social function. A man who exhibited class pride—in the day when it was possible to do so—may have been puffed up about what he *was;* but this ultimately depended on what he *did.* Thus, aristocratic pride was based ultimately on the ability to fight and administer. No pride is without fault, but pride of class may be thought of as today we think of pride of profession, toward which we are likely to be lenient.

Snobbery is pride in status without pride in function. And it is an uneasy pride of status. It always asks, "Do I belong—do I really belong? And does he belong? And if I am observed talking to him, will it make me seem to belong or not to belong?" It is the peculiar vice not of aristocratic societies which have their own appropriate vices, but of bourgeois democratic societies. For us the legendary strongholds of snobbery are the Hollywood studios, where two thousand dollars a week dare not talk to three hundred dollars a week for fear that he will be taken for nothing more than fifteen hundred dollars a week. The dominant emotions of snobbery are uneasiness, self-consciousness, self-defensiveness, the sense that one is not quite real but can in some way acquire reality.   —Lionel Trilling

In the next example, notice how the writer develops his definition throughout the paragraph so that the last sentence is the most complete formulation:

DEFINITION BY ACCUMULATED DISTINCTIONS

To describe its potentials the computer needs a new name. Perhaps as good a name as any is "information machine." This term is intended to distinguish its function from that of a power machine, such as a loom. A loom performs the physical work of weaving a fabric; the information machine controls the pattern being woven. *Its purpose is not the performance of work but the ordering and supervision of the way in which the work is done.*
                                         —Louis N. Ridenour

¶Dev

6 a-4
development by division

In developing a paragraph by division, the writer enumerates and discusses separately the main aspects of a topic, often for classifying purposes.

The material analyzed can vary in subject matter—the major kinds of job opportunities in a community, the legal requirements a candidate must fulfill, the types of people one meets while working. The writer's concern should be to keep the enumerated features or classifications distinct: they should not overlap, and they should not all be crowded into one paragraph if there are more than a few. In the following example, notice how the writer divides status into three types.

DIVISION FOR CLASSIFICATION
But the major disappointment in the book [*The Status Seekers*] is Packard's unclarified ideas about status—although the literature he himself cites could have clarified his ideas had he thought about it longer and harder. *There are at least three kinds of status, all of which the author touches upon without distinguishing. The first is* status-by-definition. If whites are defined as superior to Negroes, then any white, no matter how shiftless and ignorant, is superior to any Negro, no matter how talented and useful. *Then there is* status-by-consumption, in terms of which Bill is superior to Joe if Bill has a handsomer car, a more expensive house, or a more fashionable suit of clothes than Joe can display. *Finally there is* status-by-achievement, in which the individual is regarded as superior who, in his chosen line of endeavor, does a better job than others: the ball player who hits .375 or the scientist who solves a previously insoluble problem.
—S. I. Hayakawa

6 a-5
development by comparison
or contrast

In developing a paragraph by comparison or contrast, a writer stresses likenesses or differences.

To be effective, the paragraph should state the main point of the comparison early and should be organized so that the reader does not have to jump back and forth from one subject to another. Joseph Wood Krutch makes the point of the contrast very clear at the beginning of the following example:

CONTRAST

Sociologists talk a great deal these days about "adjustment," which has always seemed to me a defeatist sort of word suggesting dismal surrender to the just tolerable. The road runner is not "adjusted" to his environment. He is triumphant in it. The desert is his home and he likes it. Other creatures, including many other birds, elude and compromise. They cling to the mountains or to the cottonwood-filled washes, especially in the hot weather, or they go away somewhere else, like the not entirely reconciled human inhabitants of this region. The road runner, on the other hand, stays here all the time and he prefers the areas where he is hottest and driest. . . .   —Joseph Wood Krutch

One special type of comparison is *analogy,* discussed at length in chapter 3. As a method of illustration, analogy can simplify and clarify complex relationships. In the following student paragraph, for example, the writer was faced with the problem of showing how the characters in William Faulkner's short story "Spotted Horses" could continue to admire and tolerate a man who continually fleeced them. To solve this problem, the student used the apt analogy of a game of pool with Willie Hoppe, for many years the world champion.

ANALOGY FOR CHARACTERIZATION

"That Flem Snopes," says the narrator. "I be dog if he ain't a case now." The townspeople had respect for a good horse trader and Flem Snopes was that. Since money was of grotesque importance to these people who had to dig for every penny, they admired a man who could come by it easily and cleverly. Ironically, when Flem skinned someone of his last nickel and kept the fact to himself, the people would interpret Flem's silence as sheer modesty, while the victim laughed off as hopeless any thought of retribution. **Their admiration and toleration of Flem is not hard to understand. It was like a game of pool** in which you lose so decisively to Willie Hoppe that you feel no bitterness—merely a sense of pride and awe at having played the master at all. After Willie has beaten you and quietly taken off the stakes, you admit sheepishly to others you were licked before you started and put the cue back on the rack instead of taking it into some dark alley to wait for Willie. Most people didn't even try to beat the time-honored master, Flem Snopes, at his game of swindling.

Professional writers often try to make difficult abstract ideas concrete through analogy, and they take care, while developing their paragraphs, to be sure the reader understands the analogies are illustrations, not proof (see section 3b-3, part 3). In developing the following paragraph, for instance, Lincoln Barnett calls his analogy "this little fable."

ANALOGY FOR DESCRIPTION
The distinction between Newton's and Einstein's ideas about gravitation has sometimes been illustrated by picturing a little boy playing marbles in a city lot. The ground is very uneven. An observer in an office ten stories above the street would not be able to see these irregularities in the ground. Noticing that the marbles appear to avoid some sections of the ground and move toward other sections, he might assume that a [semi-magnetic] "force" was operating which repelled the marbles from certain spots and attracted them toward others. But another observer on the ground would instantly perceive that the path of the marbles was simply governed by the curvature of the field. In this little fable Newton is the upstairs observer who imagines that a "force" is at work, and Einstein is the observer on the ground, who has no reason to make such an assumption. Einstein's gravitational laws, therefore, merely describe the field properties of the space-time continuum. . . .　　　　—Lincoln Barnett

6 a-6
development by cause and effect

In developing a paragraph by cause and effect, the writer stresses the *connections* between a result or results and the preceding events.

He may begin with the causes or with the effects, but in either case he raises the question of connections and makes it the basis for his paragraph development. Many paragraphs deal with chronology or sequence; the cause-and-effect paragraph uses chronology to answer the key question *why?* or *how?* See section 5a-1.

Often, cause-and-effect paragraphs are the basis for a whole paper. The first paragraph may raise the question of causes, the second paragraph eliminate some alternatives, the third focus on the remaining likelihoods. Or the first paragraph may state the effect, the second raise the question, etc. The following student theme is given in its entirety to show this method of development. The essay concerns the function of Old Hilse, a character in Gerhart Hauptmann's play *The Weavers,* a dramatization of a revolt by impoverished Silesian weavers in central Europe during the 1840's. The writer's central question is "Why is Old Hilse even in the play?" His answer is a persuasive demonstration of *how* old Hilse changes our understanding of the play—the effect he has upon us.

CAUSES AND EFFECTS IN SEQUENCE

Why Old Hilse?

If one were to examine the contribution of Old Hilse to the plot of *The Weavers,* one would be hard put to find any excuse for his being in the play. He neither alters the course of the main action nor initiates any new actions. His speeches to the main characters are unheeded. He does not join the rebel weavers nor does he come to the defense of the manufacturers. He remains neutral in the battle, in no way affecting its outcome. His only connection with the action of the play is to be an unintentional and all-but-unnoticed casualty.

Then why are his unheeded lines ever spoken? Why is this character brought into the play at all?

The play begins with a dispute between the younger weavers and the manufacturer's buyer, builds up the weavers' discontent with their poverty and fatigue, and reaches a climax with their open rebellion. It roars towards what we hope will be its triumphant conclusion. But it runs head on into Old Hilse. Here is a man whom we fully expect to jump on the bandwagon, or at least act as a dramatic counterpoint by siding with the manufacturers. But Old Hilse just states his contempt for this particular uprising, reiterates his belief in duty, and goes back to his daily weaving. For a moment the rapidly moving picture of a community in revolt is frozen. The logic that has been leading up to the great truth of why all the weavers must kill all the owners is stopped just short of a final conclusion. The almost cornily beautiful victory of good over evil, already foreshadowed in the impoverished mass's sacking of a manufacturer's estate, falters. Old Hilse, the most respected weaver, the one most representative of simple devotion to weaving, will not join the rebellion.

In a moment the machine starts to rumble again. The drunken and possessed leaders of the rebellion rush out of Hilse's house to battle the government troops. The plot starts up again. But the reader left behind begins to question the rebels. Why won't Old Hilse join? Why does his refusal, although not altering the plan of the rebellion one bit, alter the meaning of it so greatly? Hilse is certainly not afraid. He is a wounded veteran of a much greater war. As he starts to talk about that war, the rebellion raging outside begins to shrink. It is nothing to him. What's more, it is nothing to anyone except those who are inside of it. Suddenly the story of the young weavers battling for their rights and the older ones gradually joining them becomes a pathetic example of the pattern we see in the papers almost daily, the local rebellion. This is Hilse's contribution. He is the only character who stands far enough outside the battle to see it as the futile effort it is, not as the glorious rebellion that the other weavers think it is. He has seen it all before. He can even predict jail terms for the leaders. Hilse takes us far enough from the story to see it clearly. Hilse, who is nothing to the plot's outcome, is everything to its meaning: he makes the plot change from a story in which we are as personally wrapped up as the characters into a dismal pattern of the universality of revolt born by suffering and hunger, which is doomed to be led astray by its own excesses, and thus defeated.

Notice the paper's structure: we are first shown what Old Hilse did not cause or influence and asked what purpose he did serve. Then we are shown how he interrupts our involvement in the plot and how, in the writer's opinion, he causes us to see the plot in a new perspective.

Some cause-and-effect paragraphs, like the ones preceding, are primarily persuasive. Their purpose is to make the reader feel the forcefulness of the writer's conclusions, or at least see the grounds for his conclusions. Other cause-and-effect paragraphs are primarily explanatory. Their purpose is to make the reader see a whole series of causal links and the necessary results. In the following paragraph, for example, the writer's purpose is to demonstrate why it is so hard for the poor in America to escape their suffering.

CAUSES AND EFFECTS LINKED
Here is one of the most familiar forms of the vicious circle of poverty. The poor get sick more than anyone else in the society. That is because they live in slums, jammed together under un-

hygienic conditions; they have inadequate diets, and cannot get decent medical care. When they become sick, they are sick longer than other groups in society. Because they are sick more often and longer than anyone else, they lose wages and work, and find it difficult to hold a steady job. And because of this, they cannot pay for good housing, for a nutritious diet, for doctors. At any given point in the circle, particularly when there is a major illness, their prospect is to move to an even lower level and to begin the cycle, round and round, toward even more suffering.   —Michael Harrington

6 a-7
development by a combination of methods

Depending on the nature of his material, the writer may use any combination of the methods just discussed to develop his paragraph adequately.

The following paragraph has been pulled apart to show how its topic is developed by means of definition, contrast, and example.

TOPIC
SENTENCE
London has one great advantage for the American tourist: since he knows the language, he can easily get to know the people and their culture.

↓

DEFINITION
By culture I do not mean the treasures of the British Museum or the concerts at the Royal Albert Hall. I mean, rather, the underlying assumptions, attitudes, and values which give the specific flavor to British life.

↓

CONTRAST
In other foreign countries this sense of the real life of the people is difficult to achieve. An American in Paris may be able to ask simple questions and understand simple directions, but unless he knows French very

well, he remains an onlooker, an outsider, and he misses the subtleties of the French outlook on life.

↓

EXAMPLE   In London, every native is a potential acquaintance and a source of knowledge of British life. The porter at your hotel will not only tell you how to get to Buckingham Palace; his incidental remarks may reveal a good deal about the English class system. A Cockney street merchant gave me . . . .

6 b
revision for fuller detail and development

If your instructor comments that your paragraphs are inadequately developed, you can do several things.

Examine the paragraph carefully for all vague generalities, needlessly abstract words, and clichés, and underline them.

WEAKNESSES UNDERLINED
In the early years of a child's life, his activities are free and he can be himself. He is protected from the laws of nature by our modern-day-society and its complex technology. He only has to keep out of trouble and he can do whatever he pleases. But as he gets older, he finds more and more duties and more and more responsibilities thrust upon him. He begins to lose his freedom and become a conformist.

Once underlined, such phrases as "early years" may be changed to "the first year"; "he can be himself" to "he can cry, chatter, or sleep as he pleases"; and "laws of nature" to "disease, hunger, and weather." Underlining may also suggest that other phrases are, insofar as they mean anything, untrue and need extensive revision and qualification: In what sense has a child of nine or ten who bikes to school, plays long hours afterwards, and stays overnight with friends begun to "lose his freedom" and to "become a conformist"?

> You can assist yourself in revision—or in composing the rough draft—by making a list of the concrete images, details, and examples you want to include.

If you work best from a strict outline, use the form discussed in chapter 2 for incorporating details:

I. Drama in Frost's Imagery
  A. Natural settings
     —For example, a boy climbing to top of birch tree
  B. Domestic settings
     —For example, wife crouching on stairs in "Home Burial"

If you find this technique too mechanical, at least jot down the specific items which illustrate your generalizations. You might lay out the material in short units marked for insertion where expansion seems to be needed:

> Working as a door-to-door magazine sales-man in and around St. Louis last summer gave me more than just extra spending money. It gave me a chance to meet types of people* I might otherwise never have known, and some practical experience* I am glad I had.
>
> *The last two generalizations could stand expansion.*

* Young wives of construction workers living in trailers, retired jazz musicians and news-stand operators living in boarding houses, electronic engineers in suburbs.

* How to keep temper when insulted, how to walk through a neighborhood not showing fear, how to size up a person's tastes by the way he keeps lawn or TV show he's watching.

Many underdeveloped paragraphs result from the writer's failure to distinguish between fact and opinion. For instance, the writer of the paragraph about freedom in the early years of childhood never bothered to ask himself what factual basis he had for his opinions. Having assumed as a self-evident proposition that babies lose their identity and freedom as they begin to grow up, he naturally felt he had nothing left to say after his four or five sweeping sentences. Does a child of one or two have a wider range of available choices or a more clearly defined individuality than a child of nine or eleven? Clearly, in handling topics of this complexity, a writer needs to identify his own underlying assumptions as much as he needs to question the external evidence and authority for his views. If he takes the time to do this, he is more likely to spot the flaws in his generalizations (see section 3b-3); as a result, he will find that he can think more clearly about his topic and he will discover that he has more to say. Any method you find that makes you take time to test your generalities, to see clearly and say concretely what they signify, is worth using.

SUMMARY

A well-developed paragraph gives the reader as much relevant information as he needs for a full understanding of the point. To help yourself write well-developed paragraphs, try to:
a. Use concrete diction which helps your reader see and feel the object or event, and select your details purposefully so that he cannot doubt what they illustrate.
b. Determine whether a particular method of paragraph development such as by definition or by contrast best suits your immediate ends or whether a combination of methods will be necessary.
c. Revise undeveloped paragraphs by identifying unsatisfactory passages, distinguishing the opinions which need fuller explanation and evidence, and making a list of the details and examples to be included.

REVIEW EXERCISES

6

a. This first set of examples is intended to give you practice in working with concrete diction and detail.

1. Pick one of the following topics and write two paragraphs about it. Make the diction of the first paragraph as vague, trite, and general as you can. Then, still describing the same event, make the diction of the second paragraph as concrete and clear as you can.

    a. A man shaving sleepily with a dull razor
    b. A first-year French or Spanish class reciting in unison
    c. A coed shopping for a dress
    d. A student trying to stay awake in the front row
    e. A tennis player who has lost control of his serve
    f. An inexperienced cook trying to crack eggs without breaking the yolks
    g. A teacher who cannot sit still or stay in one place
    h. A man trying to light his pipe in the wind

2. List ten or eleven details which you could use in describing one of the following. Then organize the details into a well-developed paragraph.

    a. A night crowd at a high school football game
    b. Subway or bus passengers riding home at 2 a.m.
    c. Customers in a pet shop
    d. The amusement section at a fair
    e. A public swimming pool on a hot day
    f. A college dining room at noon-time

b. This second set of exercises is intended to give you practice in working with different methods of paragraph development. Your instructor may ask you to develop one or more of your choices into paragraphs.

1. Pick one of the following and list several details you could use in developing the paragraph by specific detail.

    a. A lazy roommate
    b. A dull movie
    c. An annoying lecturer
    d. An ideal campsite
    e. A persistent salesman

2. Pick one of the following and list two extended examples for development in support of your topic sentence.
   a. The importance of the Vice Presidency as an office
   b. The difficulty in choosing a college
   c. The technique of a well-known comedian
   d. The inventiveness of a young child

3. In a short paragraph for each, define any two of the following terms. Be sure to distinguish it from other terms which are sometimes used as loose synonyms for it. For example, if you were to pick the term "chuckle," you would need to differentiate it from terms like "giggle" and "laugh."
   a. Pond
   b. Coupe
   c. Violin
   d. Pantomine
   e. Rage
   f. Bowl
   g. Macadam
   h. Biscuit
   i. The Blues (as music)
   j. Candor
   k. Parallelogram
   l. Shout

4. Choose one of the following terms and define it in a paragraph or two.
   a. Technology
   b. Propaganda
   c. Isolationism
   d. Civil rights
   e. Lobbyist
   f. Hypothesis
   g. Nationalism
   h. Labor union
   i. Deduction

5. Pick one of the following and list the main categories you would use in developing the paragraph by division.
   a. The traits of a good conversationalist
   b. The best ways to study ineffectively
   c. The types of songs popular among high school students
   d. The kinds of reading popular among college freshmen

6. Pick two of the following. For one, list the main differences you would use in developing the paragraph by contrast. For the other, list the similarities you would use in developing the paragraph by analogy.
   a. Dating in high school and dating in college
   b. Seeing the play and reading the play
   c. Doing a dissection by one's self and doing it with others
   d. Arguing and discussing
   e. The way computers "remember"
   f. A thermostat
   g. What is meant by the expression that a country has a "culture" of its own

6

h. What is meant by the expression "mathematics is a language"

7. Pick one of the following and develop it in one or more paragraphs by cause and effect.
   a. Why I have been uncertain about my major
   b. Why I have found essay tests difficult (or easy) to write
   c. Why teen-age marriages often fail
   d. How a bull session can clarify one's thinking
   e. How cars could be designed for greater safety

c. *This third set of exercises is designed to give you practice in analyzing the methods of paragraph development used by professional writers. For each of the paragraphs below, identify the method or combination of methods used by the writer. Pick out the topic sentence (or make up one if there is none) and study each paragraph carefully to see what are its main points and what kind of evidence or detail is offered in support.*

The American people, more than any other people, is composed of individuals who have lost association with their old landmarks. They have crossed an ocean, they have spread themselves across a new continent. The American who still lives in his grandfather's house feels almost as if he were living in a museum. There are few Americans who have not moved at least once since their childhood, and even if they have stayed where they were born, the old landmarks themselves have been carted away to make room for progress. That, perhaps, is one reason why we have so much more Americanism than love of America. It takes time to learn to love the new gas station which stands where the wild honeysuckle grew. Moreover, the great majority of Americans have risen in the world. They have moved out of their class, lifting the old folks along with them perhaps, so that together they may sit by the steam pipes, and listen to the crooning of the radio. But more and more of them have moved not only out of their class, but out of their culture; and then they leave the old folks behind, and the continuity of life is broken. For faith grows well only as it is passed on from parents to their children amidst surroundings that bear witness, because nothing

changes radically, to a deep permanence in the order of the world. It is true, no doubt, that in this great physical and psychic migration some of the old household gods are carefully packed up and put with the rest of the luggage, and then unpacked and set up on new altars in new places. But what can be taken along is at best no more than the tree which is above the ground. The roots remain in the soil where first they grew.

—Walter Lippmann

It is easier to say what loyalty is not than to say what it is. It is not conformity. It is not passive acquiescence in the status quo. It is not preference for everything American over everything foreign. It is not an ostrich-like ignorance of other countries and other institutions. It is not the indulgence in ceremony—a flag salute, an oath of allegiance, a fervid verbal declaration. It is not a particular creed, a particular version of history, a particular body of economic practices, a particular philosophy.

—Henry Steele Commager

It's hard to grow up when there isn't enough man's work. There is "nearly full employment" (with highly significant exceptions), but there get to be fewer jobs that are necessary or unquestionably useful; that require energy and draw on some of one's best capacities; and that can be done keeping one's honor and dignity. In explaining the widespread troubles of adolescents and young men, this simple objective factor is not much mentioned. Let us here insist on it.

By "man's work" I mean a very simple idea, so simple that it is clearer to ingenuous boys than to most adults. To produce necessary food and shelter is man's work. During most of economic history most men have done this drudging work secure that it was justified and worthy of a man to do it, though often feeling that the social conditions under which they did it were *not* worthy of a man, thinking, "It's better to die than to live so hard"—but they worked on. When the environment is forbidding, as in the Swiss Alps or the Aran Islands, we regard such work with poetic awe. In emergencies it is heroic, as when the bakers of Paris maintained the supply of bread during the French

Revolution, or the milkman did not miss a day's delivery when the bombs recently tore up London.

At present there is little such subsistence work. In *Communitas* my brother and I guess that one-tenth of our economy is devoted to it; it is more likely one-twentieth. Production of food is actively discouraged. Farmers are not wanted and the young men go elsewhere. (The farm population is now less than 15 per cent of the total population.) Building, on the contrary, is immensely needed. New York City needs 65,000 new units a year, and is getting, net, 16,000. One would think that ambitious boys would flock to this work. But here we find that building, too, is discouraged. In a great city, for the last twenty years hundreds of thousands have been ill housed, yet we do not see science, industry, and labor enthusiastically enlisted in finding the quick solution to a definite problem. The promoters are interested in long-term investments, the real estate men in speculation, the city planners in votes and graft. The building craftsmen cannily see to it that their own numbers remain few, their methods antiquated, and their rewards high. None of these people is much interested in providing shelter, and nobody is at all interested in providing new manly jobs. —Paul Goodman

Biologists used to entertain themselves by speculating as to what would happen if, through some unthinkable catastrophe, the natural restraints were thrown off and all the progeny of a single individual survived. Thus Thomas Huxley a century ago calculated that a single female aphis (which has the curious power of reproducing without mating) could produce progeny in a single year's time whose total weight would equal that of the Chinese empire of his day.

Fortunately for us such an extreme situation is only theoretical, but the dire results of upsetting nature's own arrangements are well known to students of animal populations. The stockman's zeal for eliminating the coyote has resulted in plagues of field mice, which the coyote formerly controlled. The oft repeated story of the Kaibab deer in Arizona is another case in point. At one time the deer population was in equilibrium with its environment. A number of predators—wolves, pumas, and

coyotes—prevented the deer from out running their food supply. Then a campaign was begun to "conserve" the deer by killing off their enemies. Once the predators were gone, the deer increased prodigiously and soon there was not enough food for them. The browse line on the trees went higher and higher as they sought food, and in time many more deer were dying of starvation than had formerly been killed by predators. The whole environment, moreover, was damaged by their desperate efforts to find food.   —Rachel Carson, *Silent Spring*

No subject, not even the little dogie, has produced so much good American music as the railroad—our best ballads, *John Henry, Casey Jones,* and *The Old '97;* a cycle of powerful worksongs for every aspect of railroad building; spirituals like *This Train* and *All Night Long;* love songs like *Down in the Valley* and *Careless Love;* blues verses without number, indeed the blues might be said to be half-African and half-locomotive rhythm; endless jazz tunes and pop songs such as *Yancey's Special, Blues in the Night, The Chatanooga Choo-Choo, The Fireball Mail,* and *Tuxedo Junction.* Two of the most vivid sermons ever preached on American soil were entitled—*The Black Diamond Express to Hell* and *The White Flyer to Heaven.* What a ship on the sea is to an Englishman, a droshky on the snow to a Russian, a horse on the desert to an Arab, the iron horse became to the men of North America. This early western railroad ditty ["She'll Be Comin' Around the Mountain"], anonymously composed, put the original hymn tune ("The Old Ship of Zion") out of the minds of most of us; it catches the jubilation of that halcyon day when the first steam engine came whistling and snorting into a horse-and-buggy town on the prairies.   —Alan Lomax

It is seldom that an English judge or magistrate does not at least wince or yawn when a psychiatric opinion is being read; often he speaks his mind. This is a favourite. "It is not going to hurt your victim any the less to know that you knocked her down because of some complex or other." True. Just as it is not going to hurt any the less if what knocked her down had been a falling branch or brick. We no longer think of cutting down the tree

6

or burning down the house, we've become quite rational towards inanimate things. The tree may need a prop, those bricks may need more mortar, the hooligan may need some treatment or another kind of life. The chief difference is that we know more about roofs and trees; men and women being of course more complex, and we much less willing to learn.   —Sybille Bedford

Precisely the same thing holds of a source of heat: for us to be able to convert any part of it into work the source of heat must be at a higher temperature than its surroundings. It is not only that we cannot use up the heat of ponds and lakes (I select bodies of water, because the heat capacity of water is much higher than that of stone, for instance, and because the circulation possible in water would help us to utilize the heat, if it were in any way possible to do so) and turn it into work: we could not use the heat of the furnace of a steam turbine if the whole of the engine-room were at the same temperature. We must have a condenser at a lower temperature than the furnace, if we are to convert some of the heat of the furnace into work, and the bigger the difference of temperature between the boiler and the condenser, the larger the fraction of the heat which we can turn into work. This is why to-day great efforts are being made to use steam at higher and higher pressure: the higher the pressure of the steam the higher the temperature, and the greater the efficiency. Steam in itself can do nothing: on a hot planet all the water would be steam, but no steam-engine could be run, for lack of a condenser.   —E. N. da C. Andrade

The really important question is: "What does the composer start with; where does he begin?" The answer to that is, Every composer begins with a musical idea—a *musical* idea, you understand, not a mental, literary, or extramusical idea. Suddenly a theme comes to him. (Theme is used as synonymous with musical idea.) The composer starts with his theme; and the theme is a gift from Heaven. He doesn't know where it comes from—has no control over it. It comes almost like automatic writing. That's why he keeps a book very often and writes themes down

whenever they come. He collects musical ideas. You can't do anything about that element of composing.

The idea itself may come in various forms. It may come as a melody—just a one-line simple melody which you might hum to yourself. Or it may come to the composer as a melody with an accompaniment. At times he may not even hear a melody; he may simply conceive an accompanimental figure to which a melody will probably be added later. Or, on the other hand, the theme may take the form of a purely rhythmic idea. He hears a particular kind of drumbeat, and that will be enough to start him off. Over it he will soon begin hearing an accompaniment and melody. The original conception, however, was a mere rhythm. Or, a different type of composer may possibly begin with a contrapuntal web of two or three melodies which are heard at the same instant. That, however, is a less usual species of thematic inspiration.

All these are different ways in which the musical idea may present itself to the composer.   —Aaron Copeland

Art matters not merely because it is the most magnificent ornament and the most nearly unfailing occupation of our lives, but because it is life itself. From Christ to Freud we have believed that, if we know the truth, the truth will set us free: art is indispensable because so much of this truth can be learned through works of art and through works of art alone—for which of us could have learned for himself what Proust and Chekhov, Hardy and Yeats and Rilke, Shakespeare and Homer learned for us? and in what other way could they have made us see the truths which they themselves saw, those differing and contradictory truths which seem nevertheless, to the mind which contains them, in some sense a single truth? And all these things, by their very nature, demand to be shared; if we are satisfied to know these things ourselves, and to look with superiority or indifference at those who do not have that knowledge, we have made a refusal that corrupts us as surely as anything can. If while most of our people (the descendants of those who, ordinarily, listened to Grimm's Tales and the ballads and the Bible; who, exceptionally, listened to Aeschylus and Shakespeare)

6

listen not to simple or naive art, but to an elaborate and sophisticated substitute for art, an immediate and infallible synthetic as effective and terrifying as advertisements or the speeches of Hitler—if, knowing all this, we say: *Art has always been a matter of a few,* we are using a truism to hide a disaster. One of the oldest, deepest, and most nearly conclusive attractions of democracy is manifested in our feeling that through it not only material but spiritual goods can be shared: that in a democracy bread and justice, education and art, will be accessible to everybody. If a democracy should offer its citizens a show of education, a sham art, a literacy more dangerous than their old illiteracy, then we should have to say that it is not a democracy at all, but one more variant of those "People's Democracies" which share with any true democracy little more than the name. Goethe said: The only way in which we can come to terms with the great superiority of another person is with love. But we can also come to terms with superiority, with true Excellence, by denying that such a thing as Excellence can exist; and, in doing so, we help to destroy it and ourselves.　　　—Randall Jarrell

GOOD SENTENCES

7 *sentence unity*

a unrelated ideas and excessive detail
b subordination

8 *sentence coherence:*
parallelism and pronouns
dangling and misplaced modifiers
confusing shifts
mixed and incomplete constructions

a parallelism
b faulty reference of pronouns
c dangling modifiers
d misplaced modifiers
e confusing shifts
f mixed constructions
g incomplete constructions

9 *sentence emphasis: weak and wordy sentences*

a weak sentences
b wordy sentences
c wordy constructions

7

sentence unity

A sentence is unified if all its parts contribute to one single statement or impression.

Much of what has been said about paragraphs applies to sentences. Like the good paragraph, the good sentence has *unity, coherence,* and *emphasis.* The good sentence avoids irrelevant details and ideas: its details and ideas contribute to one *unified* thought. It has clearly connected parts and a consistent order: accurately placed modifiers, unambiguous pronoun reference, and parallel structure make the statement *coherent.* It stresses the main ideas: important material is placed in the *emphatic* positions. Though these characteristics overlap, for purposes of discussion it is more convenient to treat each in a separate chapter. For treatment of sentence coherence, see chapter 8. Sentence emphasis is discussed in chapter 9.

7 a
unrelated ideas and
excessive detail

By eliminating unrelated ideas and cluttering details and by subordinating less important points, the writer leaves the reader no doubt about his meaning. Disunified sentences are usually the result of wandering attention or incomplete analysis; in short, they are caused by *the writer's failure to keep his topic and his reader clearly in mind.*

7 a-1
unrelated ideas

Remember what your main point is, and include in your sentence ideas that contribute to it.

Sometimes, unrelated ideas creep into a sentence when the writer temporarily forgets what his main point is.

UNRELATED Mac always brings out a person's sense of humor, and if a person can't learn to joke about things, he will make himself and everyone else miserable.

What is the sentence supposed to be about: Mac or the value of humor? If it is part of a character sketch of Mac, then the generalization about humor should be omitted.

UNRELATED The captain of a ship, whether he commands a tugboat or the *Queen Elizabeth,* a giant sister-ship to the *Queen Mary* and one of the fastest, most costly liners on the Atlantic, leads a very lonely life.

The Queen Elizabeth *is mentioned here only to provide a contrast with a tugboat. All other information about the liner is unnecessary.*

IMPROVED The captain of a ship, whether he commands a tugboat or a giant liner like the *Queen Elizabeth,* leads a very lonely life.

The relationship between two ideas may be clear to the writer but the sentence may baffle the reader if the unifying principle is only implied (see also section 3a):

OBSCURE RELATIONSHIP Being from San Diego, I wear only half my pajamas.

The sentence suggests the interesting if unintended generalization that all people living in San Diego wear only "half" their pajamas. The student has omitted a logical step in the cause-and-effect relationship.

IMPROVED Since I come from San Diego, which is warm most of the year, I wear only my pajama bottoms.

OBSCURE RELATIONSHIP   Maturing faster because of parents' divorcing does not hold true in all cases. The child may become timid and insecure.

Why, in the first place, should a child's maturing be hastened by a divorce? The writer is assuming a connection between the child's shock at the divorce and his growth. This connection should be made explicit.

IMPROVED   When parents divorce, *the shock may hasten* the maturing of the child. But divorce may, in some cases, retard maturity and make the child timid and insecure.

Even though two ideas belong together in the sense that one ought to follow the other, they do not necessarily belong in the same sentence. Putting them together in one sentence may suggest a closer relationship than actually exists.

FALSE UNITY   After looking at the house, I left the key with the real estate agent, and I hope you will soon find another tenant.

IMPROVED   After looking at the house, I left the key with the real estate agent. I hope you will soon find another tenant.

7 a-2
excessive detail

Use only enough detail in a sentence to make your point.

Length alone does not make a sentence good or bad. By using parallel structure, accurate punctuation, and carefully selected connectives, an experienced writer can compose long, well-unified sentences. If, however, a sentence contains too many ideas or details, none of them will stand out. The sentence will seem overcrowded and pointless. If you must bring in further details, use them to build additional sentences into a unified paragraph.

OVERCROWDED   Sculpture is one of the oldest arts known to man and the earliest known examples date from the Old

Stone Age, or Paleolithic period, over 20,000 years before the time of Christ, many pieces of ancient sculpture having been found in caves or old burial places in various parts of the world.

Here, the writer has unselectively copied from his note cards and crammed the bits of information into one sentence. He should break it into at least two sentences and simplify the wording.

IMPROVED Sculpture is one of the oldest arts known to man and the earliest examples date from more than 20,000 B.C. Many ancient pieces have been found in caves or old burial places.

OVERCROWDED On the forward end of the boat I built a little deck of plywood, which extended about one third of the way aft and into which I cut a hole for the mast, made of two pieces of plywood glued together, and I made the boom in the same way.

Especially in narratives, a writer may obscure his central thought by excessive coordination and subordination. Avoid loosely related "and . . . and" clauses. Revise the House-that-Jack-built sentence made up of "who . . . who . . . who" or "which . . . which . . . which" clauses.

IMPROVED On the forward end of the boat, I built a little deck of plywood and cut a hole in it for the mast. I made both the mast and the boom by glueing two pieces of plywood together.

OVERCROWDED When the cry for woman's suffrage was first heard there was immediate opposition to it, which continued for a long time until people finally began to realize that women were entitled to the same rights as men, and in 1920 the Nineteenth Amendment was ratified.

This sentence includes too many ideas: the beginning of woman's suffrage movement, opposition to it, continued opposition, gradual change of public opinion, and the ratification of the Nineteenth Amendment. It should be broken down into at least two sentences.

IMPROVED When the cry for woman's suffrage was first heard there was immediate opposition to it, and this opposition continued for a long time. Gradually, however, people realized that women were entitled to the same rights as men, and in 1920 the Nineteenth Amendment was ratified.

SUMMARY

1. Bring into the sentence only related thoughts and relevant details. Develop unrelated ideas in separate sentences.
2. Make logical relationships as explicit as possible so that the reader can immediately see the connection of ideas.
3. Eliminate details and ideas which obscure the main idea of the sentence.

EXERCISES

a. Point out unrelated ideas or obscure connections in the following sentences and revise the sentences to make them more unified.

1. As a young man, Conrad led an active adventurous life, and he began writing novels when he was well past thirty.
2. One of the great advantages of our system of government is that American citizens may work wherever they want to, and at present jobs are plentiful in America.
3. Many countries have trees which make good timber, and lumbering is carried on throughout much of the world.
4. The changed political conditions do not mean that we shall have a socialist government; they do mean that our government will be much more centralized, and in the future we will probably have to import more and more of our raw materials.
5. Moderators on television have to practice hard to develop pleasant speaking voices; it is very important that they acquire a sense of timing so that programs aren't rushed at the end.

7

b. Revise the following sentences to eliminate excessive or irrelevant details.

1. After his attacks on slave owners in Kansas had earned him a reputation as a violent enemy of slavery, John Brown moved his men to Virginia, took the small town of Harpers Ferry, was defeated and captured by a small detachment of marines under the leadership of Colonel Robert E. Lee, and soon after was tried and hanged for treason, becoming a martyr in the eyes of Northern abolitionists.

2. The Basques are marked by an exceptional pride of race and great physical sturdiness and endurance, as well as great conservatism and self-respect, and their language is different from any known tongue.

3. Borrowing a pen from the salesman, who had several of the cheap ball-point type which businessmen give away and which often leak, I signed the contract.

4. I was caught in the late afternoon turnpike traffic, which was packed so tightly around me that bumpers were almost touching and cars were barely moving, and I was late to work, which didn't surprise me because I had lost so much time on the road.

5. The technician was living near Philadelphia, Pennsylvania, one of the largest cities in the country and part of the great metropolitan area which reaches from Boston to Wilmington, Delaware, when his company transferred him.

7 b
subordination

Subordination means putting less important details in less conspicuous constructions—dependent clauses, participial phrases, appositives, etc

The important ideas in a sentence should go into main clauses; less important ideas should go into subordinate clauses or into phrases.

This kind of sentence structure enables you to specify more precisely the relationship between parts of a sentence and to achieve unity.

7 b-1
primer sentences

Primer sentences, short and jerky sentences like those found in a second-grade reader, are usually a sure sign that the writer has not evaluated his material. Since every detail is put as a main clause, no one action or idea seems more important than another.

> **PRIMER SENTENCES** The train was three hours late. There had been a freight wreck ahead somewhere. We finally reached Riverbank. The station was dark and deserted.
>
> **SUBORDINATED** The train was three hours late *because* of a freight wreck ahead, and the station was dark and deserted *when* we finally reached Riverbank.

Although writers like Hemingway and Sherwood Anderson skillfully employ short, simple sentences, the inexperienced writer should strive for longer, unified sentences with the less important ideas subordinated. Otherwise, the result is likely to be:

> **PRIMER SENTENCES** Thurber sticks to his subject and does not wander off into the darkness. For example, in his essay on the word "which," he makes his point. Then he is finished with that subject. He does not put in any words which are irrelevant to his purpose. All of his ideas pertain directly to his subject.
>
> **SUBORDINATED** Thurber sticks to his topic *without wandering or irrelevancies*. In his essay on the word "which," for example, he makes his point *directly* and then is finished with the topic.
>
> *The italicized passages in the revision show how whole sentences and clauses can be reduced to subordinate phrases and words.*

SU

7 b-2
avoiding false coordination

When sentence elements are joined by *and, but,* or *so,* the coordinating conjunction implies that the elements are of equal weight and importance.

Just as the reader expects ideas of lesser importance to be placed in subordinate grammatical form, so he expects ideas of equal value to be placed in coordinate grammatical form. For example, Henry Adams, in his autobiography *The Education of Henry Adams,* uses coordination skillfully to assess the value of a Harvard education around 1858:

> Sometimes in after life, Adams debated whether in fact it had not ruined him **and** most of his companions, **but**, disappointment apart, Harvard College was probably less hurtful than any other university then in existence. It taught little, **and** that little ill, **but** it left the mind open, free from bias, ignorant of facts, **but** docile. The graduate had few strong prejudices. He knew little, **but** his mind remained supple, ready to receive knowledge.

If elements are not really equal in importance, do not use a coordinating conjunction. Subordinate *one* of the elements.

FALSE COORDINATION   In English we had to learn many rules of grammar, and very few of these rules are used today.

IMPROVED   Few of the many grammar rules we had to learn in English are used today.

IMPROVED   *Although* we had to learn many rules of grammar in English, very few of these rules are used today.

Note that more than one revision is possible.

FALSE COORDINATION   The explanation had examples to go with it and they were clear, and I understood it.

IMPROVED I understood the explanation *because* it had clear examples.

IMPROVED I understood the explanation *because* it had examples and *because* they were clear.

By the subordinating "because," the writer shows the cause-and-effect relationships among the ideas more accurately. He also avoids the "and . . . and . . . and" type of sentence.

7 b-3
faulty subordination

Do not put the main idea of a sentence in a subordinate construction.

When the main idea of a sentence is placed in a dependent clause or a modifying phrase, the resulting "upside-down" subordination makes the sentence weak. For example:

FAULTY SUBORDINATION The night watchman walked past the building, noticing that the door was unlocked.

The reader is startled by the phrase "noticing that the door was unlocked." The writer has given minor emphasis to his main idea.

IMPROVED *When* (or As) he walked past the building, the night watchman noticed that the door was unlocked.

FAULTY SUBORDINATION Ruth Benedict is the author of *Patterns of Culture*, in which she praises the Zuñi Indians for their ceremonial life and its cooperative attitude toward the natural world.

IMPROVED In her *Patterns of Culture*, Ruth Benedict praises the Zuñi Indians for their ceremonial life and its cooperative attitude toward the natural world.

In some cases, of course, the context alone determines which ideas are relatively more important, and which are relatively less important. If you were stressing your own experience in a narrative, the following sentence would be satisfactory:

> I used to work for the Arco Electronics Company, which went bankrupt today.

If you were writing a report on the Arco Electronics Company, you would subordinate the first idea:

> The Arco Electronics Company, where I used to work, went bankrupt today.

Usually the reader will have clear, normal expectations of what is more important, what is less so.

7 b-4
excessive subordination

Revise sentences which have excessive subordination.

As suggested in the discussion of excessive detail, the long sentence of many clumsy "who . . . who . . . who" or "which . . . which . . . which" clauses should be rewritten. Such sentences not only obscure the main idea but also fatigue the reader, especially if they come in a series.

EXCESSIVE SUBORDINATION The examples are not very clear in the books which are used in the courses which are required for freshmen who didn't pass the placement tests. They don't receive much help in the review sections which only meet once a week, which is why many freshmen who buy these books won't use them.

REVISED Freshmen who failed placement tests and are in required elementary courses get little help from the textbooks chosen. They complain that the examples are vague and that the weekly review sections are inadequate. Many freshmen won't use the texts at all.

Sub

SUMMARY

1. Place the most important idea of a sentence in the main clause; place less important ideas in subordinate clauses, phrases, or words.
2. Revise primer sentences by making them into longer, more unified sentences with the less important ideas subordinated.
3. If elements are not really equal in importance, do not use a coordinating conjunction like "and" or "but." Subordinate one of the elements.
4. Do not place the main idea of a sentence in a subordinate construction.
5. Revise sentences which have excessive or clumsy subordination.

EXERCISES

a. Revise the following primer sentences into longer sentences in which ideas are effectively subordinated.

1. Emma was handsome. She was clever and rich. Her home was comfortable. She had a happy disposition. She seemed to unite some of the best blessings of existence. She was almost twenty-one. During these years, there had been very little to distress her. There had not been much to vex her, either.

2. Writing for a college newspaper can be good experience. The student is on his own. He doesn't have a teacher to give him his stories. He has to find them for himself. Also his copy isn't corrected and edited by a teacher. If he doesn't learn to do it himself, the editor may drop him.

3. These planes carried small cannons. A few bombs were placed under the wings. Sometimes a torpedo was added. They were also equipped with self-sealing gas tanks.

4. I am a law-abiding citizen, but I will discuss my reasons for disliking policemen.

b. Revise the following sentences by subordinating the less important ideas. Be prepared to explain the choices you make and the form of subordination you have used.

1. The potter must roll the clay out on a flat surface, and a surface that the clay will not stick to.
2. Five hundred men were too many to meet at one time, and so instead the Council was divided into ten smaller groups.
3. The job was interesting, and the pay was good, but finally I decided not to accept it and I regretted my decision later.
4. Hawthorne and Melville were contemporaries, and Melville was one of the first to recognize Hawthorne's genius as a writer.
5. Scientists are continually developing new photographic equipment, and now they have devised ways of photographing planets as far away as Mars by rockets which relay the pictures back to Earth.
6. I got the note from my parents, and I gave it to my teacher, but he just scowled at me, but finally he said I could take the afternoon off.

c. Revise the following sentences by putting the main ideas in main clauses and less important ideas in subordinate clauses. Be prepared to explain why you have chosen certain ideas as the main ones and to explain the form of subordination you have used.

1. An especially big wave rolled in, when I finally managed to get my line unsnagged.
2. Many of his home run records still unbroken and his life-time batting average one of the highest ever achieved, Babe Ruth batted for the Yankees.
3. The ocean was choppy, causing the fishermen to have little luck and to return to the pier disappointed.
4. The population of Latin America, ranging from Indians who live as their ancestors did hundreds of years ago to highly educated men and women in modern cities like Buenos Aires and Rio de Janeiro, is varied.
5. He was trying to kill a bee inside the car, driving off the road as a result.

6. Contact lenses are worn next to the eyeballs and have advantages over ordinary glasses, since contact lenses are invisible, are kept unfrosted by the eyelids, and correct faulty corneas.

7. The horse came up to the first jump, when he stumbled and threw Janet off.

d. Revise the following student sentences by eliminating the excessive subordination.

1. In 1666 when he sent a beam of white light through a glass prism which broke the beam up into bands of colored lights which resembled a rainbow, Isaac Newton showed that what we normally think of as white light is actually made up of light which consists of different colors, a discovery which revolutionized the science of optics, which was in its infancy before Newton.

2. When I bought my parrot from the pet store on the Mall, where I had visited several times and spent hours gazing at the cages because I so badly wanted a bird of my own, I was so excited that I could hardly contain myself as I rushed home to begin training him from the booklet which I had also bought at the store.

3. Socrates was also famous for his bravery and for being a soldier when he fought at Delium in 424 B.C. and at Amphipolis in 422 B.C., although after the naval battle of Arginusae in 406 B.C. he spoke against the citizens when they unjustly demanded the death of ten generals who had been unable to bury those who were killed in battle.

4. The encyclopedia says that naturalism is a literary form which was developed in accordance with a philosophic belief which says that man is an animal who has no soul and that he is conditioned by his heredity and by the environment into which he is born so that he does not have free will but only sexual and hunger drives which he cannot control because they are so powerful.

5. At the beginning of the story, which takes place in Sicily at some unknown time in the past, Verga makes

us realize that the main character is called "La Lupa," which means the wolf, because the villagers are superstitious people who believe in the devil and other evil forces that can take human form.

e. Revise the following sentences to improve their unity. Be prepared to explain the changes you have made.

1. Louise was Jonathan's girl and eventually they planned to get married and move away from town.

2. The swimming pool was intended for college students only, but is now open to townspeople as well.

3. The train was late, causing me to miss my appointment and lose the client.

4. The picture which won first prize was in water color. It was an abstract painting. Most people criticized it, but the judges liked it.

5. The first book I consulted lacked an index, and next I tried an almanac.

6. The Greek word *papyros* originally meant thin sheets of paper made from a certain Egyptian reed, from which we have borrowed our modern word *paper* and which now means any kind of writing material.

7. The United Nations, which was founded in San Francisco more than twenty years ago when many of the major diplomats of the world were there, has increased greatly in size, many of the new members being the small nations which have recently gained their independence.

8. Freud grew up in Vienna, doing some of his most creative psychoanalytic research in that city.

9. There were about ten boys out for wrestling, and we only had four weeks before our first match, so we worked very hard to get in condition, but three of our best men caught the flu and so we didn't do well against our opponents.

10. The match burned his fingers. He tried to light his pipe in the wind, and he dropped it on the ground when he burned himself.

8

sentence coherence:
parallelism and pronouns
dangling and misplaced modifiers
confusing shifts
mixed and incomplete constructions

A sentence is *coherent* when its parts are clearly connected and it has a consistent order.

The literal meaning of the word *cohere* is "to stick together."
When a sentence is well stuck together, the reader is not
thrown off by faulty reference of pronouns or by dangling
modifiers. He is not confused by unnecessary shifts in tense
or voice or by mixed constructions. The parts of the sentence
are clearly related by devices like parallel structure; the sentence is an orderly, consistent whole.

S coh

8 a
parallelism

In parallel structure, similar or logically related ideas are placed in the same kinds of grammatical constructions.

To express similar or logically related ideas, the writer parallels a noun with a noun, an infinitive with another infinitive, a subordinate clause with another subordinate clause. (For a discussion of parallel paragraph structure, see section 5 b-4.) For example, in jotting down ideas for a theme on what a college should help do for a student, you might have written:

> Make you examine your values
> Learning to become more objective in his views
> To help student appreciate real merit

Looking over this list, you discover that *examining one's values, becoming more objective,* and *appreciating real merit* are similar in that they are all desirable ends of a college education. They are parallel ideas. By putting these similar ideas in similar grammatical constructions, you emphasize their likeness.

PARALLEL IDEAS IN PARALLEL INFINITIVE PHRASES A college education should help a student

> to examine his own values,
> to become more objective,
> and
> to appreciate real merit.

PARALLEL IDEAS IN PARALLEL NOUN PHRASES Our colleges ought to have lit up in us

> a lasting relish for the better kind of man,
> a loss of appetite for mediocrities,
> and
> a disgust for cheapjacks.

In these two examples, William James relates some goals of a college education by paralleling them, first in infinitive phrases, then in noun phrases.

COMPLEX PARALLEL STRUCTURE

But | to have spent one's youth at
college in contact with the || choice and
rare and
precious,

and yet | to be
still || a blind prig
or
vulgarian, unable || to scent out
human
excellence
or
to divine it
amidst its acci-
dents,

| to know it only when || ticketed and
labelled and
forced on us by others,

this indeed should be accounted the very ||| calamity and
shipwreck of
higher
education.

*Here, to state emphatically what is the failure of a college edu-
cation, James has used a complex, tightly-controlled parallel
structure.*

8 a-1
faulty parallelism

The coordinating conjunctions *and, or, nor, but* are
sure signs of compound construction. Use them only
to connect parallel grammatical structures.

FAULTY   He likes to dance and skiing.
Infinitive paralleled with a gerund.
PARALLEL   He likes to dance and *to ski.* Or: He likes *dancing* and
skiing.

FAULTY Every player is taught to work with the team and that good sportsmanship must be shown.
Here, "and" awkwardly joins a phrase beginning with "to" and a clause beginning with "that."
PARALLEL Every player is taught **to work** with the team **and to show** good sportsmanship.
"And" now joins two phrases, each beginning with "to."

8 a-2
faulty parallelism of elements in a series

Sentence elements in a series (a, b, and c) should express parallel ideas and be parallel in form.

Faulty parallelism of elements in a series is one of the commonest errors in student writing.

FAULTY She is **young**, well **educated**, and **has** poise.
The first two elements are adjectives, but the last is a verb.
PARALLEL She is **young**, well **educated** and **poised**.
All three elements are parallel as adjectives.

FAULTY The new subway moved passengers more **rapidly**, **economically**, and with greater **comfort** than the bus system did.
PARALLEL The new subway moved passengers more **rapidly**, **economically**, and **comfortably** than the bus system did.

FAULTY Harrison signed up as the camp counselor in charge of evening **programs, sailing, swimming,** and **to lead** occasional weekend trips.
When a series is long, special care should be taken to keep all items parallel.
PARALLEL Harrison signed up as the camp counselor in charge of evening **programs, sailing, swimming,** and occasional weekend **trips**.

8 a-3
faulty omissions

To make a parallel construction clear, you will often need to repeat a preposition, an article, a relative pronoun, a subordinating conjunction, an auxiliary verb, or the sign of the infinitive.

Failure to make a parallel repetition can result in seriously confusing sentences.

FAULTY The advisor told the girl that she spent far too much time in useless fretting and she needed confidence in herself. *The omission of "that" to introduce the second subordinate clause causes misreading.*
PARALLEL The advisor told the girl *that* she spent far too much time in useless fretting *and that* she needed confidence in herself.

FAULTY Frank needed Elaine because she was his reminder of his past glory and she would also help get him into the right circles through her family.
PARALLEL Frank needed Elaine *because* she was his reminder of his past glory *and because* she would also help him get into the right circles through her family.

FAULTY The vineyard is often visited by tourists who sample the wine grapes, and especially connoisseurs.
PARALLEL The vineyard is often visited *by* tourists who sample the wine grapes, *and* especially *by* connoisseurs.

8 a-4
faulty parallelism in
correlatives

Correlative conjunctions (*either . . . or, neither . . . nor, not only . . . but also, both . . . and, whether . . . or*) should be followed by parallel sentence elements.

S coh

FAULTY Blake is *not only* famous as a poet, *but also* for his art.

"Not only" is followed by the adjective "famous" with a prepositional phrase modifying it. "But also" is followed by a prepositional phrase.

PARALLEL Blake is famous *not only* **for his poetry** but also **for his art.**

FAULTY The doctor wondered *whether* he should rely on a skin test *or* to send the patient to the hospital for a complete diagnosis.

"Whether" is followed by a subordinate clause; "or" is followed by an infinitive.

PARALLEL The doctor wondered *whether* **to rely** on a skin test *or* **to send** the patient to the hospital for a complete diagnosis.

FAULTY He *either* is a liar *or* a remarkably naive person.

"Either" is followed by a verb and its noun complement. "Or" is followed by a noun and its adjectives.

PARALLEL He is *either* a **liar** *or* a remarkably naive **person.**

8 a-5
faulty parallelism in *who* and *which* clauses

Be sure that a *who* clause precedes an *and who* clause and that a *which* clause precedes an *and which* clause.

FAULTY In the middle of the sleepy village is a statue dating from 1870 *and which* shows General Lee on horseback.

PARALLEL In the middle of the sleepy village is a statue *which* dates from 1870 *and which* shows General Lee on horseback.

FAULTY He is a man of strong convictions *and who* always says what he thinks.

PARALLEL He is a man *who* has strong convictions *and who* always says what he thinks.

CORRECT He is a man of strong convictions who always says what he thinks.
Fault corrected by omitting the coordinating conjunction.

Do not join a relative clause to its main clause by *and* or *but*.

FAULTY *He* appeared before the committee with a long written statement, *but which* he was not allowed to read.
CORRECT *He* appeared before the committee with a long written statement, *but he* was not allowed to read it.
Fault corrected by changing relative clause to a main clause.

8 a-6
using parallelism effectively

Parallel structure can be an incisive way for a writer to organize and give form to his thinking. It requires the writer to see the pattern of relationships among his ideas. The lucidity and power in Lincoln's speeches and writing, for example, cannot be separated from his use of parallel structure. In his works, as in the works of many other great writers, parallel structure harmonizes not only the elements within the sentence but also the relationships among the sentences. Notice the climax Lincoln achieves near the end of his "Address at Cooper Institute" by parallelism within and among his sentences:

> If slavery is right, all words, acts, laws and constitutions against it are themselves wrong, and should be silenced and swept away. If it is right, we cannot justly object to its nationality—its universality; if it is wrong, they cannot justly insist upon its extension—its enlargement. All they ask we could readily grant if we thought slavery right; all we ask they could as readily grant, if they thought it wrong. Their thinking it right and our thinking it wrong is the precise fact upon which depends the whole controversy.

S coh

To be effective, however, items which are placed in parallel structure should be parallel in sense. Used carelessly, parallel structure can lead to an illogical series or an awkward sequence of ideas.

> MISLEADING During his last year in law school, he rose to the top of his class, worked on the legal review, and married the day after graduation.
> *He was no longer in law school the day after graduation.*
> *The series is misleading and must be broken up.*

REVISED During his last year in law school, he rose to the top of his class and worked on the legal review. He married the day after graduation.

> INCOHERENT His slumping business, his friends, and even his wife Mary could in no way offer him a chance to find the happiness he had known while in college.
> *The three items are not parallel in meaning. A man might reasonably be expected to find a chance for happiness in those closest to him, his friends and his wife. But he would hardly be expected to find happiness in a "slumping business." The series is illogical and cannot stand.*

REVISED His friends and even his wife Mary could in no way offer him a chance to find the happiness he had known while in college.

> AWKWARD The independent voter is the one who wants to vote for the best man, listens to the candidates, reads up on the issues, thinks about the evidence, and then makes up his mind.
> *Greater separation would make the ideas clearer.*

REVISED The truly independent voter wants to vote for the best man, regardless of party: he listens to the candidates, reads up on the issues, and thinks about the evidence. Then he makes up his mind.

EXERCISES

a. Break each of the following sentences down into several shorter sentences. Then compare your version with the original:

notice how each writer has used parallel structure to give his ideas coherence, and be prepared to discuss why he chose the items and constructions he did.

1. In these short volumes I have tried to set down some aspects of the evolution of life upon this island, since the ages when it lay as nature made it, a green and shaggy forest, half-waterlogged, while here and there, on the more habitable uplands, the most progressive of the animals gathered his kind into camps and societies, to save himself and his offspring and his flocks from wolves and bears and from his fellow-man—down to the very different scene of our own sophisticated times.

—G. M. Trevelyan

2. I please myself with imagining a State at last which can afford to be just to all men, and to treat the individual with respect as a neighbor; which even would not think it inconsistent with its own repose if a few were to live aloof from it, not meddling with it, nor embraced by it, who fulfilled all the duties of neighbors and fellow-men.

—Thoreau

3. One of the basic grievances of this older generation against the younger of today, with its social agitation, its religious heresy, its presumptive individuality, its economic restlessness, is that all this makes it uncomfortable. . . . Through so much of the current writing runs this quiet note of disapprobation. These agnostic professors who unsettle the faith of our youth, these "intellectuals who stick a finger in everybody's pie in the name of social justice," "these sensation-mongers" who unveil great masses of political and social corruption, these remorseless scientists who would reveal so many of our reticences—why can't they let us alone?   —Randolph Bourne

b. Revise the following sentences by giving parallel structure to coordinate ideas.

1. The bandleader told us to wear our uniforms next time and that we should expect a long rehearsal.
2. When I was in grade school, my parents spent a lot of

time on my homework with me, and then when I got to high school letting me do it myself.

3. The columnist argued that sports stars should be well paid because of their relatively short period of greatness and that they must achieve security for later on.

4. Among the primitive uses of fire were protection from wild animals and for preparing food.

5. The congressman argued we need foreign aid to keep friendly relations with other peoples as well as preserving the health of their economies.

c. Examine the following sentences for parallel structure. Identify the cause of faulty parallelism in each and make the needed correction.

1. Applicants for the position must be United States citizens, willing to work abroad, and qualify under security regulations.

2. In the remedial reading clinic he learned how to coordinate his eye movements, how to scan for information, and how frequent reviewing for key ideas helps.

3. He spends every spare moment reading camera magazines, pricing telephoto lenses, and on the mounts which he uses for his slides.

4. The opera's opening performance was spirited, colorful, and with many people attending.

5. By this time the guests were showing signs of boredom, hunger, and some of them were beginning to leave.

6. The critics said that he had no sense of plot nor ear for dialogue, and he ought to give up trying to write plays.

7. During the summer, they planned to hitchhike along Route 40, to stop at interesting places, and take sidetrips whenever they felt like it.

8. Machiavelli is referring to those rulers who are not strong enough to be consistently aggressive but when an opportunity arises, will take advantage of their neighbors.

d. Revise the following sentences so that the correlatives are followed by elements that are parallel in grammatical form.

1. John Brown was either regarded as a patriotic martyr or a crazed fanatic.
2. The beakers were difficult to fill, not only because their necks were narrow but also they were slippery and hard to hold.
3. The bumper crop of rice neither helped the farmer nor were the customers helped.

e. Revise the following sentences, culled from student themes, for parallel structure.
1. Will Rogers was a man of great wit and who often delighted his audiences with stories of his experiences and which he told in a drawl.
2. At the campground we met a Mr. Osborn from somewhere near San Francisco and who had his whole family with him.
3. Colleges are not interested in teaching students to be geniuses; they are concerned with the student's outlook on life in general and how they prepare for their life beyond college.
4. And on these hunting trips, Sam teaches the boy when to kill and when not to, ability, patience, and endurance.
5. If you get ambitious, you might even shoot nine holes of golf from your new four-cylinder golf cart, or with your neighbor go bowling at that new air-conditioned alley, or you might even go and play miniature golf.
6. The hero is masculinity personified: he is lazy and easy-going, rough and ready, has athletic grace and sex appeal.

8 b
faulty reference of pronouns

The antecedent of every pronoun should be immediately clear to the reader.

A pronoun usually refers to a definite person or thing. The relative pronoun *which* may in some cases refer to a clause or

S coh

phrase, but even then the antecedent should be readily identifiable. For coherence, pronouns should be placed as close as possible to their antecedents. To catch faulty reference of pronouns in a first draft, read the paper aloud.

8 b-1
ambiguous reference

Do not use a pronoun in such a way that it might refer to either of two antecedents. If there is any possibility of doubt, revise the sentence to remove the ambiguity.

AMBIGUOUS   Virginia told her sister that she was unforgiving.
Who was unforgiving—Virginia or her sister?
CLEAR   Virginia confessed to her sister, "I am unforgiving."
CLEAR   Virginia said to her sister, "You are unforgiving."

AMBIGUOUS   In *Nostromo* Conrad's style is ironic and his setting is highly symbolic, so that it sometimes confuses the reader.
Does "it" refer loosely to Nostromo, *Conrad's style, his setting, or a combination of these?*
CLEAR   Conrad's ironic style and highly symbolic setting in *Nostromo* sometimes confuse the reader.
CLEAR   In *Nostromo*, Conrad's style is ironic, and his highly symbolic setting sometimes confuses the reader.

8 b-2
remote reference

If a pronoun's antecedent is remote enough to cause possible misreading, either repeat the antecedent or recast the sentence.

Although a pronoun need not be in the same sentence as its antecedent, the antecedent should be immediately clear.

Ref

REMOTE   Two major highways converge at the sign, each lined with huge, ugly billboards rising above the corn stalks and obscuring the gently rolling hills. It is a convenient location for hitching rides.

The pronoun "it" is too removed for its antecedent "sign."

CLEAR   The major highways converge at the sign, each lined with huge . . . . The *sign* is a convenient location for hitching rides.

Antecedent repeated.

CLEAR   Two major highways converge at the sign, a convenient location for hitching rides. Each highway is lined . . . .

The sentences have been recast.

REMOTE   The waitress locked the door, slapped at the flies, and then sat down wearily to rest for a minute before cleaning up the litter. But they gave her no peace.

The antecedent "flies" is too remote.

CLEAR   The waitress locked the door, slapped at the flies . . . . *But* the *flies* gave her no peace.

REMOTE   By the end of Oedipus' life he had gained self-knowledge.

A noun used as an adjective, especially the possessive form of the noun, is usually too inconspicuous to serve as an antecedent.

CLEAR   By the end of his life *Oedipus* had gained self-knowledge.

REMOTE   The Tzotzil Indians are only nominal Catholics, using its symbols and adapting them to the traditional Mayan religion.

Antecedent of "its" has to be inferred from the noun "Catholics."

CLEAR   The Tzotzil Indians are only nominal Catholics, using the symbols and names *of the Church* and adapting them . . . .

REMOTE   The botanist told us the plants' names which were all around us.

CLEAR   The botanist told us the names of the *plants which* were all around us.

S coh

8 b-3
loose use of *this*, *that*, or *which*

In informal usage, the relative pronouns *this*, *that*, and *which* are frequently used to refer to the whole idea of a preceding clause or sentence. In formal usage, these pronouns are usually expected to have a particular word as their antecedent. No hard and fast rules can be given here. Sometimes the broad reference is clear and a change would be awkward.

ACCEPTABLE BROAD REFERENCE   The game ended a little before ten, which gave us plenty of time to catch our train home.
ACCEPTABLE BROAD REFERENCE   At first glance, the desert seems completely barren of animal life, but this is an illusion.

Frequently, however, broad reference makes a sentence sound awkward. It may also be ambiguous if the preceding clause contains a noun which might be mistaken for the antecedent. If you are in doubt, recast the sentence to eliminate the pronoun or give the pronoun a definite antecedent.

LOOSE   The beginning of the book is more interesting than the conclusion, which is very unfortunate.
On the first reading, the pronoun "which" seems to refer to "conclusion," although it is intended to refer to the whole main clause.
CLEAR   Unfortunately, the beginning of the book is more interesting than the conclusion.
The misleading pronoun has been eliminated.

LOOSE   In the eighteenth century, more and more land was converted into pasture, which had been going on to some extent for several centuries.
CLEAR   In the eighteenth century, more and more land was converted into pasture, *a process which* had been going on to some extent for several centuries.
The vague reference has been corrected by the inclusion of the summarizing noun "a process" to give the pronoun "which" an antecedent.

LOOSE   The government tries to stop swindlers from taking advantage of the loopholes in our tax laws. This is not easy.
CLEAR   The government tries to stop swindlers from taking advantage of the loopholes in our tax laws. *Its job* is not an easy one.

8 b-4
indefinite use of *it, they,* and *you*

English contains a number of idiomatic expressions in which the impersonal use of the pronoun *it* is correct: "It is hot," "it rained all day," "it is late." The pronoun *it* is also used correctly in sentences like "It seems best to go home at once," in which *it* anticipates the real subject, *to go home at once.* Avoid, however, the unexplained *it,* the *it* that needs an antecedent and has none.

VAGUE   It says here that Nevada has less crime than California.
The expression "it says that . . . ." is an example of a colloquial usage which is inappropriate to college writing.
CLEAR   The *book* (or the author) says that Nevada has less crime than California.

The indefinite use of *they* is always vague and usually sounds childish.

VAGUE   If intercollegiate sports were banned, they would have to develop an elaborate intramural program.
CLEAR   If intercollegiate sports were banned, *each college* would have to develop an elaborate intramural program.

VAGUE   Thirty years ago there was no such thing as a hydrogen bomb; they didn't even know how to split the atom.
CLEAR   Thirty years ago there was no hydrogen bomb; *scientists* did not even know how to split the atom.

The indefinite use of the pronoun *you* to refer to people in general is widespread, as in "You can't trust anyone these days" or "In Sparta you had to be strong to survive." Formal usage, however, still prefers the impersonal pronoun *one* or a passive verb unless the context clearly implies a definite audience or person addressed.

INFORMAL   You shouldn't take sulfa drugs without a doctor's prescription.

FORMAL   One should not take sulfa drugs without a doctor's prescription.

STANDARD   Sulfa drugs should not be taken without a doctor's prescription.

EXERCISES

a. Revise the following sentences by correcting the ambiguous reference of pronouns.

1. The runner lunged towards the tape, threw out his chest, and snapped it.
2. Sarah and her roommate went to a production of *The Emperor Jones,* after she said that O'Neill was her favorite dramatist.
3. It wouldn't hurt people to read about criminals because they live in a different kind of world and they don't have to follow their example.
4. Both parents were there when the twin brothers graduated together, and we couldn't help noticing how happy they were.
5. She mixed the sugar with eggs and milk, which dissolved quickly.

b. Revise the following sentences in which the reference of pronouns is vague.

1. After driving in the desert temperature, we were cooled that evening by mountain breezes, ice cubes, and long, icy showers. It was a record.
2. Under Roosevelt's leadership, the Democratic party, which had not really been united under one man for some years, came together effectively for a time. His-

torians tend to agree that this was a case of the right man at the right moment.

3. The hives buzzed with activity, and the bee-keeper covered himself with netting before going after the honey and then motioned for us to follow at a distance. They were about fifty feet away.

4. In Joyce's novel, he delights in complex puns and in playing with words.

5. The spider gently shook the strands of his web as he scurried towards the fly and the moth. Although they were barely visible, they were obviously strong.

6. Engineering is the profession that applies scientific knowledge to the building of such things as bridges, harbors, and communication systems. This is my ambition.

7. No two critics I have read share the same views about the degree of Don Quixote's madness. That is the controversy.

8. Ethics must not be understood to be the same thing as honor because this is not the case.

9. When there is no harmony in the home, the child is the first to feel it.

10. Most of the students at the work camp were inexperienced, and many of them had never seen raw poverty before, but on the whole they were up to it.

11. It says in the brochure that in England they drink tea instead of coffee.

12. You can be sure that the college won't liberalize women's hours because they feel responsible to parents, or so they say, anyhow.

c. Revise the following student sentences to eliminate the faulty reference of pronouns.

1. The trunks were too bulky and much too awkward to cart around, so they made smaller and more compact ones.

2. The narrator thought only of his present happiness and showed no regard for his future well being, which is

clearly demonstrated during his last two years of college and his three years of marriage.

3. The article starts out with a quotation from James Madison which says that a government with a standing military force could enslave the people because they may feel like taking powers that do not belong to them.

4. Fielding's *Shamela* successfully uses farcical incident and character development as tools for his satire in the novel.

5. Since the white settlers held the Indians to be of no significant value, they regarded their rights as equally nonexistent. This is exemplified by several incidents in Kroeber's account.

6. On the other hand, in Shakespeare's tragedies the characters fall because of their own faults, which often is true in real life.

8 c
dangling modifiers

Normal sentence order in English is subject, verb, and complement, with modifiers either before or after the word modified.

This sentence order permits considerable flexibility in the placing of subordinate elements, as you will discover through practice. There are, however, two general cautions you ought to observe for the sake of coherence:

(a) Place modifiers as close as possible to the words they modify.

(b) Do not confusingly split related parts of the sentence.

A modifier is a "dangling modifier" when there is no word in the sentence for it to modify. Study the following sentence:

modifier	*word modified*
Swimming *out into the lake,*	*the* **water** *felt cold.*

In the sentence "Swimming out into the lake, the water felt cold," the writer took it for granted that the reader would assume that somebody was swimming. But the only noun in the main clause is *water*, and the participial phrase cannot logically modify *water*—the *water* was not *swimming out into the lake*.

Note the position of the dangling modifier: *almost all dangling modifiers occur at the beginning of a sentence*. They can be corrected in either of two ways:

(1) By supplying the noun or the pronoun which the phrase logically describes:

> *modifier*　　　　　　　　　　*word modified*
> **Swimming** out into the lake,　**I** felt the water grow colder.

(2) Or by changing the dangling construction into a complete clause:

> As I swam out into the lake, the water felt colder.

8 c-1
dangling participial phrases

> 　　　　　　　*modifier*　　　　　　　　　　*word modified*
> **DANGLING**　**Walking** along the trestle,　a **train** suddenly appeared.
> *The sentence is grammatically illogical: do trains walk?*
> 　　　　　　　*modifier*　　　　　　　　　*word modified*
> **IMPROVED**　**Walking** along the trestle,　**I** suddenly saw a train.
> **IMPROVED**　**As I** walked along the trestle, **I** suddenly saw a train.

> **DANGLING**　The mountains were snow-covered and cloud-less, **flying** over the Rockies.
> *Dangling modifiers at the end of a sentence are less frequent than those at the beginning, but they are often confusing and always awkward.*
> **IMPROVED**　When **I** flew over the Rockies, the mountains were snow-covered and cloudless.
> **IMPROVED**　I saw snow-covered, cloudless mountains **while flying** over the Rockies.

DANGLING   Having followed directions carefully, my **cake** was a great success.

IMPROVED   Since **I** had followed directions carefully, my cake was a great success.

8 c-2
dangling gerunds

modifier

DANGLING   After **explaining** my errand to the guard,

word modified

an automatic **gate** swung open to let me in.

The gate can't explain; one must infer the subject of "explaining."

IMPROVED   After **I** had explained my errand to the guard, an automatic gate swung open to let me in.

modifier   *word modified*

DANGLING   Before **climbing** the mountain, our **lunches** were packed in bags.

IMPROVED   Before **climbing** the mountain, **we** packed our lunches in bags.

8 c-3
dangling infinitives

modifier

DANGLING   To **be considered** for college,   the aptitude

word modified

test must be taken.

IMPROVED   To be considered for college, a **student** must take the aptitude test.

DANGLING   In order to become a top entertainer, all types of audiences must be pleased.

"All types of audiences" are not going to become "a top entertainer."

IMPROVED   In order to become a top entertainer, an **actor** must please all types of audiences.
The agent capable of the act is specified.

8 c-4
dangling elliptical clauses

Be sure that the implied subject of an elliptical clause is the same as the subject of the main clause, or that the omitted subject and verb are supplied.

Subject and main verb are sometimes omitted from a dependent clause (*while going* instead of *while I was going,* or *when a child* instead of *when he was a child*). If the subject of such an elliptical clause is not stated in the rest of the sentence, the construction may dangle.

DANGLING   When six years old, my grandmother died.
DANGLING   At the age of six, my grandmother died.
In both examples, the implied subject of the elliptical clause, "I," is omitted. Correct the dangling modifier by expanding it to include *subject and verb.*
IMPROVED   When **I was** six, my grandmother died.
The elliptical clause has been expanded.

DANGLING   While sleeping, the covers were kicked off her bed.
The implied subject of the elliptical clause is "she." Make it the subject of the main clause.
IMPROVED   While sleeping, **she kicked** the covers off her bed.

An alternate method is to make the implied subject of the elliptical clause the subject of a dependent clause:
IMPROVED   While **she** was asleep, **she kicked** the covers off her bed.

DANGLING   Do not apply paint until thoroughly stirred.
IMPROVED   Do not apply the paint until **it** has been thoroughly stirred.

S coh

8 c-5
permissible introductory expressions

Some verbal phrases, like *judging from past experience, considering the situation, granted the results,* and *to sum up,* have become well-established as introductory phrases and need not be attached to any particular noun. Often, these stock phrases express some kind of mental process:

ACCEPTABLE Judging from past experience, he is not to be trusted.

ACCEPTABLE Granted the results, what do they prove?

ACCEPTABLE To sum up, all evidence suggests the decision was a fair one.

Absolute phrases need not refer to any particular noun. An absolute construction consists of a participle with a subject (and sometimes a complement) grammatically unconnected with the rest of the sentence and usually telling when, why, or how something happened. See section 17b for further discussion of this kind of verbal phrase.

CORRECT The floodwater having receded, people began returning to their homes.

CORRECT The air being cold, we took blankets with us.

EXERCISES

a. Revise the following sentences to eliminate the dangling modifiers.

1. When waiting for the dentist, every sound from the office makes me nervous.
2. After correcting my original calculations, the problem was finally solved correctly.
3. To be a good story teller, the voice ought not to be too monotonous.
4. Having seen Beckett's *Waiting For Godot,* my attitude toward modern drama has changed completely.

8

5. The directions were clear, and my trouble could have been prevented, if followed correctly.
6. By working in the cafeteria, the leftover food was mine.
7. After hurrying to answer the phone, the operator told the woman the other party had hung up.
8. In order to see the comet in detail, a small telescope was set up in the backyard.
9. The zoning petition was widely supported, after having canvassed many people in the neighborhood and stirred up concern about the proposed high-rise apartment building.
10. To boil quickly, the burner should be turned all the way on.
11. Being covered with plastic, I did not expect the car seats would be cool, having sat in the hot parking lot for several hours.
12. The summer school director was surprised by the heavy enrollment, thus hiring several extra teachers to handle the overflow of students.
13. At last able to earn my car insurance, my parents allowed me to buy my own car.
14. Although tired and out of practice, the last set of the tennis match was too much of a personal challenge for me to resist.
15. The electric typewriter would not back-space, thus causing a substantial repair bill.

b. Analyze the following student sentences to determine what errors in word order or omitted parts have caused the dangling modifiers. Then, making whatever changes are necessary, revise the sentences so that they are coherent.

1. By beautifully describing several scenes, the story is made much more realistic.
2. By using this irony, the reader can form his own judgment of the characters in the story.
3. Another sentence well illustrates the repression and restraint in every-day conversation when speaking of anything offensive: "Mrs. Carpenter passed away last night in a home, after years of mental problems."

4. Being a conceited fool, I must treat him carefully.
5. In describing her physical beauty it is evident that she has no peers.

8 d
misplaced modifiers

Since word order is crucial to meaning in English, try to place modifiers as close as possible to the words they *are intended* to modify.

Consider, for example, what happens in the following sentences when the adverb *only* is moved about in it:

The notice said **only** [said *merely*] that clients were invited to see the exhibit which was on the third floor.

The notice said that **only** clients [clients *alone*] were invited to see the exhibit which was on the third floor.

The notice said that clients were invited **only** [invited for the *sole* purpose of] to see the exhibit which was on the third floor.

The notice said that clients were invited to see the exhibit which was on the third floor **only** [third floor *alone*].

Some modifying phrases and dependent clauses can be moved around to various positions in the sentence. An introductory phrase, for example, can sometimes be shifted from the beginning to the middle of the sentence:

Regardless of the astronomers' doubts, Jim was convinced that Mars had life on it.

Jim was convinced, ***regardless of the astronomers' doubts,*** that Mars had life on it.

Similarly, introductory clauses can sometimes be moved from the beginning to the middle or end of the sentence.

> *Whatever the public may think,* I am sure that Picasso will be remembered as one of the greatest artists of our times.

> I am sure, *whatever the public may think,* that Picasso will be remembered as one of the greatest artists of our times.

> I am sure that Picasso will be remembered as one of the greatest artists of our times, *whatever the public may think.*

This freedom, however, has its dangers. Movable modifiers may be placed so as to produce misreadings or real ambiguities. *Such difficulties are particularly likely to arise when two movable modifiers describe the same word.* Unlike the dangling modifier, which cannot logically modify any word in the sentence, the misplaced modifier seems to modify the wrong word or phrase in the sentence:

> **AMBIGUOUS** The picture on the wall *which* he painted sold for a high price.
> *Which did he paint—the picture or the wall?*
> **AMBIGUOUS** This morning at the market I saw my old friend Hubert Waring getting a cooked turkey *in his shorts.*

8 d-1
misplaced adverbial modifiers

To avoid ambiguity, position adverbial modifiers carefully.

> **AMBIGUOUS** I have followed the advice *faithfully* given by the manual.
> **REVISED** I have *faithfully* followed the advice given by the manual.
> *The adverb has been placed nearer the word it is intended to modify.*

AMBIGUOUS   The woman scolded the boy for playing with matches *severely*.

REVISED   The woman *severely* scolded the boy for playing with matches.

See section 8 d-3 for a discussion of ambiguity caused by *squinting modifiers*.

8 d-2
misplaced phrases and clauses

MISPLACED PHRASE   He lost the chance to make large profits *through the work of imitators and plagiarists*.

CLEAR   *Through the work of imitators and plagiarists,* he lost a chance to make large profits.

MISPLACED PHRASE   Hamlet stabs Laertes with a poisoned sword *in the last act*.

CLEAR   *In the last act* Hamlet stabs Laertes with a poisoned sword.

MISPLACED CLAUSE   I gave her a book for her birthday *which I had recently read about*.

CLEAR   For her birthday I gave her a book *which I had recently read about*.

Notice that even greater clarity has been achieved by also moving the phrase "for her birthday."

MISPLACED CLAUSE   He searched around and found an old bus schedule in the drawer *that was out of date*.

CLEAR   He searched around and found in the drawer an old bus schedule *that was out of date*.

8 d-3
squinting modifiers

Avoid placing a modifier in such a position that it may refer to either a preceding word or a following word.

SQUINTING   The child who lies *in nine cases out of ten* is frightened.

CLEAR   *In nine cases out of ten,* the child who lies is frightened.

SQUINTING   That horse with the knee injured *recently* returned to competition.

CLEAR   That horse with the *recently* injured knee returned to competition.

CLEAR   That horse with the injured knee returned to competition *recently*.

Notice that while the meaning of each of these examples is clear, it is different in each example.

8 d-4
split constructions and
infinitives

Avoid the needless splitting of grammatical constructions.

Separating the parts of a verb phrase, subject and verb, or an infinitive by an inserted modifier can give the reader an awkward jolt.

AWKWARD   The operator told him that he *should, if he expected to get his call through, place* it soon.

The verb phrase is needlessly broken up by the modifier.

IMPROVED   The operator told him that he *should place* his call soon, *if he expected to get it through.*

AWKWARD   I, more than the rest of my family, *have been losing* sleep since we got a color television set.

Subject and verb are needlessly separated by the modifier.

IMPROVED   More than the rest of my family, *I have been losing* sleep since we got a color television set.

Split infinitives, that is, infinitives with a modifier between the *to* and the verb form (*to personally supervise*) may be awkward, especially if the modifier is long.

S coh

AWKWARD   I should like *to, if I ever get the chance, take* a trip to Mexico.

IMPROVED   I should like *to take* a trip to Mexico *if I ever get the chance.*

Frequently, however, an adverb fits most naturally between the two parts of an infinitive:

ACCEPTABLE   Some young couples regard children as a nuisance, but as they grow older they begin *to actually look* forward to having a family.

If the modifier is moved, the emphasis is slightly changed: ". . . but as they grow older they actually begin *to look forward.* . . ."

ACCEPTABLE   We expect in the coming year *to more than double* our assets.

If the modifier is moved, awkwardness results: "We expect in the coming year more than to double our assets."

EXERCISES

a. Revise the following sentences to correct the misplaced adverbs, phrases, and clauses.

1. She wore a ribbon in her hair which was a light pink.
2. Mrs. Spenser only wanted us to read good books.
3. The film about the building of the pyramids that I saw downtown was interesting.
4. The dean told me I could return to school in his phone call.
5. He observed the training diligently ordered by the coach.
6. The store offered to pension off all employees thinking of retirement for no apparent reason.
7. We camped in a small shelter near the edge of the cliff which had been unused for months.
8. The library's policy is that students are not to return books to the shelves that are lying on tables.
9. Often she would spend hours on the edge of the beach

watching her son dig a hole or build a sand castle with half-closed eyes.
10. She forgot all about the roast in the hot oven which she had bought just that morning for supper.

b. Revise the following sentences by correcting the squinting modifiers.
1. He wrote his book on gambling in Iowa.
2. I promised during the evening to call her.
3. A school dropout, like his brother, he became a gang member.

c. Revise the following sentences by correcting the split constructions and split modifiers.
1. At the end of the period we were told to promptly hand in our bluebooks.
2. The pharmacist told her she should, since she needed the medicine in such a hurry, have the doctor phone the prescription immediately.
3. The term *reactionary* can be applied to political, social, economic (or a combination of the three) beliefs.
4. After nicking a submerged rock, the canoe began to slowly but steadily leak and to gradually settle deeper in the water.
5. Bills which Congress was only a few years ago unwilling to bring out of committee have recently, by overwhelming majorities, been passed.

d. Analyze the following student sentences to determine what errors in word order or omitted parts have caused the dangling and misplaced modifiers. Then, making whatever changes are necessary, revise the sentences so that they are coherent.
1. The author had his character walking over five thousand miles in a year's time, which is almost impossible, taking in ideas of weather conditions and environment.
2. Wild and primitive, with hidden snags and rapids on one side, jungle and savage natives on the other, danger is ever present.

3. During the past four months he has been squeezed out of the race for governor entirely by the Lieutenant Governor and is now a candidate for the United States Senate.

4. I believe that a story like this could have been true, for the greater majority of events.

5. Being at work, James said that because the date had been set for 5:30 he would have to change his clothes there.

6. Valuable experience can be gained at school which will always be a source of satisfaction to the individual.

7. Having broken my own leg, the author's description is very vivid and brings back unpleasant memories.

8. Mr. Waugh here presents everyone as some kind of dunderhead in the story with the exception of Paul Pennyfeather who remains in the background absorbing the whole spectacle.

9. He was hit by a rotten egg walking back to his apartment one night.

8 e
confusing shifts

Structural consistency makes sentences easier to read. If the first clause of a sentence is in the active voice, do not shift to the passive voice in the second clause unless there is good reason for the change. Similarly, avoid shifts in tense, mode, or person within a sentence unless they reflect an intentional shift in focus.

8 e-1
confusing shifts of voice
or subject

Shifting from the active to the passive voice almost always involves a change in subject; thus a shift in voice may make a sentence doubly confusing.

Shift

SHIFT IN SUBJECT AND VOICE   After *I* finally *discovered* an unsoldered wire, the *dismantling* of the motor *was begun*.
The subject shifts from "I" to "dismantling." The voice shifts from the active "discovered" to the passive "was begun."

CONSISTENT   After I finally discovered an unsoldered wire, *I dismantled* the motor.

The sentence would be logically consistent if both verbs were in the passive voice: "After an unsoldered wire was found, the motor was dismantled." But the passive voice is unnecessary here (see section 9b-1).

SHIFT IN VOICE   *He left* the examination after his *answer had been proofread*.

Who proofread the answer?

CONSISTENT   He left the examination after *he had proofread* his answer.

SHIFT IN SUBJECT   The *museum* held a special exhibit of giant fern fossils, and school *children* received free admission.

The subject shifts from "museum" to "school children."

CONSISTENT   The *museum held* a special exhibit of giant fern fossils *and admitted* school children free.

One subject only.

8 e-2
confusing shifts of person or number

One common shift in student writing is from the third person (*he, she, they, one*) to the second person (*you*); another is from a singular number (*a person, one, he*) to a plural (*they*). These errors usually occur when the writer is not thinking of a particular individual but of anybody or everybody and is stating some vague general truth applicable to all.

CONFUSING SHIFT IN PERSON   When *you* try hard enough, *one* can do almost anything.
Confusing shift from the second to the third person.
CONSISTENT   When *you* try hard enough, *you* can do almost anything.
CONSISTENT   When *one* tries hard enough, *one* [or he] can do almost anything.

CONFUSING SHIFT IN PERSON   *I* could find only one fault with my new gun. When *you* fired it, gas would leak through the action.
Confusing shift from first to second person.
CONSISTENT   *I* could find only one fault with my new gun. When *I* fired it, gas leaked through the action.

CONFUSING SHIFT IN NUMBER   When *a person* gets an early start, *they* can work more efficiently.
Confusing shift from singular to plural number.
CONSISTENT   When *a person* gets an early start, *he* can work more efficiently.

For discussion of a similar problem, see also section 23b on pronoun-antecedent agreement.

8 e-3
confusing shifts of mood or tense

If you begin a sentence with an order or command (*imperative* mood), do not shift without reason to a statement (*indicative* mood).

CONFUSING SHIFT IN MOOD   First stir in the flour; then you should add the butter and salt.
The first clause is an order, the imperative mood; the second clause is a statement giving advice, the indicative mood.
CONSISTENT   First stir in the flour; then add the butter and salt.
Both clauses in the imperative mood.

Shift

ACCEPTABLE   After you have stirred in the flour, add the butter and salt.
First clause modifies the imperative verb "add."

> If you begin a sentence in the past tense, do not switch to the present unless you have good reason to do so.

CONFUSING SHIFT IN TENSE   I *stood* on the starting block and *looked* tensely at the water below; for the first time in my life I *am* about to swim the 50-yard freestyle in competition.
Confusing shift from past to present.

CONSISTENT   I *stood* on the starting block and *looked* . . . I *was* about to swim . . . .

CONSISTENT   I *stand* on the starting block and *look* . . . I *am* about to swim . . . .

CONFUSING SHIFT IN TENSE   At the beginning of the *Divine Comedy*, Dante *finds* that he has strayed from the True Way into the Dark Wood of Error. As soon as he *realized* this, Dante *lifted* his eyes in hope to the rising sun.
When you use the historical present, the tense normally used for summarizing plots of narratives, take special care not to lapse into the past tense.

CONSISTENT   At the beginning of the *Divine Comedy*, Dante *finds* that he has strayed from the True Way into the Dark Wood of Error. As soon as he *has realized* this, Dante *lifts* his eyes in hope to the rising sun.

See also section 26b for a discussion of tense sequence.

EXERCISES

a. Correct shifts in voice, person, number, mood, or tense in the following sentences.
1. After I finished planting my garden, the seeds were watered daily.
2. The individual builds up an unconscious dislike, which is shown by his attitude in class.

3. The matinee was enjoyed by all the children because they saw two monster films.

4. A person can always find something to criticize if they look hard enough.

5. In the school I attended, you had just five minutes between classes, and that was not enough time for most of us.

6. Suppose a man was going about five miles over the speed limit and got a ticket: from that time on you would probably dislike policemen.

7. Don't ride the clutch; you should keep your left foot off the pedal.

8. Because he was so naive, Candide listens to almost anybody he meets.

9. Parson Adams went to London to try to sell his sermons and finds out that people are neither kind nor generous; he does not worry about taking much money with him for the trip because he thought that people would be hospitable to him.

b. Analyze the following student sentences to determine the cause and the type of confusing shift you find. Then, making whatever changes are necessary, revise the sentences so that they are coherent.

1. Thus, in *The Way of All Flesh*, Butler is telling his readers to look ahead; he tells them not to be caught without knowing what is going on around you.

2. Nearly everything said about the academy implies that Mistress Pinkerton was greedy: Pinkerton favors the rich girls, mistreats her instructress Becky Sharp, and was miserly.

3. Of course, knowing how to use one's leisure is also important, but I do not think that it is up to the college to more or less arrange your social life, as many colleges do.

4. Fifty years ago, your house was the center of your everyday life; today, we Americans practically live in our cars.

5. The expression "ouch" is likely to be used anytime by

anyone who unexpectedly hurts themselves in some way.
6. Tests are only given to find out what the student has remembered about the material being tested on, not what the person beside you learned.

8 f
mixed constructions

Do not begin a sentence with one construction and conclude it with another.

English is full of alternate constructions, and it is fairly easy to confuse them in a first draft and to produce a monster with the head of one sentence and the tail of another. If you mix constructions, the results will be incoherent, and the reader may get the unfortunate impression that your thinking is as chaotic as your writing.

MIXED   I was really getting beaten up; every hold I tried, my opponent would counter it.
In the second clause, the writer has two correct alternatives, neither of which he has chosen. The initial phrase has no grammatical connection to the rest of the sentence.
CORRECT   I was really getting beaten up; every hold **that I tried** was countered by my opponent.
The subject of the second clause is now "hold"; it is modified by the adjective clause "that I tried."
CORRECT   I was really getting beaten up; **every time I tried a new hold** my opponent would counter it.
The second clause now contains an adverbial phrase, "everytime [i.e., whenever] I tried a new hold," which modifies the main verb "would counter."

Not all mixed constructions are so easily diagnosed. *You may have to read longer, more complex sentences aloud two or three times to identify the error.* You can, however, avoid many mixed constructions by remembering some of their most common causes.

S coh

8 f-1
mixed comparisons

Many mixed constructions involve comparisons. The writer has jumbled together nonparallel sentence structures that represent two different ways of making a comparison. One structure or the other must be chosen as the form for making a consistent and parallel comparison (see also Incomplete Constructions, section 8g-3).

> MIXED   The amateur mechanic will find plastic *much easier to work with than with metal.*
> CORRECT   The amateur mechanic will find plastic much easier to work with *than metal.*
> CORRECT   The amateur mechanic will find *it* much easier to work *with* plastic *than with* metal.

8 f-2
illogical subjects and
complements

Using a modifying phrase or clause as subject or complement of a verb often produces a badly mixed construction. For example:

> MIXED   By defining the term "socialism" accurately will save us argument.
> *The prepositional phrase "By defining the term 'socialism'" cannot be the subject for the verb "will save."*
> CORRECT   By defining the term "socialism" accurately, *we* will save argument.
> CORRECT   An accurate definition of the term "socialism" will save us argument.

> MIXED   Because he ran out of gas made him late.
> *A subordinate adverb clause cannot be used here as the subject.*

Mix

CORRECT Running out of gas made him late.
Simple sentence
CORRECT He was late because he ran out of gas.
Complex sentence

A frequent cause of mixed constructions is the illogical use of "when" or "where" as part of the complement of "is"—the "is when" or "is where" habit:

> **MIXED** One thing which keeps me from enlisting *is when* I think of kitchen police.
> *What* thing *will keep the writer from enlisting? Not "when I think of kitchen police": the clause is a modifier, not a thing. What is needed to complete the sentence is some kind of substantive.*

CORRECT One thing which keeps me from enlisting is the *thought* of kitchen police.

> **MIXED** An accident *is where* the causes of an event are unknown.
> *An adverb clause is misused as a noun; the verb "is" needs a substantive here.*

CORRECT An accident is *an event* whose causes are unknown.

> **MIXED** The good performance of American teams at the Olympics *is because* the American athletes have been well-trained.

CORRECT American teams perform well at the Olympics because the American athletes have been well-trained.

ACCEPTABLE INFORMAL ENGLISH The *reason* American teams perform so well at the Olympics *is because* the American athletes have been well-trained.

Usage has established "the *reason* . . . *is because* . . ." construction as acceptable in all but formal English, although some writers and teachers prefer "the *reason* . . . *is that* . . ." even in informal English. They prefer the noun "reason" to be complemented by a noun clause. In most cases, however, either construction is wordy. Economize by dropping "the reason" and using simply "because": American teams have performed very well at the Olympics because they have been well-trained. See section 9c for further discussion of wordiness.

8 g
incomplete constructions

Sentence constructions are incomplete if words and expressions necessary for grammatical completeness and clarity are omitted.

Sometimes, the omissions are caused by carelessness; the remedy is more careful proofreading.

INCOMPLETE Worse still, he had a seven day journey∧the fort.
"To" is needed to complete the meaning of the predicate.
INCOMPLETE The very sound of the poem gives the feeling∧fleeting light and life.
"Of" completes and clarifies the predicate's meaning.

In other cases, the omissions result from the writer's failure to think through the implications of his phrasing. Some common symptoms of this failure are the incomplete compound verb and the ambiguous comparison.

8 g-1
incomplete verb forms

Do not omit auxiliary verbs needed to complete a grammatical construction.

When the two parts of a compound construction are in *different tenses,* the auxiliary verbs should usually be fully written in so that their meanings will be clear and logical.

INCOMPLETE   Fishing *has* and always *will be* a profitable industry in Alaska.
"Be" is the proper auxiliary for "will" but not for "has."
One cannot say "Fishing has be and always will be . . . ."
COMPLETE   Fishing *has been* and always *will be* a profitable industry in Alaska.

When there is *no change* in tense, part of a compound verb can be omitted:

ACCEPTABLE   Tickets will be sent to all students who have signed up for the trip and [who have] paid the fee.

In sentences whose predicate is the linking verb *to be,* do not omit necessary parts:

INCOMPLETE   He *was lecturing* and the students *taking* notes.
The singular "was" cannot be used with the plural "students."
COMPLETE   He was lecturing and the students *were taking* notes.

8 g-2
idiomatic prepositions

Be sure to include in compound constructions all necessary idiomatic prepositions.

English idiom requires that certain prepositions be used with certain adjectives and verbs: we say, for example, "interested *in,*" "aware *of,*" "devoted *to.*" And we expect others "to object *to,*" or "to accede *to,*" not to "object or accede *with,*" our plans (see section 12e for a list of major idiomatic phrases).

INCOMPLETE   He was *oblivious* and *undisturbed by* the noise around him.
COMPLETE   He was *oblivious to* and *undisturbed by* the noise around him.

S coh

INCOMPLETE   No one could have been more *interested* or *devoted to* his students than Mr. Beattes.

COMPLETE   No one could have been more *interested in* or *devoted to* his students than Mr. Beattes.

8 g-3
incomplete and
inexact comparisons

Many problems in sentence coherence arise from the use of incomplete and inexact comparisons.

1 idiomatic comparisons

In comparisons do not omit words necessary to make a complete idiomatic statement.

INCOMPLETE   He is as tall, if not taller than his brother.
As it stands, the sentence says that he is "as tall . . . than his brother."
COMPLETE   He is *as* tall *as* his brother, if not taller.

INCOMPLETE   Leonardo had one of the greatest, if not the greatest, minds of all times.
Two idioms: "one of the greatest minds" and "the greatest mind."
COMPLETE   Leonardo had one of the greatest *minds,* if not the greatest *mind,* of all time.

2 incomplete comparisons

Comparisons should be complete, logical, and unambiguous.

INCOMPLETE   Her salary was lower than a typist.
Is a typist low?
COMPLETE   Her salary was lower than *that of* a typist.
COMPLETE   Her salary was lower than a *typist's.*

INCOMPLETE   The food here costs no more than any other restaurant.

Can one buy the food or the restaurant at the same low price?

COMPLETE   The food here costs no more than *it does* at any other restaurant.

Watch out especially for the illogical use of *than, any,* and *any of.*

ILLOGICAL   The Empire State Building is taller than any building in New York.

"Any building in New York" includes the Empire State Building.

REVISED   The Empire State Building is taller than **any other** building in New York.

3 inexact comparisons

A comparison is inexact if the reader cannot tell what is being compared with what, or if the standard of comparison is not indicated.

INEXACT   Claremont is farther from Los Angeles than Pomona.

CLEAR   Claremont is farther from Los Angeles than Pomona *is.*

CLEAR   Claremont is farther from Los Angeles than *it is* from Pomona.

In the two revisions, both terms of the comparison are completely filled in.

INEXACT   The city's educational television station now produces more varied shows.

Than what? Than it used to? Than other stations in other cities? Than commercial television? The standard of comparison *has not been indicated.*

CLEAR   The city's educational television station now produces more varied shows *than it used to.*

S coh

INEXACT   Philsoc Gas gives more and better mileage for the dollar.

Than what? Mule teams? Many commercials and advertisements only pretend to give information: by conveniently omitting any standard of comparison, they do not commit themselves to any real claims.

If clearly indicated by the context, the standard of comparison need not be specified:

CLEAR   Boulder Dam is big, but the Grand Coulee Dam is bigger.

Note that the words *so, such,* and *too* when used as comparatives are completed by a phrase or clause indicating the standard of comparison.

CLEAR   I'm **so** tired **that I could drop.** I had **such** a small breakfast **that I was starving by noon,** and when we stopped for lunch, I was **too** tired **to eat.**

EXERCISES

a. In the following student sentences, analyze the constructions that have been mixed. For each mixed construction, write out the correct alternative or alternatives the student overlooked. Then choose the alternative you think is the most effective and be prepared to explain your choice.

1. Since cheating in schools instigates distrust on a large scale that I think all people caught cheating should be punished as a lesson to all.
2. Because Joyce's stories are written with the greatest skill makes each and every character come alive before the reader's eyes.
3. In the container is where the experiment takes place.
4. For college students, I feel that teaching assistants who read papers for the professors are really a disadvantage to the student.

5. Milton also uses this theme of sexuality to show the weakness in man for being susceptible to such temptation.

6. It would be hard for me to say what the outlook on life a person with this disease would have.

7. My good scores on time tests were because I started off relaxed and confident, sitting in the proper position and my typewriter all set.

8. In choosing the class play, we found small reading groups much easier to work with than with the whole committee together.

9. In my high school, which is rated as one of the best in the state, it is my opinion that it was much too easy.

10. Sophistication, then, is when the simplicity of youth is lost.

11. Loneliness is an experience to which most people have come to know from time to time.

12. As the volume of sound increases in the earphones, the nearer the submarine is approaching.

13. In my study of campus slang, to get an A on a test or in a course is where you "ace" it.

14. It was only when I heard the whistle give three sharp toots, I remembered the lifeguard's warning.

15. Just because a few boxers have been killed is no reason to ban the whole sport.

16. Of course, if I decide to become an engineering major doesn't mean that it is too late to change later on.

17. I found the movie's version of the story easier to follow than in the book.

b. Revise the following sentences by filling out the incomplete or inexact constructions.

1. The Japanese are at least as inventive as the United States or Germany.

2. Disneyland is as large, if not larger than any other amusement park in the country.

3. At first Macbeth tries to hide from himself the fact that he is capable and ready to commit murder.

4. The Hondas and Yamahas weigh less and are cheaper.

5. I was planning and still do to attend our next class re-union.

6. My father complained that his income tax was higher than last year.

7. The distributor was cleaned and the points adjusted.

8. Some Europeans have more contempt for American women than American men.

9. Vale did some of her best work and learned a great deal from her high school history teacher.

10. Because of their climate and soil, Florida and California raise more citrus than all the states put together.

11. According to our map of Arkansas, Fort Smith is farther from Little Rock than Pine Bluff.

12. The house we built ourselves cost far less than a contractor.

13. As your Class Secretary, I have and will continue to send you all the news that I receive about the class of '66.

14. Trying to analyze my good points and weaknesses made me a happier and secure person.

REVIEW EXERCISES

The following student sentences contain faults discussed in the preceding chapter on coherence—faulty parallelism, faulty reference of pronouns, dangling and misplaced modifiers, confusing shifts, and mixed and incomplete constructions. Identify the cause or causes of faulty coherence in each sentence, and then revise the sentence so that it is clear.

1. Entering the door, after walking up several steps made of concrete, there is a policeman, sitting behind his desk, who will gladly give you any needed information.

2. The politician has dinners given, circulars printed, and attends rallies.

3. If someone knows that a certain person is a "cheat," they wouldn't want to be around them and they wouldn't trust him.

4. By the way he tells the story is indication enough of how Updike feels.

5. I found Charlie Macklin to be the closest thing to perfection, but at the same time still being human, than any other I have either read about or known in real life.

6. Pulled through a broken window with pieces of glass scattered about, a fireman rescued a lady in her home early this morning, which was blazing.

7. One advertisement shows a washing machine "growing" to be ten feet tall, and in a different commercial for soap portrays a giant in your washer who labors to clean your clothes.

8. Some occupations in which following directions might not be important are where a man is an artist, a potter, a novelist, or some other creative artist.

9. Although surprising to students, this writer feels that in most questionable cases, the uncertainty of science should be presented for what it is.

10. It is quite insulting to offer repeatedly friendly greetings but to receive either no reply at all or only a cold stare.

11. While personally finding nothing to recommend Marx's system, it is fitting to examine him in order to see how and why so many people have believed in it.

12. He certainly didn't look like a man of my father's age and he certainly didn't have a particle of dignity that I so commonly associated with my father of having.

13. Paul has different ideas about schooling than the school system.

14. Just because our campus radio station plays so much popular music is no reason for the college to cut its funds.

15. The Lilliputians are much more like the human race than the giants.

16. I was then counseled which is a very confusing process which I won't go into.

17. After being locked in the cabin about two hours, our first roll call of the evening took place.

9

sentence emphasis:
weak and wordy sentences

Like a guest at a party, a writer may be correct, well-mannered, and dull. He stiffly enunciates or self-consciously mumbles his words, seldom raising or lowering his voice—and never is guilty of being interesting. His sentences lack force and impact: either they dwindle away into a feeble series of details and subordinate constructions or they are wordy and repetitious. To revise such sentences, the writer must remind his reader which ideas are the most important and stress them accordingly.

9 a
weak sentences

If your sentences are weak because they lack variety and emphasis, you need to become more sensitive to the movement of your prose. Familiarity with a greater range of sentence patterns will help you acquire this sensitivity. You can also improve your sentences by eliminating trailing constructions, anticlimaxes, and ineffective repetition.

9 a-1
sentence patterns

Since the basic pattern of the typical English sentence is subject-verb-object (or complement), most of your sentences will follow it. But since modifying words, phrases, and clauses can be moved about within this pattern, you should experiment to see what changes produce what effects. A *loose sentence,* for example, starts with the main idea and finishes with subordinate ones. It reports information or conveys feelings directly and naturally.

LOOSE   I will pick up the car later, probably when I get off work.
The main idea, "I will pick up the car," comes first.
LOOSE   I can feel the loneliness that haunted him as I read between the lines of his letters.
The main idea is "I can feel the loneliness that haunted him"; the sentence straightforwardly begins with it and concludes with the subordinate clause.

A *periodic sentence,* on the other hand, suspends its main idea until the end or near the end to achieve a summary or climax.

PERIODIC   As I read between the lines of his letters, I can feel the loneliness that haunted him.
PERIODIC   If any sign had been needed of the central place which the automobile had come to occupy in the mind and heart of the average American, it was furnished when the Model A Ford was brought out in December, 1927. Since the previous spring, when Henry Ford had shut down his gigantic plant, scrapped his Model T and the thousands of machines which brought it into being, and announced that he was going to put a new car on the market, the country had been in a state of suspense.   —Frederick Lewis Allen
PERIODIC   Frost's seriousness and honesty; the bare sorrow with which, sometimes, things are accepted as they are, neither exaggerated nor explained away; the many, many poems in which

there are real people with their real speech and real thoughts and real emotions—all this, in conjunction with so much subtlety and exactness, such classical understatement and restraint, makes the reader feel that he is not in a book but in a world, and a world that has in common with his own some of the things that are most important in both. —Randall Jarrell

As these examples suggest, the long periodic sentence, if employed discriminatingly, is a highly effective way of varying the rhythm of your prose. But it should be used only when the subject matter itself implies suspense or deserves climactic summary. Too many long periodic sentences can make your writing sound stilted and "literary." Many shorter sentences can be written loosely or periodically with equal ease; the form chosen depends upon the intended emphasis.

LOOSE The rally ended abruptly when Koufax struck out the pinch hitter.
PERIODIC When Koufax struck out the pinch hitter, the rally ended abruptly.
LOOSE Edison finally perfected the light bulb, after dozens of frustrating attempts.
PERIODIC After dozens of frustrating attempts, Edison finally perfected the light bulb.

Actually, some of the best sentences you will write will be *balanced*; that is, they will be sentences—often compound or compound-complex ones—whose parallel elements are equal in length and movement.

BALANCED While Shakespeare introduces many strong secondary characters who add color and depth, Ibsen concentrates on the development of his primary characters alone. From Aunt Julia in *Hedda Gabler*, we learn of Tesman's marriage, his university ambitions, and his studying even during his honeymoon; but at no time do we know enough about Aunt Julia herself to decide whether she is a meddling old woman or a sympathetic character. So it is with the rest of the secondary characters: if we take them away, we have no play; but if we analyze their function, we find they are merely needed props.

The student who wrote this used the balanced contrast in the first sentence as the basis of his paper. Comparisons and contrasts are often most naturally and effectively made in balanced sentences.

Sometimes, you can use balanced sentences of parallel structures to make a point vigorously:

BALANCED   I hate to see anything that occupies more space than it is worth. I hate to see a load of bandboxes go along the street, and I hate to see a parcel of big words without anything in them.
—William Hazlitt

Periodic and balanced sentences are not ends in themselves; rather they are means to heighten and stress important ideas. Much of the time, the loose sentence is the most natural, straightforward way to express an idea. But by experimenting with periodic and balanced sentences, you will discover a wider range of sentence patterns to work with and you will become more sensitive to the rhythm and movement of your prose.

9 a-2
trailing constructions

Important words should be placed at the beginning or end of the sentence.

These are the emphatic positions, especially at the end. By sticking minor elements into the middle of the sentence, the least emphatic position, you save key spots for key ideas, and you avoid the sentence which trails away into a tangle of subordinate elements.

TRAILING   Ursula leaped to save the collie from the oncoming car, although she was afraid of dogs.
Read aloud and note that the weaker part of the sentence

is placed in the most emphatic position—the end. Reading papers aloud is an excellent way to catch such sentences.

EMPHATIC   Although she was afraid of dogs, Ursula leaped to save the collie from the oncoming car.

TRAILING   It is in this scene that Lear finally realizes that he has been deceived by the promises that his older daughters have made to him earlier in the play when he thought they were being sincere and didn't see them for what they really were.

Read aloud and note the fatigue the sentence causes. Wordiness often produces trailing sentences. See sections 9b-2 and 9c-1 for treatment of two more kinds of wordiness problems.

EMPHATIC   In this scene Lear finally realizes that he has been deceived by the promises of his older daughters.

Pruned of such redundant phrases as "earlier in the play" and such clauses as "when he thought they were being sincere," the sentence has emphasis.

TRAILING   I quit regretfully when the strain in the office became too great because of inadequate staff and insufficient money for extra help.

Here, the subordinate elements are essential but misplaced.

EMPHATIC   When the strain of working with inadequate staff and money became too great, I regretfully quit the office.

9 a-3
anticlimax

Build a climax by arranging the items in an increasing order of importance and by placing the most important idea last.

A series of related items should follow an order of increasing importance. If they do not, emphasis disappears and an unintentional anticlimax may occur.

EMPHASIS BLURRED Einstein was a deeply philosophical man, a very great mathematician, and an amateur violinist.
EMPHATIC Einstein was an amateur violinist, a deeply philosophical man, and a very great mathematician.

ANTICLIMAX When the gorilla lunged at the bars, I fell back against my brother, bashed my head against his nose, and dropped my peanuts.
CLIMACTIC When the gorilla lunged at the bars, I dropped my peanuts, fell back against my brother, and bashed my head against his nose.

Used sparingly, the intentional anticlimax can nicely satirize pretense or point out comic incongruity, as when Dryden mocks one of his enemies:

> The midwife laid her hand on his thick skull,
> With this prophetic blessing: *Be thou dull;*
> Drink, swear, and roar, forbear no lewd delight
> Fit for thy bulk, do anything but write.

The laziest and least emphatic way to complete a series is to use such catchall expressions as *and others, etc., and the like.* These tags are occasionally used—and useful—to show that a *random* list is not exhaustive, or to point out that the reader and writer have the same topic in mind and need not multiply illustrations. But it is usually better to avoid these end tags since they suggest that the writer has run out of examples or is too sluggish to specify them.

9 a-4
ineffective repetition

Use repetition of words and ideas only to gain an intended emphasis and clarity.

Deliberate use of repetition to build up a sustained prose rhythm and to emphasize a key feeling or idea can be quite

S emp

powerful. Ineffective repetition, however, flattens out a sentence's rhythm and squashes its key ideas. The repetition is ineffective because it is careless: the sentence becomes wordy and dull, and the reader cannot find an intended climax or focus.

FOCUS LOST If *one* examines the *story* carefully, *one* will find that the hidden symbolism in the *story* makes the *story* stand for something more than *one* first found in the *story*. *The repetition of "story" and "one" obscures a simple idea—that if one reads the story carefully, he discovers a symbolism which deepens it.*

INEFFECTIVE After having opened your *presents, you* find that *you* have received just about every conceivable *present* in the world, except the *present you* have been hinting about during the preceding months.

Effective repetition usually takes the form of parallel structure: the writer intentionally gives the same word or phrase the emphatic positions in the sentence or sentences (see also sections 5b-3 and 5b-4 for discussions of sentence coherence based on repetition and parallelism).

EMPHATIC *It is hot* in Rickston, and *it is hot* on a Saturday morning when into the town come the farmers with their wives and their kids with faces rough and red from the sun. This is *a hot* town on *a hot* highway, and it is even *hotter* when you have to go twenty miles over dust that rises a hundred feet behind your car to get to the highway in the first place.   —student theme

EMPHATIC Every great literature has always been allegorical—allegorical of some view of the whole universe. The *Iliad* is only great *because all life* is a battle, the *Odyssey because all life* is a journey, and the Book of Job *because all life* is a riddle.
                                                                —G. K. Chesterton

As these examples suggest, ineffective repetition results in wordy, dull sentences. Repetition effectively and discriminatingly used leads to a strengthened, clearer sentence structure. It is a first step toward really powerful writing.

SUMMARY

1. Experiment with periodic and balanced sentences to discover a wider range of sentence patterns to work with and to become more sensitive to the rhythm and movement of your prose.

    a. If employed selectively, the long periodic sentence is a highly effective way to vary your prose rhythms and gain suspense; but it should only be used when the subject matter itself implies suspense or deserves climactic summary.

    b. Balanced sentences are often particularly effective for making comparisons and contrasts.

2. Important words should be placed at the beginning or end of the sentence.

3. Build a climax by arranging items in an increasing order of importance and placing the most important idea last.

4. Use repetition of words and ideas only to gain an intended emphasis and clarity.

EXERCISES

a. Analyze the techniques employed to gain emphasis in the following student sentences: the use of periodic and balanced sentences, the placement of words in key positions, the use of climactic order, and effective repetition. If you think some of the sentences are weak, revise them and be prepared to explain your changes. If you think some of the sentences are too labored and self-consciously emphatic, tame them, and be prepared to explain your changes.

    1. Ada's large, dark eyes, usually so clear and full of laughter, were lack-lustre and were sunk in deep circles of worn brown skin, and her naturally dark skin looked

sallow and overlaid with a fine mask of lines. Against her mother's countenance, Ada's was a pale, young, and confused face.

2. We are all foreigners. Although we live in the United States and claim the title "American," foreign blood runs through our veins. The first generation of our family came to America for opportunities and independence. But America did not greet them with the fruitfulness they had expected. Instead, they found that the hard road to success was one they had to travel by themselves, despite the barrier of their foreign language and foreign ways. Naturally, they wanted their children to become more successful than they themselves had been. I am one such child.

3. The initial setting of *All My Sons* presents Joe Keller as a "good" sort of man. He is placed in the institution of the home with all the goodness involved in the connotations of that holy place. He is just a neighborly, good-humored family man, respected, admired, and deeply loved by his son. The story of his life is the standard American one—poor, ignorant but hard-working man works his way to economic security by the grime of his hands and the sweat of his brow. Everything goes along smoothly until the war comes along and disrupts it all.

4. G. K. Chesterton has said, "Only those will permit their patriotism to falsify history whose patriotism depends on history." Such men, according to Chesterton, do not love their country; they love a theory about their country. To judge from the history books I used in school, the American patriot's theory depends on a West that was conquered only by white cowboys, the rugged sort who spent most of their time fighting other cowboys or Mexicans and Indians. Yet from a recently published book, *The Negro Cowboys*, written by Philip Durham and Everett L. Jones, I learned that there were more than 5,000 Negro cowboys, and that they lived together with the white cowboys and shared the same hardships. I learned that it was a unit of Negro cavalry

who captured Geronimo and that it was a Negro cowboy who helped bring in Billy the Kid. Though the Negro cowboys broke horses, herded cattle, and occasionally turned renegade, it has taken until 1965 for a history of their deeds to be published. Until now, I have been given a falsified history, a patriot's theory of our country's history.

b. Analyze the techniques used in the following sentences to gain emphasis.

1. A true university can never rest upon the will of one man. A true university always rests upon the wills of many divergent-minded old gentlemen, who refuse to be disturbed, but who growl in their kennels.

—John Jay Chapman

2. There is a certain expression that comes on a middle-to-upper income bracket Frenchman's face when he is about to déguster something really good, cheese, wine, any sort of culinary specialty, that starts out as a sudden interior break in the train of conversation. Silence; he is about to have a gastronomic experience. Then as the fork or glass nears his mouth, his eyes and ears seem to have blanked out; all is concentrated in the power of taste. There follows a stage when the critical faculties are gathering, the head is bent, eyes wander, lips and tongue are working over the evidence. At last comes the climactic moment of judgment, upon which may hang the mood of the meal and with it who knows what devious changes in the course of love, commerce, or the body politic. —Eleanor Clark

3. No man is an island, entire of itself; every man is a piece of the continent, a part of the main. If a clod be washed away by the sea, Europe is the less, as well as if a promontory were, as well as if a manner of thy friend's or of thine own were: any man's death diminishes me, because I am involved in mankind, and therefore never send to know for whom the bell tolls; it tolls for thee. —John Donne

c. Revise the following sentences to eliminate the trailing construction by placing the more important words at the beginning or end of the sentence.

1. The Industrial Revolution has progressed during the last two centuries, changing the life of everyone in Europe and now having its effect on the people in Africa and Asia.
2. I like to watch television, although I don't get much of a chance because I don't get home from practice until after six and then have to eat my supper before I start my homework, which isn't finished before 10:30.
3. A scientific fact is one in which the conditions by which the fact was discovered can be duplicated by someone else, achieving the same result.
4. The remote setting of the village answers the questions of why there is so much ignorance among the people who live in it, it would seem.
5. He strongly opposed the motion for several reasons which he had.

d. Revise the following sentences as necessary to gain greater emphasis.

1. To cool off that evening, she drank a coke, a pitcherful of iced tea, and a glass of water.
2. I want a job that pays well, has challenging work, and offers advancement.
3. She was valedictorian in her senior year after doing average work in her freshman and sophomore years and beginning to show her real abilities in her junior year.
4. There are two holidays which I especially enjoy, these being Christmas and spring vacation.
5. The worst driver of all is the driver who is positive he couldn't cause an accident and who doesn't care if other people are careless, speeding, or not quite sober, because he is sure that nothing can happen to him while he is driving.
6. In grade school hardly a week passed without my being beaten up by the older boys, scolded by the teacher, teased by the girls, etc.

7. The turtle nipped the boy on the finger when he put a finger into its box.
8. The two roommates finally saw each other again, many years later at a professional convention in New York, in a hotel lobby.
9. The pickets began their dramatic sit-in when the manager of the building scoffed at their requests.
10. The silent films produced America's greatest comedians, including Harry Langdon, Buster Keaton, Charlie Chaplin, and many others who could be mentioned.

9 b
wordy sentences

Be as concise as clarity permits, but note that conciseness is *not* the same as brevity.

Wordiness dilutes the strength of a piece of writing and makes sentences as flat and watery as weak coffee. In avoiding wordiness, you will find it helpful to keep in mind the distinction between brevity and conciseness. A *brief* statement does not give detail; for example, "I failed on the job." A *concise* statement may give precise detail so long as it does not waste words: "Last month I sold only 60 percent of the quota set by the company." Brevity is not always a virtue; there are times when a fairly detailed statement is required. But it is always good to be concise.

9 b-1
excessive use of the passive voice

Whenever possible, use the active voice to give your sentences strength and conciseness.

The unnecessary use of the passive voice causes many wordy, unemphatic sentences. Use it only when the receiver of an action *is more important* than the doer, or when the doer is unknown (see section 12b).

S emp

WEAK PASSIVE   The picnic was enjoyed by everybody who went on it in the afternoon.

Not only does the passive voice make unemphatic sentences but it also tempts the writer into windy identification of the doer—here, the clause "who went on it in the afternoon."

CONCISE ACTIVE   Everybody enjoyed the afternoon picnic.

Often, the passive voice causes vagueness as well as wordiness:

VAGUE PASSIVE   Criticism is created in this manner because these actions and thoughts of the main character are caused by the character's rebellious attitude towards society of which he is a member.

In what "manner" is "criticism" created? The student became lost in his of's and by's.

CONCISE ACTIVE   The main character's rebellious attitude provokes criticism from his society.

The passive voice, of course, has its own restricted usefulness. If the doer of the action is unknown or irrelevant to the statement, the passive is appropriate. Examine the following sentences:

CORRECT PASSIVE   The painting **was stolen** in 1925.

   Three purses and eight packages **were left** in municipal buses last week.

In both of these sentences, since the writer does not know the specific doers, he is forced to use the passive. He could say "A thief or thieves stole . . ." or "Passengers left . . ."; but these alternatives are awkward and shift the emphasis.

CORRECT PASSIVE   Trespassers **will be prosecuted.**

   The new dormitory **is** just about **finished.**

No one cares about who will do the prosecuting or who has been building the dormitory. What matters are the threat and the nearly-finished building.

9 b-2
redundant phrases and clauses

Check all sentences carefully to eliminate deadwood.

Sentences filled with *deadwood*—phrases and clauses which carelessly repeat what has already been said or which mean nothing in themselves ("It is my opinion that it is most desirable that . . .")—merely force the reader to stumble along and hack his way towards the path of clear meaning (see also "Exact Diction," chapter 12 and "Effective Diction," chapter 13).

1 phrases

When a writer is not thinking of the *meanings* of his noun or verb, he is especially likely to tack on a redundant phrase.

DEAD   *In this modern world* of today, because everything in this country *of ours* has become so large *in size,* the individual feels isolated *by himself* and unable to cooperate *together* with others.

CLEARER   Today, because everything in this country has become so large, the individual feels isolated and unable to cooperate with others.

DEAD   I worked on my costume for the New Year's party *celebration* from nine A.M. *in the morning* until six P.M. *in the evening;* I took such pains because *of the fact* the silk was expensive *in cost.*

CLEARER   I worked on my costume for the New Year's party from nine A.M. until six P.M.; I took such pains because the silk was expensive.

DEAD   When the poet writes *in his poem* that the character was never "odd in his views," he *means* to imply the man was a conformist *by the standards of his society in all aspects of his life.*

CLEARER   When the poet writes that the character was never "odd in his views," he implies the man was a conformist.

S emp

Some other redundant phrases include:

attractive *in appearance*	the reason *why*
close to *the point of*	red *in color*
connected *up* with	repeat *again*
different *in a number of ways*	several *in number*
expert in *the field of*	square *in shape*
fundamental principles	a *very* important *thing* to

2 clauses

The redundant *who, which,* or *that* clause often occurs when the writer carelessly says the same thing twice in slightly different words.

> **DEAD**   Over the years, Smathers becomes suspicious because he is being exploited *by people who* want to take advantage of *him and use him.*
> *The student ignored the meaning of the word "exploited."*

> **DEAD**   The criticisms I will make are major ones *which* ought to be given careful consideration because of their importance.
> *If anything is "major" (or "basic" or "fundamental"), then by definition it "ought to be given careful consideration because of its importance."*

> **DEAD**   We like to be appreciated and admired for our talents *which* we possess and we hope to be praised for our achievements *that* we have attained as individuals.
> *The student forgot the meaning of the word "our."*

9 c
wordy constructions

Always use the simplest, most direct phrasing that you can.

Answering a young man's question about how to become a good writer, the English wit Sydney Smith once said: "You should cross out every other word. You have no idea what vigor it will give to your style." Though exaggerated, the advice has its point (see also chapter 13 on effective diction).

9 c-1
reducing predication

Find the precise verb that expresses your meaning.

One cause of wordy sentences is the use of the verb *to be* and a clumsy complement instead of a precise verb and its object. The results are sometimes ludicrous:

WORDY *It should be observed* whether your dog is choosing weeds, rubbish, or other things not part of his usual diet. If he *is participating in such an action, you may be assured that this action is the symptom of his having worms.*
CLEAR Notice whether your dog eats weeds, rubbish, or other things not part of his usual diet. If he does, he has worms.
Note the economizing: "Notice" for "It should be observed"; "eats" for "is choosing"; "does" for "is participating in such an action"; "he has worms" for "you may be assured that this action is the symptom of his having worms."

WORDY If the *draft is not my course of action two or three years* from now, the *alternatives will be my obtaining of* a master's degree or *establishing* my own business.
The sentence is not only wordy but inexact: "the draft" is not a "course of action."
CLEAR If the army doesn't draft me in the next two or three years, I will either take a master's degree or establish my own business.

As George Orwell comments in "Politics and the English Language," many of the weak verb phrases in common use are the result of laziness.

WORDY Franklin *made contact with* sympathetic French officials and *played a role in obtaining* help for the Colonies.
CLEAR Franklin *located* sympathetic French officials and *obtained* help for the Colonies.

WORDY The pill *had the desired effect of* tranquilizing the dog and *served the purpose of* keeping him asleep until the end of the trip.
CLEAR The pill *kept* the dog asleep until the end of the trip.

Occasionally, you may want to use the longer forms for a particular kind of emphasis, but *usually* you will find the shortest form is the best.

9 c-2
reducing modification

Make your modifying constructions as simple and direct as you can.

Needlessly complicated modifiers can also cause wordiness (see also section 7b-4 on problems in sentence unity caused by excessive subordination.

1 economy of phrases

WORDY I am especially interested *in the* testing *in connection with* personnel work *due to the fact that* I like to work with people.
CONCISE I am especially interested in personnel testing because I like to work with people.
Notice the pompous, offending phrases in the original and the single-word substitutions in the revision.

2 economy of clauses

WORDY Late that night I *proceeded to catch* a subway *which would take me uptown.*
CONCISE Late that night I caught an *uptown* subway.

WORDY Most of the Indians live and die within their "municipio," *which is the limited area that includes the related members,* and *their concept of what the outside world is like* is hazy.

CONCISE Most of the Indians live and die in the *limited area* of their "municipio," and their *knowledge of the outside* world is hazy.

WORDY *When we made scenery* for our plays that summer, we used whatever available materials *we could find, which included* finger paints and shelf paper.

CONCISE We made scenery for our plays that summer *from* any available materials, *including* finger paints and shelf paper.

SUMMARY

1. Use the active voice to strengthen your sentences.
2. Use the passive voice *only* when the receiver of the action is more important than the doer or when the doer is unknown.
3. Check all sentences carefully to eliminate deadwood.
4. Always use the simplest, most direct phrasing that you can.
   a. Strive for the precise verb that expresses your meaning.
   b. Strive for economical modifiers.

EXERCISES

a. One way to alert yourself to wordy sentences is to write them deliberately. For each sentence in the following exercises, give yourself 5 points if you succeed in making it wordier without adding anything to the meaning. Perfect score 150.

(1) Pad out each of the following sentences by using the passive.
   1. The football team won all of its home games last season.
   2. Lock all doors and leave the keys at the desk.
   3. The Valley String Quartet decided to hold extra rehearsals during the week and agreed to postpone other activities.

S emp

4. He cut the wood with his ax.
5. Some college students choose medicine as a career as early as the beginning of their sophomore year.

(2) Pad out each of the following sentences by adding dead phrases.

1. Many writers dislike personal publicity because the lionizing keeps them from their work.
2. The apartment rooms were small, boxlike, and painted in a hideous green.
3. The City Council agreed to work with the Board of Education to determine the principles for zoning schools and homes.
4. In 1960, Kennedy won by a very small majority.
5. Sometimes I study from 8 P.M. to 2 A.M.

(3) Pad out each of the following sentences by adding dead clauses.

1. While reviewing my class notes, I discovered several illegible sentences.
2. A sprinter in the hundred yard dash fell and cut his knee on the cinders.
3. The manager of the resort personally greets all new guests.
4. High school drop-outs are encouraged to take federally-financed remedial courses in reading and writing.
5. The firm hired by the township took a poll of all registered voters and reported its findings.

(4) Pad out each of the sentences by using the verb *to be* and a clumsy complement to replace the precise verb.

1. I like musical comedies and I collect record albums of them.
2. David Riesman, author of *The Lonely Crowd,* thinks many Americans lack a firm sense of individuality.
3. Mrs. Spaulder lives in Cincinnati but teaches school in the suburbs.
4. Distance bicycling requires stamina and ten gears.
5. He has given up cigarettes and now he feels better.

(5) Pad out each of the following sentences by replacing the simple verb with a phrase, a clause, or a sentence.

1. Moss blanketed the forest rocks.
2. As a federal negotiator, Arthur Goldberg valued compromises and settled several major labor disputes.
3. During his long coaching career, Alonzo Stagg made many innovations in football strategy.
4. I think that changes in dance fads reveal changes in the mood of the times.
5. The aspirin stopped the headache and relieved the backache.

(6) Pad out the following sentences by expanding the modifiers into phrases and clauses.

1. A *mano* is a hand stone for grinding corn in a large hollowed stone *metate*.
2. A biographer lacks the artistic freedom of a novelist because the biographer cannot invent his character or move him about as he pleases.
3. Since Paul was tired when he took the Civil Service examination, he missed several easy questions and did poorly on familiar topics.
4. A number of educational theories and practices still regarded as dangerously "modern" and "progressive" date back to Rousseau.
5. If my mother, born in the Kentucky backwoods, had stayed there and spoken only with her childhood friends, she would never have had to change her speech habits; only when she moved north and began associating with teachers and business people did she realize how much people scorned her grammar and pronunciation.

b. Reduce the wordiness in the following student sentences. Be prepared to explain your changes.

1. It is my intention to be affiliated with some large automobile manufacturer in connection with sales of cars and accessories.
2. There are all too many instances of condemnation of a person by his fellow men before "sufficient knowledge" has been found.
3. I was especially interested in going to the University of

Southern California because of the fact that it was near home.

4. Respect is the individual's personal ability to be aware of another person's unique individuality.

5. Owing to the fact that quick action was taken by this employer, a major crisis was averted.

6. He is often thought to have a lack of responsibility; hence, he is not trusted to any great extent by those who know him.

7. I am now very sorry that I didn't find reading a meaningful and worthwhile experience when I was younger.

8. The reason that Lincoln kept in close contact with his generals by writing them letters was that he felt that he was responsible as commander-in-chief for the running of the war.

c. This is a brief review exercise: Make the following sentences more forceful by proper subordination and the elimination of trailing construction, anticlimactic constructions, and unnecessary words.

1. The common cold is a communicable disease which can be passed on by one person to another.

2. Political scientists attempt to regard political events with an unbiased attitude, attempting also to find and apply scientific principles which are valid.

3. Our whole civilization is becoming very lax—lax about raising our children, lax about crime rates, lax about credit buying.

4. In assessing the local political situation, one cannot leave out of account the fact that Roberts won over Mrs. Ackwell by a majority of the voters who went to the polls.

5. She is certainly not worried about her financial resources, for she puts on an act at the Flamingo Club, bringing her in over $500 a week.

6. Parts of Asia and Europe have already become communistic, but the people in the countries which have turned communist do not know what communism is in its pure form, I think.

10
uses of the dictionary

Like all languages, English is continually changing. New words are added as names are required for new inventions, discoveries, and ideas: *laser, meson, transistor, sputnik, cybernetics, apartheid.* Old words acquire new meanings as they are used in new ways: *half life* (physics), *snow* (television), *stylus, cartridge* (high-fidelity recording). Some old words disappear as the need for them vanishes; a whole vocabulary dealing with horse-drawn vehicles is on its way out. Words gain or lose prestige: *strenuous* and *mob* are now standard words, although they were once considered slang. *Aryan* acquired such disreputable associations through its use by the Nazis that most writers avoid it today.

A dictionary is an attempt to record the current uses and meanings of words. Popular notions not withstanding, a dictionary does not try to prescribe what a word should mean. Rather, like any factual account, it attempts to be accurate— to discriminate among the meanings the word now has. Large, unabridged dictionaries include a history of the past meanings

D

of words, biographical and geographical data, guides for pronunciation, spelling, and punctuation, and a variety of other useful information. The large dictionaries in established widespread use in most college libraries include:*

> *The Oxford English Dictionary,* 12 volumes and Supplement, Clarendon Press, Oxford, 1933. (This is the standard historical dictionary of the language; it traces and illustrates the development of each word from its earliest appearance to the present.)
> *Webster's New International Dictionary of the English Language,* Second Edition, G. & C. Merriam Co., 1954.
> *Webster's Third New International Dictionary of the English Language,* G. & C. Merriam Co., 1961.

Unabridged dictionaries are invaluable for occasional reference but too bulky for constant use. More practical for the student to own is one of the following abridged desk dictionaries. All are reliable, but some instructors may have preferences, which they will indicate.

> *Webster's New Collegiate Dictionary,* G. & C. Merriam Co., Springfield, Mass.
> *Webster's New World Dictionary,* The World Publishing Company, Cleveland.
> *American College Dictionary,* Random House, New York.
> *Funk and Wagnalls Standard College Dictionary,* Harcourt, Brace & World, Inc., New York.

10 a
abbreviations and symbols

To use a dictionary effectively, you must understand the abbreviations and symbols it uses. These are explained in its introductory section. Here are entries from four collegiate dictionaries and one unabridged dictionary.

*Another recent candidate in the unabridged reference field is *The Random House Dictionary of the English Language* (1966).

Dict

spelling & syllabication

↓

etymology

↓

*im·ply (im-plī′), v.t. [IMPLIED (-plīd′), IMPLYING], [ME. implien; OFr. emplier; L. implicare < in-, in + plicare, to fold], 1. to have as a necessary part, condition, or effect; contain, include, or involve naturally or necessarily: as, drama implies conflict. 2. to indicate without saying openly or directly; hint; suggest; intimate: as, his attitude implied boredom. 3. [Obs.], to enfold; entangle. —SYN. see suggest.

↑

usage label

pronunciation

↓

meanings

↗

†im·ply (im·plī′) v.t. ·plied, ·ply·ing 1. To involve necessarily as a circumstance, condition, effect, etc.: An action implies an agent. 2. To indicate or suggest without stating; hint at; intimate. 3. To have the meaning of; signify. 4. Obs. To entangle; infold. — Syn. See INFER. [< OF em-plier < L implicare to involve < in- in + plicare to fold. Doublet of EMPLOY.]

— Syn. 1. Imply and involve mean to have some necessary connection. Imply states that the connection is causal or inherent, while involve is vaguer, and does not define the connection. 2. Imply, hint, intimate, insinuate mean to convey a meaning indirectly or covertly. Imply is the general term for signifying something beyond what the words obviously say: his advice implied confidence in the stock market. Hint suggests indirection in speech or action: our host's repeated glances at his watch hinted that it was time to go. Intimate suggests a process more elaborate and veiled than hint: she intimated that his attentions were unwelcome. Insinuate suggests slyness and a derogatory import: in his remarks, he insinuated that the Senator was a fool.

full discussion of synonyms

Inflected forms

⁀

■ im·ply (ĭm plī′), v.t., -plied, -plying. 1. to involve as a necessary circumstance: speech implies a speaker. 2. (of words) to signify or mean. 3. to indicate or suggest, as something naturally to be inferred, without express statement. 4. Obs. to enfold. [ME implie(n), t. OF: m. emplier, g. L implicāre enfold, entangle, involve]

D

***im·ply** \im-'plī\ *vt* [ME *emplien*, fr. MF *emplier*, fr. L *implicare*]
1 *obs* **:** ENFOLD, ENTWINE   **2 :** to involve or indicate by inference,
association, or necessary consequence rather than by direct statement   **3 :** to contain potentially   **4 :** to express indirectly   **syn**
SEE INCLUDE, SUGGEST

↑

synonyms

quotation of usage in an unabridged dictionary

†**im·ply** \əm'plī\ *vt* **implied; implied; implying; implies** [ME
emplien, implien, fr. MF *emplier*,
fr. L *implicare* to infold, involve,
implicate, engage — more at EM-
PLOY] **1** *obs* **:** ENFOLD, ENTWINE,
ENWRAP   **2 a :** to indicate or call
for recognition of as existent,
present, or related not by express statement but by logical
inference or association or necessary consequence ⟨enrollment
in the college *implies* willingness on the part of the student to
comply with the requirements and regulations of the college
—*Bull. of Mt. Saint Mary's College*⟩ ⟨the philosophy of
nature which is *implied* in Chinese art —Lawrence Binyon⟩
⟨democracy *implies* a number of freedoms⟩ ⟨emergency and
crisis ~ conflict —H.S.Langfeld⟩   **b :** to involve as a necessary concomitant (as by general or logical implication, by
signification, or by very nature or essence) ⟨two propositions
may ~ a third⟩ ⟨war *implies* fighting⟩ ⟨an acorn *implies* an
oak⟩   **3 :** to convey or communicate not by direct forthright
statement but by allusion or reference likely to lead to natural
inference **:** suggest or hint at ⟨the girl's evasive answer and
burning brow seemed to ~ that her suitor had changed his
mind —Edith Wharton⟩ ⟨made me sick to hear him ~ that
somebody would make a report against him —Joseph Conrad⟩
⟨the tone of the book was *implied* by shrewd advertisements
—J.D.Hart⟩   **syn** SEE INCLUDE, SUGGEST

10 b
information found in a dictionary

spelling and syllabication   When more than one spelling is given, the one printed first is usually to be preferred.
Division of the word into syllables follows the conventions
accepted by printers.

pronunciation   A key to the symbols used to indicate
pronunciation of words is usually printed on the front or back

*By permission. From *Webster's Seventh New Collegiate Dictionary,* copyright
1965 by G. & C. Merriam Company, Publishers of the Merriam-Webster Dictionaries.

†By Permission. From *Webster's Third New International Dictionary,* copyright
1966 by G. & C. Merriam Company, Publishers of the Merriam-Webster Dictionaries.

inside cover of the dictionary. Some dictionaries also run an abbreviated key to pronunciation at the bottom of each page or every other page. Word accent is shown by the symbol (′) after the stressed syllable or by (′) before it.

part of speech Abbreviations (explained in the introductory section of the dictionary) are used to indicate the various grammatical uses of a word: e.g., *imply, v.t.* means that *imply* is a transitive verb. Note that some words can be used as several different parts of speech. *Forfeit,* for example, is listed first as a noun, and its various meanings in this use are defined. Then its meaning when used as an adjective is given, and finally its meaning as a transitive verb.

inflected forms Forms of the past tense and past participle of verbs, the comparative or superlative degree of adjectives, and the plural of nouns are given whenever there might be doubt as to the correct form or spelling.

etymology The history of each word is indicated by the forms in use in Middle or Old English, or in the language from which the word was borrowed. Earlier meanings are often given.

meanings Different meanings of a word are numbered and defined, sometimes with illustrative examples. Some dictionaries give the oldest meanings first; others list the common meanings of the word first, and rarer, earlier meanings last.

usage labels Descriptive labels, often abbreviated, indicate the level of usage: Archaic, Obsolete, Colloquial, Slang, Dialectal, Substandard, Nonstandard, etc. Sometimes usage labels indicate a special field, rather than a level of usage: e.g., Poetic, Irish, Chemistry, etc. If a word has no usage label, it may be assumed to be in common use on all levels and in all fields of speech and writing; that is, it is *standard* English. Note that foreign words which are not yet naturalized and should be written in italics may be indicated by a special symbol (‖) or (‡), or by a label: *French, Italian,* etc. Usage labels are defined in the explanatory notes in the front of each dictionary. Read this explanation to be sure you understand how the labels are used.

D

synonyms Words that have nearly identical or closely related meanings often need careful discrimination to indicate the precise connotation of each. A full account of the distinctions in meaning between synonyms (for example, *suggest, imply, hint, intimate,* and *insinuate*) may be given at the end of the entry for the basic word, or cross references to its synonyms may be provided for this purpose.

EXERCISES

a. In looking up the meanings of words, try to discover within what limits of meaning the word may be used. Read the definition as a whole; do not pick out a single synonym and suppose that this and the word defined are interchangeable. After looking up the following words in your dictionary, write sentences which will unmistakably illustrate the meaning of each word.

anachronism	irony	precocious
duress	materiel	retroactive
eminent	misanthropy	sabotage
fetish	mundane	sinecure
hedonist	neologism	sophistication
imminent	nepotism	taboo
increment	ostentatious	tempera
innocuous	philanthropy	travesty

b. Look up each of the following words both in an unabridged dictionary and in an abridged one, and write a report showing how much more discriminatingly and clearly the larger volume explains the use of each word than the smaller one does. State the exact title, the publisher, and the date of both dictionaries.

Bible	Christian	court	idealism
catholic	color	evolution	liberal

c. How may the etymologies given by the dictionary help one to remember the meaning or the spelling of the following words? (Note that when a series of words has the same etymology, the etymology is usually given only with the first word of the series.)

agnostic	denouement	malapropism
alibi	homogeneous	peer (noun)
capitol	hyperbole	privilege

cohort	insidious	sacrilegious
colleague	isosceles	sarcasm
concave	magnanimous	subterfuge

d. Some dictionaries have a separate section listing all abbreviations in common use; others put abbreviations used in the main alphabetical arrangement. Look up the following abbreviations and be ready to state in class what they mean:

| at. wt. | colloq. | E.T.A. | K.C.B. | LL.D. | Pb |
| CAA | e.g. | ff. | l.c. | OHG. | q.v. |

e. Consult the dictionary for the distinctions in meaning between the members of each of the following pairs of words:

neglect and *negligence*	*contagious* and *infectious*
ingenuous and *ingenious*	*wit* and *humor*
fewer and *less*	*eminent* and *famous*
admit and *confess*	*criticize* and *censure*
instinct and *intuition*	*farther* and *further*

f. In each sentence, choose the more precise of the two italicized words. Be able to justify your choice.

1. The decadent Roman civilization was a *feminine, effeminate* civilization.
2. Her charming innocence is *childlike, childish.*
3. The problem is to assure the farm workers *continuous, continual* employment.
4. He is *continuously, continually* in trouble with the police.
5. I am quite *jealous, envious* of your opportunity to study in Europe.
6. She is so *decided, decisive* in her manner that people always give in to her.
7. If we give your class all of these privileges, we may establish *precedents, precedence* which may be unwise.
8. She always makes her health her *alibi, excuse* for her failures.

g. Find the precise meaning of each word in the following groups, and write sentences to illustrate that meaning.

1. abandon, desert, forsake
2. hate, loathe, despise
3. ludicrous, droll, comic
4. silent, reserved, taciturn
5. work, labor, toil, drudgery
6. meager, scanty, sparse
7. knack, talent, genius
8. anxious, eager, avid

11
levels of usage

The basic principle of good usage is to fit the level of your language to the situation and to the reader.

Modern linguistics has largely discarded the terms *good* and *bad, correct* and *incorrect* to describe English usage. Dictionaries *record* current uses of words, but as chapter 10 pointed out, they do not "try to describe what a word should mean." But linguists still speak of "standard," "nonstandard," and "substandard" English to indicate the difference in *stylistic status* between the usage of educated people and that of the semiliterate or illiterate. Within these three large divisions, most linguists recognize a number of status levels:

Standard English	formal and technical
	informal (or general)
	colloquial
Nonstandard English	dialectal
	slang
Substandard English	invented or coined
	illiterate
	obscene and profane

A discussion of the pragmatic approach to status or prestige in English usage may be found in the last section of chapter 15.

Use

11 a
standard English

Dictionaries do not give stylistic status labels to words which have been accepted into the language, that is, which are considered standard English, nor do they distinguish between the formal and informal levels. They usually label all nonstandard or substandard words, or uses of words, which they include. Standard words *are* labelled, however, to show special limitations in their use. Some of the common labels (and their definitions) for standard words are the following:

colloquial   characteristic of the educated person's familiar speech or conversational writing
>One reporter did a *take-off* on the President.

obsolete   no longer in general use, but found in older works of literature
>Mice and rats and such small *deer* . . . . [i.e., any small animals]   —Shakespeare

archaic   going out of use, too old-fashioned for ordinary contexts
>Dry clashed his *harness* [armor] in the icy caves . . . .
>   —Tennyson

poetic   used in poetry rather than in ordinary prose
>*Oft* in the stilly night . . . .

law   a legal term not in general use
>*Tort*, a wrongful act not involving a breach of contract.

zoology   a technical term used by scientists
>When *endoderm* is applied to embryonic structures it is equivalent to *hypoblast*.

Scottish   limited chiefly to Scotland (also, *British, Southern,* etc.)
>*Dour*, in the sense of "stern and severe."

It is impossible to draw sharp lines between the levels of Standard English. Relative differences, however, can be indicated. *Exhausted* and *fatigued* are more formal than *tired; interred* is more formal than *buried; acquire* is more formal than *get; purchase* is more formal than *buy. Hunch* used as a

D

verb is Standard Informal English. Used as a noun (*to have a hunch that* . . .) it is colloquial; it would be used freely in educated speech and often in informal writing to avoid the very formal *premonition* or *foreboding*. *Size up* is colloquial; *look over* is informal; *inspect* and *examine* might be used in either informal or formal contexts; *scrutinize* is definitely formal and is rarely heard and not often used in writing.

Study the following groupings of approximate synonyms:

formal	*informal*	*colloquial*
comprehend	understand	catch on
altercation	quarrel	row
wrathful, irate	angry	mad
goad, taunt	tease	needle
predicament	problem	jam, fix
exorbitant	high	stiff

Remember that good usage is appropriate usage, suited to the situation and to the reader. If you are writing an obituary or a formal letter of application, substandard English would be as inappropriate as a T shirt at a funeral. If you are writing a handbook of information for newcomers at a summer camp, formal English would be as incongruous as a starched shirt at a clambake. During the past fifty years, the center of common usage has moved away from the Formal level toward the Informal and Colloquial. Especially in magazines and newspapers, good writers are more apt to use colloquialisms and even slang rather than risk the stilted pompousness of Formal English in a commonplace context. Nevertheless, it is still important to be able to distinguish between Colloquial, Informal, and Formal usage, since an educated person may need to use all of these levels on occasion.

11 a-1
formal and informal English

Formal English is usually written and is appropriate to scholarly articles and criticism, official documents and formal letters, and scientific writing. Its spoken use is usually reserved for the pulpit, the court, and the legislature.

Informal or General English is the language, both written and spoken, used by the educated classes in carrying on the everyday business of the country. It is the level used in most books, magazines, newspapers, and ordinary communications. Its grammar is less conservative than that of Formal English, reflecting current tendencies in the language's development; its sentence patterns are less complex and varied, more casual and less balanced and controlled, than those of Formal English. Its vocabulary, which is not always as rich and nicely discriminating as that of Formal English, is readier to experiment with slang and the livelier words of current usage.

11 a-2
colloquial English

Colloquial English is the language of easy, familiar conversation among educated people. It occurs frequently in the most informal writing and is usually considered Standard English, though it is *usually inappropriate to college writing unless the writer is seeking a very specific effect.* Because the gradations in speech between extremely informal English, conversational speech, and slang are not always easy to make, some debate has arisen about the usefulness of the term *Colloquial,* and a few dictionaries, *Webster's Third International* for instance, have abandoned it as a label. Nonetheless, since most dictionaries and other guides to usage still employ it, the term will be retained here.

11 b
nonstandard English

Linguists may use the label *nonstandard* to embrace several categories of words which do have a limited appropriate usage in the prestige group (i.e., educated people), but which nevertheless have not become accepted as part of the standard respected vocabulary for educated speech and writing. Sometimes

D

a standard word may move into this area by being used with a different function or in a context slightly different from the historically standard one, as the word *contact* in the following example:

Be sure to *contact* me if you have any difficulty.

Two other levels of Nonstandard English are *dialect* and *slang*.

11 b-1
dialectal English

Dialect, or *Dialectal English,* refers to a usage which is considered reputable in certain areas of the country, but which has not gained nationwide acceptance (as opposed to regional words which have a measure of acceptance, such as British *tram*). These words are not necessarily nonstandard in the regions where they are found, and sometimes they are useful additions to the local vocabulary. But for general college writing, dialect should not be used when equivalent words in national currency are available. Some examples of dialectal words are:

lagniappe	bonus (Creole country)
side meat	bacon or salt pork (South)
stoop	porch (Midwest)
tonic	carbonated drink (New England)

11 b-2
slang

Slang is the label given to words with a forced, exaggerated, or humorous meaning which are often used in extremely informal contexts, particularly by persons who wish to set themselves off from the average, respectable citizen.

To call a man whose ideas and behavior are unpredictable and unconventional "a kook" and to describe his ideas as "for the birds" or "way out" apparently satisfies some obscure human urge toward irreverent, novel, and vehement expression. Some slang terms remain in fairly wide use because they are vivid ways of expressing an idea which has no exact standard equivalent: *stooge, lame duck, shot* of whiskey, a card *shark*. Such words have a good chance of becoming accepted as Standard English. *Mob, banter, sham,* and *lynch* were all once regarded as slang terms. It is conceivable that as space exploration matures, the astronaut's *go, abort, destruct,* or *splashdown* may become part of standard English.

A good deal of slang, however, reflects nothing more than the user's desire to be different, and such slang has little chance of being accepted into the language. Newspaper columnists and sports writers often use a flamboyant jargon intended to show off their ingenuity or cleverness. For centuries criminals have used a special, semisecret language, and many modern slang terms originate in the argot of the underworld: *gat, scram, squeal,* or *sing* (confess), *push* (advocate, peddle), *square*. Teen-agers and jazz addicts develop a constantly changing slang which seems intended mainly to distinguish the user as a member of a select group or inner circle.

Whatever the motive behind it, slang should be used with discretion. Its incongruity in a sober, practical context makes it an effective way of achieving force and emphasis.

ACCEPTABLE SLANG   This book is so intelligently constructed, so beautifully written, so really acute at moments—and so *phony*.

But most slang terms are too violent to fit comfortably into ordinary, everyday writing; this kind of incongruity may strike a jarring note which spoils the effect of its context.

OBJECTIONABLE SLANG   We, the undersigned students, are not *bitching* about the disciplinary measures drawn up by the Council; our *gripe* is that we are not adequately represented on the Council.

Furthermore, slang goes out of fashion very quickly, through overuse, and dated slang sounds more quaint and old-fashioned than Formal English. *Tight* has worn well, but *spifflicated* now sounds depressingly dowdy, and *smashed, boiled, crocked, fried,* and *plastered* may soon be museum pieces.

D

The chief objection to the use of slang is that it so quickly loses any precise meaning. Calling a person a *fink,* a *square,* or a *nut* conveys nothing but your feeling of dislike. *Cool,* or *crummy* are the vaguest kind of terms, lumping all experience into two crude divisions, pleasing and unpleasing. Try to get several people to agree on the precise meaning of *egghead* and you will realize how vague and inexact a term it is. The remedy is to analyze your meaning and specify it. What exactly are the qualities which lead you to classify a person under the loose term *egghead?*

If, despite these warnings, you must use slang in serious writing, do it deliberately and accept the responsibility for it. Do not attempt to excuse yourself by putting the slang term in quotation marks. If you are ashamed of a slang term, do not use it (see section 30g for further discussion of the use of quotation marks with slang).

11 c
substandard English

A *substandard* usage is one which occurs widely but not in the speech or writing of educated persons (especially those in the contemporary prestige group) because it differs from their usage in word choice or form. Usages labelled *substandard* in this handbook are, for the purposes of college level writing, incorrect. Substandard English embraces *invented or coined words, illiterate English,* and *profanity and obscenity.*

Invented words coined without authority from words in good standing and not yet generally accepted are substandard and should be avoided in writing. Advertising copywriters and industrial public relations writers are continually inventing new words (visit our *sleepwear* department, our *whisper-weight* wool dress, to be *accesorized* casually, *Torque Flite, saleswise*) which have little apparent chance of gaining general acceptance. The suffixes *ize, ism, wise* tempt many people to invent exotic words. Occasionally a coined word may justify itself and become widely accepted.

Churchill's chief strength was his basic *John Bullishness.*

But a beginning writer had better not risk such barbarisms as the following:

Hitler tried to subdue his opponents with a deliberate policy of terrorism and *torturism.*

Illiterate usages occur for the most part in the speech of the uneducated. Words of this kind (like *hain't, ain't, sot* in his ways) do not appear in most dictionaries and, except in dialogue, are definitely out of place in college writing.

Profanity and *obscenity,* long ignored by dictionaries and still looked down on by most educated persons, nonetheless exist in our language. The fact that many words held to be obscene or profane have begun to appear in dictionaries should not be construed as an upgrading of the status level of these words, but as evidence of the dictionary's wider scope and its more detailed recording of the spoken language. Usages at this level are considered by this handbook to be inappropriate for college writing.

EXERCISES

a. With the aid of a dictionary and your own linguistic judgment (i.e., your ear for appropriateness), classify the following Standard English words as Formal, Informal, or Colloquial.

1. Nebulous, vague, obscure
2. limp, flaccid, fagged
3. crank, eccentric, [a] character
4. square [to settle or repay], square [meal], square [one's shoulders]
5. hide, secrete, sequester
6. a tough one, puzzle, enigma
7. [make a] face [at], grimace
8. contend [with], fight, combat
9. irascible, cranky, grouchy
10. increase, boost, jack [up the price]

D

11. criticize, ridicule, needle
12. decline, avoid, pass [up]
13. pass [out], faint, swoon
14. necessity, [a] must, requirement
15. passion, love, relationship
16. inexpensive, [a] steal, cheap
17. snooty, pretentious, affected
18. ingenuous, naive, innocent

b. For each of the following Standard English words supply one or more slang terms and, to the best of your ability, judge which are so widespread that they have already begun to creep into highly informal writing (e.g., letters to friends; college newspaper columns) or seem likely to do so in the near future.

1. to become excited [to be turned on by, *slang*]
2. money
3. to relax
4. a skilled performer
5. to be going steady or in love
6. failure
7. to tell off
8. pleasant or enjoyable
9. to play a part
10. liquor
11. to ignore or disregard
12. complaint
13. a dull person
14. unconventional person
15. to be unfairly treated
16. puzzling

c. Pick five or six slang terms widely used around campus and ask at least five people to supply the Standard English equivalent for each term or to define the term's meanings in Standard English. Then analyze the answers by the following questions: does each slang term denote and connote the same thing or feeling to the respondents, or does each term have a wide range of meanings and associations? Are all the terms equally familiar, or is at least one not so commonly used or accepted? If one is unfamiliar, what seems to be the reason?

12
exact diction

Choose words which say precisely what you mean. A reader has the right to expect that you mean exactly what your words say. It is not enough to make sure that you can be understood; before copying out the final draft of a paper, you ought to go over it carefully to see that the words express your meaning and that you cannot be misunderstood.

12 a
vague or general diction

Choose specific rather than general terms, unless there is a good reason for being general.

A general term like *food* is a name for a whole group of specific things—from vegetable soup to T-bone steak to strawberry shortcake. If you want to make a statement about all foods, the general term is appropriate: "Food is becoming more and more expensive." But do not use the general term when concrete details and specific words are called for.

VAGUE AND GENERAL   For dinner we had some really good food.
SPECIFIC   For dinner we had barbecued steaks and sweet corn.

VAGUE AND GENERAL   He liked to argue about controversial subjects.
SPECIFIC   He liked to argue about politics and religion.

D

Note that *specific* and *general* are relative, not absolute terms. In the following list, running from specific to more general, any of the four terms might be used to refer to a famous tree growing on campus:

SPECIFIC   Charter Oak (one particular tree)
LESS SPECIFIC   oak (includes thousands of trees)
MORE GENERAL   tree (includes oaks, pines, palms, etc.)
MORE GENERAL   plant (includes trees, flowers, bushes, etc.)
Tree *is more specific than* plant *but more general than* oak.

Make your language as specific as possible. If your papers are criticized for vagueness—the most common fault in undergraduate writing—revise them by using specific and concrete words which create definite and vivid pictures in the reader's mind. In searching for the concrete word, you will clarify your thinking. By replacing the vague, general term with the specific one, you will deepen the content of your paper.

NEEDLESSLY ABSTRACT   My father showed his disapproval.
CONCRETE   My father growled, "Stop that!"

VAGUE   There are several factors which make *Tom Jones* a good movie.
CONCRETE   A vigorous plot, broad humor, and energetic acting make *Tom Jones* a lively movie.

VAGUE   One member of the Student Council has been irresponsible about performing his duties.
CONCRETE   Although he is a member of the Student Council, Pete Meyers has skipped the last five meetings.

Note that a specific statement may require no more space than a vague, indefinite one, yet it can communicate much more information.

VAGUE   One member of my family has recently begun his professional career.
CONCRETE   Last week my brother Ken joined a law firm.

12 b
abstract verbs

Whenever possible, replace abstract verbs and verb
phrases with direct, concrete verbs.

Make your verbs work. In the sentence "He made a hasty
exit" the verb is abstract, and the adjective and noun carry
what meaning the sentence has. Choose a more exact and forceful verb: "He rushed from the room," or "He fled from the
office."

Occur, took place, prevail, exist, happen, and other such
relatively static verbs, expressing a state of affairs, have legitimate uses, but they are often colorless, tossed in merely to
complete a sentence.

> WEAK   In the afternoon a sharp drop in the temperature
> occurred.
> STRONGER VERB   The temperature dropped sharply in the after-
> noon.

> WEAK   Throughout the meeting an atmosphere of increas-
> ing tension existed.
> STRONGER VERBS   As the meeting progressed, the tension in-
> creased.

Copulative verbs (*be, seem, appear,* etc.) completed by an adjective or participle are usually weaker than concrete verbs.

> WEAK   He was occasionally inclined to talk too much.
> STRONGER   Occasionally he talked too much.

> WEAK   In some high schools there is a very definite lack of
> emphasis on the development of a program in remedial
> English.
> STRONGER   Some high schools have not developed programs in
> remedial English.

Unnecessary use of the passive voice produces weak sentences.
The passive voice is appropriate when the doer of an action is

D

unknown or irrelevant to the statement, but far too often the passive is used needlessly. Usually the doer of an action *is* important, and the subject of the verb should name him (see sections 16c and 23a; see also section 9b-1).

> **WEAK PASSIVE**   The expenses were shared by everyone.
> **STRONGER ACTIVE**   Everyone shared the expenses.

> **WEAK PASSIVE**   Every night Mr. Richardson's lawn had to be watered by me.
> **STRONGER ACTIVE**   Every night I had to water Mr. Richardson's lawn.

> **APPROPRIATE PASSIVE**   Chicken and green peas were served at the banquet.
> **APPROPRIATE PASSIVE**   Lost parcels may be claimed at the office.

One final word of caution: do not, in an effort to avoid flat and colorless verbs, go to the opposite extreme and use verbs which are too explosive for their context.

> **FORCED**   Her angry words leaped at him and pounced upon him.
> **FORCED**   The evening breeze ravished her senses and cooled her forehead.

12 c
jargon and utility words

Deal directly with your subject; do not cloud your meaning with jargon.

Some writers feel that simple, direct language is dull and commonplace and prefer high-sounding synonyms or generalities—those who write "adverse climatic conditions" when all they mean is "bad weather" or "rain and winds." Official reports—of educators, social scientists, government commissions or advisory committees—are often written in stilted, roundabout, and abstract language, and the style is sometimes imitated by students who feel their statements need some arti-ficial support. So they dress up their ideas in formal, vague "official" language, with the hope of sounding authoritative and profound. Consider the following specimen:

> The leader-follower relationship must be looked upon as a field situation and such a field will be structured and sustain its structure only when the views of the leader are acceptable to the followers. The leader-follower field will be extended to the degree that the leader is seen to have authority to assume the leader role. As the relation of the leader's ap-parent right to authority is moved progressively away from the problem area confronting the group, there will be an increasing tendency for the leader-follower field to disinte-grate.

Stripped of their jargon, these sentences mean no more than:

> A group will fall apart when its members no longer agree with the views of their leader. Whatever degree of authority a leader has he gains from the group's willingness to grant it. The more the group feels that its leader is meddling, the less likely it is to follow him.

Often the writer who uses jargon is attempting to deceive him-self and his reader—to disguise from both of them the common-placeness of the thinking or the absence of any real content (see also section 13b on the additional dangers of the use of *clichés*). Certain key words betray him, however. He is addicted to *factor, case, basis, elements, phenomenon, field, objectives,* and *fundamental assumptions, in terms of, in the nature of, with reference to.* He does not, remarks the *London Times,* speak of people who go but of *personnel who proceed.* "They do not have, they are (or more often are not) in posses-sion of. They do not ask, they make application for . . . . They cannot eat, they only consume; they perform ablutions; in-stead of homes they have places of residence in which, instead of living, they are domiciled. They are not cattle, they are not ciphers, they certainly are not human beings; they are person-nel."

D

Most subjects require some technical terms with precise meanings and for exact discriminations (but see section 13c for a discussion of excessively technical writing). These terms only become jargon when they are borrowed and used loosely by those outside the field to impress others or themselves—for example, the student who talks about "the leader-follower *field*" or who speaks of his *"interpersonal relationships"* with his family. Somewhat similarly, utility words like *thing, situation,* and *emotion* are helpful and necessary at times, but when a paper is cluttered with sentences in which the writer "had a deep *emotion* over the *situation*" and will "remember this *thing* as long as he lives," there is little real content. The specific emotion, situation, or thing remains unnamed and therefore unintelligible.

12 d
inappropriate connotation

Choose words with the exact connotation required by the context.

In addition to their *denotation* (literal meaning), words have a *connotation,* a fringe of associations and overtones which makes them appropriate in certain situations but not to others. *House, home,* and *domicile* all have the same denotation—a place of residence. But their connotations are quite different: *house* emphasizes the physical structure; *home* suggests family life, warmth, comfort, affection; *domicile* has strictly legal overtones.

The connotation of each word should be appropriate to the context. One could not write a sentimental song entitled "House, Sweet House," nor could he comfortably speak of the official residence of the President of the United States as "The White Home." Similarly, he might ask a stranger, "Are you *married?*" but would not (as once did a foreign intern in a hospital) inquire, "Are you *mated?*" One learns the connotations of a word by seeing the word in different contexts. *Trip,* for instance, usually appears in a context which indicates a short distance ("to the city," or "a trip to Europe this summer," if it is a quick, short one by jet); *journey* is used for slow travel over long distances ("a journey to Australia by boat"). Your dictionary distinguishes the connotations of many near-synonyms, and special dictionaries of synonyms, like Roget's *Thesaurus* or *Webster's Dictionary of Synonyms,* are available; users should distinguish cautiously among near-synonyms.

12 e
incorrect use of idiom

Use the idiom most appropriate to your subject and your reader.

An idiom is an expression peculiar to the language and not explainable by principles of logic or the ordinary meaning of the individual words. Why do we say that a person is *on duty, in trouble,* or *at play?* The only answer is that these are idiomatic combinations. How can a foreigner who knows the words *take, in, up, down,* and *over,* deduce the meaning of *take in* (comprehend), *taken in* (fooled), *take up* (begin to consider), *take down* (humiliate), *take over* and *overtake?*

Idiom requires that some words be followed by arbitrarily fixed prepositions. Something may be *required of* all students, *compulsory for* all, *necessary to* all, or *obligatory on* all. Here are some major idiomatic uses of prepositions:

> agree *to* a proposal; *on* a procedure; *with* a person
> angry *at* or *about* something; *with* a person
> argue *with* a person; *for* or *against* or *about* a measure
> compare *to* a similar item; *with* a contrasting or dissimilar one
> correspond *to* or *with* a thing; *with* a person
> differ *from* one another in appearance; differ *with* a person in opinion
> independent *of*
> interest *in*
> listen *to* a person, argument, or sound; listen *at* the door

D

possessed *by* or *with* an idea or emotion; *by* a spirit; *of* goods

with regard *to* or *as* regards

stay *at* home

superior *to*

wait *on* a customer; wait *for* a person; wait *at* a place

Idiom demands that certain words be followed by infinitives, others by gerunds. For instance:

infinitive	*gerund*
able to go	capable of going
like to go	enjoy going
eager to go	cannot help going
hesitate to go	privilege of going

If two idioms are used in a compound construction, each idiom must be complete (see section 8g-2).

INCOMPLETE   He had no love or confidence in his employer.
COMPLETE BUT AWKWARD   He had no **love for,** or **confidence in,** his employer.
IMPROVED   He had no love for his employer and no confidence in him.

INCOMPLETE   I shall always remember the town because of the good times and the friends I made there.
COMPLETE   I shall always remember the town because of the **good times I had** and the **friends I made** there.

EXERCISES

a. Give several specific or concrete words for each general or abstract word. For example: *cloth: velvet, satin, taffeta, linen, burlap.*

1. Nouns: *examination, car, bird, goodness, clothing, surprise.*
2. Verbs: *to look, to laugh, to talk, to entertain, to walk.*
3. Adjectives: *unpleasant* person, *cold* day, *interesting* evening, *young, dark.*

b. Make the following student sentences more specific and concrete.

1. We couldn't get started on the float that night because
   of bad weather.
2. The family liked to show its financial standing by driving expensive sports cars and wearing imported clothing.
3. Many tract homes are made out of cheap materials and
   decorated in bad taste.
4. One reason that I enjoy football and basketball is that
   I like sports with real action to them.
5. During high school I had real trouble with my foreign
   language courses but in college so far I have found it
   much easier.
6. The expedition encountered a serious difficulty, which
   delayed its departure for some time.
7. By her own efforts she overcame her handicap of bad
   health and the emotional problems it caused.
8. One of my hobbies is music.
9. Something was wrong with the elevator, so they had a
   hard time getting up to the office.
10. The effect of a setting like the Grand Canyon on people
    is truly remarkable.

c. Revise the following student sentences by giving them forceful
verbs or verb forms.

1. Volpone's role in playing the game of deceiving the
   people is easily seen.
2. It was soon discovered by the new settlers that life in
   the colonies was not utopian.
3. But the ironic tone of the poem is necessary so that the
   realization that the characters are slaves to conformity
   can be made.
4. Later that afternoon a violent argument between my
   roommate and me occurred.
5. Our teacher was in a hurry to leave because there had
   been a phone call for him from his wife who was expecting a child.
6. Throughout the whole series of discussions on Student
   Values, a feeling of candor and self-examination existed.

D

7. The increasing competition for college admissions would seem to illustrate the fact that students who have only an average record are going to have trouble getting any kind of higher education.

8. Great flocks of sandpipers and gulls could be seen along the edge of the beach as we approached.

9. Only about half of the freshman class was present at the last rally and they appeared to be pretty feeble in their cheering.

d. By using jargon and utility words, inflate and obscure the following sentences.

1. Employees are asked to turn out all lights before leaving the plant.

2. While wandering through Spain, Don Quixote meets the rich and the poor, the educated and uneducated.

3. To relieve congestion, the city planners should restrict more streets to one-way traffic.

4. I took a course in public speaking to gain confidence and poise.

e. Eliminate the jargon and utility words in the following student sentences and make each sentence as intelligible as you can.

1. Education aggregates distinctive qualities in a person and impresses a characteristic individuality.

2. While in college, the student should participate in social and recreational activities if he is to gain all the advantages of a higher education.

3. The selection of a medical man thoroughly versed in the skills of his profession is a matter of supreme importance to the individual.

4. This idea of the variability of the standards of conduct would be challenged by some people in terms of the religious values they have.

5. This preconceived opinion was not based on experience or any factors of evidence; however, it gave the criticizers a mental feeling of superiority.

6. Dentistry is a good profession and has a number of aspects which are worthy of individual research.

7. Personality conflicts can cause embarrassing situations

for both parties involved if they meet at a social occasion.

8. Frost's "Mending Wall" is not outstandingly poetic, although it is well-written and artistic.

9. In the case of the student who was injured during the demonstration, this type of incident is responsible for giving the college a bad reputation, and if such an incident were to occur again there might be tragic consequences of great importance.

f. Explain the difference in connotation between the words in the following pairs.

1. violin, fiddle	9. biased, prejudiced
2. sympathy, pity	10. infant, baby
3. marsh, swamp	11. stare, gape
4. upset, agitated	12. hurt, injure
5. break, shatter	13. old, elderly
6. waste, squander	14. mutt, mongrel
7. joy, ecstasy	15. tease, torment
8. gobble, gorge	

g. For the following words, find synonyms whose connotations fit under the headings listed below.

commonplace, neutral	crude or derogatory	slang	elevated, literary
girl	slut	bod	maiden
boy			
food			
money			
complain			
go away			
car			
liquor			

h. Some of the following student sentences tell truths unintended by the writer; some are merely inappropriate in their connotations. Revise their diction for exactness.

1. His immaturity may improve with age.

2. The basic objective of the indoctrination program is to build strong class spirit and to weed out those who are leaders in the class.

3. Lee had a fine formal education and he ended up going to West Point.
4. Darwin's *Origin of the Species* began an epic of materialism.
5. Margaret Mead's book had a great success because Americans are grossly interested in sex.
6. The words that bring pictures to your mind are lovely and lush.
7. I flitted away my first three years in college.
8. Jefferson and Madison were two of the most prolific characters our nation produced at that time in history.
9. Watching attentively, I saw the tall lean stature of a man hop briskly from the car.
10. Her shrewish temper leads her to disregard common social politeness and essential consideration until she not only has debauched herself but her husband.

i. Correct the violations of English idiom in the following student sentences.

1. Shelley was washed out on the shore.
2. Most often, however, a taxpayer will cheat with his own incentive.
3. One of the main issues which came out concerned the adoption of a compulsory health program of the nation.
4. Sixth grade teachers first introduce homework to the student in any large scale.
5. If anyone does poorly in the first few games, chances are the bench will be next.
6. About his eyes are the etched lines caused by years of hard work.
7. Get a dog with a keen nose because you can teach a dog to point but you can't make him smell good.
8. Jonson thought Shakespeare knew no Latin and less Greek.
9. He has thoroughly analyzed, computed, and consulted the problem with renowned men all over the world.
10. One aspect of Joyce's writing I didn't care for was the way he exaggerated on certain unimportant parts in a story.

13

effective diction

In addition to being exact, your diction should be effective; that is, you should try to make it easy and pleasant for a reader to grasp what you are saying. An awkward, pretentious, or repetitious style will antagonize readers. Prevent this by keeping your diction natural and simple, direct and concise. Your writing need not be boring if you make it lively with fresh, unhackneyed phrases and if you shun needless technical language.

13 a
pretentious diction

Keep your language simple and direct. Avoid expressions which are deliberately pretentious, ingenious, or exotically foreign.

Written prose is usually somewhat more formal than the spoken language, but according to current taste, expository language should not be ornate or pretentious. A reader is apt to lose faith in the sincerity of the writer who decorates his sentences.

PRETENTIOUS The heavens were dark save for the myriad twinkling of God's candles, the stars which glittered like the eyes of snakes through the bitter chill of air as cold as outer space.

PLAIN AND IMPROVED The stars sparkled in a clear and bitterly cold night.

D

PRETENTIOUS It is my conviction that by examining Carr's reasoning we shall be in a position to decide as to the real validity of his hypotheses and conclusions concerning the Williamson case.

PLAIN AND IMPROVED I wish to examine Carr's theories about the Williamson case to see what truth they may have.

Rich and figurative language is not necessarily bad in itself, but it is very difficult to use well, and can often lead to grotesque effects on inappropriate occasions. People who consistently crave elaborate, ornate sentences in preference to plain statements are asking to be tricked by the advertising copywriter and the used-car salesman. Figurative language must be very good and very original to be at all useful in your writing. It is better to be simple and unpretentious than to offend readers with what the *New Yorker* sardonically calls "rich, beautiful prose."

PRETENTIOUS The installment plan equalizes all men in their ability to obtain the goods of our great industrial society and to achieve a higher standard of living.

SIMPLE AND IMPROVED Under the installment plan, both the rich and the poor have improved their standards of living.

PRETENTIOUS As the crowd slowly but surely departed from the suddenly silent stadium, the last rays of the sun were replaced by the gathering gloom of evening.

SIMPLE AND IMPROVED It was already dark as the crowd silently made its way out of the stadium.

The desire to avoid monotony is a motive that may lead untried readers into the trap of pretentious diction and a straining for ingenuity or novelty. Insecure writers often cherish the notion that they are achieving originality by avoiding ordinary words and substituting ingenious phrases.

ordinary word	strained circumlocution
dog	faithful canine friend
fish	denizen of the deep
girl	member of the fairer sex
hit	smacked the horsehide

large house	imposing edifice
man	*homo sapiens*
married	state of connubial bliss
passed	tossed the pigskin
university	institution of higher learning

Such awkward expressions may often be used in an attempt to avoid repeating an ordinary word. Although frequent repetition can be annoying, it is preferable to the sound of pretentiousness in would-be elegant variations. See chapters 12 and 7 through 9 for better ways of avoiding monotony with fresh diction and varied sentences (see also section 13e).

Foreign words and phrases, likewise, often suggest that a writer is hoping to impress readers with an inflated idea of his superior knowledge. Foreign expressions are necessary when there is no English equivalent to convey the exact meaning, as in *blitzkrieg, a priori, laissez faire, slalom.* But foreign phrases like the following should be avoided, since English equivalents are available.

foreign phrase	*English equivalent*
entre nous	between us
joie de vivre	enjoyment of life
sub rosa	secret or secretly
Sturm und Drang	storm and stress

13 b
clichés

Guard against the use of clichés. Keep alert to worn-out expressions.

"Hungry as bears" may once have been effective, but it has been worn out by constant repetition. The phrase has become a *cliché.* If it has any effect at all, it is to make one's writing sound tired and stale. While it is probably impossible for a writer to remove all clichés from his writing, he ought to eliminate as many of them as he can catch. Frank Sullivan, the *New Yorker's* "cliché expert," has been collecting trite expres-

D

sions for years without exhausting the supply. The list below illustrates the kind of hackneyed expression you should guard against.

abreast of times	last but not least
acid test	mother nature
agony of suspense	neat as a pin
all nature seemed clothed in	partake of refreshments
as luck would have it	poor but honest
beat a hasty retreat	proud possessor of
bitter end	quick as a flash
blushing bride	reigns supreme
bolt from the blue	rotten to the core
breathless silence	slow but sure
checkered career	speculation was rife
cool as a cucumber	steady as a rock
deep, dark secret	tiny tots
depths of despair	tired but happy
do justice to a meal	undercurrent of excitement
doomed to disappointment	untiring efforts
dull, sickening thud	wee small hours
fair sex	wended their way
green with envy	work like a horse
herculean efforts	working like Trojans

Avoid hackneyed quotations, literary allusions, and proverbs, such as:

truth is stranger than fiction
method in his madness
sadder but wiser
variety is the spice of life
all work and no play
never put off till tomorrow what you can do today
make hay while the sun shines
music hath charms
ignorance is bliss

The best way to eliminate trite phrases from your writing is to sharpen your awareness of them so that you don't lapse into them. The clichés in the following passage show how easy it is to fall unthinkingly into stereotyped diction:

Mr. Arbuthnot—They have not kept nor do they intend to keep . . . They have undermined the foundations . . . They constitute a threat to our democratic institutions . . . And I say to you, my fellow-Americans . . .

Q—Mr. Arbuthnot, I can tell what you're up to. . . . You're being a campaign orator again.

A—That's right. . . . Guess what kind of disclosures I plan to reveal in my speech at Wichita next week.

Q—What kind?

A—Mounting disclosures of graft and corruption

Q—Where?

A—In high places. You know, of course, what my favorite brand of faith is.

Q—No. What?

A—An abiding faith. In the destiny of our g-reat democracy.

Q—Do you still prefer your indifference callous?

A—Yes, and my national debts astronomical, my corruption shameful, my courage invincible, my violations flagrant, and my appeals ringing. . . .

Q—Your abuse is reckless, I suppose.

A—No. The other side's abuse is reckless. I do not indulge in personalities. I confine myself to solemn obligations, political expediency, disloyal elements, supreme goals, historic roles, honest toil, headlong plunges, glowing words, empty phrases, giant strides, sordid business, secret understandings, eternal vigilance, staggering costs, paramount issues, valiant sons, jaundiced critics, painful necessities, governmental folly, and the great heart land of the South, also the great heart lands of the North, East, and West. . . .

Q—Whom are you going to call upon in your speeches?

A—I speak from the heart when I say to you that my candidate is a man unafraid, a man in whom there is no guile, who is equal to the task, whose name is a household word, who has worked untiringly, who is one of the outstanding, who has embarked on a career, who has not failed his country, who is a consistent advocate of, who has answered the call, and who will resist every attempt to encroach. . . .

Q—How does your man stand, Arbuthnot?

A—On his own two feet. . . . He faces facts, or grim reality. He will lead us out of the morass. His deeds will be writ large. His words will be engraved.

Q—Where?

A—On the hearts of his countrymen.

Q—Therefore you, as a stump speaker, do what?

A—Therefore, my friends, I take great pleasure. It is my firm belief. I can unhesitatingly say. And I need not remind you. Yet I cannot agree.

Q—Whom can't you agree with?

A—I cannot agree with those who. Yet there *are* those who. I defy them.

Q—How do you speak when you defy those who?

A—I speak not as a Republican or a Democrat but as an American.   —Frank Sullivan

13 c
excessive technical terms

Minimize the use of technical terms and make plain the meaning of those few which are necessary.

In writing addressed to specialists, technical terms are appropriate, and sometimes, in writing for a general audience, technical expressions have to be used because no others are available. In such cases, be sure to explain the meanings for the nontechnical reader. Unnecessarily technical language, however, runs the risk of turning into *jargon* (see section 12e). As a general rule, writing aimed at the general reader should avoid technical terms which are not commonly understood, even though more words may be required to say the same thing in plain English.

TOO TECHNICAL This book gives an elaborate account of the construction and validation of the English placement

Fig

13
d

test for college freshmen, with a study of the predictive significance of this examination, and also discusses the adequacy of bases for homogeneous grouping in freshman English.

IMPROVED This book explains in detail how the English placement test for college freshmen was constructed and checked for reliability and validity. (Reliability means consistency of performance: a reliable test will give nearly the same results when administered a second time to the same students. Validity means that the test measures the kind of ability or knowledge it was intended to measure.) The book goes on to discuss the test's accuracy in predicting the future performance of students taking English. Finally it criticizes the methods and standards by which students are assigned to high, middle, or low ability sections in Freshman English.

13 d
mixed figures of speech and worn allusions

Be sure that figures of speech and allusions are fresh, appropriate, and consistent.

A figure of speech is a comparison, either stated or implied, between two things which are unlike except in one particular. In a *simile* a comparison between two different items is explicitly indicated by a term such as "like" or "as"; for example, James Joyce's story, "Araby," uses a simile to communicate the loneliness of a bazaar after most of the crowd has left: "Nearly all the stalls were closed and the greater part of the hall was in darkness. I recognized a silence *like that* which pervades a church after a service."

In a *metaphor* a word which normally signifies one kind of thing or action is applied to another without the use of "like" or "as." Communist countries are not literally "behind the iron curtain," yet the metaphor "behind the iron curtain" evokes a sharp image of the hostility, imprisonment, and exclusion which have existed. Similarly, when Randall Jarrell describes a college president who "crooned" his speeches in a

D

voice that "not only took you into his confidence, but laid a fire for you and put out your slippers by it and then went into the other room to get into something more comfortable," we are made to know the man and the type only too well.

English is full of what are called *dead metaphors* (the figure "sleeping metaphor" might actually be more exact), such as "the *leg* of a table," "the *hands* of the clock," and "the *arm* of government," in which we are no longer even conscious of the distinction between the literal and the metaphoric use. Occasionally the context may make one of these "wake up" or "come alive," tricking us with a mixed figure of speech.

In an *allusion* the comparison made is between some present event, situation, or person and an event or person from history or literature. Usually it is a brief reference to something which the reader is assumed to be familiar with, as when E. M. Forster says, "My lawgivers are Erasmus and Montaigne, not Moses and St. Paul." Unless he is deliberately being far-fetched or esoteric, the writer has the right to hope that his reader will look up unfamiliar allusions.

Figures of speech—especially metaphors—and allusions are used to give vividness and color to writing. To be effective, figurative language must not only avoid the trite ("She was mad as a wet hen") but also be consistent and appropriate. Strained or incongruous comparisons may be deliberately used for humorous effect as in

> And like a lobster boiled, the morn
> From black to red began to turn.

or

> Whenever he saw a spark of genius, he watered it.

But when they appear in serious writing, forced or confused figures of speech are merely distracting or unintentionally comic. The student who wrote, "The *road* to success has many slippery *rungs* and tricky *pitfalls*" obviously had done very little walking or climbing, just as the student who wrote "The empty stalls of the cowshed were like a desolate garden in late November" had not taken a good, hard look at a cowshed recently.

MIXED FIGURE This young attorney is rapidly gaining a foothold in the public eye.

13
e

Either of these metaphors is satisfactory by itself: "gaining a foothold" is drawn from mountain climbing; "in the public eye" personifies the public. But together they call up an unfortunate picture of the young attorney digging his toe into the eye of the public.

INCONGRUOUS Maddened by its voracious, sharklike appetite, the baby screamed for its bottle.

A "voracious appetite" is a characteristic of sharks, their huge jaws opening, their snapping white teeth gouging out huge hunks of bloody flesh. But the image is grotesque when used as a description of a crying child.

Sometimes, misspellings or errors in diction can produce unintentionally comic images or puns. Arguing very earnestly against short haircuts, one student wrote, "A chopped up head of hair is *pointless*"; another urged, "Maybe if we took *stalk* of foreign aid, we would be able to change it." Similarly, when a writer uses an allusion he does not understand, the results will be different from what he intended. The student who complained that among his friends "A football player is stereotyped as an *Amazon*" did not mean that tackles, guards, and quarterbacks are commonly thought of as tall, spear-bearing, breast-plated female warriors.

13 e
awkward repetition

Read a paper aloud to catch the unpleasant echo produced by needless repetition.

Sometimes a word or phrase is deliberately repeated, and the writer capitalizes on the echo for emphasis or to make a meaning clear. Deliberate repetition of a word may also be preferable to straining after synonyms. But the echo caused by the needless repetition of a word or phrase is disturbing. Reading a paper aloud is the best means to detect this awkwardness.

D

DELIBERATE REPETITION   Harriet came to spend the last week in May with us, and strangely enough the last week in May was the only time George could come for a visit.

> **AWKWARD**   He said that the orders said that uniforms must be worn.
>
> **IMPROVED**   He said that the order required uniforms to be worn.

> **AWKWARD**   Probably the next problem that confronts a parent is the problem of adequate schooling for his children.
>
> **IMPROVED**   The parent's next problem is providing adequate schooling for his children.

Particularly awkward is the repetition of a word which has two different meanings in the sentence.

> **AWKWARD**   The *object* of the expedition was to investigate the *object* which had fallen from the sky.
>
> **IMPROVED**   The *purpose* of the expedition was to investigate the object which had fallen from the sky.

> **AWKWARD**   The mother *ordered* the children to stop roughhousing in the livingroom and to put things back in *order.*
>
> **IMPROVED**   The mother ordered the children to stop roughhousing in the livingroom and to *straighten things up.*

Noticeable repetition of sounds or other poetic devices is out of place in ordinary prose.

> **OBJECTIONABLE**   Then came the time for heart-*breaking* leave-*taking.*
>
> **OBJECTIONABLE**   To keep up the dis*play,* the fountains were kept *play*ing night and *day.*
>
> **OBJECTIONABLE**   The *old* woman *sold* a *cold mould*ed jello salad.

Combinations of sounds which are difficult to pronounce should be avoided in writing, as in speech.

> **CACAPHONOUS**   Our statistics show that she should sell seven sets a day.
>
> **CACAPHONOUS**   The big black Buick backed up against the curb.

EXERCISES

a. Inflate the following sentences by using pretentious diction and circumlocutions.

1. Whenever I get tired of dormitory life and I can find the time, I take a long, quiet walk across the campus.
2. Cheap paint will fade when exposed to bright sunlight.
3. I am not sure what my major will be, but I do know I want a broad education in the liberal arts.
4. Rasmussen was high scorer on the basketball team, an excellent miler, and a fine tennis player.

b. Revise the following student sentences by changing the pretentious diction and the circumlocutions to clear, direct phrasing.

1. His restriction of the number of characters facilitates the reader's ability to follow the sequence of the action.
2. Soon a complete metamorphosis came over Macbeth and his fear of destruction was replaced by his belief that he was invulnerable and unconquerable.
3. Usually, my car is my means of transportation for getting to my job.
4. Canines are the most affectionate members of the animal kingdom.
5. Thus, it is my contention that every participant in the demonstration was a representative of the school and must therefore be prepared to take the responsibility for disgracing the school's unblemished reputation.

c. Using Frank Sullivan's "Mr. Arbuthnot" as a model, take any one of the following topics and write a hundred-word paragraph in which you employ only clichés. Subtract one point for every word which is not part of a trite phrase. A perfect score is 100.

1. A speech on the dangers of some "ism."
2. A speech on what makes up a "well-rounded person."
3. A speech on the irresponsibility or depravity of the "youth of today."

d. Revise the following student sentences by eliminating the clichés.

1. If Prendergast was good for anything he was good for nothing.

D

2. In this modern day and age, the discovery of atomic energy will lead a path to many new inventions.

3. When the news leaked out, all of us were in an agony of suspense except for my grandfather, who remained cool and collected.

4. The Suez Canal is a monument to the brave men who fought against a hostile environment and seemingly overwhelming odds.

e. Analyze the following student sentences to determine which figures of speech and allusions are effective and which are not. If a figure is mixed or inappropriate or an allusion is misleading, be prepared to explain why.

1. Thus, the young athletes are the workhorses that made the ends of the budget meet to form a vicious circle.

2. Our balloons of egotism filled with the air of freshman knowledge were soon to be pricked by the pin-points of self-awakening.

3. As the town grew, the theatre obtained a foothold and the newspaper began to plant its roots.

4. His purity and courage definitely overshadow the grid of morality placed on him, making it into a mockery.

5. This is the Achilles' heel of their position. For once a set of ideas are ruled fair game for witch-hunters, Pandora's box has been opened, and there is no ending.

6. Drinking seems to have its claw in the economy of San Francisco.

7. Our tariff wall will continue to be an unsurmountable obstacle until we throw a span across the ebb to link the rest of the world to our industrial growth.

8. Pouring through *Paradise Lost* was like wading in deep water.

9. The only time Huck's relationship with Jim is marred is when the taint of society's ideas concerning slavery intrudes upon Huck's consciousness of what he is doing.

10. A good education is the trunk for a good life for it is the origin of all the branches which are your later accomplishments.

f. Determine what word, image, or reference the writer meant to use in each of the following student sentences. In some cases, you will have to sacrifice comedy for accuracy.

1. The hazing in the dorms ought to be abolished for three pacific reasons.
2. My grade on the first test did not help my piece of mind.
3. The Japanese began to play hobby with China in 1937.
4. They believe that earthly life is a hamper to man's soul.
5. Johnson and Boswell got along so well because they complimented each other.
6. Sam said she would have to brandish the roast before she could serve it.
7. Pearl Buck early adopted the Chinese attitude towards life, death, and immorality.
8. In the room can be heard inaudible moans and grumblings.
9. The Prime Minister hoped, with the King out of the way, to take over the reigns of government for himself.
10. Females are the worst violators of this crime.

g. Revise the following sentences to eliminate pretentious language, trite phrases, inappropriate figures of speech, and awkward repetition.

1. A plumber needs to know more than just plumbing if he is going to install new plumbing fixtures in an old house.
2. To achieve good health, a person must build on the foundation of his native endowment, developing and training it for effective functioning.
3. Democracy in parts of far-off Asia is slowly being strangled by a lack of contact with democratic ideas.
4. For some students, adequate education finances are likely to be lacking.
5. The only guest still left was the lady who had sat on my left at dinner, and she left soon after.
6. Some people take a fiendish delight in not minding their own business.
7. I can hear every noise in the hall through my walls and it annoys me whenever I try to study.
8. At every meeting the senator was the center of attention and his fame grew by leaps and bounds.

9. An understanding of the Oriental viewpoint in terms of Eastern philosophies and literature would contribute greatly to bridging the gap between East and West.
10. Student activities are activities which are open to student participation.

REVIEW EXERCISES

Revise the following student sentences to make the diction more exact and effective. For each sentence, identify the error in idiom, weak verb, misleading connotation, pretentious term, or inappropriate figure and then make the necessary changes.

1. He himself was wounded in the leg but he seemed as though this was a normal event.
2. In the 18th century, form was very formal, not only in poetry but also in formal gardens, experimental architecture, and painting.
3. Public schools offer advantages which, I believe, add up to a well-rounded person.
4. We were then in eminent danger of having the avalanche come down on us.
5. In order to gain a complete education, a person might study the relationship of knowledge to philosophy and to religion.
6. The personnel are quite effective in the sense that they convey the trend of thought that existed during the time of the novel.
7. This belief is illustrated in a quote by C. S. Lewis.
8. Few people realize it but today's schools contain conditions which will guide our future American adults into strong-charactered individuals or perhaps grafty business men.
9. The name Marie is just a variance of the name Mary.
10. With the assassination of Peter I and with Napoleon climbing the steps of Russia, Alexander I ascended the throne.

14

for
8 Dec 69

glossary of words commonly misused

This glossary discusses only some of the more commonly misused words, and it should be supplemented by a good, recent dictionary for detailed information on words not included here. The usage labels employed here have been standardized as much as possible with current dictionaries and contemporary research, though a few dictionaries (*Webster's Third International,* for example) have abandoned the term *colloquial* which is retained here. Chapter 11 discusses in detail levels of usage and the contexts in which each is appropriate.

Note that the label *colloquial* means that a word is frequently used in speech and for writing in a conversational style, as distinguished from carefully edited or formal writing.

> A good working principle is to avoid colloquialisms in serious writing unless you have a special reason for using them.

In general, this handbook advocates all three levels of Standard English as a goal for educated speech, but prefers the informal and formal levels for college writing. Words here labelled *nonstandard, substandard, dialectal,* and *slang* are not appropriate in college writing. Further discussion of usage status appears in the last section of chapter 15.

D

A, An   Indefinite *articles* (see chapter 22). *A* is used before words beginning with a consonant sound, *an* before words beginning with a vowel sound. Before *h*, the *an* form precedes the few words in which the *h* is silent (e.g., an *herb*); usually the *h* is considered to be pronounced (aspirated), and the *a* form is used (e.g., a *history* book).

Above   As an adjective, preferably confined to legal documents, since many readers and writers object to its use in ordinary writing. Often used in speaking to mean *preceding* or *foregoing*.

>   COLLOQUIAL   The above remarks should be taken seriously.
>
>   PREFERRED IN WRITING   These remarks should be taken seriously.
>
>   PREFERRED IN WRITING   The lines quoted above prove the point.

Accept   Not to be confused with *except;* consult dictionary.

Ad   An abbreviated form of *advertisement* not appropriate in formal writing.

Affect   Not to be confused with *effect;* consult dictionary.

Aggravate   Means *to intensify* or *to make worse;* as *The shock aggravated his misery.* Colloquially it means to *annoy, irritate, arouse the anger of.*

Agree to, Agree on, Agree with   See section 12e.

Ain't   A nonstandard contraction of *am not, is not,* or *are not.*

Alibi   Means, in legal usage, an assertion that one was elsewhere when the crime was committed. Colloquial when used to mean *an excuse* or *to make an excuse.*

All right   All right is still the standard spelling. When used to mean *good, honest, dependable,* as in *He's an all right guy,* the phrase is slang.

Alright   Substandard for *all right.*

Already   An adverb meaning *by this time.* Not to be confused with *all ready,* which means *completely ready.*
STANDARD   The hotel was already full.
STANDARD   They were all ready to go.

Alternative   Strictly, means *choice between two things.* Now widely used to mean *a choice between more than two things,* and so defined in dictionaries.

Alumnus   A Latin word now standard in English for *male graduate* of a school. A female graduate is an *alumna* (the Latin feminine form). The plurals are, respectively, *alumni* (m.) and *alumnae* (f.); often these are pronounced almost identically.

Among   See **Between.**

Amount, Number   See **Less, Fewer.**

And etc.   A redundancy. *Etc.* is an abbreviation of Latin *et* (and) plus *cetera* (others). See **Etc.**

Anyplace, Everyplace, No place, Someplace   Colloquialisms for *anywhere, everywhere, nowhere, somewhere.*

Anyways, Anywheres   The first is dialectal for *anyway, in any case;* the second is dialectal for *anywhere.* Compare **Anyplace.**

Apt   Often considered colloquial when used to mean *likely.*

As   Dialectal when used in place of that, as in *I don't know that* (not *as*) we can go; dialectal when used in place of

D

who as in *Those who* (not *as*) *know him trust him. Because* and *since* are clearer than *as* for introducing clauses, showing causal relationship.

At about   Prefer *about* in writing; *at about* is overworked and redundant.
PREFERRED IN WRITING   He came *about* three o'clock.

Awful, Awfully   Often colloquially used as an intensive for *very* or *extremely*. Prefer the latter forms.

A while   Nonstandard when used for *awhile;* consult dictionary.

Badly   Colloquially used for *a great deal* or *very much* with verbs signifying *want* or *need.*
COLLOQUIAL   I want badly to see you.
PREFERRED IN WRITING   I want very much to see you.

Besides   Means *additionally* or *in addition to.* Not to be confused with *beside,* which is always a preposition meaning *by the side of,* as *beside the house.*

Between   Often used with more than two objects, but some speakers still distinguish *among,* as applying to more than two objects, from *between,* as applying to only two. Compare **Alternative.**

But   Often used colloquially with a negative implication (compare **Hardly**) in such idioms as *I can't help but think* = *I cannot but think* (cannot avoid not thinking) = *I must think* (preferred in writing).

But what   A colloquialism sometimes used for *that,* with a negative implication; often used with an accompanying negative or positive verb in many colloquial idioms.
COLLOQUIAL WITH NEGATIVE   I don't doubt but what he's lying. = I think he's lying.

PREFERRED IN WRITING I don't doubt that he's lying.
COLLOQUIAL WITH POSITIVE I'm not sure but what he's right. = Perhaps he is right.
PREFERRED IN WRITING I'm not sure (that) he isn't right.

Can, May Now used interchangeably to signify permission, but some speakers still distinguish *may,* as implying permission, from *can,* as implying ability.

Can't hardly See **Hardly.**

Can't help but Colloquial. See **But.**

Compare to, Compare with See section 12e.

Complected Nonstandard for *complexioned.*
NONSTANDARD A light-complected girl.
PREFERRED A light-complexioned girl.

Contact Chiefly and correctly used as a noun. It is in wide nonstandard use as a verb to mean *consult, confer, telephone, speak to, look up,* but many people find this use objectionable.
NONSTANDARD I did not contact any of my old friends during my vacation.
PREFERRED I did not telephone any of my old friends during my vacation.

Continual Not always synonymous with *continuous.* In modern usage *continual* is used of events that are intermittent but recurrent: The *continual* dripping of the rain. *Continuous* is used of time and space, and implies an absence of interruption: the *continuous* flow of the river.

Could of See **Of.**

Data, Phenomena, Strata Latin plural, not singular forms, and so used in formal scholarly writing. But the use of

D

data with a singular verb is widespread. The singular forms are *datum, phenomenon,* and *stratum.*

INFORMAL This data has been taken from the last Census Report.

FORMAL These data have been taken from the last Census Report.

Different Usually followed by *from,* but *than* is gaining acceptance.

Don't A contraction of *do not.* Not to be used in formal writing with a subject in the third person singular.

SUBSTANDARD He don't know.

PREFERRED He doesn't know.

Due When followed by *to,* widely used to mean *because of* or *owing to,* though still questioned by some when used in an adverbial phrase. *Because of* is safer in formal writing.

COLLOQUIAL The snowplow stalled due to the mounting drifts.

PREFERRED IN WRITING The snowplow's failure to reach us was due to the snow's mealy consistency.

In strict usage, "due" is an adjective. In this example, "due" modifies "failure."

FORMAL The snowplow failed to reach us because of the landslide.

Effect See **Affect.**

Either, Neither Preferably used in writing to designate one of two persons or things; colloquially, one of three or more. In formal writing, prefer *none* to *neither* when referring to one of three or more items.

COLLOQUIAL I asked Leahy, Mahoney, and McGinty, but neither of them was willing.

PREFERRED IN WRITING Leahy said that either Mahoney or McGinty would show us around.

FORMAL I asked Leahy, Mahoney, and McGinty, but none of them was willing.

Emigrate   Means *leave a country;* often confused with *immigrate* (enter a country); consult dictionary.

Enthuse   Common in speech, but to be avoided in writing. Prefer *enthusiastic.*
>   COLLOQUIAL   Everyone was enthused about the idea.
>   PREFERRED IN WRITING   Everyone was enthusiastic about the idea.

Equally as good   A confusion of two phrases: *equally good* and *just as good.* Use either of the two phrases in place of *equally as good.*
STANDARD   Their radio cost much more than ours, but ours is equally good.
STANDARD   Our radio is just as good as theirs.

Etc.   Avoid the vague use of *etc.;* use it only to avoid useless repetition or informally to represent terms that are entirely obvious from the context.
>   VAGUE   She was more beautiful, witty, virtuous, etc., than any other lady.
PREFERRED   She was more beautiful, witty, and virtuous than any other lady.
INFORMAL   Her biographers portray her as beautiful, witty, virtuous, charming, etc.

Every place   See **Anyplace.**

Except (verb)   See **Accept.**

Expect   Colloquial when used to mean *suppose, presume.*
>   COLLOQUIAL   I expect it's time for us to go.
PREFERRED IN WRITING   I suppose it's time for us to go.

Factor   Means *something which contributes to a result;* as *Industry and perseverance were factors in his success.* Should be used with an intelligent regard to its meaning (see section 12c for a discussion of *jargon*).

D

INEXACT   Being ducked in the lake is an inevitable factor in the freshman's experience.
STANDARD   Being ducked in the lake is an inevitable *part* of the freshman's experience.

Farther, Further   In careful usage *farther* indicates distance; *further* indicates degree and also means *additional.* Both are used as adjectives and as adverbs: *a mile farther, further disintegration, further details.*

Faze, Phase   Commonly confused; consult dictionary.

Fewer   See **Less.**

Fine (1)   Means *refined, delicate, free from impurity, of excellent quality: fine cutlery, fine dust, fine sense of honor, fine gold.* Widely and somewhat loosely used as an epithet of approval: *a fine person, a fine ship.* Prefer a more exact descriptive word.

Fine (2)   Colloquial when used as an adverb to mean *well* or *very well:*
COLLOQUIAL   The motor works fine. I feel fine.
PREFERRED IN WRITING   The motor works well. I feel very well.

First-rate   An adjective meaning *of the first order* or *finest class.* Colloquial as an adjective meaning *excellent* or *very good,* or as an adverb meaning *excellently* or *well.*
COLLOQUIAL   He plays tennis first-rate.
PREFERRED IN WRITING   It is a first-rate building.

Fix (1)   (noun) Colloquial for *situation* or *condition.*

Fix (2)   (verb) Widely used in the United States for *repair* or *arrange.* The expression *fix up* is a colloquialism.

Flunk   Colloquial for *fail;* not to be used in formal writing.

Former, Latter Preferably used to designate one of two persons or things, not one of three or more (compare **Either, Neither**). For designating one of three or more, say *first* or *last*.

Gentleman, Lady Used to indicate persons of cultivation, refinement, or good social standing. To indicate sex differences in compound words use *man* and *woman*.
   STANDARD   Men's clothing, cleaning woman, repairman, saleswoman.
   STANDARD   He received a gentleman's upbringing.

Get, Got, Gotten *Get to* (*go*), *get across, get by with, get over, get with* are widely used in speech but seldom acceptable or accurate enough for formal writing. Consult an unabridged dictionary for the many uses of *get*. The forms *have got* for *have* and *got to* for *must* are usually considered too informal or colloquial for college writing.

Good An adjective; should not be used in formal writing as an adverb meaning *well*.
   SUBSTANDARD   Do it good this time.
   STANDARD   Do it well this time. Do a good job.

Guy Nonstandard when used to mean *man* or *person*.

Had Have, Had of Substandard when used for *had*.
   SUBSTANDARD   If he had have (or *had of*) tried, he would have succeeded.
   STANDARD   If he had tried, he would have succeeded.

Had ought See **Ought.**

Hardly, Scarcely These words convey the idea of negation. Hence they should not be used with another negative.
   SUBSTANDARD   It was so misty that we couldn't hardly see.
   STANDARD   It was so misty that we could hardly see.

D

Hung With reference to the death penalty, *hanged* is preferred to *hung*.

Immigrate See **Emigrate**.

Imply See **Infer**.

Individual Colloquial when used indiscriminately for *person* or *men*. Formally used in this connection to mean *individual person,* as distinguished from a group.

Infer Means to reach a conclusion by reasoning from facts or premises. Not to be confused with *imply* which means to suggest or *to hint*.
  STANDARD His tone *implied* contempt; I *inferred* from this that he did not like me.

Inferior, Superior Not comparative forms, but adjectives that have the same meanings, respectively, as the comparative forms of *bad* and *good,* i.e., *worse* and *better*. They are not limited by a *than* phrase, but by a *to* phrase.
  SUBSTANDARD It was superior from every point of view than the lathe previously used.
  STANDARD This plane has proven *superior* in combat *to* the enemy's.
  STANDARD This plane is *better than* the one we had before the war.

Inside Does not require *of* following. Say simply *inside*.
  STANDARD They were trapped inside the walls.

Inside of A colloquial Americanism for *within,* in time expressions.
  COLLOQUIAL It will disappear inside of a week.
  PREFERRED IN WRITING It will disappear within a week.

Irregardless A nonstandard amalgam of *irrespective* and *regardless*. Prefer either of the latter forms.

Its, It's Often confused; its = the possessive form of *it;* it's = the contracted form of *it is.*

Just A colloquialism when used to mean *quite, very.*

    COLLOQUIAL I shall be just delighted to come.

    FORMAL I shall be delighted to come.

Kind, Sort Formal usage prefers consistency: either *this kind* (or sort) of magazine, or *those kinds* (or sorts).

Kind of, Sort of (1) Colloquial when used to mean *rather, somewhat* or *somehow.*

    COLLOQUIAL People who kind of chill you . . .

    PREFERRED IN WRITING People who somehow chill you . . .

    COLLOQUIAL I thought the lecture was sort of dull.

    PREFERRED IN WRITING The lecturer's approach to economics seemed rather dull.

Kind of, Sort of (2) Colloquial when followed by *a* or *an.*

    COLLOQUIAL What kind of a house is it? It is a sort of a castle.

    PREFERRED IN WRITING What kind of house is it? It is a sort of castle.

Latter See **Former.**

Lay Often confused with *lie. Lay* is a transitive verb meaning *to put,* or *place,* something. It always takes an object. Its principal parts are *lay, laid, laid.*

    Lie is intransitive and means *to recline* or *to remain.* Its principal parts are *lie, lay, lain.* When in doubt, try substituting the verb *place.* If it fits the context, you want some form of *lay.*

    STANDARD I lie down every afternoon.

    STANDARD I lay the paper by his plate every morning.

    STANDARD I lay down yesterday after dinner.

    STANDARD I laid the paper by his plate yesterday.

    STANDARD I have lain here for two hours.

    STANDARD I have laid the paper by his plate many times.

D

Leave, Let Do not use *leave* in the sense of *permit* or *let*.

> **SUBSTANDARD** Leave him go.
> **STANDARD** Let him go.

Less, Fewer *Less* refers to amount; *fewer* refers to number. Exact usage prefers *fewer* in speaking of things which can be counted, and *less* for amounts which are not usually counted.

> **INEXACT** Less men were hurt this year than last.
> **EXACT** Fewer men were hurt this year than last.
> **EXACT** You will need less butter with this recipe.

Let's Contraction of *let us*. Should be used only where *let us* can be used.

> **NONSTANDARD** Let's don't leave yet.
> **STANDARD** Let's not leave yet.

Liable In formal usage, not properly used in the sense of *likely* except in designating an injurious or undesirable event which may befall a person or thing.

> **COLLOQUIAL** We're liable to have a clear day tomorrow.
> **PREFERRED IN WRITING** We are likely to have a clear day tomorrow.
> **PREFERRED IN WRITING** We are liable to have a flood if the rain continues.

Like The use of *like* to introduce a clause is widespread in informal English, especially that used by advertising agencies. In formal writing *as, as if,* and *as though* are preferred.

> **COLLOQUIAL** He acted like the rest did.
> **PREFERRED IN WRITING** He acted as the rest did.
> **PREFERRED IN WRITING** I felt as if [or *as though*] I had done something generous.

Lot, Lots, A whole lot Colloquialisms for *much, many, a great deal*.

Mad Means *insane*. Colloquial when used to mean *angry*.

May of See **Of**.

Mean As an adjective means *lowly* or *base*. Colloquial when used to mean *cruel, vicious, unkind,* or *ill-tempered*. Slang when used to mean *excellent* or *formidable*; as *He serves a mean ball*.

Messrs The plural of *Mr., Messrs* should never be used without a name or names following it.

Might of See **Of**.

Most Colloquial or dialectal when used as a shortened form of *almost*.

Much See **Very**.

Must of See **Of**.

Myself Colloquial as a substitute for *I* and *me*.
> COLLOQUIAL They received help from Mary and myself.
> PREFERRED IN WRITING They received help from Mary and me.

Nice Has the primary meaning of *keen* and *precise in discrimination,* or *delicately* or *precisely made*; as a *nice judge of values, a nice distinction in meaning.* It may also mean *pleasant* or *agreeable,* but in this sense it is overused. Prefer adjectives that more exactly express the meaning.

No place See **Anyplace**.

Notorious Means of *bad repute*; as *a notorious gambler*. Not to be used for *famous, celebrated,* or *noted*.

D

Nowhere near A colloquialism for *not nearly.*

Nowheres Dialectal for *nowhere.*

Of *Could of, may of, might of, must of, should of,* and *would of* are corruptions resulting from slurred pronunciation of *could have, may have, might have, must have, should have,* and *would have.*

Off of A nonstandard usage in which *of* is superfluous.
> NONSTANDARD Keep off of the grass.
> PREFERRED Keep off the grass.

Only See **Hardly.**

Or Should not be correlated with *neither;* substitute *nor.*
> NONSTANDARD Neither the long arctic night or any other cause . . .
> STANDARD Neither the long arctic night nor any other cause . . .

Ought Substandard when combined with *had.*
> SUBSTANDARD You hadn't ought to have entered.
> STANDARD You ought not to have entered. You should not have entered.

Outside of (1) *Of* is usually superfluous and nonstandard. Say simply *outside.* Compare **Off of.**

Outside of (2) *Outside of* should not be used in writing for *aside from, except for.*
> COLLOQUIAL Outside of this mistake, it is very good.
> PREFERRED IN WRITING Aside from this mistake, it is very good.

Over with *With* is superfluous. *The regatta is over.* (Not *over with.*)

Party Means *a person* or *a group of persons taking part* (in some transaction). Colloquial when used to mean simply *person*.

STANDARD He was a party to the plot.

 COLLOQUIAL The party who wrote that article must have been a scholar.

PREFERRED IN WRITING The person who wrote that article must have been a scholar.

Percent Use *percent* (or *per cent*) only after a numeral in formal writing. Percent means literally *by the hundred* and therefore is most accurately used when there is an exact numerical statement. Percentage means, loosely, a *part* or *proportion of a whole*.

 COLLOQUIAL A large per cent were Chinese.

STANDARD Twenty percent were Chinese.

STANDARD A large percentage were Chinese.

The word *percent* should be used rather than the sign %. In strictly commercial writing, however, the sign is used, but only after numerals.

Perfect, Round, Unique Widely used in comparative, superlative, or intensive forms, but some speakers contend that this use is illogical; strict formal usage prefers *more nearly perfect, most nearly round, unique*.

Phase See **Faze.**

Phenomena A plural noun. See **Data.**

Plenty (1) Dialectal when used as an adjective before a noun. Say *plenty of*.

 DIALECTAL We have plenty time.

STANDARD We have plenty of time.

Plenty (2) Colloquial when used as an adverb meaning *very, quite*.

 COLLOQUIAL His playing is plenty good.

PREFERRED IN WRITING His playing is very good.

D

Poorly Colloquial when used to mean *not well, in poor health.*

Put in A colloquialism for *spend* or *occupy.*
> COLLOQUIAL I put in three hours trying to memorize the speech.
> FORMAL I spent three hours trying to memorize the speech.

Quite a few Colloquial for *a good many* or *a considerable number.*

Quite a little Colloquial for *a considerable amount* or *a good deal.*

Raise Often confused with *rise.* Remember that *raise* means *to cause something to rise.* Therefore *raise* must always have an object. Remember the principal parts of each verb:

STANDARD	I rise	I rose	I have risen
	I raise (something)	I raised (something)	I have raised (something)

> STANDARD I rise at six o'clock every morning.
> STANDARD I raise flowers for sale.
> STANDARD I rose at six o'clock.
> STANDARD I raised flowers for sale.
> STANDARD I have risen at six o'clock for years.
> STANDARD I have raised flowers for years.

Real Colloquial when used for *very.*

Reason is because See the last example in section 8f-2.

Reverend In formal contexts should be preceded by *the,* and should not be followed immediately by a surname.
> FORMAL The Reverend Mr. Carter   The Reverend Amos Carter
> INFORMAL Reverend Amos Carter

Right along Colloquial when used to mean *continually* or *frequently.*

Round See **Perfect.**

Say Colloquial in the sense of *give orders,* with an infinitive as object.
> COLLOQUIAL The guard said to go back.
> PREFERRED IN WRITING The guard ordered us (or told us) to go back.

Scarcely See **Hardly.**

Set A transitive verb often confused with *sit,* an intransitive verb (compare **Raise**). Remember the principal parts of each verb:

CORRECT	I sit	I sat	I have sat
	I set (something)	I set (something)	I have set (something)

The use of *set* without an object, as expressing mere rest, is nonstandard; say *sit, stand, lie, rest,* or *is set.*
> NONSTANDARD The vase sets on the mantel.
> STANDARD The vase stands (or rests) on the mantel.

Shall, Will See section 26d.

Shape Colloquially used to mean *manner, condition, state.*
> COLLOQUIAL He is in good shape for the debate.
> FORMAL He is in good condition (or thoroughly prepared) for the debate.

Should of See **Of.**

Show up A colloquialism when used intransitively in the sense of *appear, attend, come,* or *be present,* or when used transitively in the sense of *expose.*

Sit See **Set.**

D

Size up   Colloquial for *observe, scrutinize, estimate, evaluate.*

Some (1)   A colloquialism when used as an adverb meaning *a little, somewhat.*

>   COLLOQUIAL   I worked some last winter. I am some better today.
>
>   PREFERRED IN WRITING   I worked a little last winter. I am somewhat better today.

Some (2)   Colloquial when used as an intensifying adjective; as *That is some car you are driving.* A word conveying the precise meaning should be substituted.

Someplace   See **Anyplace.**

Sort   See **Kind.**

Strata   A plural noun. See **Data.**

Superior   See **Inferior.**

Sure   Colloquial when used for *certainly, undoubtedly, surely.*

Suspicion   Substandard when used as a verb.

>   SUBSTANDARD   I did not suspicion that he was coming.
>   STANDARD   I did not suspect that he was coming.

Take and   A nonstandard redundancy when used between subject and verb.

>   NONSTANDARD   It will stay if you take and put it on right.
>   STANDARD   It will stay if you put it on right.

Their, There   Often confused; consult dictionary.

This here, These here, That there, Those there   Nonstandard. Say *this, these, that,* or *those.*

Through   Colloquial when used as in the following sentence:
    COLLOQUIAL   He is through writing.
    PREFERRED IN WRITING   He has finished writing.

To, Too, Two   Sometimes confused; consult dictionary.

To (with the infinitive)   Sometimes creates the "split infinitive" problem; see section 8d-4.

Transpire   Means *to give forth* or *to become known;* as *In spite of their efforts at concealment, the secret transpired.* Nonstandard when used to mean *happen, occur.*

Try and   Often used for *try to,* but should be avoided in formal writing. Say *I must try to* (not *try and*) *find a job.*

Unique   See **Perfect.**

Up   Do not attach a superfluous *up* to verbs unless you are sure that by doing so you can make your expression more accurate and effective.
    SUPERFLUOUS   He opened up the box and divided the money up among the men.
    IMPROVED   He opened the box and divided the money among the men.

Wait on   Dialectal for *wait for.*

Want (1)   Should be followed by an infinitive, not a clause.
    SUBSTANDARD   I want you should be happy.
    STANDARD   I want you to be happy.

Want (2)   *Want in, want out,* are dialectal elliptical forms.
    DIALECTAL   Do you want in?
    STANDARD AND COMPLETE   Do you want to come in?

Want for   A colloquialism in which *for* is superfluous.
    COLLOQUIAL   I want for you to get some water.
    STANDARD   I want you to get some water.

D

14

Ways   Colloquial in such expressions as *a little ways*. In writing, the singular is preferred: *a little way*.

Where to, Where at   Colloquialisms whose prepositions are usually redundant.

> COLLOQUIAL   Where are you going to? Where is he at?
> PREFERRED IN WRITING   Where are you going? Where is he?

Who, Whom   See section 24b. *Who* is substandard when used as an object.

Wise   Often considered substandard when used as a suffix in various invented words (see section 11c).

Would have   Substandard when used in *if* clauses instead of *had*.

> SUBSTANDARD   If he would have stood by us, we might have won.
> STANDARD   If he had stood by us, we might have won.

Would of   See **Of.**

Write-up   Colloquial for *a report, a description, an account.*

You (indefinite)   See section 8b-4.

handbook

15

for 29 Sept 69
to 340

development of American English

Any living language, like a biological organism, is undergoing constant, gradual change. The English we know and use today is only one stage in a long, and presumably endless, process of gradual development. Everyone who has read Chaucer knows that his English was different from ours, and if we go back another five centuries, we find a still different stage of English— so different from that used today as to be unintelligible to all but the professional student.

Here is a sentence written by King Alfred about the year 880. It concerns the *hors-hwael,* "horse-whale," or as we say today, "the whale-horse," or *walrus:*

> Hīe habbath swīthe aethele bān on hiora tōthum, ond hiora hȳd bith swīthe gōd to sciprāpum.

All but two of these words are in common use today, but they have changed so much over the centuries as to be unrecognizable to most of us.

We might guess at the archaic verb-ending *-eth* and translate two words as "haveth" and "be-eth"—that is, *have* and *be.* A linguist who knew the facts of grammatical and phonetic change in English could interpret *bān* as "bone," *tōthum* as an old plural form of *tooth*, *hȳd* as "hide" (skin), *gōd* as "good," and *sciprāpum* as "shipropes." He would recognize *aethele* as akin to German *edel,* meaning "noble," and *swīthe* as an intensive, like *very.* If we know that *hīe* and *hiora* correspond to *they* and *their,* and that some prepositions have changed their meanings if not their written forms, we can translate:

> They have a very noble bone in their teeth (i.e., tusks), and their hide (rawhide) is very good for shipropes.

Historical linguistics is concerned with the principles of change from one stage of a language to another. Linguistic evolution is gradual: phonetic change proceeds by the accumulation of slight variations in sound which may hardly be noticed by the people who make them. Today many people pronounce "going to" as "goin to" or "gawn ta" or even "gonna"* without being aware of these differences.

Similarly, in the past the sound of English words varied slightly from speaker to speaker, or from place to place, and an increment of small changes has brought about the difference between King Alfred's English and Chaucer's, or between Chaucer's and our own. There were other kinds of change as well: new words were borrowed, old words disappeared, spellings varied, meanings shifted. But phonetic change—that is, change in the sound of the language—is basic for a linguist.

Phonetic changes are often regular enough to be generalized into principles. Old English *rāp* (pronounced to rhyme with Modern American English *top*) became something like "rawp" in Chaucer's day and has become *rope* in our own time. If you say these three words in front of a mirror, you will notice that the vowel in *top* is made with the mouth spread wide toward

---

* The spellings used here to indicate different pronunciations of "going to" illustrate some shortcomings of the English alphabet. We have no letters to indicate unmistakably the vowel sounds I have tried to suggest by "gawn ta." Linguists have provided such symbols [gɔn tə], and enough others to indicate fairly accurately all the sounds used in English. For any serious study of linguistics, learning a phonetic alphabet is indispensable.

the sides. To pronounce "rawp" you will move your lips so that your open mouth is in the shape of an approximate square. To pronounce *rope* you round your lips into a still smaller opening, even protruding your lips a little. This account is oversimplified, but it suggests a kind of principle: the change from Old English *rāp* to Modern English *rope* involves progressive rounding of the mouth. The principle can be checked by looking at similar words; Old English *bān, rād, hām,* and *stān,* have become Modern English *bone, road, home,* and *stone* by the same principle of progressive rounding.

Some of the consonants have also changed, and the changes can often be described by phonetic principles. A number of English consonant sounds can be arranged in pairs according to the way they are formed. The tongue is held in exactly the same position for pronouncing *s* and *z;* the difference lies in whether our vocal cords vibrate to produce the voiced *z* or we whisper the voiceless *s*. Here are some other examples:

voiced	*voiceless*
b	p
d	t
g	k
v	f

A change from a voiced consonant to its voiceless counterpart is fairly common, and we can find many instances in the history of English of the opposite change, from voiceless to voiced. (Notice the difference, which is not indicated by the spelling but can be heard, between the *s* in *house* and the *s* in *houses.*) But there is no simple explanation for a change from a voiceless *s* to a *g*, nor from a *d* to an *f*, and in fact such changes have seldom if ever occurred in the history of English. Phonetic change seems to occur only along what a geologist would call "natural lines of cleavage." These natural lines in language can often be explained by a careful study of the mechanisms of speech.

Historical linguists in the nineteenth century noticed that

there are marked similarities between some English words and words with the same meaning in other European languages. Consider, for example, English *mother,* Old English *modor,* Dutch *moeder,* German *mutter,* Celtic *mathair,* Latin *mater,* Greek *meter,* and Lithuanian *moter.* Such similarity can hardly have been accidental, and it raised some questions. Were these words all variants of a common original? If so, what was the original?

By comparing thousands of related words in different languages, historical linguists could note some relationships: Latin is more like Greek than like Dutch, Dutch is more like English than like Russian. Romance languages (French, Spanish, Italian, etc.) have many close similarities, and since it can be shown historically that the Romance languages have evolved from dialects of Medieval Latin, it seems a probable hypothesis that other European languages have evolved as descendants of a single very ancient language. This hypothesis is now supported by so much circumstantial evidence that it is almost universally accepted by linguists. The original parent language is called Indo-European, since some of its branches are spoken in Persia and northern India as well as in Europe. No record of Indo-European remains, since the people who spoke it had not invented a writing system. But comparative linguists have worked out a good many of the principles of phonetic change operating in the Indo-European languages and have reconstructed many words of the parent language.

Data from other sciences have contributed to our knowledge of the location and way of life of this hypothetical Indo-European people, and linguistic research has helped the historian. For example, since a good many widely separated languages in the family have similar words for *salmon, turtle, honey,* and *beech* tree, it is a fair assumption that the parent language had these words and that the speakers were acquainted with these things. The geographic limits of these animals and plants can be determined: the turtle did not live north of Germany; the beech tree did not grow naturally much to the east of the Vistula river in Poland; the line marking the occurrence of the honey bee can be drawn on a map.

Somewhere within these boundaries, in the fourth millennium, B.C. the Indo-European tribesmen lived as small farmers, who kept cows for milk, knew and used the wheel, and were organized into patriarchal families something like those of modern Europe. Paul Thieme locates the original homeland of the Indo-Europeans on the Baltic coast, between the Vistula and the Elbe, in what is now East Germany and Poland. Other linguists have placed it farther east and south, in what is now the Ukraine. But there is general agreement that the original homeland was in central Europe, rather than Asia.

During the third millennium the tribes began migrations which took them east to Persia and India, south to Italy and Greece, north to Scandinavia, and west to Spain and the British Isles. As they separated, they developed their own dialects, which eventually became the separate languages of the Indo-European family.

The changes which, over the centuries, produced the branch of the Indo-European family to which English belongs are often regular enough to be described in general "laws." For example, it can be shown that the Germanic languages (English, Dutch, German, Scandinavian, and some others) all went through a regular change of consonants in the first millennium B.C., whereas other Indo-European languages, like Greek, Latin, or Sanskrit, preserved for the most part the original consonants. In the Germanic languages, an original Indo-European voiced *b* became the voiceless *p*. Latin *labia* preserves the original *b,* but English *lip* shows the change to *p*. Similarly, Latin *turba* (crowd, group) keeps the original Indo-European consonants, but English *thorp* (village) shows, among other things, the shift of *b* to *p*.

Turba and *thorp* are thus related by being descended from a common Indo-European root, and they are called *cognates*. Words that are borrowed by one language from another usually do not show the phonetic changes that distinguish the Germanic languages from their Indo-European brothers and sisters. For example, we have borrowed the Latin stem of *turba* directly into English in such words as *turbid, turbulent,* and *disturb*. Borrowings are relatively recent; cognates go back to the early stages of each language. The words for *mother* listed on page 322 are presumably all cognates, descendants of a common Indo-European ancestor which probably sounded something like "mah-tár." Within historical times we have borrowed *maternal* and *matron* from Latin and Old French.

The following lists show other changes which make up the Germanic Consonant Shift, often called "Grimm's Law." The Indo-European consonants are represented here by roots of Latin and Greek words, instead of less familiar words from Sanskrit or Lithuanian. After each root, some English words borrowed from Latin or Greek are added in parentheses to indicate the meaning. Since they are borrowings, they preserve the original Indo-European consonants.

Indo-European *d*	becomes	Germanic *t*
ed- (*edible*)		eat
decem (*decimal*)		ten

Indo-European *g*	becomes	Germanic *k*
gen- (*generate, genus*)		kin
ager ("*field*," as in agriculture)		acre

Indo-European *p*	becomes	Germanic *f*
pyr (*pyre, pyrotechnics*)		fire
pullus (*pullet, poultry*)		fowl

Indo-European *t*	becomes	Germanic *th*
tu (*second person pronoun*)		thou
frater (*fraternal*)		brother

Indo-European *k*	becomes	Germanic *h*
cornu (*cornet, cornucopia*)		horn
canis (*canine*)		hound

With a little knowledge of Greek and Latin roots, some ingenuity, and a good dictionary, a student will be able to find other examples of the Germanic Consonant Shift and of borrowed words which preserve the original Indo-European consonants.

EXERCISES

Look up the etymologies of the following pairs of words, keeping in mind the Germanic Consonant Shift.

1. docile, teach
2. domestic, tame
3. gusto, choose
4. intrude, threaten
5. octopus, eight, foot
6. peril, fear
7. pedal, foot
8. piscatorial, fish
9. subjugate, yoke
10. tension, thin

The Indo-European family includes almost all the languages of Europe, from Scandinavia to Greece, from Russia to Ireland, and some of the languages spoken in Armenia, Persia, and northern India. Among the latter, Sanskrit is specially important to the linguist since it is the oldest recorded Indo-European language, appearing first in the *Vedas,* ancient religious books of India written down in the second millennium B.C.

There are many other language families in the world, but the only important non-Indo-European languages in Europe are Finnish and Hungarian, which belong to the Finno-Ugric family. Basque, spoken in the Pyrenees along the border between France and Spain, is a linguistic mystery; it has no known relatives and may be a lone survivor of the lost Iberian languages spoken in the Late Stone Age throughout Southern Europe.

The Germanic tribes who invaded Great Britain in the fifth century came from the low country around the base of the Danish peninsula. They conquered all of the island except Scotland and Wales and imposed their Germanic dialects on the Celts who survived the invasion. (Celtic languages still persist in Scotland, Wales, Ireland, and the Breton peninsula in France.) Old English, as the Anglo-Saxon dialects of the invaders are now called, was not written down until after the arrival of Christian missionaries from Rome in the year 597. Like their modern counterparts the world over, these missionaries wrote down the language of the natives in the Roman alphabet, and they taught English monks to write and make translations. In so doing, they rendered a great service to historical linguistics, for they provided us with the earliest specimens of the English language.

To this Old English language stock, a great many words borrowed from other languages have been added. Some Latin words used for place names in the first century, when the Roman legions established army posts throughout the island, have remained on the map. Most conspicuous is the Latin word for "camp," *castra,* which frequently appears in place names like Lancaster, Winchester, Worcester, and the like. More Latin words were borrowed when Christianity was introduced into England, and since the Renaissance, a great many Latin and Greek words, especially those dealing with education, law, and science, have been borrowed, sometimes by way of French. In the following sentence, all italicized words are of Latin origin.

> Today the *curriculum* of our *educational institutions*—*elementary, secondary,* and *collegiate*—is *administered* by *deans, superintendents, coordinators,* and *principals* as well as *professors* and other *faculty members.*

The traditional fields of study often have Greek names: *geography, theology, economics, physics, psychology, mathematics, philosophy, botany.* Modern physics has taken Greek roots to form such words as *thermodynamics, atomic, cyclotron, electronics, gamma*-ray, and *proton.*

French words were borrowed in increasing numbers after the Norman Conquest, especially in the thirteenth and fourteenth centuries. A famous passage in Scott's *Ivanhoe* reminds us that language can reflect differences in social class. The Saxon serfs in *Ivanhoe* used English words for the animals they tended: *ox, cow, sheep, swine.* Their Norman overlords had little need for the names of the animals but were interested in the end product; they used French words for the different kinds of meat that appeared on their tables: *beef, veal, mutton,* and *pork*.

French words make up the largest part of the borrowed words in our everyday vocabulary, but the English-speaking peoples have borrowed words from almost every language they have come in contact with. *Sky* and *happy* and *window* come from Scandinavian; *flannel* and *whiskey* from Celtic; *tub, yacht,* and *pump* from Dutch; *pretzel, kindergarten,* and *hamburger* from German. From Italian come words like *balcony, piazza,* and *umbrella,* as well as many terms used in music and art. Spanish has contributed *cigar, alligator, mosquito,* and many words used in the American Southwest, like *canyon, rodeo, lariat,* and *mesa.* From Hebrew have come *camel* and *sabbath;* from Arabic, *algebra* and *sugar* and *alcohol.* Many words for fruits and flowers come ultimately from Persia: *peach* and *orange, tulip* and *lilac;* and we have borrowed *tea* and *mandarin* from China, *kimono* and *tycoon* from Japan, *pajama* and *bungalow* from India, and *gong* and *gingham* from Malaysia. The list is far from complete, but it will illustrate the fact that Modern English has borrowed foreign words very freely.

EXERCISES

In a good dictionary, look up the ultimate origin of the following borrowed words:

1. alkali
2. alligator
3. amethyst
4. bamboo
5. calico
6. cherub
7. isolate
8. lute
9. Negro
10. potato
11. skipper
12. skunk
13. sirup

Since Old English times, the language with its borrowed additional vocabulary has changed steadily. Englishmen have apparently always had a tendency to telescope and shorten words —a tendency which today sometimes reduces *extraordinary* from six syllables to three: "extráwdnry." Old Englesh *hlāf-weard* (literally, "loaf-guard") meant the leader of a tribe; hlāf-dige (literally, "loaf-kneader") meant a woman. Both words were shortened in Middle English to *loverd* and *lavedi,* and they have been further shortened in Modern English to *lord* and *lady.*

Many changes in the form of words fall into regular patterns like that already mentioned in the change from Old English *rāp* to *rope.* A pattern of vowel changes, very common in German where it is called *umlaut,* also appears in Old English and has produced such pairs of words as *man* and *men, strong* and *strength, blood* and *bleed, goose* and *geese, full* and *fill, mouse* and *mice.* Voiceless consonants tend to become voiced when they occur between vowels: contrast *house* and *houses, bath* and *bather, wife* and *wives.* Especially in the vicinity of vowels like *i* or *e,* a *k*-sound may become palatalized to *ch,* as in *chill* (compare *cool*), Green*wich* (compare Ber*wick*), and Win*chester* (compare Lan*caster*). Palatalization also distinguishes verb from noun in *bake* and *batch, speak* and *speech, stick* and *stitch.* Other forms of palatalization account for pairs like *skirt* and *shirt, gard(en),* and *yard, drag* and *draw.*

Initial *k* disappeared before an *n,* and *w* before an *r,* though we still preserve a record of the earlier pronunciation in modern spelling: *knee, know, knight; wrap, wreck, wrong.* Inflectional endings, once as common in English as in Latin, have mainly eroded away. In King Alfred's time there were still three different declensions of the noun, and one of them had six different forms, illustrated in *stan, stanes, stane, stanas, stana, stanum.* Today *stone* has only two phonetic forms, *stone* and *stones,* though in spelling we distinguish two more, *stone's* and *stones'.* The inflection of verbs has been similarly simplified, and we have given up entirely the old inflection of adjectives. The final *e*'s which trouble students trying to read Chaucer aloud are vestigial remnants of earlier inflectional endings.

EXERCISES

a. The second word in each of the following pairs shows a change in form. What phonetic principles explain the various changes? Look for changes in *sound*, not in spelling.

1. calf, calves
2. disk, dish
3. food, feed
4. kirk, church
5. long, length
6. louse, lousy
7. proud, pride
8. stink, stench
9. tug, tow
10. use (noun), usable

b. Look up in a good dictionary the Old English forms of the following words, and note the consonant sounds that have been dropped in Modern English:

1. hussy
2. lanky
3. loud
4. lee
5. nit
6. rack (and ruin)
7. retch
8. ring

Just as the spoken forms of words change by slow degrees over a long period of time, so do the meanings of words. Old English *hlāf-weard* must once have meant something like "loaf-keeper," but along with the change in form to *lord* there has been a considerable change in meaning. Such semantic changes do not follow regular principles, but one can often trace the psychological connections between the different meanings of a word. *Head* means, basically, a part of the body. But it is easy to see how this meaning was extended, as a kind of metaphor, in such phrases as "head of lettuce," "head of a pin," "come to a head," "headmaster," "newspaper headline," "head on a glass of beer," "headwaters," or "headland." Latin *candidatus* originally meant "dressed in white"—i.e., in one's best toga. Since aspirants for public office dressed in white, *candidate* has come to mean a person seeking office, and the original idea of whiteness has disappeared entirely. English *hearse* came, through Old French, from Latin *hirpex*, a rake or harrow. When it first appeared in English it meant a frame with candles on which a coffin was placed. The frame with candles sticking up around the edge looked like a primitive harrow. Later the meaning changed to a device for carrying a coffin and eventually to the leading Cadillac in a funeral procession.

Some meanings are expanded, or generalized. *Gossip* originally had the fairly specific meaning of "god-parent," but it became generalized to any talkative old woman, and eventually to what she said. *Barn* at first meant a place for storing barley. *Manuscript* originally meant "written by hand," but since the invention of the typewriter, the word has been expanded to mean an author's typed or written copy, as distinguished from a printed version. By the same kind of change, an airplane can now "land" at sea.

Other words become more specialized in meaning. In Shakespeare's time, *deer* still meant any kind of wild animal ("Rats and mice and such small deer"), but today it means only one kind. *Starve* meant "to die" in Chaucer's time: the little boy in the Prioress's Tale "sterved" of a cut throat. Today the word means to die from lack of food, or even just to be very hungry.

A few words which once had a derogatory meaning have become complimentary terms. *Shrewd* used to mean harmful or malicious, from the supposedly poisonous small animal called a shrew. Today a good many people would be pleased to be described as "shrewd." Similarly, *knight* once meant a servant boy, and only under the feudal system did the word acquire its present honorific sense.

A great many words have undergone the opposite change. *Hussy* is a contraction of Old English *huswif*, "house wife," and originally had none of its present depreciatory sense. *Wanton* and *lewd* once meant simply undisciplined or untaught. A *knave* was once merely a boy, a *boor* was simply a farmer, and a *villain* a farm laborer at a villa, or village.

Folk etymology—a bad guess as to the meaning or origin of a word—may cause a change in the form of a word. *Crayfish* (American and Irish *crawfish*) comes from a misunderstanding, and hence misspelling, of Middle English *crevis*. A *penthouse* represents an English misunderstanding of Old French *apentis*, from Latin *appendix*, "an addition to." *An umpire* was originally *a nompere* (Old French *nonper*, or unequal), but the *n* of the original word was taken by the English to be the last letter of the article *an*.

15

EXERCISES

Look up the etymologies of the following words, and try to account for the changes in meaning:

1. adder (snake)
2. amethyst
3. auger
4. belfry
5. bishop
6. bridegroom
7. can (as in *ashcan*)
8. churl
9. cretin
10. marshal
11. newt
12. pretty
13. shrive
14. volume
15. wiseacre

Even a brief look at the history of English shows that changes in the form and meaning of words have been taking place at every stage of the language, and they are still going on today, in spite of the efforts of teachers and textbooks. Historical linguistics gives little encouragement to those who would guard the purity of English by fixing it in a permanent form. Changes are slow, however, and any one generation finds the language fairly stable. Dictionaries attempt to record the current state of the language, though they often include archaic or obsolete forms and meanings.

At any given stage, a language constitutes a system: certain ways of putting words together are acceptable while others are not. The system of a language at a given stage is its *grammar,* but the word *grammar* is used in other senses, too. W. Nelson Francis, in his often reprinted article, "Revolution in Grammar" (*Quarterly Journal of Speech,* October, 1954), makes some useful distinctions. The meaning just described, which Francis calls Grammar 1, is the actual structure of a language —the way in which English words *must* go together if sentences are to be acceptable to other people who speak the language. Certain patterns of verbal sounds are used by all people who speak English; other patterns are never used. When a child learns to speak English—to use these acceptable patterns—he has at least made a start at learning the grammar of English in this first basic sense. A schoolboy may not know that he knows Grammar 1, but he would find a statement like "This my is book" unacceptable and "This is my book" a perfectly normal English sentence. Even though he cannot explain *why* the first sentence is wrong, he knows that it just isn't English.

Consider the following sentences:

1. Send me your new address.
2. Send your new address to me.
3. Send to me your new address.
4. Send your new address me.

No one would object to the first two sentences, though the pattern of the second sentence is probably a little less common. The third sentence, though intelligible, sounds stilted, slightly foreign. We would not be apt to use it ourselves, though we would understand it readily if a foreigner spoke it. The fourth sentence, however, is just not English, and everyone who recognizes this knows at least a part of Grammar 1.

The second meaning of *grammar* is suggested by a phrase like "a grammar of the English language," or by the word *grammarian.* If we want to know *why* "This my is book" is wrong, we need some systematic description of the acceptable forms and patterns of words in English sentences. Such theoretical, explanatory descriptions may be called Grammar 2. The plural form "descriptions" is purposely used to indicate that there is no single correct way of describing and explaining English. Grammar 2 is any theoretical account of Grammar 1.

Language, like walking, is initially learned by trial and error. All normal children eventually learn to walk, though they may never learn exactly what happens to nerves and muscles when they are walking. Similarly, every normal child learns to speak the language of the adults around him, and he thus acquires the Grammar 1 of his particular dialect without conscious effort. If he wants to know, or is required to learn, the "theory" of the language he uses every day, he will have to study Grammar 2.

Is there any practical advantage to studying Grammar 2? There may be, though probably not so much as you think. Knowing something about the process of walking may improve our efficiency when we walk; it may help us distribute our weight properly and thus avoid weakened or flattened arches. Similarly, a knowledge of Grammar 2 may lead to greater efficiency in our use of the language; it may increase our knowledge of the possibilities of Grammar 1. It will not help much with simple sentences like "Send me your new address," but it may help us to communicate precisely more subtle or more complex meanings, or to redistribute the weight in a sentence so as to emphasize one part and play down another.

In the mind of the public, however, the chief reason for studying grammar at all is to enable us to speak and write "correct" English and to avoid "bad grammar." This is the third sense of the word in common use. Grammar 3 usually consists of prescriptive rules for "correct" English usage: Don't say "between you and I"; the preposition *between* requires a complement in the objective case. Don't say "Everyone brought their own lunch"; *everyone* is singular in number and must be followed by a singular pronoun.

Many people uncritically assume that studying Grammar

15

2, an analytic description of the language, is a necessary first step in correcting "errors" like those in the preceding paragraph, which are the main concern of Grammar 3. It may be that some grammatical analysis is useful in explaining why certain constructions are "wrong," but common sense suggests that a complete theoretical account of the structure of English is hardly necessary for correcting errors in, say, agreement of subject and verb. Furthermore, linguists in recent years have raised serious doubts about the adequacy of the traditional Grammar 2 that has been taught in our schools since the Renaissance. Intelligent students are disturbed by the many exceptions to the grammatical principles they are taught, and linguists would add to the charge of inconsistency that of incompleteness.

For one thing, traditional Grammar 2 is concerned primarily with written, rather than spoken, English, and it thus simply ignores some very important ways of signalling meaning, like accent and pitch. A classic example from C. C. Fries is this headline:

PROFESSOR RAKES LEAVES AFTER CHAPEL

If we accent the word *rakes* and pronounce it with a relatively high pitch, we produce "Professor Rakes leaves after chapel." But if we accent the second syllable of *professor* and the word *leaves,* pronouncing both with a higher pitch than we give to *rakes,* we are saying "Professor rakes leaves after chapel."

Furthermore, traditional Grammar 2 attempts to fit written English into a theoretical framework derived from classical languages. The categories of our traditional grammar were borrowed from Latin and Greek. These are both highly inflected languages, in which the relationship between words is indicated by adding an ending to the root word. English has lost most of its inflectional endings; it depends on word order, rather than word endings, to indicate the difference between "Dog bites man" and "Man bites dog." The so-called parts of speech —eight categories into which all words are supposed to fit—had some meaning in Latin. One can tell from the form that *quies* is a noun, *quiesco* is a verb, and *quietus* is an adjective. But in English the word *quiet* may be, without change of form, a noun (*peace and quiet*), a verb (*to quiet down*), or an adjective (*a quiet hour*). To apply the Latin concept of parts of speech to English words is bound to produce some confusion, since many English words fit into several categories.

One way out of the difficulty is to use terms like *noun, verb,* or *adjective* to refer to function in a sentence. That is, let function determine the part of speech, instead of vice versa. If *brick* is used to name an object, it is a noun. If it is used to describe an object (*a brick wall*), it is an adjective. This functional approach to grammatical analysis, using traditional Latin names to indicate function in a sentence, works fairly well for a rough analysis of sentence structure. But linguists have argued that new categories, derived from English as it is spoken rather than borrowed from Latin, might be more accurate and more useful.

In an effort to arrive at a Grammar 2 derived inductively from English, C. C. Fries studied fifty hours of transcribed telephone conversations among educated middle-class citizens of Michigan, analyzing their actual speech patterns. His book *The Structure of English* (New York: Harcourt, Brace and World, Inc., 1952) proposed new categories for English grammar, and they have since been modified and used by many structural linguists. Structural linguistics applies to English the objective approach used by anthropologists studying a native language in the field. Making no a priori assumptions, the structural linguist tries to limit himself to statements about the forms of words and their structure in sentences, regardless of their meaning. Structural linguists in general pride themselves on being scientific: their statements are tentative (subject to change or qualification in the light of further data), verifiable by anyone who knows Grammar 1, and objective (they describe what is, instead of what should be). Though they do not yet agree on all details of structural analysis, nor on the terminology to be used in describing it, they have already made very important discoveries about features of English which were obscured or ignored by traditional grammar.

The question remains, however, whether their categories and terminology are useful to a student hoping to "improve his English" by studying Grammar 3. There is no intention here to depreciate the very real achievements of structural linguistics. But many students will probably find some of the old terminology of traditional Grammar 2 still useful for the rough analysis needed to clarify the rules of Grammar 3. This handbook attempts to utilize some of the insights of structural analysis without discarding entirely the older terminology.

Whatever system of grammatical analysis is used, we must meet squarely a basic question raised increasingly by modern linguists: are the "errors" catalogued by Grammar 3 really errors? Is there a standard by which we can call certain usages correct and others wrong?

In some areas, like vocabulary, the answer is a qualified yes (see chapter 14). All language is based on a social agreement to attach certain meanings to verbal symbols, and we all agree that in English *bread* is something we eat, not something we build walls with. There may be slight disagreement about the exact limits of a word's meaning: whether a certain bakery product is to be called *bread* or *cake,* for example. But it is our general agreement about the meanings of English words that makes communication possible, and we can say unequivocally that Mrs. Malaprop was wrong when she referred to "an allegory on the banks of the Nile."

Since the Eighteenth century, a good many people have tried to give equally certain answers to questions about correct usage—about ending sentences with prepositions, or using contractions like *ain't.* Communication is not involved here: one construction conveys the meaning as well as the other. Is one usage right and another wrong? Among the rich varieties of expression possible in English, is there such a thing as *the* correct way of speaking or writing?

It is easy to ridicule this question as naive. To show its supposed triviality, Bergen Evans cites a hypothetical case: a student takes a mouse to a biologist with the question "Is this a correct mouse?" Such a question would seem nonsensical to a scientist. A biologist can tell about the the species, age, sex, and physical condition of a mouse, but he has no standard for determining the "correctness" of mice. Evans is implying, of course, that linguistics, like other sciences, should be descriptive rather than evaluative, and he bolsters this point by citing another hypothetical example. Suppose you want to make a grammar of the Eskimo language. The first thing you must do is to find some Eskimos. Then you must listen to what they say, record it, and by trial and error figure out how the language works. If while you are doing this, someone says, "Yes, but is this correct Eskimo?," all you can answer is, "Well, this is what they say in Baffinland." You might add that in Greenland they say it a little differently, but the implication is clear that the question is as nonsensical as the question about the correct mouse. What the Eskimos say is a fact, and all a linguist can do is record, analyze, and describe the facts. If English is what English-speaking people say and write, a linguist must base his analysis on what people are speaking and writing, without worrying about its "correctness."

Is one man's English, then, as good as the next's? Are there no errors to be corrected by Grammar 3? It depends on the meaning one attaches to the term *error*. Certainly there are differences in the way different people speak English. When these differences are conspicuous, fairly regular, and confined to a particular area, we accept them as regional dialects, like Southern or Down-East. But to a linguist, dialects are not necessarily limited to particular regions. People of different social classes in the same region may speak differently (on one side of the tracks "He don't" is common; on the other, nearly everyone says "He doesn't"), and any family is apt to have its own peculiarities of pronunciation, vocabulary, and syntax. It is probably true, in the last analysis, that no two people speak the language in precisely the same way—that is, each person has his own dialect (or idiolect, as the linguist would call it) of English. Why should any one dialect be called correct and others wrong?

The answer comes, in part, from history. In the past, the dialect of a metropolis has often gained prestige among the rural or provincial citizenry and has eventually been accepted as the standard. Modern English is a direct descendant of the dialect spoken in and around London in the fourteenth century. Furthermore, the written language of metropolitan areas has an advantage in its wider range of sentence patterns and its very much larger vocabulary, as compared with the dialects spoken in the provinces or backwoods.

But there is a sociological answer, too. In any given period there are apt to be differences between the language used by the educated classes and that used by uneducated people, rural or urban; and these differences almost always reflect different degrees of social prestige. In some countries, where society is more rigorously stratified than in the United States, speech is the determining mark of class, and thus of social prestige. Scientific accuracy would seem to require some description of the differences, including the difference in prestige, between the language used by the educated, professional and executive classes and the dialects spoken, and sometimes written, by the less educated. One might also note that while it is relatively easy for an educated person to use the language of the uneducated, it is almost impossible for an uneducated person to speak and write the dialect of the professional and administrative classes.

Grammar 2 might thus be redefined as a particular dialect of English which has special prestige because of the people who use it. A student ought to know this dialect even though he doesn't always use it. Why should we study the endless idiosyncracies of English spelling? *Beleive* is just as intelligible in written contexts as *believe,* but a person who misspells the word may lose caste in the eyes of others. Why should students be taught to write "I felt bad" instead of "I felt badly"? Because most people need to be concerned about the effect of their language on others. A person who confuses adjectives and adverbs may still communicate his meaning clearly enough, but he will reveal an ignorance of Grammar 3 which many people still regard as deplorable.

The motives behind studying Grammar 3 may thus be ultimately snobbish. The rules are often arbitrary conventions, without historical or rational justification, but they represent a level of usage found in practically all books, magazines, and newspapers; and this level of English can hardly be ignored by teachers in a fluid society in which people are constantly trying to move upward in the social scale. Since the dialect of the educated is not necessarily part of the Grammar 1 that children acquire unconsciously by imitating their elders, "good English," like good table manners and polite behavior, must be studied and learned if one is to share whatever prestige attaches to speaking and writing "correctly."

Dictionaries and handbooks of composition usually try to distinguish different levels of English usage. When descriptive labels like *provincial, slang,* or *substandard* are used, they are meant as approximate guides to the social acceptability of different kinds of English. Almost everyone recognizes examples drawn from vocabulary. *Tired* is the normal English word, appropriate in both speech and writing, to indicate the feeling which follows overexertion. *Exhausted* is a little more literary; it is more apt to appear in writing than in speech. *Fatigued* is almost purely literary; though you know the word, you have probably never actually spoken it in conversation, and if you use it in informal writing, the chances are that your style is pompous. *Tuckered out* sounds provincial, as though the speaker came from the backwoods or were deliberately affecting folksy language. *Bushed* and *beat* are slang; you would not be likely to use either term when talking to the president of your college or in a letter applying for a job. A handbook is simply shirking part of its job if it does not point out that, things being what they are, the use of *like* as a conjunction may cast doubt on the social and educational background of the writer, even though one can find many examples of the usage in speech and print.

In this handbook, the rules and the descriptive labels attached to examples of usage, are not meant to be final judgments on what is, and what is not, correct by some mythical standard of "pure" English. Our purpose is more modest and more utilitarian; we are trying, among other things, to provide a guide for the perplexed. We are saying that, in our opinion, the level of usage implied by these rules and prescriptions is that of the people who determine the prestige-values of the language: editors, writers, and educators. If you choose to violate the rules they follow, you should do so deliberately, not unwittingly.

Learning how to avoid "errors" in English may be important in a practical way, but there are better reasons than this for studying English. Any serious study of the language will sharpen one's linguistic sensibility and will thus contribute to a more important end than mere correctness: a greater facility and accuracy in using the expressive possibilities of our most valuable intellectual tool—the Grammar 1 of the English language.

15

ANALYSIS OF THE SENTENCE

16
elements of
a sentence

For any kind of grammatical analysis, it is necessary to *classify* the words and groups of words that make up a sentence. To classify means simply to group together words that are alike in some respects and to give names to the classes thus formed. *Pen, telephone, idea,* and *fluid,* for example, are alike in that they can appear after *the,* or *a,* or *this: a pen, the telephone, this idea.* They also take inflectional endings, usually a suffix including the letter *s:* telepho*nes,* flui*ds,* ide*as.* Another class is made up of words to which inflectional suffixes like *ed* can be added: *smell, smelled; cry, cried; walk, walked.* A third class consists of words to which *er* and *est* can be added: *happy, happier, happiest; swift, swifter, swiftest.*

Traditional grammar calls the words of the first class *nouns;* words of the second class, *verbs;* and words of the third class, *adjectives.* But it also widens each class to include many words that lack some of the similarities so far described but that are similar in other respects. That is, traditional grammar would include in class one above, as nouns, words like *man* even though it is inflected *man, men.* The third class could include words which do not add *er* and *est,* like *beautiful,* which is inflected *more beautiful, most beautiful.*

S|elem

In widening the classes, traditional grammar makes use of another set of similarities: it puts words into classes not merely by their position in a sentence or by their forms (the way they can be inflected), but by their *functions* in a sentence. That is, traditional grammar says that *man, pen,* and *idea* belong together in a class because they name something; whereas *rich* and *beautiful* and *cold* belong together in another class because they modify (that is, describe or limit) something.

Modern linguists have proposed alternative classifications which may well provide a more accurate and consistent analysis of grammatical structures and relationships than do the categories of traditional grammar. (W. Nelson Francis' book *The Structure of American English* [New York: Ronald Press Co., 1958] is an admirable example of a modern structural grammar.) But for the limited sort of analysis needed in a handbook, which tries merely to explain why certain constructions are "grammatical" without offering a complete system of grammar, the traditional classifications and the old names have the advantage of simplicity and familiarity. And they can be made consistent enough to be relevant and usable.

Many of the supposed inconsistencies of traditional grammar are caused by the fact that most English words can function in different ways and hence must be classified in different ways. By its form, the word *poor* seems to belong in the class with *hot* and *tall;* it can take the suffixes *er* and *est* to make *poorer, poorest.* But the sentence *The poor usually eat poor food* shows that *poor* can also be used like words of the first class described above. *The poor* belongs with *the telephone, the idea,* etc., even though it does not take an *s* suffix like *telephones.*

Into what class, then, do we put the word *poor?* The answer is no class, until we see the word used in a sentence. In a construction, the form and position indicate unambiguously the word's meaning and grammatical function. *The poor* names an economic class; in this construction, the word belongs with other names like *telephone* or *fluid.* In the construction *poor food, poor* describes the quality of food eaten by the poor; it belongs in the class with *rich, hot,* and *good.*

Once it is clear that grammatical analysis deals not with isolated words but with words used in sentences, various systems of classification are possible. For theoretical purposes, a "structural" classification is probably most satisfactory. But a structural analysis is a very complicated process which involves learning a whole new vocabulary and using a set of unfamiliar concepts. To a linguist, this difficulty does not seem serious if he can achieve completeness and accuracy in his analysis. But to the student, concerned more with his own writing than with a complete system of English grammar, learning the new system can be a considerable hardship and may be an irrelevant distraction.

16

If we classify words by their *functions* in a sentence, we have a simple and usable tool, adequate for the needs of a composition course. There are four functions of words in sentences: to name things, to assert things, to modify (describe, identify, or limit) other words, and to connect other parts of a sentence. Groups of words (what linguists call *constructions*) may have the same functions as single words: such groups are called phrases (see chapter 17) or clauses (see chapter 18). Sub-groups can be distinguished in each classification. Nouns and pronouns and gerunds (explained later) are sub-classes of the naming, or substantive, function. Adjectives and adverbs are special cases of modifiers, and so on.

Class:	substantive	assertive	modifiers	connectives
Function:	to name	to assert	to limit, describe, or explain	to join elements
Types:	nouns pronouns gerunds	verbs	adjectives adverbs participles	conjunctions prepositions

The basic unit of discourse, and the starting point of grammatical analysis, is the sentence. Sentences do a number of

S|elem

things: make requests, ask and answer questions, issue commands, and make statements. In speech they are not always explicitly complete. The single word "Going?" may serve in place of the full question "Are you going to the party?" and the answer may be the single word, "Yes," just as the answer to the question "Where do you live?" may be "On Elm Street." These answers are elliptical sentences—a short way of saying "I am going to the party," or "I live on Elm Street." Questions and answers, requests or commands are special types of the sentence, with their own grammatical characteristics. (Commands usually omit the subject; questions are indicated by a peculiar word order.) But the typical sentence in written English is a statement.

16 a
subject and predicate

A statement says something about something, and to make a statement you need to *name* what you are talking about and *assert* something about it.

The grammatical term for the word or words that name what you are talking about is the *subject*. The *predicate* is the assertion you make about the subject.

subject	predicate
Edison	invented the light bulb.
The storm	cut off our lighting.
A coyote	howled all night.
I	like spices.
He	does not like spices.

The subject is usually a noun or pronoun, though it may be a phrase or clause, as will be explained later (chapter 18). The predicate may contain a number of different words used in different ways, but the essential part is a verb, a word that asserts something. See chapter 23 for discussion of subject-verb agreement.

16 b
modifiers

It is possible to make a complete sentence of two words, a subject and a verb:

> Thunder rolled.

Few sentences, however, are as simple as this. We usually add other words whose function is to describe the subject or the verb.

> *Loud* thunder rolled *savagely*.

Here *loud* describes thunder and *savagely* describes the verb rolled. Such words are called *modifiers,* and they may be attached to almost any part of a sentence. Although modifiers usually describe, they may also indicate how many (*three* books, *few* books), which one (*this* pencil, *the* pencil, *my* pencil), or how much (*very* slowly, *half* sick, *almost too* late).

Modifiers are divided into two main classes: adjectives and adverbs. Any word which modifies a noun or pronoun is an adjective in function; an adverb is any word which modifies a verb, an adjective, or another adverb.

My very talented roommate budgets most carefully.

In this sentence, *my* and *talented* are adjectives, since they modify *roommate; carefully* is an adverb modifying the verb *budgets; most* is an adverb modifying the adverb *carefully* (it tells how carefully); and *very* is an adverb modifying the adjective *talented*.

adj.	adv.	adj.	noun	verb	adv.	adv.
My	very	talented	roommate	budgets	most	carefully.

Difficulties caused by dangling or misplaced modifiers are more fully discussed in chapter 8.

S|elem

16 c
identifying subject and verb

The analysis of any sentence begins with the identification of the simple subject and the verb. Look first for the verb: a word or group of words that states an action or happening.

> I *sprained* my wrist.
> Joe Miller *published* nothing.
> The fire *burned* out.
> He *has* never *painted* landscapes before.
> *The two parts of the verb are separated by "never."*

Some verbs merely assert that something is or was or seems to be (see section 16f):

> He *is* a fine mechanic.
> There *were* two reasons for believing his story.
> This story *seems* plausible.
> The student *looked* weary.

When you have found the verb, ask yourself the question, "Who or what ____?" putting the verb in the blank space. The answer to the question is the subject, and if you strip away the modifiers you have the *simple subject*.

> A long, dull *speech* followed the dinner.

What followed the dinner? A *long, dull speech*. But *long* and *dull* are adjectives describing *speech,* and the simple subject is *speech*.

Use of this method is especially helpful when the normal order of the sentence is inverted (that is, when the subject comes *after* the verb) or when the sentence begins with an introductory word like "there."

> Across the Alps lies *Italy*.

The verb in this sentence is *lies*. What lies across the Alps? The answer is the subject, *Italy*.

Consider the following sentence:

There is a serious **error** in the first paragraph.

In this sentence the verb is *is,* and the predicate asserts that something "is in the first paragraph." What? Certainly not the word *there*. *There* does not name anything and hence cannot be the subject; it is an idiomatic introductory word. The answer to the question is "a serious error," and *error* is the simple subject.

16 c

Note that in a sentence which asks a question the subject often comes after the verb if it is a form of the *auxiliary* verb *have* or *be* (see *auxiliary* in chapter 22).

verb	*subject*	
Have	you	the time?
Is	he	gone?

auxiliary	*subject*	*verb*	
Have	you	returned the books?
Did	she	buy	a lock?
May	they	come	in?

	auxiliary	*subject*	*verb*
What kind of lock did		you	buy?

In an imperative sentence the subject is not expressed. Since a command or request is addressed directly to someone, he need not be named.

subject	*verb*	
( )	Come	in.
( )	Shut	the door.

	subject	*verb*	
Please	( )	take this to the post office.

S|elem

A sentence may have several nouns as its subject, since it is possible to make one assertion about several things. Such a contruction is called a *compound subject*.

> *compound subject*
> **Richmond** and **Hyatt**   have been elected.
> The **trees** and **plants**   were dying.

Similarly, it is possible to use a *compound predicate*—that is, to make several assertions about one subject.

> *compound predicate*
> The car   **swerved, skidded,** and **ran** into the ditch.
> Marilyn   **changed** her clothes and **dressed** for dinner.

EXERCISES

Pick out the subjects and verbs in the following sentences. Note that either the subject or the verb may be compound.

1. After locking the door, the stewardess sat down at the rear of the plane.
2. Invisible to us, the pilot and copilot were already in their places.
3. Signs warning passengers not to smoke and to fasten their seat belts flashed on.
4. Directly beneath the signs was a door leading to the pilot's compartment.
5. Altogether there were about sixty passengers on the plane.
6. In a few moments the plane moved, slowly at first, and then roared into life.
7. After taxiing out to the airstrip, the pilot hesitated a moment to check the runway.
8. Then with a sudden rush of speed the plane roared down the runway and gradually began to climb.
9. Below us, at the edge of the airport, were markers and signal lights.
10. The football field and the quarter mile track enabled me to identify the high school.

16 d
direct object

The *direct object* is one way of completing the assertion made by a certain type of verb.

Some verbs, called *intransitive,* require nothing to complete them; that is, in themselves they make a full assertion about the subject.

> After meeting all the relatives, my cousin **left**.
> In a heavy rain, cabbage **may explode**.

Other verbs, however, are incomplete by themselves. If one says only "I bought," the reader is left hanging in mid-air and is apt to ask "What did you buy?" Words which answer such a question, and thus complete the assertion, are called *complements* of the verb (see chapter 22).

subject	*verb*	*complement*
I	bought	a scarf.

The commonest type of complement is the *direct object* of a transitive verb, illustrated in the sentence above. The direct object is usually a noun or pronoun, though it may be a phrase or a clause, and it usually names the thing acted upon by the subject.

subject	*verb*	*direct object*
My nephew	built	a water clock.
They	chased	the soccer ball.

The easiest way to identify a direct object is to say the simple subject and verb and then ask the question "What?" My nephew built what? The answer, *clock,* is the direct object of the verb *built*. Note that the direct object may be compound.

subject	*verb*	*direct object*
I	borrowed	a tent, a sleeping bag, and a gas stove.

S|elem

16 e
indirect object

In addition to a direct object, certain verbs (usually involving an act of giving), may take an *indirect object,* a complement that receives whatever is named by the direct object. Consider the following sentence:

> The Constitution grants us certain rights.

What does the Constitution grant? *Rights* is the direct object. Who receives them? *Us* is the indirect object—the receiver of what is named by the direct object *rights*. Note that the same meaning could be expressed by a phrase:

> The Constitution grants certain rights **to us**.

An indirect object is usually the equivalent of a phrase beginning with *to* or *for*.

> I gave **her** a receipt = I gave a receipt **to her**.
> I wrote **him** a check = I wrote a check **for him**.

16 f
subjective complements

Linking verbs, sometimes called copulative verbs, are those which assert, with varying degrees of assurance, that something is, or looks or sounds or seems or appears to be. Linking verbs (all forms of *be,* plus such verbs as *become, seem, appear, look, sound, feel, taste,* etc.) require a *subjective complement,* a word which completes the predicate by giving another name for the subject or describing the subject. Consider the following sentence:

> Floyd is the clerk.

In this sentence, *clerk* cannot be called the direct object, since it is merely another name for Floyd, and it can be made the subject of the sentence without changing the meaning.

> The clerk is Floyd.

(Contrast "Floyd fired the clerk," in which the direct object, *clerk,* names another person, who is acted upon by Floyd. Making *clerk* the subject of this sentence changes the meaning entirely.) A noun which serves as a subjective complement of a linking verb is usually called a *predicate noun.*

Linking verbs may also be completed by an adjective which describes the subject. Such a subjective complement is called a *predicate adjective.*

> The musical was **routine** and **unimaginative**.

Routine and *unimaginative* describe *musical,* but instead of being directly attached to the noun ("a routine, unimaginative musical"), they are joined to it by the linking verb *was* and become predicate adjectives.

EXERCISES

Pick out the subjects and verbs in the following sentences. Identify direct objects, indirect objects, predicate nouns, and predicate adjectives.

1. As a wedding present, my uncle gave us a picture.
2. It was an original ink sketching by Picasso.
3. The technique was interesting, since Picasso had used only a few brief lines.
4. It seemed a late work, according to a friend to whom I showed it.
5. We hung it in the living room and it looked good.
6. I wrote my uncle a note and thanked him for the picture.
7. We enjoyed it for several months, until my friend told us its value.

17
phrases

A group of words may have the same function in a sentence as a single word. For example, in the sentence

The train to Boston leaves in ten minutes.

the group of words *in ten minutes* modifies the verb *leaves* in exactly the same way as an adverb like *soon*. Similarly, *to Boston* functions like an adjective: it describes and identifies *train*. Such groups of words, which do not make a complete statement but which function like a single word, are called *phrases*. Phrases may be named for the kind of word around which they are constructed—prepositional, participial, gerund, or infinitive. Or they may be named by the way they function in a sentence—as adjective, adverb, or noun phrases. *To Boston* in the sentence above is a prepositional phrase used as an adjective. For a general discussion of problems in sentence structure with phrases, see chapter 8.

17 a
prepositional phrases

A preposition is usually defined as a word showing relationship which combines with a noun or pronoun (its object) to form a modifying phrase.

The following are prepositions in phrases:
"an agreement *between us*," "a motel *in New Orleans*," "slid *under the table*," "try *with all my strength*." Some of the most

common prepositions are *of, by, with, at, in, on, to, for, between, through, from.* Prepositional phrases usually modify nouns or verbs, and they are accordingly described as adjective or adverb phrases.

The lyrics *in the musical* were written *by Stephen Sondheim.*

adjective
adverb

17 b
verbals and verbal phrases

A very common type of phrase is built around a verbal, instead of a preposition. A *verbal* is a verb form used as some other part of speech. *Hunting* is a form of the verb *to hunt,* and while it may be used as part of the verb in a construction (*was hunting, has been hunting*), it may also be used as an adjective to modify a noun: *hunting dog.* For discussion of problems in sentence structure with dangling verbal phrases, see section 8c.

A verbal which modifies a noun is called a *participle.* Note that a participle may be in the past tense, as well as in the present—a *used* car, with *worn* upholstery. A participle joined with a subject (and sometimes a complement) and grammatically unconnected with the rest of the sentence is called an *absolute phrase.* It usually tells when, why, or how something happened.

ABSOLUTE PHRASE   *The floodwater having receded,* people began returning to their homes.

When a verb form ending in *ing* is used as a noun, it is called a *gerund.*

gerund
Hunting is his hobby.

In this sentence, *hunting* is a gerund since it serves as the subject of the sentence. Gerunds may also be used as the objects of verbs or of prepositions.

obj. of verb
He loves hunting and supports himself by *obj. of prep.* training dogs.

One other type of verbal is common: the *infinitive*. This is the ordinary form of the verb preceded by the particle *to* (to run, to see). Infinitives are frequently used as nouns—as subject or object of a verb.

subject
To win is his chief concern, and he hates *object* to lose.

They are sometimes used as adjectives and as adverbs (see *infinitive* in chapter 22).

Since they are verb forms, participles, gerunds, and infinitives may take objects and they may be modified by adverbs or by prepositional phrases. A verbal with its modifier and its object, or subject, makes up a verbal phrase and functions as a single part of speech, but it does not make a full statement.

INFINITIVE PHRASE The conductor ordered *me to tune my flute immediately.*
The infinitive "to tune" has a subject, "me," an object, "flute," and an adverbial modifier, "immediately." The whole phrase is the object of the verb "ordered"—What did the conductor order? He ordered me to tune my flute immediately.

PARTICIPIAL PHRASE *Climbing a silken line,* the spider was reaching his web.
Here the participle "climbing," with its object and modifier of the object, describes the spider.

GERUND PHRASE *Scaling a long slippery barracuda* takes strong hands.
Here the phrase—gerund, object, and the modifiers of the object—is the subject of the sentence.

17 c
appositive phrases

An appositive is another name for something already indicated—a noun added to explain another noun.

> Mr. Ruis, the *actor,* served as guest director.

Appositives with their modifiers may be regarded as phrases, since they function as a unit to give further information about a noun.

APPOSITIVE PHRASE The dancing was on the green, *a terraced lawn bordered with hedge and shaded by tall trees.*

For punctuation of appositives, see section 28d.

EXERCISES

Pick out the phrases in the following sentences. Identify them us prepositional, participial, gerund, infinitive, or appositive, and be ready to describe their function in the sentence.

1. On Tuesday I came home expecting to drive my car, a shiny new convertible, into the garage.
2. To my surprise, I found a ditch between the street and the driveway.
3. A crew of men had begun to lay a new water main along the curb.
4. Hoping that I would not get a ticket for overnight parking, I left the car in the street in front of the house.
5. For three days a yawning trench separated me from my garage.
6. Finding a place to park was difficult, since all the neighbors on my side of the street were in the same predicament.
7. By Friday the workmen had filled up the ditch, but my car, stained with dust and dew, looked ten years older.
8. I had to spend the weekend washing and polishing it.

18
clauses

Any group of words which makes a statement—that is, which contains a subject and a predicate, the key part of which is the *finite verb* (see definitions, chapter 22)—is called a *clause*. Except for elliptical questions and answers, every sentence must contain at least one clause.

18 a
independent and dependent clauses

Though all sentences must contain a clause, not all clauses are sentences. Some clauses, instead of making an independent statement, serve only as a subordinate part of the main sentence (see item 5, section 20a—dependent clauses as sentence fragments). Such clauses, called *dependent* or *subordinate*, perform a function like that of adjectives, adverbs, or nouns. *Independent clauses,* on the other hand, are capable of standing alone as complete sentences. They provide the framework to which modifiers, phrases, and dependent clauses are attached in each sentence; and any piece of connected discourse is made up of a series of independent clauses. For discussion of problems with clauses in sentence structure, see sections 8c and 8d.

"While I was sitting on the steps" is a clause, since it contains a subject, *I* and a verb, *was sitting.* But it is a dependent clause; in meaning it is incomplete (what happened?) and it would normally be used as a modifier. Its purpose is to tell *when* something happened, and the complete sentence should state *what* did happen.

| *dependent clause* | *independent clause* |
| While I was sitting on the steps, | I wrote a letter. |

18 b

A dependent clause is usually connected to the rest of the sentence by a relative pronoun (*who, which,* or *that*) or by conjunctions like *although, as, because, if, since, when,* or *where.* These are called subordinating conjunctions because they introduce clauses which are elements of a sentence rather than an independent statement. Notice how the addition of a subordinating conjunction to an independent clause makes the clause dependent. Let us begin with two independent clauses, each a complete sentence:

| *independent clause* | *independent clause* |
| We stayed home. | It was beginning to snow. |

Adding the subordinating conjunction *because* to the second clause makes it dependent; written as a separate sentence, it would now be a fragment (see section 20a, item 5). If correctly joined to the preceding clause, however, it modifies the verb *stayed,* giving the reason for our staying.

| *independent clause* | *conj. & dependent clause* |
| We stayed home | **because** it was beginning to snow. |

18 b
adverb clauses

An *adverb* or *adverbial clause* is a dependent clause used to modify a verb or an adjective or adverb in the main clause.

ADVERB CLAUSE   I went **where I was told to go**.
The adverb clause "where I was told to go" modifies the verb "went."

ADVERB CLAUSE   He dieted **because he was overweight**.
The adverb clause "because he was overweight" modifies the verb "dieted."

18 b

ADVERB CLAUSE   The trip was as pleasant **as they had hoped**.
The adverb clause "as they had hoped" modifies the adjective "pleasant."

ADVERB CLAUSE   The train arrived sooner **than they had expected**.
The adverb clause "than they had expected" modifies the adverb "sooner."

18 c
noun clauses

A *noun clause* functions as a noun in the sentence. It may be a subject or a complement in the main clause, or the object of a preposition or of a gerund.

NOUN CLAUSE   **That he couldn't jump twenty-two feet** was obvious.
The noun clause is used as the subject of the sentence.

NOUN CLAUSE   He said **that he could jump only twenty feet**.
The noun clause is used as the direct object of the verb "said."

NOUN CLAUSE   Sell it to **whoever will buy it**.
The noun clause is used as the object of the preposition "to."

NOUN CLAUSE   Keep out of trouble by doing **what comes naturally**.
The noun clause is used as the object of the gerund "doing."

18 d
adjective clauses and relative pronouns

A dependent clause used to modify a noun, pronoun, or substantive in the main clause is called an *adjective clause.*

ADJECTIVE CLAUSE The salesman *we met yesterday* showed us his library, *which includes all the first editions of Hemingway.*

The adjective clause "we met yesterday" modifies the noun "salesman"; the adjective clause "which includes all the first editions of Hemingway" modifies the noun "library."

Adjective clauses are usually introduced by a *relative pronoun,* which serves both as a pronoun and as a subordinating conjunction. Its function can be seen by some examples.

Ken was a leader; Ken never failed us.

This sentence consists of two independent clauses, but it would be more idiomatic to substitute a pronoun for the second "Ken."

Ken was a leader; *he* never failed us.

If, instead of using the personal pronoun *he,* we substitute the relative pronoun *who,* the second clause becomes dependent.

Ken was a leader *who* never failed us.

"Who never failed us" no longer will stand as an independent sentence; but when it is joined to the first clause, it functions as an adjective, modifying *leader.*

The relative pronouns *who* (and *whom*), *which,* and *that* always have two functions: they serve as subordinating conjunctions, connecting dependent clauses to independent ones, but they also function like nouns, as subject or complement in the dependent clause. Often the relative pronouns can be omitted—I received the book (*which, that*) I ordered.

The correct use of *who* and *whom* depends upon your ability to analyze the function of the relative pronoun in a dependent clause. See chapter 8 and section 24b. For punctuation of dependent clauses, see section 28g.

18 EXERCISES

Find the simple subject and verb of each clause in the following sentences. Point out the main clauses and the dependent clauses, and be prepared to state the function in each sentence of each dependent clause.

1. The movie director who did much to perfect the one-reel Western as a distinct genre was D. W. Griffith.
2. Shortly after he had entered movies in New York, Griffith achieved immediate success with his first film, which he directed in 1908.
3. Between 1908 and 1913, while he was directing Westerns, Griffith continually worked with techniques which, though they had been introduced by others, were developed and refined by him.
4. Griffith was delighted by the Western because it offered opportunities for spectacle and scope.
5. He found that the Western was an ideal genre in which to experiment with close-ups and with cross-cutting, the techniques he employed to build narrative suspense.
6. Some critics have pointed out that Griffith was more interested in dramatic situations which lent themselves to lively visual treatment than he was in the details of plot or conventional justice.
7. He would willingly let the villains go free whenever he felt the dramatic situation warranted it.
8. The close-up of the outnumbered settlers grimly hanging on and the panoramic view of the battle seen from afar were characteristic Griffith shots.
9. In 1915, Griffith produced *The Birth of a Nation,* the first great spectacle movie.

19
types of sentences

Sentences are traditionally classified, according to their structure, as simple, complex, compound, and compound-complex.

19 a
simple sentences

A *simple sentence* consists of one independent clause, with *no* dependent clauses attached, although it may have modifying phrases.

SIMPLE   The *subject* children hurriedly *verb* left for school.

SIMPLE   *mod. phrase* Slumped in the bottom of a skiff, *sub* I *verb* floated peacefully along.

Simple sentences are not necessarily short and jerky, but their over-use is apt to make one's writing seem both choppy and childish. So-called "primer" style is caused by a succession of short simple sentences. The remedy is to combine some of them into complex sentences (see section 7b).

19 b
complex sentences

The *complex sentence* contains one independent clause and one or more dependent clauses, which express subordinate ideas.

COMPLEX   *independent clause*   •   *dependent clause*
We lost touch with the Carters   after they moved.

COMPLEX   *ind. clause*   *dependent clause*
He was a man   who had many close friends.

COMPLEX   *dependent clause*
Although the spray contained endrin,
dependent clause   *independent clause*
which may harm people,   he used the poison on tomato plants.

The complex sentence has the advantage of flexibility; it can be variously arranged to produce variety of sentence pattern. It also provides selective emphasis, since the subordination of dependent clauses throws the weight of the sentence on the main clause.

19 c
compound sentences

The *compound sentence* consists of two or more independent clauses.

COMPOUND   *ind. clause*
He notified the office,   *and*   *ind. clause*
the manager corrected the error.

COMPOUND   *ind. clause*
This sentence is compound   ;   *ind. clause*
it has two main clauses.

S|type

Problems in parallel structure of compound sentences are treated in section 8a.

19 d
compound-complex sentences

When a compound sentence contains dependent clauses, the whole is sometimes described as a *compound-complex sentence*.

dependent clause
COMPOUND-COMPLEX Although the critics gave it good reviews,

independent clause
the play never attracted the public,   and

independent clause
the producers closed it reluctantly after two weeks

dependent clause
because they could not afford the losses.

For problems in subordination, see section 7b, and for parallelism, see section 8a.

EXERCISES

Classify the following sentences as simple, compound, complex, or compound-complex. Identify the subject, verb, and complement, if any, of each clause. Describe the function of each dependent clause. Describe phrases both by kind (prepositional, participial, etc.) and by function (adverb, adjective, etc.).

1. When Renaissance physicians began to study human anatomy by means of actual dissection, they concluded that the human body had changed since the days of antiquity.

S|type

2. Galen, an ancient Greek physician, was generally accepted as the authority on anatomy and physiology.

3. His theory of the four humors, blood, phlegm, bile, and black bile, was neat and logical, and authorities had accepted it for centuries.

4. Similarly, his account of the structure of the human body, revised by generations of scholars and now appearing in many printed editions, was generally accepted.

5. If dissection showed a difference from Galen's account, the obvious explanation was that man's structure had changed since Galen's time.

6. One man who refused to accept this explanation was Andreas Vesalius, a young Belgian physician who was studying in Italy.

7. Asked to edit the anatomical section of Galen's works, Vesalius found many errors in it.

8. Galen said that the lower jaw consisted of two parts, but Vesalius never found such a structure in his own dissections.

9. Vesalius finally concluded that Galen was describing the anatomy of lower animals—pigs, monkeys, and goats—and that he had never dissected a human body.

10. His realization that Galen could be wrong was a stimulus to Vesalius' own major work, a fully illustrated treatise on the human body based on actual observation.

20
sentence fragments

Every sentence must contain at least one independent clause.

In writing, it is necessary to mark the end of each sentence by a period. A careless writer, by putting the period in too soon, may seriously mislead the reader by cutting off a piece of the full sentence. If the piece does not contain an independent clause, the result is a *sentence fragment*. For example:

> The purpose of reciting five minutes in French was to encourage imitation of the recording. *Thus putting emphasis on intonation, rhythm, and pronunciation.*

This was meant to be one complete sentence. As it is written, however, the last part is a fragment, a participial phrase without subject or verb. This phrase should be attached to the previous sentence:

> The purpose of reciting five minutes in French was to encourage imitation of the recording, thus putting emphasis on intonation, rhythm, and pronunciation.

Frag

types of sentence fragments

Learn to recognize the types of sentence fragments most likely to occur in your writing and learn how to correct them.

The great majority of fragments fall into a few basic types. By learning these types, you can discover which kind(s) you are most prone to and correct them before the final draft. (For discussion of other incomplete constructions, see section 8g.)

1 appositive phrase

FRAGMENT   One thing I admire very much is a person with a strong character. *A person who will stand up for what he believes.*

CORRECTED   One thing I admire very much is a person with a strong character—a person who will stand up for what he believes.

FRAGMENT   A major economic problem is the number of unemployable people. *The uneducated and unskilled who already have families to support.*

CORRECTED   A major economic problem is the number of unemployable people—the uneducated and unskilled who already have families to support.

2 prepositional phrase

FRAGMENT   The receptionist was expected to appear efficient and serene, but it was impossible. *With the telephone ringing constantly and salesmen arriving every half hour for appointments.*

CORRECTED   The receptionist was expected to appear efficient and serene, but it was impossible. The telephone rang constantly and salesmen arrived every half hour for appointments.

The fragment might have been simply added to the preceding sentence, but making it into a separate sentence avoids a long trailing construction.

FRAGMENT The committee to elect Jensen spent long hours canvassing homes and mailing out brochures. *In the hope of a big turn-out of voters.*

CORRECTED The committee to elect Jensen spent long hours canvassing homes and mailing out brochures. It hoped for a big turn-out of voters.

3 participial phrase

FRAGMENT He had good reason for coming to college and choosing the one he did, unlike some of his classmates. *Having planned for several years to become a doctor.*

CORRECTED Unlike some of his classmates, he had good reason for coming to college and choosing the one he did, having planned for several years to become a doctor.

FRAGMENT I was surprised at the commotion in the magazine's office. Reporters, copywriters, and secretaries were rushing all over the place. *Running up and down the aisles, conferring with the editors, and talking in little groups.*

CORRECTED I was surprised at the commotion in the magazine's office. Reporters, copywriters, and secretaries were rushing all over the place, running up and down the aisles, conferring with the editors, and talking in little groups.

4 infinitive phrase

FRAGMENT The entire freshman class met that night in the gym with just one angry purpose in mind. *To get rid of hazing and the sophomore leaders.*

CORRECTED The entire freshman class met that night in the gym with just one angry purpose in mind: to get rid of hazing and the sophomore leaders.

FRAGMENT After a good deal of arguing, I finally received permission from my parents. To work for *Project Head Start that summer and perhaps even during the fall semester.*

CORRECTED After a good deal of arguing, I finally received permission from my parents to work for Project Head Start that summer and perhaps even during the fall semester.

Frag

5 dependent clause

FRAGMENT The first car was trying to get far enough ahead to pull off safely. *While the second car kept close in an effort to pass.*

CORRECTED The first car was trying to get far enough ahead to pull off safely, while the second car kept close in an effort to pass.

Note that the fragment could have been corrected by omitting the conjunction "while" and making two complete sentences.

FRAGMENT After so many weeks of worrying, I was grateful to learn of the college's loan funds. *Because I didn't know where I could turn for help or see how I could take a part-time job.*

CORRECTED After so many weeks of worrying, I was grateful to learn of the college's loan funds because I didn't know where I could turn for help or see how I could take a part-time job.

Usually the best way to correct a sentence fragment is to join it to the sentence of which it is logically a part. Sometimes, however, it is better to change the fragment into a full sentence, by adding a verb, a subject, or whatever else is lacking.

20 b
permissible incomplete sentences

Certain elliptical expressions are equivalent to sentences because the missing words are clearly understood. Such permissible incomplete sentences include the following:

1 questions and answers in conversation

Why not?   How much?
Because it's late.   Two dollars.

2 exclamations and requests

At last!
This way, please.

Radar Speed Check
Compare this example with similar traffic signs, such as
"Unlawful to Litter Highway."

3 transitions
So much for the first point.
Now to consider the next question.

In addition, fragments are sometimes deliberately used for particular effects, especially in narrative or descriptive writing. In most expository writing, however, there is seldom occasion or excuse for writing sentence fragments.

ACCEPTABLE Outwardly a rough, gruff person. Inwardly a warm, tender father. This is Paw Sexton.
ACCEPTABLE They turned left. "We took the wrong road again. No log fence here." Ralph drove back to the intersection. Impossible. The second time they twisted the directions.

EXERCISES

a. For each of the following student sentences, identify the cause of the fragment and correct it in whatever way seems most effective.

1. When you really get down to it, homework is more likely to be assigned in the academic subjects. Whether they are English, math, science, or some language.

2. One thing which I dislike very much is a person with a mean streak. A person who will go out of his way to do harm to others.

3. Some people would question whether or not he could even survive in the wilderness just because of the environment. The sun being so very hot in the day, and it being so cold at night.

4. During the day the eel lies buried in the mud or concealed under rocks or in seaweed. But at night begins its prowling for food.

5. As this much summary indicates, the first part of the

Frag

story is deceiving. So far, just another tale about a college boy—maybe the all-American ideal—who gets his girl and job and is living on easy street.

6. For some people, life is only boring or painful. Especially if the person has no purpose, no goal in life.

7. The number of the very rich and the very poor having been reduced, leaving most Americans in one large middle class.

8. I now think that my high school was too progressive in some ways. Meaning that it didn't teach how to read and write correctly.

9. The head librarian threatened to close the stacks to all students. Because the cost of replacing stolen books was mounting each year.

10. Tyrone Guthrie's movie production of *Oedipus Rex* was very impressive. Although it took me awhile to get used to the masked actors.

b. For each of the following sentences, identify the cause of the fragment and correct it in whatever way seems most satisfactory.

1. Many people still believe the old superstition that men are stronger than women. Although it has been proved that women are better able to withstand shock and exposure.

2. Some students just aren't suited for boarding-school life. In which case it is much better for them to go to day schools.

3. The City Council's decision to limit speed on a road in the campus but not on a street near an elementary school seemed ridiculous. Since small children are less able to cross streets responsibly.

4. Long hours of practice after classes, the weekends usually taken up with games, and most evenings spent in study. Athletes have little time for working their way through college.

5. In New England there are many colleges for men only. The reason being that they were founded primarily to train the clergy.

6. Historians are interested only in the more civilized societies that have existed in the past. The ones that have produced great works of art, science, or technology.

7. Every month, the entire research staff spends a full day together in informal conference. To discuss at length current problems and propose and criticize new ideas.

8. To Lowell, the canals on Mars appeared as fine, straight lines from 100 to over 1,000 miles in length. Not really straight lines, of course, but parts of great circles.

20

9. A description of being lost in the Grand Canyon when Schuyler's life was saved by a discarded semi-rotten orange.

10. Books being a means of communication whereby a writer can share his experience with thousands of men, in his own time and in the future.

11. Thanks to the movies, I have seen many remote parts of America. From the wheat fields of Alaska to the cactus deserts of southern Arizona.

12. The distance between the stars is immense. So immense that it is difficult to find a unit of measurement which will help one grasp it imaginatively.

21
comma splices and fused sentences

21 a
comma splices

Do not join two main clauses with only a comma between them (comma splice).

COMMA SPLICE   I'm sure that the teen-agers of today didn't invent cheating, it must have been going on for quite a long time.

COMMA SPLICE   Next the potter rolls the clay between his hands, this gets out the air bubbles.

A comma splice (sometimes called a "comma fault") is two or more main clauses separated *only* by a comma. The result can be either a misreading, as in

I wonder if he is thinking, he probably won't tell.

or a failure to show clear sequence and relationship as in

There was an extremely heavy rain on Monday night, after the storm was over, the streams were overflowing.

You can catch many comma splices in revision by reading your paper aloud: if you drop your voice or pause conspicuously at a comma, check the sentence to see if it is two separate statements.

If you cannot distinguish main clauses from each other or from subordinate clauses, reread chapter 18 carefully. To use any of the following methods for correcting comma splices, you must be able to recognize main clauses.

21 a-1
subordination of one main clause

Revise the comma splice by subordinating one of the main clauses.

COMMA SPLICE   The banks were closed, John couldn't get the necessary money.
SUBORDINATION   *Since* the banks were closed, John couldn't get the necessary money.

COMMA SPLICE   There are many good reasons for working in the summer, only a few of them can be discussed.
SUBORDINATION   There are many good reasons for working in the summer, only a few *of which* can be discussed.
or
SUBORDINATION   *Of* the many good reasons for working in the summer, only a few can be discussed.

COMMA SPLICE   The dealer repossessed the car, the payment wasn't made.
SUBORDINATION   The dealer repossessed the car *when* the payment wasn't made.

Subordination is one effective correction for a comma splice; it shows the dependence of one idea upon another. But be sure you mean such dependence before you correct the comma splice by subordination.

CS

coordination of clauses by conjunction

Revise the comma splice by using a coordinating conjunction to join the two main clauses if you want to give them equal emphasis.

COMMA SPLICE We will add another room to the house this summer, painting will have to wait until next year.
COORDINATION We will add another room to the house this summer, *but* painting will have to wait until next year.

COMMA SPLICE Reading is partly a matter of personal taste, every reviewer ought to keep this fact in mind.
COORDINATION Reading is partly a matter of personal taste, *and* every reviewer ought to keep this fact in mind.

COMMA SPLICE As the development of the atomic bomb, the computer systems, and guided missiles shows, technology, indeed basic scientific research itself, is often determined by political and military considerations, many people do not recognize this interdependence and instead naïvely regard changes in technology as changes which simply "happen."
COORDINATION As the development of the atomic bomb, the computer systems, and guided missiles shows, technology, indeed basic scientific research itself, is often determined by political and military considerations; *but* many people do not recognize this interdependence and instead regard changes in technology as changes which simply "happen."

The most usual pattern is the coordinating conjunction (*and, but, for, nor, or*) preceded by a comma. When long, complex clauses punctuated internally by commas are joined, a semicolon along with a coordinating conjunction may be needed to show the main division of the sentence.

21 a-3
coordination of clauses by
semicolon

Revise the comma splice by using a semicolon to join the two main clauses.

COMMA SPLICE   First I replaced the foundation, then I added another story.
SEMICOLON   First I replaced the foundation; then I added another story.

21 a-4
separation of clauses into sentences

Revise the comma splice by making each main clause into a sentence.

COMMA SPLICE   There was an extremely heavy rain on Monday night, after the storm was over, the streams were overflowing.
TWO SENTENCES   There was an extremely heavy rain on Monday night. After the storm was over, the streams were overflowing.

Whether you should use a semicolon or period will depend upon your intended meaning.

There are no hard and fast rules telling which of these four methods of correcting comma splices should be used. Judgment is required to decide what the sentence is intended to say. Often it is best to recast the sentence entirely.

21 b
commas with short
independent clauses

Use commas to join short independent clauses in a series only when you are striving for special narrative effects or emphasis.

CS

Short, closely related independent clauses in a series are occasionally joined only by commas. Such punctuation is often used in narratives, more sparingly in formal writing. But unless you are writing a narrative and have permission to use it, or unless you are an experienced writer, you should avoid this punctuation.

**21
b**

ACCEPTABLE The wind blew, the shutters banged, the children trembled.

ACCEPTABLE She comes, she looks, she purchases.

21 c
clauses linked by
conjunctive adverbs

Two main clauses linked by a conjunctive adverb require a semicolon or a period between them.

One of the commonest forms of the comma splice is the use of the comma between two main clauses linked by a conjunctive adverb. Such conjunctive adverbs as *also, besides, hence, however, instead, moreover, then,* and *therefore* are all conventionally preceded by a semicolon or period when they introduce a second independent clause.

COMMA SPLICE I hadn't read the text very carefully, therefore I was surprised by how well I did on the test.
CORRECTED I hadn't read the text very carefully; therefore I was surprised by how well I did on the test.

COMMA SPLICE He didn't like the movie at all, consequently he willingly left before intermission.
CORRECTED He didn't like the movie at all. Consequently, he willingly left before intermission.

Omitting the semicolon or period before the conjunctive adverb can result in grotesque misreading:

> The sergeant had command of his temper and his men, also the general who was reviewing that day was in a good mood.

One way to tell a conjunctive adverb from a pure conjunction is to try to change its position in a sentence. A conjunctive adverb need not stand first in its clause:

CONJUNCTIVE ADVERB   The children were expected to stay indoors on rainy afternoons; they could not, *however,* resist the challenge of a mud fight that one afternoon.

CONJUNCTIVE ADVERB   The children were expected to stay indoors on rainy afternoons; *however,* they could not resist the challenge of a mud fight that one afternoon.

21 d
fused sentences

Do not fuse two main clauses by omitting punctuation between them (a fused sentence).

FUSED SENTENCE   He took the job he was offered otherwise he would have had to borrow more money.

The fused sentence is a worse error than the comma splice since it often results in more serious misreadings. To correct a fused sentence you should either rewrite it entirely or you should use the other means for correcting the comma splice (see sections 21a-1 through 21a-4).

REWRITTEN   To avoid borrowing money, he took the job he was offered.

CORRECTED   He took the job he was offered; otherwise he would have had to borrow more money.

CS

EXERCISES

a. In the following student sentences, revise the comma splice or fused sentences by whatever means seems most effective. Be prepared to explain the reasons for the means you choose.

1. The offense had thrown every conceivable blocker at Tom, after five men had run him down and walked on him, the runner came through the hole and Tom missed him.
2. No one wants him, he is an outcast from life's feast.
3. On most report cards there is a special place for marking effort this is put there so that the teacher can show how hard a student has tried.
4. Nick is trying to relive an experience, thus he must have everything just as it once was, and nothing must go wrong which would spoil the occasion.
5. I obeyed my elders, but I always weighed the facts and formed my own judgments, apparently this independence of mine made some adults angry.
6. But why shouldn't carols be played in shops and stores it's all in the spirit of Christmas.
7. But Huck doesn't pray, instead he thinks of all the times that Jim has been good to him.
8. Once in her room she did a few dance steps, looked at her unmade bed, and shrugged unconcernedly, then she glanced out the window in hopes of catching sight of her little brother.
9. But with the first of September the warm days were over, cold winds began to blow, stirring up freshly turned dirt in the graveyard, and causing old Charles to cast apprehensive glances at the sky.

b. Revise each of the following comma splices or fused sentences by using subordination.

1. Congress passed the bill only after long hours of debate there was strong feeling on both sides.
2. Ironically, the population migration has been especially great to places like Arizona, New Mexico, and

Southern California, these are places with a limited water supply.

3. Whenever she was about to take a picture, she gave a nervous giggle, this giggling was an odd habit.

4. There was a long string of gas stations outside the city, any driver could fill up easily.

5. We found the sea too choppy for sailing or swimming, we stayed on shore.

21

c. Correct any comma splices you find by whatever means seems best and be prepared to explain your choice. Mark with a C any sentences that may stand unrevised.

1. Permission was not granted for the interview, however the reporters never gave up hope.

2. The new dictionary was more than a revision of the old one, the compilers had redefined the entries and included many more examples of usage.

3. The critic wrote that as the commercials became longer and more offensive, the shows became shorter and more innocuous, also he felt advertisers ought to be forced to watch.

4. Mary and her sister are identical twins, though they don't dress alike, indeed they resent being expected to act alike.

5. The jet is faster than the propeller airplane of World War II and can, moreover, fly at higher altitudes.

6. In speech class he announced he would give a demonstration-lecture on how not to pack a suitcase, after he was finished, the other students clapped reluctantly.

7. The counsellor gathered the paddles, came down to the pier, and untied the canoe, then he waited while the campers climbed in.

8. From the top of Whiteface, you can see miles of rolling mountain country, its valleys are studded with lakes and streams.

9. The medical insurance was cheap and comprehensive, according to its advertisers, the people who bought it soon claimed otherwise.

22

definitions of grammatical terms

Absolute phrase See section 17b.

Active voice See **Voice**.

Adjective A part of speech used to describe or limit the meaning of a substantive. There are the following kinds:

> DESCRIPTIVE   a *true* friend, a *poor* man.
> LIMITING   a boy, *an* apple, *the* man.

Notice that many kinds of pronouns regularly perform the function of an adjective:

> POSSESSIVE   *my* book, *his* sister, *your* house.
> DEMONSTRATIVE   *this* chair, *these* papers.
> INTERROGATIVE   *whose* hat? *which* one?
> INDEFINITE   *any* card, *each* boy, *some* candy.

Adverb A part of speech used to modify a verb, an adjective, or another adverb. An adverb answers the questions: *Where? When? How? Why?* or *To what extent?*

> He bowed *politely*.
> *"Politely" modifies the verb "bowed."*

A **very** old woman came in.
"Very" modifies the adjective "old."

He was **too** much absorbed to listen.
"Too" modifies the adverb "much."

Substantives may be used adverbially:

He walked **two miles**.
"Two miles" modifies the verb "walked."

He walked **two miles** farther.
"Two miles" modifies the adverb "farther."

Antecedent   A word, phrase, or clause to which a pronoun refers (see section 23b).

I saw the **house** long before I reached **it**.
"House" is the antecedent of "it."

This is a **problem which** cannot be solved without calculus.
"Problem" is the antecedent of "which."

Appositive   A substantive attached to another substantive and denoting the same person or thing. A substantive is said to be *in apposition* with the substantive to which it is attached (see section 17c).

George, my **cousin**, was enjoying his favorite sport— **sailing**.
"Cousin" is in apposition with "George"; "sailing" is in apposition with "sport."

Article   The word *the* is called the definite article; the word *a* or *an* is called the *indefinite article*. Articles can be classed with adjectives.

Auxiliary   When the verbs *be, have, do, shall, will, may, can, must,* and *ought* assist in forming the voices, modes, and tenses of other verbs, they are auxiliaries.

I *was* given a message.
He *should have* known better.
He *has been* gone a week.

Cardinal number Any of the numbers *one, two, three, four,* etc., denoting quantity, in distinction from *first, second, third,* etc., which are *ordinal numbers* and which show sequence. Both cardinal and ordinal numbers can function as adjectives.

Case The inflection of a noun (girls', friend's) or pronoun (she, her, hers) to show its relationship to other words. In English, pronouns are classified into three cases (see chapter 24).

1. NOMINATIVE (OR SUBJECTIVE) *I* spoke; *they* listened; *she* dozed.
The inflected pronoun functions as subject.

2. OBJECTIVE John tossed *me* the ball. I collided with two other players and knocked *them* down.
The inflected pronoun functions as object.

3. POSSESSIVE (OR GENITIVE) *His* anger and *mine* were identical. *Our* scores were higher than *theirs*. They wondered *whose* grade was the highest.
The inflected pronoun shows possession or a similar relationship.

In modern times, English nouns are inflected only to indicate the genitive case: *Jerry's* money and *Sarah's* money was invested at their *parents'* advice; this allayed the *relatives'* fear about the *boy's* education and the *girl's* future.

Clause A group of words containing a subject and predicate (see chapter 18). Clauses that can stand alone as complete sentences are *independent* (*principal* or *main*) clauses. Clauses that are not by themselves complete in meaning are *dependent* (*subordinate*) clauses. Subordinate clauses are used as nouns, adjectives, or adverbs. They are usually introduced by subordinating words.

We heard him **when he came in**.
"We heard him" is the main clause; "when he came in" is the subordinate clause.

That she will be late is certain.
Subordinate clause used as a noun.

The woman **who spoke to us** is our neighbor.
Subordinate clause used as an adjective.

He will come in **when he is ready**.
Subordinate clause used as an adverb.

Clauses that play the same part in a sentence, whether they are main or subordinate, are called *coordinate clauses*.

The bell rang and **everyone stood up**.
Coordinate main clauses.

He left **because he did not like the work** and **because the pay was low**
Coordinate subordinate clauses.

Comparison Inflection of an adjective or adverb to indicate an increasing degree of quality, quantity, or manner.

POSITIVE DEGREE   Their house is **cold**.
COMPARATIVE DEGREE   Their house is **colder** than ours.
SUPERLATIVE DEGREE   Their house is the **coldest** in town.

When adjectives have one or two syllables, the comparative degree is usually formed by adding *er* to the positive; and the superlative degree is usually formed by adding *est* to the positive. Adjectives of more than two syllables, and most adverbs, form the comparative degree by placing *more* before the positive; and the superlative degree is usually formed by placing *most* before the positive. Some adjectives have irregular comparison: e.g., *good, better, best; bad, worse, worst* (see section 25c).

Def

Complement   Traditionally, a word or phrase added to a verb to complete the sense of the statement. It may be the direct object of a transitive verb, an indirect object, or a predicate noun or adjective (see sections 16d, 16e, 24c and 25a).

DIRECT OBJECT: A big wave swamped our *boat*.
INDIRECT OBJECT: I paid *him* the money.
PREDICATE NOUN: Our destination was *Corsica*.
The referee called Sanchez the *winner*.
PREDICATE ADJECTIVE: The waves were *enormous*.
A limber branch made the tree-house *shaky*.

"Corsica" and "enormous" are called subjective complements (see section 16f). "Shaky" and "winner" are sometimes called objective complements (see **Objective complement**).

Complex sentence   See section 19b.
Compound sentence   See section 19c.
Conjugation   The inflected forms of a verb which show person, number, tense, voice, and mode. The following is a simplified conjugation of the indicative mode of the verb *See:*

	Active Voice	*Passive Voice*
PRESENT TENSE		
sing. 1.	I see	I am seen
2.	you see	you are seen
3.	he (she, it) sees	he is seen
pl. 1.	we see	we are seen
2.	you see	you are seen
3.	they see	they are seen
PAST TENSE		
sing. 1.	I saw	I was seen
2.	you saw	you were seen
3.	he saw	he was seen

Active Voice	Passive Voice
pl. 1. we saw	we were seen
2. you saw	you were seen
3. they saw	they were seen

FUTURE TENSE

sing. 1. I shall see	I shall be seen
2. you will see	you will be seen
3. he will see	he will be seen
pl. 1. we shall see	we shall be seen
2. you will see	you will be seen
3. they will see	they will be seen

PERFECT TENSE

sing. 1. I have seen	I have been seen, etc.
2. you have seen	
3. he has seen	
pl. 1. we have seen	
2. you have seen	
3. they have seen	

PAST PERFECT TENSE

sing. 1. I had seen	I had been seen, etc.
2. you had seen	
3. he had seen	
pl. 1. we had seen	
2. you had seen	
3. they had seen	

FUTURE PERFECT TENSE

1. I shall have seen, etc.	I shall have been seen, etc.

See section 26d on *Shall-Will*. See also **Principal parts.**

Conjunction A part of speech used to connect words, phrases, and clauses. There are the following kinds:

COORDINATING Pure, or simple, conjunctions: *and, or, nor, but, for, yet.*

Def

COORDINATING Correlatives: *either . . . or, neither . . . nor, both . . . and, not only . . . but* [*also*].

SUBORDINATING Conjunctions introducing adjective clauses: *that, when, where, while, whence,* etc.

SUBORDINATING Conjunctions introducing adverbial clauses: *when, while, where, because, so that, although, since, as, after, if, until,* etc.

Coordinating conjunctions (see section 21a-2) connect sentence elements that are logically and grammatically equal; i.e., they may connect two subjects or two verbs or two adjective clauses, etc. Subordinating conjunctions (see section 21a-1) connect subordinate (or dependent) clauses with their principal (or independent) clauses.

Conjunctive adverb An introductory adverb, or sentence modifier, which indicates the relationship between principal clauses: *however, moreover, therefore, nevertheless, also, hence, consequently, then, furthermore,* etc. Between independent clauses it must be reinforced by a semicolon or by a coordinating conjunction (see section 21c).

Coordinate Sentence elements that are parallel in grammatical construction are coordinate. In the sentence *He and she talked lengthily and earnestly, and at last agreed, he* and *she* are coordinate; *talked* and *agreed* are coordinate; *lengthily* and *earnestly* are coordinate.

Copula, or Linking verb A verb, like *to be, to seem, to appear, to become,* which acts mainly as a connecting link between the subject and the predicate noun or predicate adjective.

Correlative conjunctions Coordinating conjunctions used in pairs:

> *both* my father *and* my mother
> *neither* my father *nor* my mother
> *not only* deceived us *but also* accused us of deception.

Declension See **Inflection.**
Demonstrative See **Adjective** and **Pronoun.**

Direct address A grammatical construction in which the speaker or writer addresses a second person directly.

> *Mary,* wait for me.
> *Friends, Romans, countrymen,* lend me your ears.

Direct object See **Object** and section 16d.

Elliptical expression An expression which is grammatically incomplete, but the meaning of which is clear because the omitted words are implied.

> ELLIPTICAL *If possible,* bring your drawings along.
> COMPLETE *If it is possible,* bring your drawings along.

Finite verb A term used to distinguish a verb which makes an assertion and can serve as a predicate from infinitives, participles, and gerunds, which cannot serve as predicates. See **Verbals.**

> FINITE VERB The alarm *rang* and I *got* up.
> VERBAL The *ringing* alarm awoke me and I hurried *to get* up.

Genitive See **Case** and sections 24e and 24f.

Gerund A verb form ending in *ing* and used as a noun. It should be distinguished from the present participle, which also ends in *ing* but is used as an adjective. (See **Participle.**)

> SUBJECT OF VERB *Fishing* is tiresome.
> OBJECT OF VERB I hate *fishing.*
> OBJECT OF PREPOSITION I have a dislike of *fishing.*
> PREDICATE NOUN The sport I like least is *fishing.*

Like a noun, the gerund may be modified by an adjective. In the sentence *They were tired of his long-winded preaching, his* and *long-winded* modify the gerund *preaching.* A noun or pronoun preceding a gerund is normally in the genitive case—e.g., *his* fishing. Since a gerund is a verb form, it may take an object and be modified by an adverb.

> He disapproved of our **taking** luggage with us.
> *"Luggage" is the object of the gerund "taking."*

> Our success depends upon his **acting** promptly.
> *"Promptly" is an adverb modifying the gerund "act-ing."*

Idioms An expression whose meaning cannot be determined from the literal meaning of the individual words, but which as a whole is understood and used by speakers of a particular language or region.

> He **was taken in** by the practical jokes.
> **Every now and then,** I **have a mind to tell him off.**
> **Between you and me,** I think you **had a hand in this.**
> She was **out of her head** for awhile, but she finally **pulled herself together.**

Imperative See **Mode.**
Indicative See **Mode.**
Indirect object See **Object** and section 16e.
Infinitive That form of the verb usually preceded by *to. To* is called *the sign of the infinitive.*

The infinitive has two tenses, present and perfect, and if the verb is transitive, both active and passive voices.

Since it is a verb form, the infinitive can have a subject, can take an object or a predicate complement, and can be modified by an adverb.

> We asked **her** to come.
> *"Her" is the subject of "to come."*

> They asked to meet **him.**
> *"Him" is the object of "to meet."*

> We hope to hear **soon.**
> *"Soon" is the adverbial modifier of "to hear."*

The infinitive may be used as a noun.

subject
To meet her is a pleasure.

predicate complement
His chief delight is **to tease** her.

object of verb
He wished **to see** the dog.

The infinitive may be used as an adjective.

noun modified   *modifier*
He gave me a **book**   **to read**.

predicate adjective
He is **to be congratulated**.

The infinitive may be used as an adverb.

verb modified
He **waited** to see you.

adj. modified
We are **happy** to help.

adv. modified
He's old **enough** to travel alone.

Inflection   A change in the form of a word to show a change in meaning or use. Nouns may be inflected to show number (*man, men*) and the genitive case (*dog, dog's*). Pronouns may be inflected to show case (*he, him*), person (*I, you*), number (*I, we*), and gender (*his, hers*). Verbs are inflected to show person (I *go*, he *goes*), number (she *is*, they *are*), tense (he *is*, he *was*), voice (I *received* your letter, your letter *was received*), and mode (if this *be* treason). Adjectives and adverbs are inflected to show

Def

relative degree (*strong, stronger, strongest*). The inflection of substantives is called *declension;* that of verbs, *conjugation;* that of adjectives and adverbs, *comparison.*

Intensive pronoun   When the pronouns *myself, himself, yourself,* etc., are used in apposition, they are called intensives because they serve to intensify or emphasize the substantives that they are used with; e.g., *I myself will do it. I saw the bishop himself.* When one of these words is used as the object of a verb and designates the same person or thing as the subject of that verb, it is called a *reflexive pronoun;* e.g., *I hurt myself. They benefit themselves.*

Interjection   An exclamation that has no grammatical relation with the rest of the sentence; e.g., *oh, alas, please.*

Interrogative pronoun   See **Pronoun.**

Intransitive   See **Verb.**

Irregular verb   A verb which forms its past tenses by a change of the root vowel: *sing, sang, sung; drink, drank, drunk.* Such a verb is sometimes called a *strong verb.* See section 26c for a table of irregular verbs.

Linking verb   See **Copula.**

Mode (mood)   Inflection of a verb to indicate whether it is intended to make a statement or command or to express a condition contrary to fact.

The *indicative mode* is used to state a fact or to ask a question.

> The wind is blowing.
> Is it raining?

The *imperative mode* is used to express a command or a request.

> Do it immediately.
> Please answer the telephone.
> Come up for a drink when you are in our neighborhood.
> Kindly take your feet off the table.

The *subjunctive mode* is used to express a wish, a doubt, a concession, a condition contrary to fact (see section 26e). In speech and in all but "edited" writing, the subjunctive mode has largely been replaced by the indicative.

WISH I wish that I **were** able to help you.
CONDITION CONTRARY TO FACT If she **were** older, she would understand.

22

Modify To limit the meaning of a word either by describing what the word refers to (*sour* oranges) or by indicating quality or degree: *very* hot, *deeply* hurt, *few* words. Adjectives, adverbs and substantives may function as modifiers. See **Adjective** and **Adverb**. See also section 16b, "modifiers."

Nominative See **Case** and chapter 24.

Nonrestrictive modifier A dependent clause or phrase which adds information without limiting the meaning of the word it modifies. See section 28d.

Noun A part of speech: a noun names a person, place, thing, or abstraction. There are the following kinds:

A *common noun* is the name applied to all the members of a group of persons, places, things, or abstractions; e.g., *man, village, book, courage*. Common nouns are not usually capitalized.

A *proper noun* or *proper name* is the name of a particular person, place, or thing, or event; e.g., *Adlai Stevenson, Chicago, Domesday Book, Revolutionary War*. Proper nouns are capitalized.

A *collective noun* is the name of a group or class considered as a unit; e.g., *flock, class, group, crowd, gang, team*.

Nouns may also function as modifiers; e.g., *town hall*.

Number Inflection of verbs, nouns, and pronouns to indicate singular or plural.

Object The *direct object* (see section 16d) of a verb names the person or thing that completes the assertion made by a transitive verb. It answers the question *what* or *whom*.

Father dried the *dishes* and broke a *plate*.
I trusted *him* and followed his *advice*.

The *indirect object* (see section 16e) of a verb is the person or thing to which something is given or for which something is done. The indirect object can usually be made the object of the preposition *for* or *to*.

I built my *wife* a shelf. = I built a shelf *for my wife*.
I wrote *him* a letter. = I wrote a letter *to him*.

Objective (accusative)   See **Case** and chapter 24.

Objective complement   Either a noun or an adjective that completes the predicate by telling something about the direct object.

> *noun*
> They called him a *fool*.
> *adj.*
> I like my coffee *hot*.

Ordinal number   See **Cardinal number**.

Participle   A verb form used as an adjective. The present participle ends in *ing*; e.g., *eating, running*. The past participle ends in *ed, d, t, en, n* or is formed by vowel change; e.g., *stopped, told, slept, fallen, known, sung*.

Since a participle is a verbal adjective, it has the characteristics of both a verb and an adjective. Like an adjective, it modifies a substantive:

> The *inquiring* reporter stopped him.
> *Encouraged* by his help, she continued her work.
> *Having* just *returned* from my vacation, I had not heard the news.

Like a verb the participle may take a direct or an indirect object and may be modified by an adverb:

22

Wishing us success, he drove away.
"Us" is an indirect object, "success" a direct object, of the participle "wishing."

Stumbling awkwardly, he came into the room.
"Awkwardly" is an adverb modifying the participle "stumbling."

Parts of speech The classification of words according to the special function that they perform in a sentence: nouns, pronouns, verbs, adjectives, adverbs, etc.

Passive voice See **Voice** and section 9b-1.

Person Inflection of verbs and personal pronouns to indicate the speaker (*first person*), the person spoken to (*second person*), and the person spoken of (*third person*).

FIRST PERSON   I am, we are; I go, we go.
SECOND PERSON   you are; you go.
THIRD PERSON   He is, they are; he goes, they go.

Phrase A phrase is a group of words without a subject and predicate, and used as a single part of speech—as a substantive, verb, adjective, or adverb. See chapter 17.

Predicate A group of words that makes a statement or asks a question about the subject of the sentence (see section 16a). Thus in the sentence *Jim drove the car, drove the car* is the predicate, for it tells what the subject *Jim* did. The predicate always contains a finite verb, or a verb phrase; e.g., *drove, was driving.*

The *simple predicate* is the verb alone. The *complete predicate* is the verb and its modifiers and complements.

Jim drove the car into the garage.
"Drove" is the simple predicate. "Drove the car into the garage" is the complete predicate.

Predicate adjective, Predicate noun See **Complement.**

Preposition A part of speech that shows the relationship

Def

between a substantive and another word in the sentence; e.g., *in, on, into, to, toward, from, for, against, of, between, with, without, before, behind, under, over, above, among, at, by, around, about, through.* The word that completes the meaning of the preposition is called the object of the preposition. In English many words may be used as either prepositions or adverbs, their classification depending on their function in the sentence. If they are followed by a substantive which, with them, forms a phrase, they are prepositions (see section 17a); if by themselves they modify a verb, they are adverbs.

> *prep.*
> He stood *behind* the chair.
> *adverb*
> He walked *behind.*
> *prep.*
> He is *in* the bank.
> *adv.*
> He came *in* while we were there.

Principal clause   See **Clause** and chapter 18.

Principal parts   In English, the three forms of a verb from which all other forms are derived (with the exception of the verb *to be*). They are (1) the present infinitive, (2) the past tense, and (3) the past participle: *send, sent, sent; choose, chose, chosen; swim, swam, swum.* All present and future tense forms, including the present participle, are derived from the first principal part: I *send,* he *sends,* we *will send.* The second principal part is used for the simple past tenses: he *sent,* I *chose,* you *swam.* Compound past tenses and the forms of the passive voice employ the third principal part: he *has chosen,* they *had swum,* the package *was sent,* or *may be sent, is being sent, will be sent,* etc.

In learning a foreign language or in correcting unconventional English, one must know the principal parts of the irregular verbs (see section 26c).

Pronoun   A part of speech, a word used to refer to a sub-

Def

stantive already used (or implied). Pronouns may be classified as follows:

1 **PERSONAL:** *I, you, he, she, it,* and their inflectional forms.
   I listened to *her.*

2 **DEMONSTRATIVE:** *this, that, these, those* (see section 23b-5).
   This is my favorite book.

3 **INTERROGATIVE:** *who, which, what.*
   Who can answer this question?

4 **RELATIVE:** *who, which, that,* and compounds like *whoever* (see section 18d).
   The house *that* they bought was built many years ago.

5 **INDEFINITE:** *any, anyone, some, someone, no one, nobody,* etc. (see section 23a-5).
   Everyone is invited.

6 **REFLEXIVE:** *myself, yourself,* etc.
   I hurt *myself.*

7 **INTENSIVE:** *myself, yourself,* etc.
   He *himself* is to blame.

8 **RECIPROCAL:** *each other, one another.*
   John and Mary looked at *each other.*

Regular verb A verb which forms its past tenses by adding *ed* or *t: start, started; dream, dreamed* or *dreamt; buy, bought.* Also called a *weak verb.*

Relative pronoun A pronoun (*who, which,* or *that*) used with a double function: to take the place of a noun and to connect clauses as does a subordinating conjunction (see section 18d).

Restrictive modifier A dependent clause or phrase intended to define or limit the word it modifies (see section 28d).

Sentence An independent utterance, usually including a

Def

subject and predicate, which can stand by itself and is set off by capitalization of its beginning and a period or other terminal punctuation at the end. A sentence may range in length from one word (Why?) or short phrases (What an absurd idea!) to a main clause (I saw him sitting on the fence.); but it is grammatically independent and therefore is considered a self-contained unit. See chapter 16.

From the point of view of structure, sentences are classified as simple, compound, complex, or compound-complex. See chapter 19.

From the point of view of meaning or function, sentences may be classified as follows:

1. A *declarative sentence* asserts something about a subject.
   The man felt ill and called the doctor.

2. An *interrogative sentence* asks a question.
   When is he coming?

3. An *imperative sentence* expresses a command.
   Call him again.

4. An *exclamatory sentence* expresses strong feeling.
   How stupid can you get!

For further discussion, see chapters 7, 8, and 9; see also chapter 20, especially for the discussion of so-called "incomplete" forms.

Strong verb   See **Irregular verb.**

Subject   The part of the sentence or clause naming the person or thing about which something is said. The subject of a sentence is usually a noun or pronoun, but it may be a verbal, a phrase, or a noun clause. The subject can most easily be determined by phrasing the predicate as a question, using *who* or *what* as a temporary subject. The answer to such a question is the subject. See sections 16a and 23a.

NOUN   Beyond the ridge lay a high *plateau.*
What lay beyond the ridge?

VERBAL   Nowadays *flying* is both safe and cheap.
PHRASE   *To err* is human.
CLAUSE   *That he will be promoted* is certain.

The *simple subject* is a substantive, usually a noun or pronoun. The *complete subject* is the simple subject and its modifiers.

> The young trees that we planted last year have grown tall.
> *"Trees" is the simple subject. "The young trees that we planted last year" is the complete subject.*

Subjective complement   See **Complement** and section 16f.
Subjunctive   See **Mode** and section 26e.
Subordinate clause   A dependent clause. See section 18a.
Substantive   Any word or group of words used as a noun. It may be a noun, a pronoun, a clause, an infinitive, or a gerund.
Superlative   See **Comparison.**
Tense   A characteristic of verbs shown by different forms that indicate time of the action. There are six tenses: the present tense, the past tense, the future tense, the perfect (present perfect) tense, the past perfect tense, and the future perfect tense. See **Conjugation** for examples. See chapter 26 for discussion.
Transitive verb   See **Verb.**
Verb   A part of speech whose function is to assert that the subject exists, acts, has characteristics, or is related to some other quality or state (He *cut* the corn; he *is* the doctor). The verb may be a word or a group of words, but in either case its form changes to indicate time, person, mode (He *was saying* that I *am* too young but *should have* a chance next year).

a. A *transitive verb* is a verb which requires a direct object (noun or other substantive) to complete its meaning.

He *shut* the *door.*
"Door" completes the statement by telling what was shut.

They *greeted her.*

   b. An *intransitive verb* is a verb which is not accompanied by a direct object (see section 16d).

After a heated argument, he *left.*
The child *sat* near the fire.

   c. A copula, or *linking verb,* acts mainly as a connecting link between the subject and the predicate noun or predicate adjective.

That *seems* correct.
She *felt* warm.

Verbals Forms of a verb (*stealing, stolen, to steal*) used as nouns, adjectives, or adverbs. See **Gerund, Participle, Infinitive,** and section 17b.

Voice Inflection of a verb to indicate the relation of the subject to the action expressed by the verb. A verb is in the *active voice* when its subject is the doer of the action. A verb is in the *passive voice* when its subject is acted upon.

ACTIVE VOICE I rang the bell.
The subject "I" did the act of "ringing."

PASSIVE VOICE The bell was rung by me.
The subject "bell" was acted upon by "me."

Weak verb See **Regular verb.**

GRAMMATICAL USAGE

23 *agreement: subject and verb*
                                      pronoun and antecedent

a   subject-verb agreement
b   agreement of pronouns with antecedents

24 *case*
a   compound constructions
b   *who* with dependent clauses
c   complement of *to be*
d   pronoun after *than, as, but*
e   possessives
f   possessive with gerund

25 *adjectives and adverbs*
a   adjectives with certain linking verbs
b   *ly* form of adverbs
c   comparatives and superlatives

26 *tense and mode of verbs*
a   tenses to indicate time
b   sequence of tenses
c   principal parts of irregular verbs
d   *shall* and *will*
e   subjunctives

23

agreement:
subject and verb
pronoun and antecedent

23 a
subject-verb agreement

Make subject and verb agree in number: singular subjects require singular verbs; plural subjects require plural verbs.

FAULTY AGREEMENT   Pets *requires* care.
FAULTY AGREEMENT   John and Herb *plays* chess.
CORRECT   *Pets require* care.
Plural subject "pets" takes plural verb "require."

CORRECT   *John* and *Herb play* chess.
Compound subject "John and Herb" takes plural verb "play."

Violations of this rule occur when the writer does not know which word is the subject, or when the writer is not sure whether the subject is singular or plural. If you have trouble making a subject and verb agree, reread section 16c and pay particular attention to the discussion of the simple subject—

Agr

the subject stripped of its modifiers. To correct faulty agreement of subject and verb, you must first be able to identify the simple subject.

23 a-1
verb and simple subject

Make the verb agree with the simple subject; do not be misled by modifying phrases or clauses which intervene between the simple subject and its verb.

WRONG The *suggestion* of two councilmen, a teacher, and three parents **were** accepted.
The simple subject is "suggestion" and the verb must be singular to agree with it. The intervening prepositional phrases are modifiers.
CORRECT The *suggestion* of two councilmen, a teacher, and three parents **was** accepted.

WRONG A *program* of two Bergman films **were shown** at the movie house.
CORRECT A *program* of two Bergman films **was shown** at the movie house.

Modifying elements such as "accompanied by," "as well as," "including," and "together with" which suggest a plural idea *do not* change the number of the subject.

CORRECT The *prisoner,* accompanied by guards and his lawyer, **was** in the courtroom.
CORRECT The *property,* including the guest house and the extra garage, *is* up for rent.

If the predicate is the verb *to be* and the predicate noun is plural, the verb must still be singular when the subject is singular. *The verb should agree with the subject, not the predicate noun.*

WRONG The first *thing* which caught my eye *were* the tuna boats.

CORRECT The first *thing* which caught my eye *was* the tuna boats.

If the verb precedes the subject, take care to determine the subject and make the verb agree with it.

Faulty agreement is especially likely to occur in sentences containing *there is, there are* or in statements of quantity.

WRONG There *is* a *million laughs* in this bouncy little musical comedy.

CORRECT There *are* a *million laughs* in this bouncy little musical comedy.

WRONG There *are* a long *list* of jobs to be done before we can leave.

CORRECT There *is* a long *list* of jobs to be done before we can leave.

CORRECT There *are* a *number* of jobs to be done before we can leave.

WRONG Around us in every direction *was miles* of empty beach.

CORRECT Around us in every direction *were miles* of empty beach.

CORRECT Around us in every direction *was* a vast *expanse* of empty beach.

In informal English, a singular verb is occasionally used when a compound subject follows it.

FORMAL In the office there *are* a *desk,* a *chair,* and a filing *cabinet.*

INFORMAL In the office there *is* a desk, a chair, and a filing cabinet.

For discussion of problems of agreement involved with parallel or sequential sentence structure, see section 8a or 8e-1.

Agr

23 a-2
plural subjects with *and*

Consider most subjects plural if they are joined by *and*.

CORRECT Mathematics and science *are* my best subjects.
CORRECT The hiring, training, and evaluating of workers *are* administrative duties.

This convention has certain exceptions, however. First, if a compound subject refers to the same person or thing, it takes a singular verb.

CORRECT The young bachelor and man-about-town *was* finally trapped into marriage.

Second, when *each* or *every* is used to modify the compound subject, a singular verb is used.

CORRECT *Each* soldier and sailor *was* given a complete examination.
CORRECT *Every* camera and light meter in the shop *has* been reduced in price.

23 a-3
singular subjects with *or, nor*

Two or more singular subjects joined by *or* or *nor* usually take a singular verb. When one subject is singular and one is plural, the verb agrees with the subject nearer it.

CORRECT Neither the producer nor the consumer *was* treated fairly.
CORRECT Either the local tourist bureau or a good road map *is* a good source for scenic route information.
CORRECT Neither John nor his brothers *like* golf.

In informal English, a plural verb is occasionally used when a *neither . . . nor . . .* construction expresses a plural idea.

ACCEPTABLE   Neither the union nor the company *seem* to be seriously interested in changing the retirement age.

23 a-4
antecedents of *who, which, that*

With the relative pronouns *who, which,* and *that,* use a singular verb for a singular antecedent, a plural verb for a plural antecedent.

CORRECT   Betsey is the kind of *woman who prefers* to live in an apartment.
Antecedent of "who" is "woman."

CORRECT   This is the only *one* of the radio units *which is* soldered.
Antecedent of "which" is "one." The sentence means, "Of all the radio units, this is the only one which is soldered."

CORRECT   This is the best of the *typewriters that are* in working order.

23 a-5
indefinite pronouns

The indefinite pronouns *each, either, someone, somebody, nobody, anyone, everyone, everybody* take singular verbs.

CORRECT   *Each* of the accountants *was* questioned by an outside examiner.
CORRECT   *Nobody is* willing to take a chance.
CORRECT   *Somebody has* been holding up the line for the last hour.

Agr

None, neither, some, more, most, and all may be either singular or plural, depending on the context and the intended meaning.

CORRECT *None* of this money *is* to be spent for clothes.
CORRECT *None* of the dresses *are* paid for.
CORRECT *Most* of the pie *has* been eaten.
CORRECT *Most* of the students *know* the answer to that question.

23 a-6
collective nouns

**23
a-5**

When a collective noun refers to the group or quantity as one unit, use a singular verb; when the noun refers to individual units, use a plural verb.

Nouns which refer to a group of people—*class, committee, team, family,* etc.—are collective nouns. You can emphasize either the group as a whole or its individual members.

CORRECT The *committee was* unanimous in its recommendations.
CORRECT The *class were* unable to agree on a day for the party.
Many writers would feel this sentence to be awkward, even though correct, and would rephrase it: "The members of the class were unable. . . ."

CORRECT A large *number* of votes *is* required.
CORRECT A large *number* of notes in his journal *are* inaccurate.

23 a-7
singular nouns with
plural forms

Some nouns may be plural in form but singular in meaning; consult a good dictionary if there is any doubt.

Some abstract nouns which are plural in form are grammatically singular—e.g., *aesthetics, economics, linguistics, mathematics, news, physics, semantics.*

CORRECT   Physics *was* the hardest course I had in high school.

Note that certain nouns ending in *s* have no singular form and are always plural: *trousers, scissors, measles, forceps.* Some nouns ending in *ics (athletics, politics, statistics)* may be either singular or plural, often with a distinction in meaning.

CORRECT   Athletics [the collective activity] *builds* the physique.
CORRECT   Athletics [particular sports and teams] *are* his favorite pastime.
CORRECT   Statistics *is* my most difficult course.
CORRECT   Statistics *show* that . . . .

**23
a-7**

Words like *data* and *strata* are Latin plurals, but there is a strong tendency in current English to treat them as collective nouns, which may be either singular or plural.

CORRECT   We must classify all the data that *have* been collected.
ACCEPTABLE   This data *was* collected in a survey.

EXERCISES

a. In the following student sentences, determine the cause of the faulty agreement and supply the correct form of the verb.
  1. In addition, there is the students who cheat because they have never been taught differently.
  2. The author's portrayal of the guests and the games add up to an extremely vivid picture of that particular society, with its petty concerns and rituals.
  3. Another of the unpopular activities that take place during freshman week are the roll calls.
  4. The theme of suffering, its causes and its consequences, are treated by Shakespeare, Tolstoy, and Conrad.
  5. The first thing which catches your eye are the headlines.

6. The fact that the children are so beautiful and so intelligent add to their goodness and make ghosts appear even more evil.

7. Everyone else in the story have readjusted to their roles, and Pam is the only one who is injured by the experience.

8. But their way of expressing themselves are totally different.

9. The typical high school student who come to this college does have problems.

10. These products of automation may have made life more pleasant but has reduced the population from hard-working pioneers to button-pushing time-servers.

23 a

b. Give reasons for using the singular or the plural verb form in the following sentences.

1. Every one of the nine men on the team (is, are) important.

2. The close relationship with professors and fellow students (makes, make) the small college the choice of many entering freshmen.

3. Doug sprawled in the chair and knocked over one of the most expensive lamps which (was, were) in the store.

4. There (has, have) never been hard feeling between the families on this street.

5. The symptoms of lead poisoning (varies, vary) with each individual case.

6. Next in the waiting line (was, were) an elderly lady and her grandson.

7. He believes that athletics (improves, improve) school morale.

8. Up (goes, go) the gun, and each of the runners (becomes, become) tense.

9. The doctor said that there is always a possibility the infection will return but that so far there (has, have) been no signs of its recurrence.

10. In some countries such punishments as beating, whipping, and solitary confinement (is, are) still used.

11. The family (takes, take) its annual vacation during August.
12. A majority of the hospital's patients (has, have) some kind of medical insurance.
13. The flour and ground rice (is, are) thoroughly mixed to form the dough.
14. Either the *Times* or the *Tribune* (is, are) a reliable source of news.
15. The catcher, as well as the pitcher and the coach, (was, were) arguing furiously with the umpire.
16. The measles on my arms and face (itches, itch) terribly.
17. Measles (is, are) a frequent childhood disease; mumps (is, are) another.
18. Nearly half the class (wants, want) to put off the examination, but a majority of the students (is, are) ready to take it now.

**23
b**

23 b
agreement of pronoun and
antecedent

Make pronouns agree in number with their antecedents.

FAULTY AGREEMENT   A *person* pays good money to a genealogist to look up *their* ancestors so that *they* may be boastful.

FAULTY AGREEMENT   *Either* the janitor or the plumber must have eaten *their* lunch here.

CORRECT   The *janitor* [singular antecedent] must have eaten *his* [singular pronoun] lunch here.

CORRECT   *People* [plural antecedent] pay good money to a genealogist to look up *their* [plural pronoun] ancestry.

For general treatment of problems in pronoun agreement and faulty reference, see section 8b.

Agr

23 b-1
singular pronouns with indefinite antecedent

In formal writing use a singular pronoun for such antecedents as *each, either, neither, someone, somebody, anyone, everybody, no one, nobody, person, man, woman.*

CORRECT   *Each* of us was on *his* best behavior.
CORRECT   *Neither* of the twins wished to show that *his* feelings were hurt.
CORRECT   I think a **person** should mind *his* own business.
Notice that "he," "his" are used when the antecedent refers to both sexes, or when the gender is unknown.

In speech and in informal writing the plural pronoun *they* is often used when there is a plural meaning implied or when the singular pronoun is stilted or awkward.

AWKWARD   *Everyone* there agreed to say what *he* thought.
ACCEPTABLE   *Everyone* there agreed to say what **they** thought.
ACCEPTABLE   Almost **everybody** has a bulky-knit sweater as part of *their* basic wardrobe.

Such antecedents as *any, each, every,* and *someone* are among the pronouns which most frequently take a plural pronoun in speech and informal writing. Usually, this informal usage is frowned upon in college writing.

23 b-2
collective noun antecedents

If the antecedent is a collective noun, use a singular pronoun to emphasize the group as a whole, a plural pronoun to emphasize the separate members.

CORRECT   The *audience* showed *its* approval by applause.

CORRECT   The *family* could never agree about *their* shares of the property.

INCONSISTENT   The *jury is* about to return and give *their* verdict.

If the verb shows the antecedent to be singular, consistency requires that the pronoun referring to it also be singular.

CORRECT   The *jury* is about to return and give *its* verdict.

23 b-3
plural antecedents with *and*

Consider most antecedents plural if they are joined by *and.*

When two or more antecedents are connected by *and,* the pronoun referring to them is usually plural.

CORRECT   The *boy* and his *father* started on *their* vacation last Monday.

CORRECT   My father encouraged *Henry* and *me* not to postpone *our* trip.

This convention has certain exceptions, however. First, if the two antecedents refer to the same thing or person, they may take a singular pronoun (see agreement of subject and verb, section 23a-2).

CORRECT   The young *sculptor* and *ceramicist* was elated when *his* enamelled bronze mobile won first prize.

Second, if the antecedents are modified by *each* or *every,* they may take a singular pronoun (see agreement of subject and verb, section 23a-2).

CORRECT   *Each stump* and *shrub* had to be pulled out by *its* roots.

Agr

23 b-4
plural antecedents with *or, nor*

When two or more singular antecedents are connected by *or* or *nor,* the pronoun referring to them is singular; when one of the antecedents connected by *or* or *nor* is singular and the other plural, the pronoun agrees with the nearer.

CORRECT Neither *Senator Taft* nor *Senator Neuberger* lived *his* entire term of office.

CORRECT Either the *secretary* or the *members* of the committee may submit *their* grievances.

23 b-5
agreement of demonstrative pronouns

When a demonstrative pronoun (this, these) is used as an adjective, it should agree in number with the noun it modifies.

WRONG *These kind* of sheep can be found in Kansas.

CORRECT *This kind* of sheep can be found in Kansas.

The demonstrative adjective modifies the singular noun "kind," not the plural noun which follows "kind".

CORRECT *These kinds* of sheep can be found in Kansas.

WRONG *Those sort* of pipes are hard to ream.

CORRECT *That sort* of pipe is hard to ream.

EXERCISES

a. In the following student sentences, determine the cause of the faulty agreement and supply the correct form of the pronoun.
1. Neither Macbeth nor the Emperor Jones cared how they got what they wanted.
2. I really believe that a person should never ask another person for advice on their problems.

3. These kind of scrimmages can be very bruising.
4. Each camper was supposed to bring their own bedding.
5. Now that everything was perfect, he was going to make sure they stayed that way.
6. Out of school and out of his allowance, Paul has to accept a job as a teacher in a second rate preparatory school, where he encounters hypocrisy and bullying and is unable to ignore it.
7. Neither character knew that he was to become a man until they had already stepped across the threshold from adolescence to manhood.
8. Dorm meetings are always a spectacle because someone always loses their temper.
9. Upon release, the prisoner's attitude toward society is determined by their treatment in prison.
10. When he took the wrong turn, we lost our way and caused ourself a lot of trouble.

b. Give reasons for using the singular or plural form of the pronoun in the following sentences. Be prepared to say which pronoun forms would be acceptable in speech and informal writing but would be discouraged in college writing.

1. Maybe some day each person will have (his, their) own helicopter for commuting to the city.
2. Nobody needs servants because nobody has more housework than (he, they) can manage.
3. The school was preparing to put on (its, their) annual May Day Dance.
4. Any parent hopes to get the best education possible for (his, their) children.
5. The congregation were divided in (its, their) feelings about the new minister.
6. Neither Faulkner nor T. S. Eliot won the Nobel Prize in literature until well after (he, they) had written (his, their) most important works.
7. Each man and woman must make (his, their) own decision.
8. The United States has to look out for the rights of (its, their) citizens.

24

case: pronouns and nouns

The case of a noun or pronoun is the form it takes to show its use in a sentence. The inflectional form of a noun (*girl's*) or pronoun (*she, her, hers*) shows its relationship to neighboring words. Although English nouns used to have many case forms, they now have different endings only to indicate the possessives. But most pronouns have three case forms: *nominative* (or subjective) in which the inflected pronoun functions as the subject of a verb; the *possessive* (or genitive) in which the inflected pronoun shows possession; and the *objective,* in which the inflected pronoun functions as object.

NOMINATIVE:	I	we	he	she	they	who
POSSESSIVE:	my	our	his	her	their	whose
OBJECTIVE:	me	us	him	her	them	whom

Most people use the correct case without deliberate or conscious choice. But a few constructions sometimes cause trouble.

24 a
compound constructions

A noun and a pronoun used in a compound construction should be in the same case; the same principle applies to constructions like *we boys* and to appositives.

WRONG   My father and *me* often hunt together.
CORRECT   My father and *I* often hunt together.
In the compound construction "My father and I," I is a subject of the verb "hunt."

WRONG   Professor Steiner invited my father and *I* to come to his house on Thursday evening.
CORRECT   Professor Steiner invited my father and *me* to come to his house on Thursday evening.
Because a construction like "my father and I" is so commonly used as the subject of a sentence, it is easy to slip into using the same form even when the objective case is needed.

WRONG   Between you and *I,* Porter doesn't have a chance to win.
CORRECT   Between you and *me,* Porter doesn't have a chance to win.
The compound construction "you and me" is the object of the preposition "between."

WRONG   My father always spanked *we* boys for staying out too late.
CORRECT   My father always spanked *us* boys for staying out too late.
The construction "us boys" is the object of the verb "spanked."

WRONG   Most of the float was designed by two members of the class, Howard and *I.*
CORRECT   Most of the float was designed by two members of the class, Howard and *me.*
Since "two members" is the object of the preposition "by," the appositives must be in the objective case.

Ca

who with dependent clauses

Determine the proper case form of the pronoun *who* by noting whether the pronoun is used as subject or object in the dependent clause.

When in doubt about the case of the relative pronoun *who,* substitute a personal pronoun for the relative. If *he* (*she*) or *they* fits the context, use *who;* if *him* (*her*) or *them* fits the context, use *whom.*

24 b

CORRECT Here is a man **who** can explain "new math."
*Equivalent to: Here is a man; he can explain "new math."
"Who" is the subject of the dependent clause "who can explain . . . ."*

CORRECT Here is a man **whom** I told you about.
Equivalent to: Here is the man; I told you about him. "Whom" is the object of "I told you about."

A parenthetical expression, like *I think* or *he says,* intervening between a relative pronoun and its verb does *not* change the case of the pronoun.

> **WRONG** The woman **whom** I thought would take the survey did not.
> **CORRECT** The woman **who** I thought would take the survey did not.
> *The relative pronoun "who" is the subject of the verb "would take" in the dependent clause "who would take the survey."*

The pronoun *whoever* is sometimes incorrectly put into the objective case because it appears to be the object of a preceding preposition.

> **WRONG** Reservations will be made for **whomever** sends ticket money.

CORRECT   Reservations will be made for **whoever** sends ticket money.
"Whoever" is the subject of "sends," not the object of "for." The object of "for" is the whole clause, "whoever sends ticket money."

CORRECT   There are extra bluebooks for **whoever** needs them.

In formal writing, the interrogative pronouns *who* and *whom* are used exactly like the relative pronouns.

CORRECT   **Who** is coming to the party?
CORRECT   **Whom** are you expecting at the party?
"Whom" is the object of "are expecting."

In speech and in much informal writing, there is a decided tendency to use *who-* as the interrogative form whenever it begins a sentence, no matter what its construction in the sentence. *Whom* is usually avoided unless it directly follows a preposition. Since the use of *who* and *whom* is still often picked on as a crucial test of literacy, it is safer in formal writing to use the formal case form.

ACCEPTABLE   **Who** are you expecting for dessert?
FORMAL   **Whom** are you expecting for dessert?
ACCEPTABLE   **Who** are you driving with?
CORRECT   With **whom** are you driving?

24 c
complement of *to be*

In formal writing, the complement of the linking verb *to be* should be in the nominative case.

CORRECT   The members of the delegation are you, your brother, and I.
CORRECT   We hoped the speaker would be President Markson, but it was not he.
CORRECT   May I speak to Professor Poynter? This is he.

In speech and informal writing, the form "It is me" is widely accepted, and analogous forms such as "I thought it was her" and "It wasn't us" are commonly used. So far as college writing is concerned, however, these forms are most likely to occur in dialogue, when they are appropriate to the speaker.

When the infinitive form of *to be* is used, its complement is usually in the objective case, although in some formal writing the nominative is used.

CORRECT I wouldn't want to be him.
FORMAL I would not want to be he.

24 d
pronoun after *than, as, but*

Determine the case of a pronoun after *than* or *as* by its use in the elliptical clause of which it is a part.

Most commonly the pronoun following *than* or *as* is the subject, but occasionally it may be the object.

CORRECT My cousin is taller than **I.**
"Than I" is a shortened form of "than I am."

CORRECT They take more photographs than **we.**
"Than we" is a shortened form of "than we do."

CORRECT I can type as well as **he.**
"As he" is a shortened form of "as he can type."

CORRECT He chooses you more often than **me.**
"Than me" is a shortened form of "than he chooses me."

"But" is sometimes used as a preposition meaning "except." When so used, *but* is followed by the objective case.

CORRECT By morning everyone had left the house but **me.**

24 e
possessives

Ordinarily, use the *s* possessive with nouns referring
to persons and living things; use an *of* phrase for the
possessive of nouns referring to inanimate objects.

AWKWARD The hive of the bees was near the sourwood
trees.
IMPROVED The bees' hive was near the sourwood trees.

AWKWARD The door's jamb was warped beyond repair.
IMPROVED The jamb of the door was warped beyond repair.

Although the *of*-phrase is usually more graceful for the possessive of inanimate objects, good usage approves of many exceptions to these conventions. Even with persons, an *of*-phrase
rather than the possessive *'s* should be used when the modifying noun is separated from the word it modifies by a phrase or
clause.

WRONG The man who was the moderator's voice was
rasping.
IMPROVED The voice of the man who was the moderator was
rasping.

Expressions designating time or measure (*a day's journey, a
month's wages*) and expressions implying personification (*for
pity's sake, the law's delay*) normally make use of the form *'s*
rather than an *of*-phrase. The double genitive, which uses both
an *of*-phrase and *'s*, is acceptable in informal writing.

CORRECT A friend of my aunt, a friend of my aunt's, one of my
aunt's friends

24 f
possessive with gerund

A noun or pronoun modifying a gerund is usually in
the possessive case.

Ca

CORRECT *Julie's giggling* during the movie annoyed those around her.

CORRECT I applaud *your winning* the contest.

CORRECT Everyone approved of *his applying* for a scholarship.

This convention has several exceptions, however. To begin with, when the emphasis is upon the noun or pronoun preceding the verbal (the word ending in *ing*), the verbal may be interpreted as a modifying participle.

CORRECT We saw **Mary** crying.

The noun "Mary" is taken to be the direct object and the verbal "crying" is taken to be a modifying participle. What would "We saw Mary's crying" mean literally?

CORRECT I found *him* washing the dishes.

Second, the possessive is not used before the gerund when the pronoun is separated from the gerund.

CORRECT Who ever heard of *anyone* in his right mind *making* such a decision.

EXERCISES

a. For the following student sentences, identify the errors in case form and supply the proper case form.

1. My uncle almost never asked Peter and I to do any chores around the farm that summer; even though he was much older than us, he treated us as equals who could see what needed doing.
2. The book disappointed me because the man whom I suspected would be the killer didn't turn out to be the guilty one.
3. My parents have always objected to me motorcycling without a crash helmet.
4. Registration was so confusing that most freshmen ended up asking advice of whomever seemed to know what was going on.

5. Working as precinct doorbell ringers was quite an experience for we high school students who were on vacation and had the time.

6. Our team lost in the final rounds of the state debate tournament when we ran up against a team that was more experienced than us.

b. In each sentence, choose the proper case form and be prepared to explain your choice:

1. My brother is a better skier than (I, me).

2. If Harvey hadn't finished college, my parents would never have permitted Betty and (he, him) to get married.

3. There was no comment from the two members (who, whom) I thought were sure to protest.

4. All the students (who, whom) I talked to seemed to like the new coach.

5. My father used to nag us—my sister, her friends, and (I, me)—about using his pipe cleaners to make bracelets, but we didn't pay much attention to him.

6. All the family went to the funeral but (I, me).

7. The new dictator won't be sure of (who, whom) he can trust.

8. His father objects to (him, his) watching sports every spare minute he can.

9. As for his wife and (he, him), they always prefer to go to the shore.

10. The Holes have not lived here as long as (we, us).

11. That year we finally had a teacher (who, whom) won the respect of all of (we, us) students (who, whom) she had in class.

12. I do not want to find myself in the position where the job has me, instead of (me, my) having the job.

13. Only two members of the family are double-jointed in the thumb, my mother and (I, me).

14. Another good reason for (him, his) joining the Coast Guard is the chance for special training.

15. The ten remaining tickets will be given to (whoever, whomever) applies first.

25
adjectives and adverbs

Distinguish between adjectives and adverbs and use the form required by the construction of a sentence: use adjectives to modify nouns and pronouns; use adverbs to modify verbs, adjectives, or adverbs.

Most adverbs are formed by adding *ly* to the adjective: *clear, clearly; immediate, immediately.* But note that some adjectives end in *ly: friendly, manly, womanly.* A few adverbs have the same form as the adjective: *far, much, little, right, fast.* The dictionary will tell you whether a word functions as an adjective or an adverb, or both. For a general discussion of modifiers, see section 16b.

> **WRONG**   The car stopped quite *sudden.*
> **CORRECT**   The car stopped quite *suddenly.*
> *"Suddenly" is an adverb modifying the verb "stopped."*

> **CORRECT**   The car came to a *sudden* stop.
> *"Sudden" is an adjective modifying the noun "stop."*

For discussion of problems in sentence structure with adjectives, adverbs, and other modifiers, see sections 8c and 8d.

25 a
adjectives with certain
linking verbs

Verbs like *become, seem, appear,* as well as verbs indicating the use of the five senses (*look, feel, sound, taste, smell*), are often used to link an adjective to the subject of the sentence.

		looked	
		seemed	
CORRECT	The swimmer	*felt*	cold.
		became	
		sounded	

Do not use an adverb as the complement of a linking verb.

    WRONG   I felt *terribly* about my mistake.
CORRECT   I felt *terrible* about my mistake.

    WRONG   The melon tasted *sweetly.*
CORRECT   The melon tasted *sweet.*

Note the distinction in use between the adjectives and adverbs in the following sentences.

The repairman felt the joint **carefully.**
adverb modifying "felt"

Watching him, I felt **uneasy.**
adjective complement of "felt"

Since pollen makes me sneeze, I smelled the flower
cautiously.
adverb modifying "smelled"

To my relief, it smelled **fresh.**
adjective complement of "smelled"

Adv

I felt **bad** about her illness.
adjective complement of "felt"

I felt **badly** bruised.
adverb modifying "bruised"

25 b
ly form of adverbs

If an adverb can take the same form as the adjective but also can take an *ly* ending (*slow, slowly; loud, loudly*), prefer the *ly* form in formal writing.

In informal writing and in speech, especially in short imperative sentences, the adverbial form without *ly* is often used when the adverb follows the verb. In formal writing, the form *ly* is preferred, and whenever the adverb precedes the verb, the form *ly* is required.

ACCEPTABLE   Drive slow. You may have to stop quick. The box was buried deep in the sand.
CORRECT   You should drive slowly on wet pavements. By good luck I was able to stop quickly. He dug deeply into the wet soil.

The following adjectives are often used in popular speech to modify a verb or adjective. In writing, use the corresponding adverb or an intensive like *very*.

adjectives	*adverbs*
good	well
most	almost
real	really
some	somewhat, some (before a numeral)
sure	surely

MISUSED IN WRITING   I slept **real good** last night.
CORRECT   I slept **very well** last night.

MISUSED IN WRITING   He was **sure** glad to see them again.
CORRECT   He was **very** glad to see them again.

MISUSED IN WRITING   She is *some* better today.
CORRECT   She is *somewhat* better today.
CORRECT   There is *some* improvement in her condition.

25 c
comparatives and
superlatives

For formal writing, distinguish between the comparative and superlative degree of adjectives and adverbs.

The comparative is used in speaking of two persons or things—he was the *taller* of the two; a diamond is *harder* than an emerald. The superlative is used in speaking of three or more persons or things—he was the *tallest* man on the team; a diamond is the *hardest* rock there is. In speaking and informal writing this distinction is not always observed, and the superlative is often used in comparing two persons or things.

CORRECT   He was the more influential of the two stockholders.
CORRECT   He was the most influential of all the stockholders.
ACCEPTABLE   Of the two styles offered, the first was the most popular.

According to logic, adjectives like *perfect, round, unique* should not have comparative or superlative forms; a thing is either perfect or not perfect, round or not round. Formal writing tends to avoid expressions like *more perfect, rounder than, most unique,* preferring *more nearly perfect, more nearly round, unique.* But comparative, superlative, and intensive forms of such adjectives are very commonly used in both speech and in writing.

ACCEPTABLE   We, the people of the United States, in order to form a more perfect union . . . .
ACCEPTABLE   The Guggenheim Art Museum has a very unique design.

Adj

EXERCISES

a. Correct the use of adjectives and adverbs in the following student sentences as may be necessary to bring the sentences up to the level of standard *written* English.

1. I told my advisor I'm going to continue Spanish so I can learn at least one foreign language real good.
2. The trick worked as perfect as we had hoped.
3. By looking real close at the ballot, I could see somebody had changed it.
4. A small minority of students have given this university a real bad image.
5. At the end of the play, he finds that defeat tastes bitterly.

b. Correct the use of adjectives and adverbs as may be necessary to bring the following sentences up to the level of standard *written* English.

1. If you listen close, you should be able to hear it quite distinct.
2. The colors in the living room contrasted harshly and looked shockingly.
3. People today live more secure because of new drugs and antibiotics.
4. I am sure I didn't do too good on the objective part of the final.
5. The sky was clear and the air smelled freshly.
6. On the trip through the laboratory we were shown several of the seemingly impossibilities of recent technology.
7. An exciting documentary affects me quite different from a dramatized story about the same thing.
8. We were real pleased that so many people were willing to help.
9. That disastrous Thursday started out quite normal.
10. The sunset was beautiful that evening, but the sky looked threateningly the next morning.
11. During the whole time that Blaisdel was chairman, business went along very smooth.

26
tense and mode of verbs

The tense of a verb is its inflectional form to indicate distinctions of time. There are six principal tenses in English.

PRESENT   I *know* this is the right thing to do.

PAST   I *mowed* the lawn, and my sister *pruned* the bushes.

FUTURE   I *will fly* to Denver next month.

PRESENT PERFECT   I *have tried* to encourage him, but he *has* never *dared* to dive.

PAST PERFECT   Although she *had driven* for five years, she never made long trips.

FUTURE PERFECT   He *will have arrived* before we get to the station.

For discussion of sentence problems with shifted tense, mode, and form of verbs, see section 8e. For treatment of problems with the passive voice, see section 9b-1.

26 a
tenses to indicate time

Be sure your tenses accurately indicate the time you intend.

Note that the English system of tenses does not treat the past as one single time. The simple past tense (I *sang*) indicates an

T

event which occurred at a specific time in the past. The present perfect (I *have written* my paper) indicates any time up to the present. The past perfect (He *had finished* the assignment by the time I arrived) indicates that one past event has preceded another.

ILLOGICAL   When he *died*, his fellow citizens *realized* how much he *contributed* to the community, and since then they *collected* funds for a memorial.

CORRECT   When he *died*, his fellow citizens *realized* how much he *had contributed* to the community, and since then they *have been collecting* funds for a memorial.

26
a

ILLOGICAL   These fossils are the remains of animals that *have lived* and *died* before the dawn of history.

CORRECT   These fossils are the remains of animals that *lived* and *died* before the dawn of history.

ILLOGICAL   Until now the weather *was* dry.

CORRECT   Until now the weather *has been* dry.

CORRECT   Until the middle of March the weather *had been dry*, but in April, spring showers *began*.

For discussion of sentence problems involving shifts of tense, see section 8e-3.

26 b
sequence of tenses

Let the tense of the verb in the main clause govern the tense of the verb in a subordinate clause.

The following sentences illustrate consistent sequence of tenses.

CORRECT   When the button *is pressed*, the motor *begins* to run. When he *pressed* the button, the motor *began* to run. If you *will press* the button, the motor *will begin* to run.

Now that he *has pressed* the button, he *can begin* to test the motor.

When he *had pressed* the button, he *began* to test the motor.

An infinitive should be in the present tense, *unless* it represents an action earlier than that of the governing verb.

ILLOGICAL   July 14, 1789, must have been a great day *to have been* alive.

CORRECT   Bliss was it in that dawn *to be* alive,
But *to be* young was very Heaven!   —Wordsworth

ILLOGICAL   Only then did I realize that it was a mistake *to choose* the life of an astronaut two years ago.

CORRECT   Only then did I realize that it was a mistake *to have chosen* the life of an astronaut two years ago.

Ordinarily, the past participle should be used to represent action earlier than that of the governing verb. The present participle indicates action at the time expressed by the verb.

ILLOGICAL   *Entering* the course two weeks late, he soon *found* it too difficult.

CORRECT   *Having entered* the course two weeks late, he soon *found* it too difficult.

CORRECT   *Entering* the course two weeks late, he *expected to find* it difficult.

Statements that are permanently true should be put in the present tense (sometimes called the "timeless present"), even though the main verb is in the past.

ILLOGICAL   He *insisted* that the Amazon River *was* longer than the Nile.

CORRECT   He *insisted* that the Amazon River *is* longer than the Nile.

T

ILLOGICAL   Copernicus *found* that the Sun *was* the center of our planetary system.
CORRECT   Copernicus *found* that the Sun *is* the center of our planetary system.

The present tense is often used in book reviews and criticism for statements of permanent truth regarding a work of art or for summarizing the plot of a novel, play, or movie. In statements relating the events of an author's life, the past tense would normally be used.

CORRECT   The setting of Hawthorne's short stories *is* the New England village that he *knew* so well.
The settings of the short stories are still the same; Hawthorne knew them in the past.

CORRECT   Oliver La Farge's novel *is* the story of a young Navajo whose wife *seeks* revenge for her mistreatment by the white man.

For general discussion of problems involving shifts in tense, see section 8e-3.

26 c
principal parts of irregular verbs

Know the principal parts of irregular verbs.

Irregular verbs are a small group which, instead of forming their past tenses by adding *ed* (*start, started*), change the vowel to indicate the past tense and the past participle (*begin, began, begun*). The principal parts consist of 1) the present infinitive (*begin*); 2) the past tense (*began*); 3) the past participle (*begun*). All tense forms can be derived from the three principal parts with the exception of the irregular verb *to be*. The first principal part is the basis for all present and future tenses, including the present participle; the second principal part is used for the simple past tense—"I began the job yesterday." The third principal part is used in all the compound tenses: "I have begun," "he had begun," "the job was begun," etc.

In the speech of uneducated people and children, errors in the use of principal parts of the irregular verbs are common: "I threwed the ball," "We brung it home," "He has went home." The following list gives the principal parts of some irregular verbs which are apt to be confused. For discussion of problems with shifts in person or number of verb forms, see section 8e-2.

present	simple past	past participle
begin	began	begun
bid *(offer)*	bid	bid
bid *(command)*	bade	bidden
bite	bit	bitten
blow	blew	blown
break	broke	broken
bring	brought	brought
burst	burst	burst
choose	chose	chosen
come	came	come
dive	dived (dove)	dived
do	did	done
draw	drew	drawn
drink	drank	drunk
eat	ate	eaten
fall	fell	fallen
fly	flew	flown
forget	forgot	forgotten (forgot)
freeze	froze	frozen
get	got	got (gotten)
go	went	gone
grow	grew	grown
know	knew	known
lie	lay	lain
ride	rode	ridden

26
°C

T

ring	rang (rung)	rung
rise	rose	risen
run	ran	run
see	saw	seen
shrink	shrank (shrunk)	shrunk (shrunken)
sing	sang	sung
speak	spoke	spoken
spring	sprang (sprung)	sprung
steal	stole	stolen
swim	swam	swum
swing	swung	swung
take	took	taken
throw	threw	thrown
wear	wore	worn
write	wrote	written

26 c

26 d
shall and *will*

Be familiar with the few remaining distinctions that
exist between *shall* and *will*.

More space is devoted to the distinctions between the auxiliary
verbs *shall* and *will* than the topic deserves. But, despite the
fact that many writers and speakers get around the problem
by using contractions (*I'll, we'll, they'll*) and despite divided
usage, these distinctions are sometimes regarded as a sign of
literateness and must be discussed.

To express the simple future (the tense which shows an
event yet to occur), the general American practice is to use
will—"I will go, we will go, you will go, he (she, it, they) will
go." A few writers still observe the very formal distinction for
the simple future: *shall* is used in the first person—"I *shall*
join you and we *shall* go together"; *will* is used in the second
and third person—"You and he *will* be late" (see examples under *conjugation* in chapter 22). But, as has been suggested, this
distinction is ignored by most speakers and writers.

To express determination, promise, or prophecy, both *shall* and *will* are used. According to the formal view, *will* is used in the first person (We *will* pay, despite the inconvenience) and *shall* is used in the other two persons (You and he *shall* do as I tell you). But in the United States usage is divided: *will* is often used for all three persons, the stress upon and the context of the word giving it emphasis rather than the form—"He *will* succeed next time, and won't (will not) they be surprised." On the other hand, *shall* is sometimes used, especially in the second and third persons, because it is more emphatic—"You *shall* do as you are told, and the others *shall* too." Such alternative constructions as "I *must* go buy it" and "They *have* to return it" can also express determination.

In questions, *shall* is often used with the first person plural as a polite substitute for *let's*—"Shall we begin" for "Let's start." *Shall* is also used with the first person singular in questions: "Shall I turn out the light?" But *will* and the contraction *'ll* are used in questions like—"Will I (you, he, they) pass?" "How'll I (you, he, they) find out the results?"

26 e
subjunctive

Be familiar with the few remaining uses of the subjunctive.

Subjunctive forms (*be* or *were* for *am, are, is; had been* for *was;* etc.) are used much less than formerly. In speech, the subjunctive has almost disappeared, except in formulas like "If I were you . . . ." Still, informal writing often uses, and very formal writing demands, the use of the subjunctive on a few occasions:

1 condition contrary to fact
CORRECT   I wish I *were* younger.
INFORMAL   I wish I *was* younger.
CORRECT   If I *were* you, I would refuse.
CORRECT   If this *were* a Saturday, we would be at the lake.

T

2 after *as if* or *as though*

CORRECT   The hound acts as if he *were* sick.

INFORMAL   The hound acts as if he *is* sick.

CORRECT   They act as though they *were* lost, and they probably are.

3 indirect imperative

CORRECT   The terms of the will require that the fund *be spent* on education.

CORRECT   I request that he *close out* the account now.

4 motions and resolutions

CORRECT   I move that the minutes *be approved*.

CORRECT   Resolved, that this question *be submitted* to a committee.

EXERCISES

a. For the following student sentences, identify any incorrect verb forms and be prepared to explain how they are incorrect and to give the proper form.

1. If you do well in one particular subject, you would probably leave that until last so you could concentrate more on the subjects you do poorly in.

2. Unlike the officers, he had a feeling of responsibility for his fellow man; however, the court cannot judge a man on what he thinks or thought, but only by what he does or did.

3. At the inn, Fielding gives the reader his first good look at this young woman, whom he portrayed as the "flower" of womanhood and with a figure "bursting through her stays."

4. She quickly arose the interest of everyone in our class.

5. He had a deep wound in the leg, but he acted as if it was a small scratch that hardly bothers him.

b. Correct any errors in the use of verbs in the following sentences.

1. She wore a faded blue dress, and her shoes, gray from lack of polish, were once white.
2. The astronomer said that the moon was approximately 293,000 miles from the earth.
3. For the reader who had never run across advertising of this kind, a further explanation may be necessary.
4. Zephyr, our cat, would lay on the floor for hours and played with a ball of string.
5. He should have like to have told what he thought of her.
6. The dog begun to growl when I started to ride down the pavement.
7. If I had chose physics as my major, I wouldn't have all these papers to write.
8. It was a serious mistake to have been so candid.
9. The book had laid right where I had put it.
10. The water level began to raise, and by noon it had rose ten feet.
11. She recognized the boy who had spoke to her at the dance.
12. By evening we had drank most of the water in the canteen.

c. For each of the following sentences choose the proper verb form and be prepared to justify your choice.
1. I wouldn't tolerate such noise if I (were, was) you.
2. He moved that the motion (is, be) approved.
3. His mother insists that he (come, comes) in right now.
4. If Alaska (was, were) a warmer state, its population would be larger.
5. He acts as if he (was, were) drunk, and he probably is.

REVIEW EXERCISES

Correct all grammatical errors in the following sentences.
1. Most ski accidents are the results of someone being careless or thinking they are more skillful than they really are.

T

2. But along with increased speed comes many new problems in jet design.
3. Their bird was setting right on the perch, right where they left him three hours earlier.
4. The adolescent feels that if they do not conform, they will be unpopular.
5. Intercollegiate sports, even though the whole student body does not participate in it, provides amusement for most of the students.
6. Certain basic traits in man, such as his love of power, is a real obstacle to a peaceful world.
7. I know several people in my class whom I'm convinced scarcely opened a book in four years.
8. Criminals receive very fair trials in our country in that he is considered innocent until proved guilty.
9. His favorite reading matter are novels, preferably science fiction.
10. According to the report, the company will give a bonus to whomever exceeds his quota.
11. Extra work was assigned to we students who came in late.
12. Every time any of us open a newspaper, we read of new trouble abroad.
13. The foreman of the lumber gang told Stan and I to report early the next morning.
14. Anyone with a little practice can learn to drive, can't they?
15. Within the broad limits of the assignment there are a great variety of topics for students to choose from.

26

PUNCTUATION

27
end punctuation

27 a
period

Use a period to mark the end of a declarative or imperative sentence.

CORRECT This is an example of a declarative sentence.

CORRECT Use a period at the end of a sentence like this.

A period is also used after abbreviations, like *Dr., Mr., Ph.D., etc., A.D., Calif., Inc.* For the proper use of abbreviations see chapter 39.

Three spaced periods (. . .), called ellipsis marks, are used to indicate the omission of a word or words from a quoted passage. If the omitted words come at the end of a sentence, a fourth period is needed.

CORRECT We hold these truths to be self-evident: that all men . . . are endowed by their Creator with certain unalienable rights. . . .

Similarly, three (or four) periods are sometimes used in dialogue and interrupted narrative to indicate hesitation and pauses. Beginning writers should use these with caution.

P|.?!

CORRECT He inspired uneasiness. That was it! Uneasiness. Not a definite mistrust—just uneasiness—nothing more. You can have no idea how effective such a . . . a . . . faculty can be.
—Joseph Conrad, *Heart of Darkness*

27 b
question mark

Use a question mark after a direct question.

CORRECT Where did you find such information?
CORRECT How much of the White Sands is gypsum?
CORRECT Looking at me, the officer said, "Where do you live?"

An indirect question should be followed by a period, not a question mark.

CORRECT He asked what had caused the delay.
CORRECT I wonder how many Americans walk to work these days.

A request which is phrased as a question for politeness' sake is followed by a period.

CORRECT Will you please send me your latest catalog.

27 c
exclamation

Exclamation marks are appropriate only after statements with unusual emphasis of spoken exclamation.

This mark is seldom appropriate to expository writing. Do not use it to lend force to flat statements or ironic remarks.

27
b

28

the comma

The chief uses of the comma are to separate coordinate sentence elements and to set off subordinate constructions in a sentence. That is, a single comma may be required to separate x from y: ___x___ , ___y___ . But two commas may be needed to set off x from the rest of the sentence: _____ , ___x___ , _____ . In addition, a comma is occasionally used to prevent misreading: to separate words which might be erroneously grouped together by a reader.

28 a
to separate independent clauses

Two independent clauses joined by a coordinating conjunction (*and, or, nor, but, for*) should be separated by a comma.

Note that the comma is always placed before the conjunction.

CORRECT   I failed German in my senior year of high school**, *and*** it took me a long time to regain any interest in foreign languages.

CORRECT   She went through the motions of studying**, *but*** her mind was elsewhere.

Very short independent clauses need not be separated by a comma if they are closely connected in meaning.

CORRECT   The bell rang and everyone left.

, | com

Coordinating conjunctions are often used to join the parts of a compound predicate: that is, two or more verbs with the same subject. In such a sentence a comma is not required to separate the predicates. However, if the two parts are long or imply a strong contrast, a comma may be used to separate them.

CORRECT We *measured* the potassium and *weighed* it on the scale.

CORRECT Mr. Fossum *demonstrated* the differences between preserving wood with oil and with shellac**, and** advised the use of oil for durable table tops.

CORRECT To our dismay, the suede could not be *washed* at home **nor** could it be *dry cleaned* at an ordinary place**, but had to be sent** to a specialist.

When the clauses of a compound sentence are long and are also subdivided by commas, a stronger mark of punctuation than a comma may be needed to separate the clauses from each other. For this purpose a semicolon is regularly used (see section 29b).

28 a

CORRECT For purposes of discussion, we shall recognize two main varieties of English, Standard and Nonstandard**;** and we shall divide the first type into Formal, Informal, and Colloquial English.

EXERCISES

Place commas or semicolons wherever needed in the following sentences and be prepared to justify your choice of punctuation.

1. Seven legislators from the southern part of the state changed their votes and with their aid the bill was passed.
2. The student with a late paper may explain that he is just recovering from the flu or he may claim that his new glasses give him a headache and thus prevent him from writing.

3. Liberals are seldom violently partisan and are often accused of having no principles at all.
4. The truck pulled up at the roadside and the sergeant led us into the woods.
5. New cars must be built according to requirements of safety but this cannot make up for careless drivers operating them.
6. Three of the editors argued that the article was biased and malicious and voted to reject it in spite of the distinguished name of the author.
7. You may correct the sentence by changing the participle to a dependent clause or you may omit the participial phrase altogether.
8. The teller at the bank a man I had never seen before looked dubiously at the check I offered him and even though I knew the check was good I could feel a guilty look freezing on my face as his doubts increased.

28 b
to separate elements in series

> Separate words, phrases, or clauses in a series by commas.

The typical form of a series is *a, b,* and *c.* A series may contain more than three parallel elements, and any of the coordinating conjunctions may be used to connect the last two. The series as a whole should *not* be separated from the rest of the sentence (see also section 8a-2).

SERIES OF ADJECTIVES The shy devil-fish blushes in blue, red, green, or brown.

SERIES OF PHRASES Water flooded *over the riverbed, over the culverts, and over the asphalt road.*

SERIES OF PREDICATES The bear *jumped away from the garbage can, snarled at the camper, and raced up the tree.*

SERIES OF NOUNS *Resistors, transistors, capacitors, and connectors* are small electronic parts.

SERIES OF INDEPENDENT CLAUSES Stone was hauled twelve

miles, casing was built as the hole deepened, and a well 109 feet deep was completed in Greensburg, Kansas.

The comma before the last item in a series is omitted by some writers, but its use is generally preferred since it may help prevent misreading. The abbreviation *etc.* at the end of a series is always set off by commas.

CORRECT   The dean discussed the usual dormitory complaints: closing hours, noise, visiting hours for men, etc.

If *all* the elements of a series are joined by coordinating conjunctions (*a and b and c*), no commas are necessary to separate them.

CORRECT   We packed her bag and bought her ticket and put her on the train.

28 c
uses with coordinate elements

Know the comma's uses with other coordinate elements.

Adjectives modifying the same noun should be separated by commas if they are coordinate in meaning. Coordinate adjectives are those which could be joined by *and* without distorting the meaning of a sentence.

CORRECT   Bus lines provide inexpensive, efficient transportation. *The adjectives are coordinate: transportation which is "inexpensive" and "efficient."*

Sometimes, however, an adjective is so closely linked with the noun that it is thought of as part of the noun. Such an adjective is not coordinate with a preceding adjective.

CORRECT   Paynes bought a spacious summer cabin. *This does not mean "a cabin which is spacious and summer." "Summer" indicates the kind of cabin; "spacious" describes the summer cabin.*

Note that numbers are not coordinate with other adjectives and are not separated by commas.

CORRECT   They screened in two large, airy outdoor porches.
"Two" and "large" should not be separated by a comma. But since the two outdoor porches were "large" and "airy," a comma is used to separate these two coordinate adjectives.

Coordinate words or phrases which are sharply contrasted are separated by commas.

CORRECT   He is ignorant, not stupid.
CORRECT   Our aim is to encourage question and debate, not criticism and argument.

An idiomatic way of asking a question is to make a direct statement and add to it a coordinate elliptical question. Such a construction should be separated by a comma from the direct statement.

CORRECT   You will come with us, won't you?
CORRECT   He won't test on last semester's units, will he?

Another idiomatic construction which requires a comma is the coordinate use of adjectives like *the more . . . , the more . . . .*

CORRECT   The faster the bird, the higher the metabolism.
CORRECT   *The more* a candidate meets voters, *the more* he may learn about their concerns.

EXERCISES

Insert commas where they are required in the following sentences, and give a reason for each comma.

1. The curry sauce called for regular milk coconut milk and cream.
2. Painted surfaces should be washed with a detergent sanded lightly and covered with a thin coat of plastic varnish.
3. Everyone knows that the more you swim regularly the more you can control your breathing.

28
c

, | com

4. I painted the house a warm deep pearl gray.
5. Playgrounds have been built in the downtown areas of New York Los Angeles and San Francisco.
6. For some years Mr. Neighbor has lived in a big sprawling modern house on top of a hill.
7. I put the brushes in place wound the coil and adjusted the contact points.
8. You haven't signed the contract have you?
9. I believe that a state lottery can be useful because it can provide revenue for education increase employment and relieve the tax burden.
10. I judge a person of any race by what he says and how he acts not by the color of his skin.

28 d
to set off
nonrestrictive modifiers

Set off nonrestrictive modifiers by commas.

This rule applies to dependent clauses, participial phrases, and appositives. A modifier is nonrestrictive when it can be omitted without changing the main idea of the sentence. A nonrestrictive modifier gives additional information about the noun to which it refers. A restrictive modifier, on the other hand, restricts the meaning of the word to which it refers to one particular group or thing. If it is omitted, the main idea of the sentence is changed. One check is to read the sentence aloud: if the voice pauses and drops slightly before and after the modifier, the modifier is probably nonrestrictive; if the voice is sustained and unhesitant before and after the modifier, the modifier is probably restrictive and *is not* set off by commas.

1 nonrestrictive clauses and phrases
Note that *two commas* are required to set off a nonrestrictive modifier in the middle of a sentence; one comma is sufficient if the modifier is at the beginning or end of the sentence.

NONRESTRICTIVE CLAUSE   My faculty advisor, *who had to sign the program card,* was very hard to find.
If the clause were omitted, some information would be lost, but the sentence would still make the same point: that my advisor was hard to find.

RESTRICTIVE CLAUSE   A faculty advisor *who is never in his* office makes registration difficult.
Omitting the clause here changes the sense completely. The purpose of the clause is to limit the statement to a certain kind of faculty advisor—those who are never in their offices.

		nonrestr. clause
CORRECT	I found the letter under the door,	*where the postman had put it.*

		restrictive clause
CORRECT	The letter was still	*where the postman had put it.*

		nonrestrictive phrase
CORRECT	The beaded dress,	*hanging loosely from shoulder to knee,* fits in a most peculiar manner.

CORRECT   We have had no complaints on merchandise damaged
restrictive phrase
because of careless packaging.

**28
d**

Notice how the meaning of a sentence may be altered by the addition or the omission of commas:

CORRECT   The board sent questionnaires to all members, who are on Social Security.
Nonrestrictive clause. The sentence implies that all members are on Social Security.

CORRECT   The board sent questionnaires to all members who are on Social Security.
Restrictive clause. The questionnaire is sent to some members, those on Social Security.

,|com

EXERCISES

Insert commas in the following sentences to set off nonrestrictive clauses and participial phrases. In doubtful cases, explain the difference in meaning produced by the insertion of commas.

1. King Leopold of Belgium who was Queen Victoria's uncle also gave her a great deal of advice.
2. Many people who have never been to the United States think of it as a country of wealth and luxury where everyone lives on the fat of the land.
3. Some years ago I lived in a section of town where almost everyone was a Republican.
4. With the advent of the jet engine which is more efficient at high than at low altitudes aircraft could attain greater heights.
5. The astronaut who must train responses for any circumstance was calm when launching was called off at the last minute.
6. The average student hoping to get a C without too much work should stay out of Economics 152.
7. We shall have to hire a caretaker if you can't find time to keep the place neat and orderly.
8. The packing plant where I worked all summer earning over $1000 is on the Aleutian Islands.
9. New planes which are already being tested weigh over two thousand tons which will enable them to transport several hundred passengers.
10. The average American woman tired of last year's clothes and seeking something new is an easy prey for the fashion designers who capitalize on herd psychology and the craving for novelty.

2 nonrestrictive appositives

Appositives are usually nonrestrictive and hence are set off by commas. If, however, an appositive puts a necessary limitation upon its noun, it is restrictive and no punctuation is necessary.

NONRESTRICTIVE APPOSITIVE Scientists working with cryogenics have produced temperatures within a thousandth of a degree

28
d

of absolute zero, *approximately 459.7 below zero Fahrenheit.*
RESTRICTIVE APPOSITIVE The noun *cryogenics* comes from a
Greek word meaning "icy cold."

Note that an appositive used to define a word is often introduced by the conjunction *or*. Such appositives are always set
off by commas to distinguish them from the common construction in which *or* joins two coordinate nouns.

CORRECT   The class found a fine specimen of pyrite, **or** *fool's
gold.*
CORRECT   We couldn't decide whether to plant phlox or coral
bells.

Note that an abbreviated title or degree (K.C.B., USMC,
M.D., Ph.D.) is treated as an appositive when it follows a
proper name.

CORRECT   He was introduced as Robert Harrison, *L.L.D.,* and
he added that he also held a Ph.D. from Cornell.

**28
d**

EXERCISES

In the following sentences, set off all nonrestrictive dependent
clauses, participial phrases, and appositives. Be able to justify
your answers.

1. Workers in other fields of social science particularly
   sociology and psychology are rapidly inventing new
   techniques.
2. The term deciduous is used to indicate plants which
   shed their leaves each year.
3. Paris a world center of fashion determines what the
   average woman living in a Midwestern town will be
   wearing next year.
4. Mark Twain born and raised in Missouri was well qualified to describe river life in his most famous novel
   Huckleberry Finn which has been translated into every
   major language.

5. The only shrub growing in the yard was an *Osmathus* or sweet olive.

6. Not being familiar with geology I couldn't see that the sharp hill was really a fault.

7. We met two prominent alumni from St. Louis Rev. Ralph Harrison D.D. and Captain Henry King USN both of whom were attending class reunions.

8. The Olympic Games copied from the ancient Greek festival still retain a part of their original purpose the promotion of understanding and good will.

9. A student who has not yet discovered what he wants to major in should learn all he can about the world in which he must some day take his place.

28 e
to set off parenthetic elements

**28
e**

Set off parenthetic elements by commas.

Parenthetic is a general term describing explanatory words or phrases which are felt to be intrusive and subordinate. That is, they interrupt the normal sentence pattern to supply additional, supplementary information, and they are accordingly set off by commas or other punctuation marks. In the widest sense of the term, nonrestrictive modifiers are a kind of parenthetic element. Many other sentence elements may become parenthetic if they are removed from their regular place and inserted so that they interrupt the normal order of a sentence.

For example, adjectives normally are placed before the words they modify: *Two tired, hungry boys came into camp.* If the adjectives are inserted elsewhere in the sentence, they become parenthetic and should be set off: *Two boys, tired and hungry, came into camp.* Similarly, it is possible to rewrite a sentence like *I am certain that space science will bring some unexpected discoveries* so that one clause becomes parenthetic: *Space science, I am certain, will bring some unexpected discoveries.*

CORRECT   The minutes, I regret to say, need several additions.
CORRECT   The discovery that mammals can learn to breathe under water may, in the opinion of some experts, lead to a technique which will prevent drowning.

28 f
conventional uses

Know the conventional uses of the comma and the occasions when they can be omitted.

Transitional words and phrases, like *however, moreover, indeed, consequently, of course, for example, on the other hand,* are usually set off by commas, especially when they serve to mark a contrast or the introduction of a new point. In short sentences where stress on the transitional word is not needed or desired, the commas are often omitted.

CORRECT   The beginning violinist needs patience. For example, six lines of music can have 214 bowing variations.
CORRECT   The best beef should be bright red and be marbled with pure white fat. However, a customer may be fooled by tinted lighting which, in fact, cheats the buyer.
CORRECT   The court ruled, consequently, that no damages could be collected.

Notice that *however* is sometimes used as a regular adverb, to modify a particular word rather than as a sentence modifier, and that when so used it is not set off by a comma.

CORRECT   However much he diets, he does not lose enough weight.
Since "however" modifies "much," it is not set off.

1 dates and addresses
Additional elements of dates and addresses and references are set off by commas. If only one element (day of month, year, city, etc.) appears, no punctuation is needed.

CORRECT   April 4 is her birthday.
CORRECT   New York is her native state.
CORRECT   Act IV moves toward the climax.

But if other elements are added, they are set off by commas.

CORRECT   April 4, 1953, is the date of her birth.
CORRECT   The return address was 15 South Main Street, Oxford, Ohio.
CORRECT   The quotation is from *King Lear*, II, ii, 2.

2 direct address, interjections, yes and no

Nouns used as terms of direct address, interjections, and the words *yes* and *no* should be set off by commas.

CORRECT   Miss Kuhn, would you like to be a teaching assistant?
CORRECT   This preposterous charge, ladies and gentlemen, reveals my opponent's ignorance.
CORRECT   Oh, yes, we have a more expensive rental.

**28
f**

3 quotation expressions

Quotation expressions such as *he said* are set off by commas when used with a direct quotation.

CORRECT   "When I was young," he said, "seeing a monoplane was exciting."

Do not use a comma to set off an indirect quotation.

CORRECT   The jeweler said that he could reset the sapphire.
CORRECT   They told us that they had sent a wire.

When the quotation contains two independent clauses and the quotation expression comes between them, a semicolon may be required to prevent a comma fault (see section 21a).

CORRECT   "Please try," he said; "you could win."
CORRECT   "Please try," he said. "You could win."
CORRECT   "I'd like you to try," he said, "but I won't insist."

For other rules regarding the punctuation of direct quotations, see sections 30a, 30b, and 30e.

4 absolute phrase

An absolute phrase should be set off by commas. An absolute construction consists of a participle with a subject (and sometimes a complement) grammatically unconnected with the rest of the sentence and usually telling when, why, or how something happened.

CORRECT The gale having quieted, highway workers began to clear fallen trees and signs from the roads.

CORRECT The marks on her transcript didn't annoy her, grades representing only part of her education.

EXERCISES

Insert commas where they are required to set off parenthetic elements or to follow conventional usage.

1. Money is not to be sure the only problem that people worry about.
2. Yes I have lived in Minnesota most of my life, but I was born in Seattle Washington.
3. My uncle formerly one of the richest men in Woodstock promised to put me through college.
4. In the first place there is no evidence Mr. Jones that my client was driving a car on July 14 1965.
5. Teaching of course has certain disadvantages class size being what it is.
6. "Come over here" said Mr. Newman "you can see the car from this window."
7. The study of Latin or any other foreign language for that matter helps to clarify English grammar.
8. My cousins tired and wet returned from their fishing trip at sunset.
9. Stricter laws it is argued would be of no use without more machinery for their enforcement.
10. Portland Maine was not as I remember an unpleasant place for a boy to grow up in.

28 g
to set off dependent clauses

A dependent clause coming first in the sentence is usually set off by a comma; if a dependent clause follows the main clause, a comma is used when the clause is nonrestrictive.

CORRECT If you see him, tell him to write me soon.
Introductory adverbial clause, set off by a comma.

CORRECT Since the melting point of tallow is 127° Fahrenheit, slow-burning candles are made with beeswax.

CORRECT Tell him to write me as soon as he can.
Restrictive adverbial clause following main clause.

CORRECT Take a trip abroad now, even if you have to borrow some money.
Nonrestrictive adverbial clause following main clause.

28 g

An introductory verbal phrase (participial, gerund, or infinitive) is usually followed by a comma. A prepositional phrase of considerable length at the beginning of a sentence may be followed by a comma.

participial phrase

CORRECT Suffering from disease, overcrowding, and poverty, the people of Manchester were prime victims of the early Industrial Revolution in England.

gerund phrase

CORRECT After seeing the poverty and unfair treatment of the working class people, Mrs. Gaskell wrote several protest novels.

infinitive phrase

CORRECT To understand Hemingway's uneasy friendship with F. Scott Fitzgerald, one must know something of Hemingway's attitude toward Fitzgerald's wife, Zelda.

long prepositional phrase

CORRECT Soon after his first acquaintance with Fitzgerald, Hemingway took an intense dislike to Zelda.

28 h
to prevent misreading

Use a comma to separate any sentence elements that might be incorrectly joined in reading and thus misunderstood. *This rule supersedes all others.*

MISLEADING   Ever since he has devoted himself to athletics.
CLEAR   Ever since, he has devoted himself to athletics.

MISLEADING   Inside the house was brightly lighted.
CLEAR   Inside, the house was brightly lighted.

CORRECT   Soon after, the minister entered the chapel.
CORRECT   To elaborate, the art of Japanese flower arranging begins with simplicity.

28 i
misuse of the comma

Using commas where they do not belong is a more flagrant error than omitting them where they might be expected.

Leaving out a comma may be the result of carelessness, but putting one in the wrong place is positive evidence of ignorance. Modern practice is to use less, rather than more, punctuation in narrative and expository prose. A good working rule for the beginner is to use no commas except those required by the preceding conventions.

Listing all the circumstances in which a comma should not be used would be an endless task. Here are some examples of the kinds of serious errors due to excessive punctuation. In all the following sentences, the commas should be omitted.

INCORRECT   His ability to solve the most complicated problems on the spur of the moment, never failed to impress the class.
The comma erroneously separates subject and predicate.

, | com

INCORRECT   The men who lived in the old wing of the dormitory, unanimously voted to approve the new rules.
If the clause is restrictive, no commas should be used; if the clause is nonrestrictive, two commas are required. Using one comma here is a glaring example of ignorance.

INCORRECT   During chapel, the minister announced, that the choir would sing Handel's *Messiah* for Easter.
The comma erroneously separates an indirect quotation from the rest of the sentence.

INCORRECT   Gigi is so tall, that she makes her own dresses.
The comma erroneously splits an idiomatic construction: so tall that.

Do not put a comma before the first member or after the last member of a series, unless the comma is required by some other rule.

**28
i**

INCORRECT   For lunch I usually have, a sandwich, some fruit, and milk.
The comma after "have" separates the whole series from the rest of the sentence. It should be omitted.

INCORRECT   Rhode Island, New Jersey, and Massachusetts, were the most densely populated states in 1960.
The comma after "Massachusetts" erroneously separates the whole series from the rest of the sentence.

CORRECT   Rhode Island, New Jersey, and Massachusetts, in that order, were the most densely populated states in 1960.
The comma after "Massachusetts" is required to set off the parenthetic phrase "in that order."

EXERCISES

a. Some of the following student sentences omit necessary commas, while others contain unnecessary and misleading ones.

Punctuate the sentences correctly and be prepared to justify each comma you use and the eliminations you make.

1. The person who used to speak precisely and clearly, may now mumble and run his words together the way his favorite television or radio star does.
2. Some parents feel there should be a limit to the amount of homework which students are assigned but I feel most teachers are quite reasonable about the amount given.
3. When one cheats, he cheats no one, but himself.
4. Even if the student does get away with cheating for a long period of time when this student enters college, will he be better prepared?
5. This purity of spirit combined with the courage to stand up for what he believes, makes Huck the great character that he is.
6. Finally when Ike is fully initiated the chase begins.
7. A certain coffee commercial is amusing because it uses puppets, and is different from other advertisements.
8. The skeptical writer proposes questions hoping for answers.
9. He states that, "The play remains a fine source book for an intensively searching but as yet not consistently dramatic play."
10. The band, bunting and fireworks were planned but these were not enough to assure the parade's success.
11. It is soon evident, in the story, *Lucky Jim*, by Kingsley Amis, that Margaret is unstable, and that Dixon feels insecure and inferior.
12. He is apparently disgusted with his job, and the rest of his environment.
13. Yet, even in football he did not do outstandingly well.
14. Their faces, like the faces of the rest of the villagers are grotesque and primitive.
15. When he sat next to her he couldn't even talk to her.

28

29
the semicolon

The semicolon indicates a greater break in the sentence than does the comma. Its most important use is to separate two independent clauses when no conjunction joins them. It is also used whenever a comma is not adequate to indicate a separation.

29 a
to separate principal clauses

When the independent clauses of a compound sentence are not joined by a conjunction, a semicolon is required.

The conjunctive adverbs (*so, therefore, however, hence, nevertheless, moreover, accordingly, besides, also, thus, still, otherwise,* etc.) are inadequate to join two independent clauses. A semicolon is required to separate two independent clauses not connected by a pure conjunction. Using a comma instead produces a comma splice (see section 21a).

CORRECT   I do not say that these stories are untrue; I only say that I do not believe them.

CORRECT   In India fourteen main languages are written; several hundred dialectical variations are spoken.

COMMA SPLICE   Our plan was to sail from Naples to New York, however, an emergency at home forced us to fly instead.

CORRECT   Our plan was to sail from Naples to New York; however, an emergency at home forced us to fly instead.
CORRECT   From the high board, the water looked amazingly far away; besides, I was getting cold and tired of swimming.
CORRECT   The loan account book must be sent with each monthly payment; otherwise, there may be disputes as to the amount still owing.

If the clauses are short and closely parallel in form, commas are frequently used between them even if conjunctions are omitted.

CORRECT   The picture dimmed, the sound faded, the TV failed. The curtains fluttered, the windows rattled, the doors slammed.

As a means of combining sentences into compound sentences, the semicolon may easily be overworked. If a conjunction expresses the relationship between two sentences, use the conjunction. *The semicolon should be reserved for use when the relationship between the two statements is so clear that it is unnecessary to state it explicitly.*

**29
b**

29 b
to separate when commas
are inadequate

Even when two independent clauses are joined by a coordinating conjunction, a semicolon may be used to separate the clauses if the clauses are long or are subdivided by commas.

CORRECT   The Northwest Ordinance of 1787, drafted by Jefferson, is generally noted because it established government of territory North of Ohio and West of New York; *yet* one of its most important statutes was the allocation of land and support for public schools.

; | semi

CORRECT   In recognition of her services, the principal was given a farewell dinner, a record, and a scroll; *and* a new elementary school was named after her.

A semicolon is used to separate elements in a series when the elements contain internal commas. That is, when a comma is not a strong enough mark of separation to indicate the elements of a series unmistakably, a semicolon is used instead.

> AMBIGUOUS   One day of orientation was led by Mr. Joseph, a chaplain, Mrs. Smith, a French teacher, and the Dean.
> *How many led orientation?*

CORRECT   One day of orientation was led by Mr. Joseph, a chaplain; Mrs. Smith, a French teacher; and the Dean.

CORRECT   Bibliography may include Randall Jarrell, *Poetry and the Age*; Northrup Frye, *Anatomy of Criticism*; and Edmund Wilson, *The Shock of Recognition*.

29 b

Be sure that semicolons separate coordinate elements. Using a semicolon to separate an independent clause and a subordinate clause is an error similar to writing a sentence fragment, and just as serious.

> INCORRECT   Young people tend to reject parental authority; while they are searching for other adults as models.

CORRECT   Young people tend to reject parental authority, while they are searching for other adults as models.

EXERCISES

a. Some of the following student sentences contain semicolons which are unnecessary or incorrect, while other sentences lack needed semicolons. Correct the punctuation and be able to justify each semicolon you use or omit.

  1. Joseph is reluctantly picked up by a passing stage-coach; and then only after one of the passengers notes that they could be held legally responsible if a naked stranger should die for lack of aid.

2. More understandable than any of his other criticisms are his remarks about the educational system, however, even these are not very specific.

3. Our technology has developed the telephone for the talebearer; the car for the speedster; and the elevator for children.

4. A novel dealing with the affectations of a past society may become dated, and one must consider this possibility when judging it, otherwise, the book will suffer undue criticism.

5. He was not admitted to the honor society; although he was a good athlete and a top student.

b. In the following sentences, cross out semicolons which are unnecessary or incorrect and add semicolons where they are needed. Be able to justify your corrections.

1. The second edition of the book, published in 1922, is relatively scarce and hard to find; but the third edition, published four years later, can be seen in almost any store selling old books.

2. In most respects the hotel is admirably located, it is near the corner of Fifth Avenue and 52nd Street, within walking distance of most mid-town points of interest.

3. I might ask here; "What is the most important thing in life?"

4. The sculptor can work for more than a week on the same clay model; because clay can be kept soft and workable by the application of wet towels.

5. The average person is not financially able to do a great deal of traveling to distant countries, and therefore he will probably never have the chance to see most of the places he reads about.

6. Sometimes I get so interested in a book that I stay up until I finish it; regardless of whether I have classes the next morning or not.

7. Since air is dissolved by water at the surface only, the shape of an aquarium is important, too small an opening may cause an oxygen deficiency.

8. I don't mean to criticize the hospitality of the University; actually when I go there I am always received most cordially.
9. On the postcard was a reproduction of a water color by John Piper, it showed the interior of Ingelsham Church.
10. "Get off at the next main intersection," said the bus driver, "the park entrance is two blocks to the right."

c. Explain the punctuation in the following sentences. In order to do so, you will need to distinguish between principal clauses, subordinate clauses, and phrases.

1. There are no set rules which an actor must follow to become proficient in his art; however, there are certain principles regarding the use of mind, voice, and body which may help him.
2. The book covered the life of Lotta Crabtree from birth to death; it painted her as one of the most colorful figures of early California.
3. Her forehead was wrinkled, her mouth was firm and tense, but her eyes had a dreamy, reminiscent look.
4. The unconscious sailor would then be taken to an outbound ship to be sold to the captain at a price ranging from $100 to $300, depending on how pressed the captain was for men; and he would regain consciousness somewhere in the Pacific Ocean, without the slightest idea of where he was or where he was going.
5. Among the colorful figures in the book are Johnny Highpockets, a simple-minded settler; Charley Tufts, formerly a professor at Yale; and the author of the book himself.

29

30

quotation marks

30 a
to enclose direct quotation

Use quotation marks to enclose a direct quotation,
but not an indirect quotation.

A direct quotation is a part of a sentence which gives the exact
words of a speaker. An indirect quotation is the writer's paraphrase of what someone said.

> **INCORRECT**   He said "that he would call."
> *This is an indirect quotation, since it does not give his
> exact words.*

CORRECT   He said that he would call.
CORRECT   He said, "I will call."
Since this gives his exact words, it is a direct quotation.

The expression *he said* is never included within the quotation
marks. If the actual quotation is interrupted by such an expression, both halves must be enclosed by quotation marks. For
punctuation of *he said* expressions, see section 30b.

CORRECT   "I am interested," he said, "so let's talk it over."
CORRECT   "It all began accidentally," Jackson said. "My remark was misunderstood."

30 b
to quote several sentences

If a quotation consists of several sentences, uninter-
rupted by a *he said* expression, use one set of marks
to enclose the entire quotation.

Do not enclose each separate sentence. If a quotation consists
of several sentences, put quotation marks at the beginning of
each paragraph and at the end of the last paragraph.

CORRECT   Barbara replied, "On Tuesday night? My husband
and I would love to come. I'll tell him right away."

CORRECT   Poor Richard has a number of things to say about diet:
"They that study much, ought not to eat so much as those
that work hard, their digestion being not so good.

"If thou art dull and heavy after meat, it's a sign thou hast
exceeded the due measure; for meat and drink ought to refresh
the body and make it chearful, and not to dull and oppress it.

"A sober diet makes a man die without pain; it maintains
the senses in vigour; it mitigates the violence of the passions and
affections."

A quotation within a quotation is enclosed with single quotation marks. Be sure to conclude the original quotation with
double marks.

CORRECT   The lecture began, "As Proust said, 'Any mental
activity is easy if it need not take reality into account.'"

30 c
to indicate implied speech

Quotation marks are frequently used for implied
speech, but are not customarily used for unspoken
thoughts.

CORRECT   He tried to cry, "She is there, she is there," but he
couldn't utter the words, only the sounds.   —Jan de Hartog

CORRECT It was a momentary liberation from the pent-up anxious state I usually endured to be able to think: At least I'm not them! At least I'm not those heavy, serious, righteous people upstairs. —Robert Lowry

30 d
misuse in paraphrase

Use quotation marks around material directly quoted from another writer, but not around a paraphrase of an author's ideas (see also section 43g).

CORRECT John Selden pinpoints our attitude toward virtues when he defines humility: "Humility is a virtue all preach, none practise, and yet everybody is content to hear. The master thinks it good doctrine for his servant, the laity for the clergy, and the clergy for the laity."

CORRECT John Selden describes humility as a virtue we all praise, but few practice. We expect to observe it in those who deal with us, while overlooking our own chances to be humble.

If you quote only a few words from a well-known writer and work them into your own sentence, quotation marks may be omitted.

CORRECT During childhood it was easy to see that others should share toys, but during adulthood the reverse is less easy: do unto others as you would have them do unto you.

But quotation marks should be used if the audience may not recognize a quotation or if the limits of the direct quotation need to be indicated or if special emphasis is to be placed upon the quoted words.

CORRECT The student court, though fair, levied painful sentences which "made the punishment fit the crime."

CORRECT Despite all efforts to modernize and improve life, the world still suffers from what William Blake called "mind-forg'd manacles."

" | quot

When a borrowed quotation runs to several lines of print, it may be set off by indenting and single-spacing. Quotation marks *should not* be used when the quoted material is so indicated (see also section 36c).

CORRECT

T. S. Eliot begins the essay "Tradition and the Individual Talent":

> In English writing we seldom speak of tradition, though we occasionally apply its name in deploring its absence. We cannot refer to 'the tradition' or to 'a tradition'; at most, we employ the adjective in saying that the poetry of So-and-so is 'traditional' or even 'too traditional.' Seldom, perhaps, does the word appear except in a phrase of censure. If otherwise, it is vaguely approbative, with the implication, as to the work approved, of some pleasing archaeological reconstruction.

30 d

A quotation of more than one line of poetry should be set off by indenting and single-spacing, without quotation marks. Be sure to keep the line lengths exactly as they are in the original.

CORRECT   Boileau has captured a quality inseparable from fine satire:

> But satire, ever moral, ever new,
> Delights the reader and instructs him too.
> She, if good sense refine her sterling page,
> Oft shakes some rooted folly of the age.

30 e
punctuation with quotation marks

At the end of a quotation, a period or comma is placed inside the quotation mark; a semicolon or colon is placed outside the quotation mark.

CORRECT "Quick," said my cousin, "hand me the flashlight."
CORRECT The bride and groom said, "I do"; the ladies in the audience wept.
CORRECT I have only one comment when you say, "All men are equal": I wish it were true.

A question mark or exclamation mark goes inside the quotation mark if it applies to the quotation only, and outside the quotation mark if it applies to the whole sentence.

CORRECT My mother asked, "Did you arrive on time?"
CORRECT Did the invitation say "R.S.V.P."?
CORRECT He called irritably, "Move over!"
CORRECT Above all, don't let anyone hear you say, "I give up"!

30 f
to indicate titles

Titles of books, poems, plays, musical compositions, etc., may be enclosed in quotation marks, but the preferred practice is to italicize titles of whole publications or works and to use quotation marks for the titles of chapters, articles, etc.

Titles of paintings and other objects of art are regularly enclosed in quotation marks.

CORRECT The fourth section of Isak Dinesen's *Out of Africa* is entitled "From an Immigrant's Notebook."
CORRECT Carl Orf's cantata *Carmina Burana* opens and closes with "Fortune, Empress of the World."

30 g
misuse for humorous emphasis or
with slang

Do not use quotation marks for humorous emphasis or as an apology for slang.

" | quot

If occasionally you want to indicate that a word or phrase should be heavily stressed or deserves special attention, use italics. Humor or irony should be indicated by the context. Using quotation marks to call attention to an ironic or humorous passage is like poking your listener in the ribs when you have reached the point of a joke.

As to slang, if you use it at all, take full responsibility for it. Do not apologize for a phrase by putting it in quotation marks. If you are ashamed of it, don't use it (see section 11c).

EXERCISE

Insert quotation marks where they are necessary in the following sentences.

1. The Dean replied that he knew very well freshmen had trouble getting adjusted. But he added it doesn't usually take them eight months to find themselves.
2. I hope said Professor Painter that someone can identify a quotation for me. It's from the end of a sonnet, and all I can remember is Like a lean knife between the ribs of Time.
3. President Turini, according to the *Alumni Magazine,* believed that the chief values of a liberal education were nonmaterial; but on another page he was quoted, in the course of a speech delivered in Seattle, as saying that a college education is essential for any man who does not plan to marry money.
4. The janitor—they call him a custodial engineer now— dragged the filing case in and grunted Where do you want it? When he had put it in the corner, I started to say Thank you, but he had disappeared.
5. I asked whether Professor Lawrence still began his first lecture by saying My name is Lawrence and I wish I were not here, as he always did when I was in college.
6. The program said that the musical Hello, Dolly is based on Thornton Wilder's play The Matchmaker.

31
the apostrophe

The chief uses of the apostrophe are to indicate the possessive case of nouns and indefinite pronouns, to mark the omission of letters in a contracted word or date, and to indicate the plural of letters or numerals.

31 a
possessive case

Nouns and indefinite pronouns which do not already end in *s* form the possessive by adding an apostrophe and an *s*.

CORRECT	a man's shirt	men's shirts
	Auden's essays	children's toys
	one's dignity	Cole Porter's songs

Plural nouns which end in *s* (*boys, girls*) form the possessive by adding an apostrophe only.

CORRECT	girls' hockey	ladies' gloves
	boys' jackets	the Ellises' orchard
	princesses' jewels	the Neilsons' garage

Singular nouns which end in *s* (*Thomas, waitress*) form the possessive by adding an apostrophe and an *s* if the *s* is to be pronounced as an extra syllable.

’|apos

CORRECT	Thomas's poems	Lewis's philosophy
	Miss James's house	King James's reign
	a princess's jewels	a waitress's tip

But if an extra syllable would be awkward to pronounce, the possessive is formed by adding the apostrophe only and omitting the second *s*.

CORRECT	Socrates' questions	Higgins' motorbikes
	Moses' life	Euripides' plays

Despite a long set of complicated rules for dealing with such words, in actual practice usage is divided. Both *Yeats's* and *Yeats'* can be found in reputable publications. Note, however, that in all instances the apostrophe comes after the complete nominative form of the word.

WRONG	Edgar Lee Master's poetry
CORRECT	Edgar Lee Masters' poetry

WRONG	Aristophane's comedies
CORRECT	Aristophanes' comedies

WRONG	Dicken's novels
CORRECT	Dickens's novels

The personal pronouns *never require an apostrophe*, even though the possessive case ends in *s*.

CORRECT his, hers, its, ours, yours, theirs

In joint possession the last noun takes the possessive form. In individual possession each name should take the possessive form.

JOINT POSSESSION   Marshall and Ward's St. Paul branch
INDIVIDUAL POSSESSION   John's, George's, and Harold's separate claims

In compound words the possessive form is usually added to the last word.

CORRECT   my sister-in-law's visit

Note also these preferred forms: *someone else's book; somebody else's opinion.* The general pattern is as follows:

	singular	*plural*
CORRECT	sister-in-law's	sisters-in-law's
	mother-in-law's	mothers-in-law's

31 b
contractions

Use an apostrophe to indicate omitted letters in contracted words and dates.

Apostrophes may be used to indicate the omission of sounds and syllables by speakers, but they should be used sparingly.

CORRECT	haven't	doesn't	isn't	it's	o'clock
	have not	does not	is not	it is	of the clock
CORRECT	the class of '65, the hurricane of '38				

31 c
plural of letters and numerals

The plural of letters and of numbers is formed by adding *'s*.

The plural of a word considered *as a word* may be formed in the same way.

CORRECT   His *W*'s were like *M*'s, and his *9*'s like *G*'s.
CORRECT   Her conversation is too full of *you know*'s punctuated by *well*'s.

' apos

EXERCISE

Insert apostrophes, or an apostrophe and *s*, where they are required in the following sentences.

1. Grandma Moses paintings were very popular Christmas cards a few years ago.
2. In spite of its reputation, Hughes restaurant is not popular with the students; its too expensive.
3. Dont take Charles promises too seriously.
4. He ordered fifty cents worth of ground beef at Ross market.
5. The mens dormitories are always open, but the girls residence halls close at midnight.
6. Members of the class of 60 wore sport shirts covered with letters, bright crimson Hs and Cs.
7. Brooks and Callahan store isn't as large as Otis department store.
8. The Davises car was parked on our driveway, right behind Travis sports car.
9. Too many *ands* will weaken anyones writing.
10. Don't take anyone elses word for it; trust your own experience.
11. Keats poems are more like Tennysons than like Brownings.
12. A fifteen minute walk every day may save five dollars worth of doctors prescriptions.
13. My brothers boat was not working, so we borrowed a launch belonging to the Willises.
14. Our future mothers-in-laws disagreements about the wedding plans caused our elopement.
15. Its too bad he doesn't have the money for the trip.

31

32
the colon

The colon is a rather formal mark of punctuation, and it is not widely used in informal writing if a semicolon or dash will serve instead. The colon is primarily an introductory mark, and its proper uses are listed below.

32 a
to introduce formal list, quotation, or statement

The principal use of the colon is to introduce a formal enumeration or list, a long quotation, or an explanatory statement.

CORRECT   Consider these three viewpoints: political, economic, and social.

CORRECT   Tocqueville expresses one view: "In the United States we easily perceive how the legal profession is qualified by its attributes . . . to neutralize the vices inherent in popular government . . . ."
The quotation continues.

CORRECT   I remember which way to move the clock when changing from Daylight Saving Time to Standard Time by applying a simple rule: spring ahead, fall backwards.

Note that a list introduced by a colon should be in apposition to a preceding word; that is, the sentence preceding the colon should be grammatically complete without the list.

:|colon

UNDESIRABLE   We provide: fishing permit, rod, hooks, bait, lunch, boat, oars.

CORRECT   We provide the following items: fishing permit, rod, boat, oars, etc.

CORRECT   We provide the following: fishing permit, rod, lunch, boat, etc.

CORRECT   The following items are provided: fishing permit, rod, lunch, boat, etc.

32 b
between main clauses

The colon may be used between two principal clauses when the second clause explains or develops the first.

CORRECT   Intercollegiate athletics continues to be big business, but Robert Hutchins long ago pointed out a simple remedy: colleges should stop charging admission to football games.

CORRECT   Some feel that outlawing a drug only complicates the problem: the user then deals with criminal elements.

32 c
conventional uses

A colon is used after a formal salutation in a business letter.

CORRECT   Dear Sir: Dear Mr. Harris: Gentlemen:

A colon is used to separate hour and minutes in numerals indicating time.

CORRECT   The train leaves at 9:27 A.M., and arrives at Joplin at 8:15 P.M.

In bibliographical references, a colon is used between the place of publication and the name of the publisher.

CORRECT   New York: Oxford University Press

Between the parts of a Biblical reference a colon may be used.

CORRECT   *Proverbs* 28:20

33
the dash

Since the dash (made in typing by *two* hyphens placed without space between them) is a rather dramatic mark of punctuation, it should not be used indiscriminately in place of commas, semicolons, or periods. It indicates a stronger degree of separation than the comma. The overuse of dashes may suggest that the writer is careless, or that he does not know how to use the other marks of punctuation, or that he is striving to gain emphasis by the easy device of emphatic punctuation rather than by exact and vivid diction or effective sentence structure.

33 a
as a separator

A dash is used, as a separator, to indicate that a sentence is broken off or to indicate a sharp turn of thought.

CORRECT

The application requested a transcript and had space to enter extra-curricular activities, interests, hobbies -- need I say more?

CORRECT

From noon until three o'clock, we had an excellent view of all that can be seen of a battle -- i.e., nothing at all.

--Stendahl

On a typewriter, a dash appears as two hyphens, as in the two examples above.

– dash

33 b
to set off appositives or parenthetic elements

Dashes may be used to set off appositives or parenthetic elements when commas are insufficient.

CORRECT Three pictures—a water color, an oil, and a silk screen—hung on the west wall.
If the commas were used to set off "a water color, an oil, and a silk screen," the sentence might be misunderstood to refer to six pictures. The dashes make it clear that only three pictures are meant.

CORRECT By the time the speech was over—it lasted almost two hours—I was dozing in my chair.
Since the parenthetic element is an independent clause, commas would be insufficient to set it off clearly.

Modern writers often use a dash to emphasize an important or contrasting appositive.

CORRECT The body is a thing, the soul is also a thing; man is not a thing, but a drama—his life.   —Ortega y Gasset

33 c
to mark a summarizing statement

When a sentence begins with a list of substantives, a dash is commonly used to separate the list from the summarizing statement which follows.

CORRECT Relaxation, repose, growth within—these are necessities of life, not privileges.

CORRECT The chance to sit on a committee with no big issues to debate, the prospect of introducing bills which will never be reported, the opportunity to write speeches that will rarely be delivered—these are not horizons toward which an able man will strain.   —Harold Laski

34

parentheses and brackets

34 a
parentheses

Parentheses, like dashes and commas, are used to enclose or set off parenthetic, explanatory, or supplementary material.

34
a

Arbitrary rules indicating which marks to use cannot be laid down, but in general commas are the weakest marks, dashes are stronger, and parentheses are strongest. Commas are most frequently used, and are usually sufficient when the parenthetic material is very closely related in thought or structure to the rest of the sentence. If the parenthetic material is long or if it contains commas, dashes would customarily be used to set it off. Parentheses are most often used for explanatory or supplementary material of the sort which might be put in a footnote—useful information which is not essential. Parentheses are also used to enclose numbers which mark an enumeration within a sentence.

CORRECT   It was, perhaps, this very sensibility to the surrounding atmosphere of feeling and speculation, which made Rousseau more directly influential on contemporary thought (or perhaps we should say sentiment) than any writer of his time. And this is rarely consistent with enduring greatness in literature.
—James Russell Lowell

CORRECT His last story ("Success à la Steinberg") lacked imagination and any relevance to the cartoonist named in the title.

CORRECT In general, the war powers of the President cannot be precisely defined, but must remain somewhat vague and uncertain. (See Wilson's *Constitutional Government in the United States.*)

CORRECT The types of noncreative thinking listed by Robinson are (1) reverie, or daydreaming, (2) making minor decisions, (3) rationalizing, or justifying our prejudices.

34 b
brackets

Brackets are used to enclose a word or words inserted in a quotation by the person quoting.

CORRECT "For the First Amendment does not speak equivocally. It prohibits any law 'abridging the freedom of speech, or of the press.' *It must be taken as a command of the broadest scope that explicit language, read in the context of a liberty-loving society, will allow.*" [Italics added.]

or

CORRECT "The diarist pulls his character up by the roots every evening, and finds the soil of human nature,—the humus,—out of which it must needs grow, clinging to its radicles. Then he mourns over himself as did the saintly Brainard as 'inexpressibly loathsome and defiled,' calling himself so vile 'that [he] dared not look anybody in the face,' . . . ." —Jonathan Edwards

The word *sic* (meaning *thus*) enclosed in brackets is sometimes inserted in a quotation after a misspelling or other error to indicate that the error occurs in the original.

CORRECT "I have often heard diverse Ladies vent loud feminine complaints of the wearisome varieties and chargable [*sic*] changes of fashion: I marvell [*sic*] themselves prefer not a Bill of redresse [*sic*]." —Nathaniel Ward

EXERCISES

a. Study the use of colons, dashes, parentheses, and brackets in the following sentences.

1. And so far as they [those who go to college for social reasons] are concerned, the remedy is plain: a stern insistence on the part of the college authorities that they demonstrate a right to be there.   —Richard Burton

2. A sense of the value of time—that is, the best way to divide one's time into one's various activities—is an essential preliminary to efficient work.—Arnold Bennett

3. And watching the white clouds so bright against the intense blue, Ashurst, on his silver-wedding day, longed for—he knew not what.   —John Galsworthy

4. It had never occurred to me that he was a real Communist (I had never, so far as I knew, met one) until, looking over the proofs of a forthcoming book, I read the assertion that he had been a Party member.

—Bradford Smith

5. Clubs, fraternities, nations—these are the beloved barriers in the way of a workable world; these will have to surrender some of their rights and some of their ribs.

—E. B. White

b. Insert colons, dashes, parentheses, and brackets as they are needed in the following sentences.

1. Each of its large rooms there were no separate cells in this prison housed some twenty prisoners.

2. I took part in a number of activities in high school the rally committee, dramatics, *Ayer* staff the *Ayer* is our annual, and glee club.

3. He joined the Quakers and became an occasional speaker the Quakers have no ordained ministers at their meetings in Philadelphia.

4. According to an inscription on the flyleaf, the book had been owned by Alburt *sic* Taylor.

5. The sect permits dancing but forbids some other seemingly innocent recreations card playing, for example, is banned as being the next thing to gambling.

6. According to the *Mason Report* Stearns testified as fol-

P

lows "I made his John Brown's acquaintance early in January 1857, in Boston."

7. The midnight programs at the Varsity Theater feature horror films, science-fiction thrillers, movies of strange monsters from the sea you know the kind of thing.

REVIEW EXERCISES

a. Some of the following student sentences contain incorrect or misleading punctuation, while others lack needed punctuation. Correct each sentence and be prepared to justify your changes.

1. The author mentions spontaneous and joyous effort, but what is a spontaneous and joyous effort.

2. Lincoln born in 1809 in Kentucky, was brought up in a poor family in the woods.

3. What would imply greater silence and quiet meditation than the numerous s's in the sentence.

4. You have a carwash for your car; a combination washer and dryer for your laundry; and a portable dishwasher for your dishes.

5. His goal had been to set up camp at this particular place along the river—No other place would do even though other places would have been faster to get to, and now he had done it.

6. It is the setting that is significant; without the setting there would be no story.

7. Now we reach the inevitable question; how does our liberally educated man make use of his knowledge when he enters the business world?

8. However, Bernard Shaw's main purpose is not to show the tragedy of St. Joan (that is already quite evident) but to explain the character of St. Joan.

b. Punctuate the following sentences. Be ready to give a reason for any mark of punctuation you use.

1. In our new house the kitchen the bathroom and the utility rooms will have plain wood floors

2. Under the system just established a student from a family which cannot afford to send a child away to

34

college will have a chance for a scholarship especially if he is interested in science or engineering

3. Reading gives enjoyment to many friendless lonely people but it will not encourage them to go out and make friends

4. Man lives in groups small animals live in groups even plants sometimes live in groups

5. The following men will report to the Infirmary Wednesday October 3 at 4 30 for medical examinations Appleby Peter Catlin Bill Hadly Charles Stevenson Robert

6. Jan was born in Vienna Austria on January 14 1945 in a fashionable residential area

7. The student if he is lucky enough to pass the test may register for the next course in the sequence

c. Punctuate the following paragraphs and be ready to give a reason for each mark used.

1. I could tell without turning who was coming. There wasnt a big flat-footed clop-clop like horses make on hard-pack but a kind of edgy clip-clip-clip. There was only one man around here would ride a mule at least on this kind of business. That was Bill Winder who drove the stage between Reno and Bridgers Wells. A mule is tough all right a good mule can work two horses into the ground and not know it. But theres something about a mule a man cant get fond of. Maybe its just the way a mule is just as you feel its the end with a man whos that way. But you cant make a mule part of the way you live like your horse is its like he had no insides no soul. Instead of a partner youve just got something else to work on along with the steers. Winder didnt like mules either but thats why he rode them. It was against his religion to get on a horse horses were for driving

Its Winder Gil said and looked at Davies and grinned. The news gets around dont it

P

I looked at Davies too in the glass but he wasnt showing anything just staring at his drink and minding his own thoughts

Winder wouldnt help Davies any we knew that. He was edgy the same way Gil was but angry not funning and you couldnt get at him with an idea

Gabe Hart was with him on another mule. Gabe was his hostler a big ape-built man stronger than was natural but weak-minded not crazy but childish like his mind had never grown up. He was dirty too he slept in the stables with his horses and his knees and elbows were always out of his clothes and his long hair and beard always had bits of hay and a powder of grain chaff in them. Gabe was gentle though not a mean streak in him like there genrally is in stupid very strong men

—Walter Van Tilburg Clark

34

2. When Father Urban was able to continue he was again speaking to the audience at large. Differences of opinion can occur in any organization human or divine large or small yes even in the best-run families between husbands and wives so I've been told. Laughter. People who perhaps hadn't entirely trusted the speaker until he dealt with the red head and then hadn't been far from carrying him around the room on their shoulders were now in a mood to get cozy with him. Now don't misunderstand me. I'm not saying that differences of opinion are a good thing in themselves but I do think there's a lot to be said for taking them for what they often are healthy manifestations of the democratic process. Clapping here and there but Father Urban could tell it wasn't going to catch on and so quickly before this would be unnecessary he raised his hand for silence. Now that we're on the subject let me tell you of another difference of opinion in which I was involved recently. For many years I traveled out of Chicago

but now as some of you may know I'm stationed
right here in Minnesota and very happy to be here
let me say. Where I am was known until recently
as the Retreat House of the Order of St Clement.
Quite a mouthful you say and I agree. There are just
four of us there three priests and a brother and we
got to wondering if we couldn't find another name
for the place which by the way I hope you'll all find
time to visit Catholic or not it makes no difference to
us. Just stop in and say hello. Well one of our men
the one in charge as it happened was all for calling
the place Mount St Clement whereas I was more for
St Clement's Hill and so we called it that. Here
Father Urban did a double-take. Say I wonder how
that happened he cried and drew another fine laugh
and that was it. Waving and saying Good night
Good night he sat down certain that he'd repaired
a good part of the damage done by Wilf and the
crusade and also that he'd put the Hill on the map
for a lot of people who really mattered in the community. The audience gave him a wonderful hand,
almost a standing ovation.   --J. F. Powers

3. A few teachers and college administrators have begun to discover that student-made films say as much
or more about students their present frustrations and
aspirations as about film-making itself. Some contend that these movies are the best guides to the
intellectual and emotional world of students and
that even a cursory glance will provide penetrating
insights into what is really behind the recent up-
heavals at Berkeley and other institutions. On a
kind of hunch the American Council on Education
a relatively conservative organization in higher education has screened dozens of student-made films to
learn more about what undergraduates are thinking.
No one has clarified the reasons why these films are
so revealing but most people believe that it has a

P

great deal to do with the fact that students are expressing themselves in a medium which they feel is their own and which therefore they can trust.

Not unexpectedly student films are characterized by a spirit of revolt they are anti-establishment anti-system anti-conformity. In some pictures this takes the form of a relatively clear statement. Take The Bulb Changer a whimsical comedy produced by a Northwestern student in which the title character completely fouls up an entire community's trafficlight system after he suffers an injustice at the hands of his superior at the local bureaucracy.

More often however the "message" in a student film is stated obliquely. A film entitled Another Yesterday made by two undergraduates at the University of Pennsylvania's Annenberg School of Communication is ostensibly a documentary account of the humdrum life of a young Negro prizefighter. We follow him from the time he awakes at 600 A M and starts his roadwork until he returns from the gym to his dingy one-room apartment following a 900 P M workout. Boxing is his profession but most of the time he devotes to it is actually moonlighting before and after his regular job as a stevedore. Part of the sound track gives us the highlights of a boxer's day a straightforward professionally composed narrative. The startling element however is an interwoven narration spoken flatly and without emotion from Camus' novel The Stranger for example Mother died today or was it yesterday it doesn't really matter.

In this second narrative thread the film-makers felt they had captured the essence of what was really going on. Predictably they waited until the last minute to add the sound assuming that their teacher wouldn't understand and would veto the whole project.   --David C. Stewart

35 *spelling*

35
spelling

Misspelling of common words is regarded by the general public as a sure sign of lack of education. College graduates cannot afford to be poor spellers. They need not be, since most misspelling is a habit and habits can be changed with a little effort.

The first step is to make a list of words which you misspell. Have someone give you a series of spelling tests on the words listed in section 35e. These are all common words frequently misspelled. Difficult words like *asphyxiate* or *symbiosis*, which occur infrequently in ordinary writing, need not be learned, since you can consult a dictionary for the spelling of any word which is obviously difficult.

Add to the list all words which are misspelled on your themes, and study the list. Look carefully at the letters of each word, pronounce the word a syllable at a time, write the word repeatedly to fix the pattern in your mind. Invent mnemonic devices—pictures, jingles, associations—to help you remember particular spellings. For example, a student might remember the distinction between *capital* and *capitol* by associating capitAl with WAshington and capitOl with dOme. Learn the more common prefixes and suffixes, and analyze words to see how they are formed. For example:

    disappoint = dis + appoint
    dissatisfied = dis + satisfied
    misspelling = mis + spell + ing
    really = real + ly
    unnecessary = un + necessary
    undoubtedly = un + doubt + ed + ly

35

```
government = govern + ment
carefully = care + ful + ly
incidentally = incident + al + ly
```

See how many words in the list of *Words Commonly Misspelled* can be analyzed into a root word with prefixes or suffixes. If you find exceptions, look for an explanation in the Spelling Rules.

When you have finished the final draft of a paper, proofread it carefully before you hand it in. (Proofread for spelling errors separately if you have trouble with spelling.) It is no excuse to say that you knew the correct spelling of a word but that your pen slipped. Misspellings due to typographical errors or general carelessness are still misspellings.

35 a
trouble spots in words

Learn to look for the trouble spots in words and concentrate on them.

35

Common words are almost always misspelled in the same way. That is, a particular letter or combination of letters is the trouble spot, and if you can remember the correct spelling of the trouble spot, the rest of the word will take care of itself. Look for the trouble spots in words and concentrate on them. *Receive,* like *deceive, perceive,* and *conceive,* is troublesome only because of the *ei* combination; if you can remember that it is *ei* after *c,* you will have mastered these words. To spell *beginning* correctly, all you need to remember is the double *n.*

Careful pronunciation may help you to avoid errors at trouble spots. In the following words, the letters in italics are often omitted. Pronounce the words aloud, exaggerating the sound of the italicized letters:

accident*ally*	February	li*a*ble
candi*d*ate	gener*ally*	library
everybody	laboratory	literature
occasion*ally*	recognize	surprise

probably	sophomore	temperament
quantity	strictly	usually

Many people add letters incorrectly to the following words. Pronounce the words, making sure no extra syllable creeps in at spots indicated by italics.

athletics	entrance	mischievous
disastrous	height	remembrance
drowned	hindrance	similar
elm	lightning	umbrella

Trouble spots in the following words are caused by a tendency to transpose the letters italicized. Careful pronunciation may help you to remember the proper order.

children	perform	prejudice
hundred	perspiration	prescription
irrelevant	prefer	tragedy

35 b
similar words frequently confused

Learn the meaning and spelling of similar words.

Many errors are caused by confusion of such words as *effect* and *affect*. It is useless to spell *principal* correctly if the word that belongs in your sentence is *principle*. The following list distinguishes briefly between words which are frequently confused.

accept	*receive*	affect	*to influence* (verb)
except	*aside from*		
access	*admittance*	effect	*result* (noun)
excess	*greater amount*	effect	*to produce* (verb)
advice	noun	aisle	in church
advise	verb	isle	*island*

Sp

all ready	*prepared*
already	*previously*
allusion	*reference*
illusion	*misconception*
altar	*shrine*
alter	*change*
alumna	a woman
alumnae	women
alumnus	a man
alumni	men
angel	*celestial being*
angle	*corner*
ascent	*climbing*
assent	*agreement*
berth	*bed*
birth	*being born*
boarder	*one who boards*
border	*edge*
breath	noun
breathe	verb
capital	*city*
capitol	*building*
choose	present
chose	past
clothes	*garments*
cloths	*kinds of cloth*
coarse	*not fine*
course	*path, series*
complement	*to complete*
compliment	*to praise*

confidentially	*secretly*
confidently	*with confidence*
conscience	*sense of right and wrong*
conscious	*aware*
corps	*squad*
corpse	*dead body*
costume	*dress*
custom	*manner*
council	*assembly*
counsel	*advice*
dairy	*milk room*
diary	*daily record*
decent	*proper*
descent	*slope*
desert	*wasteland*
dessert	*food*
device	noun
devise	verb
dual	*twofold*
duel	*fight*
formally	*in a formal manner*
formerly	*previously*
forth	*forward*
fourth	*4th*
ingenious	*clever*
ingenuous	*frank*
its	*of it*
it's	*it is*

35 b

later	subsequent	respectfully	with respect
latter	second of two	respectively	as relating to each
lead	metal		
led	past tense of verb lead	shone	cf. shine
		shown	cf. show
loose	adjective	stationary	adjective
lose	verb	stationery	noun
peace	not war	their	possessive
piece	a portion	there	in that place
		they're	they are
percent	part of a hundred	to	go to bed
percentage	rate	too	too bad, me too
		two	2
personal	adjective		
personnel	noun	weather	rain or shine
		whether	which of two
principal	most important	who's	who is
principle	basic doctrine	whose	possessive
quiet	still	you're	you are
quite	entirely	your	possessive

35
c

35 c
spelling rules

Learn the available spelling rules.

Spelling rules apply to a relatively small number of words, and unfortunately almost all rules have exceptions. Nevertheless, some of the rules may help you to spell common words which cause you trouble, especially those words formed with suffixes.

It is as important to learn when a rule may be used as it is to understand the rule itself. Applied in the wrong places, rules will make your spelling worse, instead of better.

Sp

1 final silent e

Drop a final silent *e* before suffixes beginning with a vowel (*ing, age, able*). Keep a final silent *e* before suffixes beginning with a consonant (*ful, ly, ness*).

hope + ing = hoping	hope + ful = hopeful
love + able = lovable	nine + teen = nineteen
stone + y = stony	arrange + ment = arrangement
guide + ance = guidance	late + ly = lately
plume + age = plumage	pale + ness = paleness
white + ish = whitish	white + wash = whitewash
write + ing = writing	sincere + ly = sincerely
dote + age = dotage	bale + ful = baleful

Learn the following exceptions:

dyeing	hoeing	gluey	awful
ninth	truly	duly	wholly

The *e* is retained in such words as the following in order to keep the soft sound of *c* and *g*:

noticeable	courageous
peaceable	outrageous

35 c EXERCISE

Following the rule just given, write the correct spelling of each word indicated below.

use + ing	pale + ing
use + ful	manage + ment
argue + ment	peace + able
guide + ance	write + ing
hope + ful	advantage + ous
outrage + ous	refuse + al
nine + teen	waste + ful
pale + ness	hope + less
immediate + ly	absolute + ly
please + ure	sure + ly
manage + able	manage + ing

2 doubling final consonant

When adding a suffix beginning with a vowel to words ending in one consonant preceded by one vowel (*red, redder*), notice where the word is accented. If it is accented on the last syllable or if it is a monosyllable, *double* the final consonant.

pre**fer** + ed = preferred	**ben**efit + ed = benefited
o**mit** + ing = omitting	**pro**fit + ing = profiting
oc**cur** + ence = occurrence	**dif**fer + ence = difference
red + er = redder	**tra**vel + er = traveler

Note that in some words the accent shifts when the suffix is added.

re**fer**red	**ref**erence
pre**fer**ring	**pref**erence

There are a few exceptions to this rule, like *transferable* and *excellent*; and a good many words that should follow the rule have alternate spellings: either *worshiped* or *worshipped; traveling, traveler,* or *travelling, traveller.*

EXERCISE

Make as many combinations as you can of the following words and suffixes. Give your reason for doubling or not doubling the final consonant. Suffixes: *able, ible, ary, ery, er, est, ance, ence, ess, ed, ish, ing, ly, ful, ment, ness, hood.*

occur	scrap	ravel	man	libel
happen	red	kidnap	vassal	will
begin	equip	hazard	sum	skill
god	commit	read	stop	expel
shrub	equal	rid	clan	rival
glad	profit	level	avoid	jewel

3 words ending in y

If the *y* is preceded by a consonant, change the *y* to *i* before any suffix except *ing.*

Sp

lady + es = ladies   lonely + ness = loneliness
try + ed = tried   accompany + es = accompanies
study + ing = studying

The *y* is usually retained if it is preceded by a vowel:

valleys   monkeys   displayed

SOME EXCEPTIONS   *laid, paid, said.*

EXERCISE

Add suffixes to the following words. State your reason for spelling the word as you do.

mercy	relay	hardy	bounty	medley
duty	study	wordy	jockey	galley
pulley	essay	fancy	modify	body

4 *ie or ei*

When *ie* or *ei* is used to spell the sound *ee*,
Put *i* before *e*
Except after *c*.

achieve	grieve	retrieve	ceiling
belief	niece	shield	conceit
believe	piece	shriek	conceive
brief	pierce	siege	deceit
chief	relief	thief	deceive
field	relieve	wield	perceive
grief	reprieve	yield	receive

SOME EXCEPTIONS   *either, leisure, neither, seize, weird.*

35 d
hyphenation

Consult a dictionary if in doubt about hyphenation.

A hyphen is used, under certain circumstances, to join the parts of compound words. Compounds are written as two separate words (*city hall*), as two words joined by a hyphen (*city-state*), or solid as one word (*cityfolk*). In general, the hyphen is used in recently made compounds and compounds still in the process of becoming one word. Because usage varies considerably, no arbitrary rules can be laid down. When in doubt consult the latest edition of an unabridged dictionary. The following "rules" represent the usual current practice.

1 compound adjectives

Words used as a single adjective *before* a noun are usually hyphenated.

blue-green sea three-quarter binding
strong-minded woman matter-of-fact statement
far-sighted proposal so-called savings
well-informed leader old-fashioned attitude

When these compound adjectives *follow* the noun, they usually do not require the hyphen.
CORRECT   The snow-covered mountains lay ahead.
CORRECT   The mountains are snow covered.
When the adverb ending in *ly* is used with an adjective or a participle, the compound is not usually hyphenated.
CORRECT   highly praised organization, widely advertised campaign.

**35
d**

2 prefixes

When a prefix still retains its original strength in the compound, use a hyphen.

In most instances, however, the prefix has been absorbed into the word and should not be separated by a hyphen. Contrast the following pairs of words:

ex-president, excommunicate   pre-Christian, preconception
vice-president, viceroy   pro-British, procreation

Note that in some words a difference of meaning is indicated by the hyphen:

She recovered her strength.
She re-covered her quilt.

Sp

3 compound numbers

A hyphen is used in compound numbers from twenty-one to ninety-nine.

CORRECT   twenty-six, sixty-three, *but* one hundred thirty.

4 hyphen to prevent misreading

Use a hyphen if necessary to avoid ambiguity.

AMBIGUOUS   A detail of six foot patrolmen was on duty.
CLEAR   A detail of six foot-patrolmen was on duty. *Or*
A detail of six-foot patrolmen was on duty.

EXERCISE

Should the compounds in the following sentences be written solid, with a hyphen, or as two words? Consult a recent edition of a good dictionary.

1. We need an eight foot rod.
2. All the creeks are bone dry.
3. He gave away one fourth of his income.
4. The United States is a world power.
5. He was our go between.
6. She is very good looking.
7. The younger son was a ne'er do well.
8. Let us sing the chorus all together.
9. They are building on a T shaped wing.
10. She is getting a badly needed rest.
11. Are you all ready?
12. The leak was in the sub basement.
13. He was anti British.
14. She does her work in a half hearted manner.
15. I don't like your chip on the shoulder manner.
16. She always was old fashioned.
17. A high school course is required for admission.
18. I do not trust second hand information.
19. He is as pig headed a man as I ever knew.
20. He will not accept any thing second rate.

35 d

35 e
words commonly misspelled

Master the correct form of the most commonly mis-spelled words.

The following list is composed of some ordinary words that are often misspelled. If you learn to spell correctly those which you usually misspell, and if you will look up in a dictionary words which are obviously difficult or unfamiliar, your spelling will improve remarkably.

Have a friend test you on these words—fifty at a time. Then concentrate on the ones you miss. To help you remember correct spellings, trouble spots are italicized in many of the following words.

absence	amateur	bargain
absorption	among	basically
absurd	analysis	becoming
abundant	annually	beginning
academic	apology	believe
accidentally	apparatus	benefited
accommodate	apparent	boundary
accumulate	appearance	brilliant
accurate	appetite	Britain
achievement	appreciate	business
acquainted	appropriate	calendar
acquire	arctic	candidate
across	argument	career
additionally	arithmetic	category
address	arrangement	cemetery
adequately	article	certain
aggravate	ascend	challenge
airplane	association	changeable
allotment	athletic	changing
allotted	attacked	Christian
all right	attendance	column
already	audience	coming
altogether	available	commission
always	awkward	committee

35
e

Sp

comparatively
competent
competition
conceit
concentrate
condemn
confidence
conqueror
conscientious
conscious
consider
consistent
contemporary
continuous
controlled
convenience
coolly
copies
courteous
criticism
dealt
deceive
decision
definitely
descendant
describe
description
desirable
despair
desperate
dictionary
different
difficult
dining room
disappear
disappoint
disastrous
discipline

disease
dissatisfied
dissipate
divide
doctor
dying
effect
eighth
eliminate
embarrass
emphasize
entirely
entrance
environment
equipped
especially
etc. (et cetera)
exaggerate
exceed
excellent
exceptionally
exercise
existence
exorbitant
expense
experience
explanation
familiar
fascinate
feasible
February
fictitious
finally
foreign
forty
friend
gauge
government

grammar
guard
harass
hardening
height
hindrance
humorous
hurriedly
hypocrisy
illiterate
imagination
imitation
immediately
incidentally
incredibly
independent
indispensable
infinite
initiative
intelligence
interest
involve
irrelevant
irresistible
itself
jealousy
knowledge
laboratory
laid
led
leisure
library
license
literature
loneliness
lose
luxury
magazine

maintenance
manufacturer
marriage
mathematics
mattress
meant
medieval
merely
miniature
municipal
murmur
mysterious
necessary
neither
nineteen
noticeable
nowadays
nucleus
obstacle
occasionally
occurred
occurrence
omission
omitted
opinion
opportunity
optimism
origin
paid
pamphlet
parallel
paralyzed
parliament
particularly
partner
pastime
perform
perhaps

permanent
permissible
persistent
personnel
persuade
physical
pleasant
politician
possess
possible
practically
preceding
predominant
prejudice
preparation
prevalent
primitive
privilege
probably
procedure
proceed
profession
professor
prominent
pronunciation
prove
psychology
pursue
quizzes
really
receive
recognize
recommend
reference
referred
religious
reminisce
repetition

representative
rhythm
ridiculous
sacrifice
safety
scene
schedule
secretary
seize
sense
separate
sergeant
severely
shining
siege
similar
sincerely
soliloquy
sophomore
specimen
speech
stopping
strenuous
stretch
studying
succeed
suppress
surprise
susceptible
syllable
sympathize
temperament
tendency
thorough
together
tragedy
transferred
truly

**35
e**

Sp

typical	until	village
tyranny	using	villain
undoubtedly	usually	weird
unnecessary	vengeance	writing

EXERCISES

1. Write the infinitive, the present participle, and the past participle of each of the following verbs (e.g., *stop, stopping, stopped*):

prefer	slam	hop	acquit
profit	begin	differ	commit
drag	equip	recur	confer

2. Write the following words together with the adjectives ending in *able* derived from them (e.g., *love, lovable*):

dispose	compare	imagine
move	console	cure
prove	blame	measure

3. Write the following words together with their derivatives ending in *able* (e.g., *notice, noticeable*):

trace	marriage	damage
service	charge	peace
change	place	manage

4. Write the singular and the plural of the following nouns (e.g., *lady, ladies*):

baby	remedy	treaty	turkey
hobby	enemy	delay	decoy
democracy	poppy	alley	alloy
policy	diary	attorney	corduroy
tragedy	laundry	journey	convoy

5. Write the first and third persons present indicative, and the first person past, of the following verbs (e.g., *I cry, he cries, I cried*):

fancy	spy	vary	worry
qualify	reply	dry	pity
accompany	occupy	ferry	envy

6. Study the following words, observing that in all of them the prefix is not **diss** but **dis:**

dis + advantage	dis + obedient
dis + agree	dis + orderly
dis + approve	dis + organize
dis + interested	dis + own

7. Study the following words observing that in all of them the prefix is not **u** but **un:**

un + natural	un + numbered
un + necessary	un + named
un + noticed	un + neighborly

8. Study the following words, distinguishing between the prefixes **per** and **pre.** Keep in mind that **per** means **through, throughout, by, for;** and that **pre** means **before.**

perform	perhaps	precept
perception	perspective	precipitate
peremptory	perspiration	precise
perforce	precarious	precocious
perfunctory	precaution	prescription

9. Study the following adjectives, observing that in all of them the suffix is not **full,** but **ful:**

peaceful	forceful	healthful
dreadful	shameful	pitiful
handful	grateful	thankful
graceful	faithful	cupful

10. Study the following words, observing that in all of them the ending is not **us,** but **ous:**

advantageous	specious	fastidious
gorgeous	precious	studious
courteous	vicious	religious
dubious	conscious	perilous

11. Study the following words, observing that in all of them the suffix **al** precedes **ly:**

accidentally	terrifically	exceptionally
apologetically	specifically	elementally
pathetically	emphatically	professionally
typically	finally	critically

35

12. Study the following words, observing that the suffix is not *ess*, but *ness*:

clean + ness	plain + ness	stern + ness
drunken + ness	stubborn + ness	keen + ness
mean + ness	sudden + ness	green + ness

13. Study the following words, observing that the suffix is not *able*, but *ible*:

accessible	discernible	imperceptible
admissible	eligible	impossible
audible	feasible	incompatible
compatible	flexible	incredible
contemptible	forcible	indefensible
convertible	horrible	indelible
intelligible	perceptible	responsible
invincible	permissible	sensible
invisible	plausible	susceptible
irresistible	possible	tangible
legible	reprehensible	terrible

14. Study the following groups of words:

ain		*ian*	
Britain	curtain	barbarian	guardian
captain	fountain	Christian	musician
certain	mountain	civilian	physician
chieftain	villain	collegian	politician

15. Study the following groups of words:

ede		*eed*
accede	precede	exceed
antecede	recede	proceed
concede	secede	succeed

16. Fill the blanks with *principal* or *principle*. *Principle* is always a noun; *principal* is usually an adjective. *Principal* is also occasionally a noun: the *principal* of the school, both *principal* and *interest*.

    1. The _____ will be due on the tenth of the month.

    2. His refusal was based on _____ .

    3. This is my _____ reason for going.

35

  4. The _____ has asked that we hold our meeting tomorrow.

  5. He did not even know the first _____ of the game.

  6. Can you give the _____ parts of the verb?

17. Fill the blanks with **affect** or **effect:**

  1. I do not like her _____ed manner.

  2. An entrance was _____ed by force.

  3. The _____ upon her is noticeable.

  4. The law will take _____ in July.

  5. It will be an _____ive remedy.

  6. The hot weather will _____ the crops.

  7. There was no serious after _____ .

  8. She _____ed ignorance of the whole matter.

18. Fill the blanks with **passed** or **past. Passed** is the past tense or past participle of the verb **pass; past** can be an adjective, noun, adverb, or preposition.

  1. We _____ your house.

  2. She went _____ me.

  3. He whistled as he _____ by.

  4. He is a man with a _____ .

  5. He is a _____ master at the art of lying.

  6. He is _____ his prime.

  7. Many years _____ before he returned.

  8. It is long _____ bedtime.

19. Fill the blanks with:

a) **Its** (pronoun in the possessive case) or **it's** (contraction of **it is**).

  1. _____ raining.

  2. The cat has had _____ supper.

  3. The clock is in _____ old place again.

  4. _____ now six years since the accident.

  5. I think that _____ too late to go.

b) **Your** (pronoun in the possessive case) or **you're** (contraction of **you are**).

  1. _____ mistaken; it is _____ fault.

  2. _____ position is assured.

  3. _____ to go tomorrow.

  4. I hope that _____ taking _____ vacation in July.

35

c) *There* (adverb or interjection), or *their* (pronoun in the possessive case), or *they're* (contraction of *they are*).

1. It is _____ turn.
2. _____ ready to go.
3. _____ , that is over with.
4. _____ car was stolen.
5. _____ back from _____ trip.

d) *Whose* (pronoun in the possessive case) or *who's* (contraction of *who is*).

1. _____ turn is it?
2. There is the man _____ running for mayor.
3. _____ responsible for this?
4. _____ book is this?
5. He is one _____ word can be trusted.
6. Bring me a copy of _____ Who.
7. _____ ready to go?

20. Circle the italicized word which is spelled correctly in each of the following sentences. Consult Section 35b if necessary.

1. Everyone is going **accept, except** me.
2. People came to him every day for **advice, advise,** and he was always ready to **advice, advise** them.
3. At so high an altitude it was hard to **breath, breathe.**
4. His **breath, breathe** came in short gasps.
5. One of the sights of Washington, D. C. is the **Capital, Capitol.**
6. Albany is the **capital, capitol** of New York.
7. Before dinner I had time to change my **clothes, cloths.**
8. The tickets were sent with the **complements, compliments** of the manager.
9. The country was as dry and dreary as a **desert, dessert.**
10. The shack in which we **formally, formerly** lived is still standing.
11. It's **later, latter** than you think.
12. The winners were **lead, led** up onto the stage.
13. Button the money in your pocket so you won't **lose, loose** it.

35

MECHANICS

36 *manuscript*

a   paper and legibility
b   arrangement on page
c   arrangement of quotations
d   correcting the manuscript

37 *capital letters*

a   proper nouns
b   titles of persons
c   other titles
d   to open sentences and quotations
e   lines of poetry
f   letters

38 *writing numbers*

39 *abbreviations*

40 *use of italics*

a   in titles
b   proper names
c   foreign words and phrases
d   words and letters as such
e   for emphasis

41 *syllabication*

36
manuscript

Before a paper is handed in it should be carefully edited and corrected. An instructor has no way of knowing whether an error—in spelling, for example—is a result of ignorance or of hasty typing and careless editing. Do not expect him to give you the benefit of the doubt. The following rules are designed to make your paper easier to read.

36 a
paper and legibility

Use 8½" x 11" paper and write clearly in ink, or type neatly.

Paper should be 8½ x 11 inches in size, unless your instructor specifies some other kind. It should be unruled if you type your themes. If you use ruled paper for handwritten themes, the lines should be widely spaced to prevent crowding. Themes should be either typed or written in ink—black or blue-black; pencil is difficult to read. Write legibly. An instructor or an editor cannot do full justice to a manuscript if he has to puzzle it out, one word at a time. Do not crowd your writing. Leave enough space between consecutive lines to permit editing. Write each word as an entity without gaps between the letters. Do not decorate letters with unnecessary flourishes; use plain forms. Simple, clear handwriting which can be easily read predisposes the reader in your favor. Conversely, handwriting which must be deciphered word by word makes it almost impossible for a reader to appreciate what you have written.

36 b
arrangement on page

Observe the following conventions for arrangement of material.

1. Write on one side of the sheet only.
2. Leave a generous margin—at least an inch and a half—at the left side of each page and at the top. Leave about an inch of margin at the right side and at the bottom.
3. In typewritten manuscript, double-space the lines except in footnotes or in questions set apart on the page. In handwritten manuscript, leave an equivalent space between lines. Use alternate lines on narrow lined paper.
4. Number all pages except the first in the upper right-hand corner. Use Arabic numerals, not Roman.
5. Indent uniformly for paragraphs. The usual indentation for typewritten manuscript is five spaces. Indent about an inch in handwritten manuscript.
6. Center the title at least two inches from the top of the page, or on the first line if you use ruled paper. Leave extra space between the title and the first line of the composition.

36 c
arrangement of quotations

Observe the following conventions in reproducing quotations.

1. A quotation of only a few words may be incorporated into the text.

CORRECT

Irma Rombauer describes the Dobos Torte as a cake

that "looks rich, is rich and enriches all who eat it."

2. An extended quotation of verse or prose is usually set off from the main text by these methods (e.g., pp. 468, 578):
   a. It begins on a new line.
   b. It is usually separated from the text by extra spacing.
   c. In typewritten manuscript it is usually single spaced.
   d. In handwritten manuscript it is usually given a wider margin than the text and is enclosed in quotation marks. In typewritten manuscript where it is clearly differentiated from the text by single spacing, the margin often remains the same, and the quotation marks are usually omitted.

CORRECT

The first hint of Virginia Woolf's inquiry into the possi-

bilities of the English language comes in an essay on

Addison:

. . . compositions of Addison will live forever. Since every moment brings proof that our mother tongue is more lusty and lively than sorts with complete sedateness or chastity, we need only concern ourselves with the vitality of Addison.

Woolf did not reveal precisely what she meant by

"lusty" until 1921. . . .

3. A quotation of poetry should be divided into lines exactly as the original is divided. If an entire line of verse cannot be written on one line of the page, the part left over should be indented.

36 c

CORRECT

Allons! the inducements shall be greater,
We will sail pathless and wild seas,
We will go where winds blow, waves dash, and the
    Yankee clipper speeds by under full sail.
                --Walt Whitman

4. The text following a quotation should begin on a new line, indented if it begins a new paragraph, or flush with the left-hand margin if it continues the paragraph containing the quotation.

CORRECT

Boswell quotes Johnson in 1773 as being against perpetual copyright on the grounds of public welfare:

> For the general good of the world, therefore, whatever valuable work has been created by an author, and issued out by him should be understood as no longer in his power, but as belonging to the public; at the same time the author is entitled to an adequate reward.

This conception of literature being in the public domain, after an author has been properly regarded, was also held by Fielding. . . .

5. When quoting a dialogue of more than one speaker from a story, novel, or play, the quotation should be exactly as it appears (including paragraphing and punctuation) in the original.

CORRECT

'Never mind, Dick; kiss my hand,' she said, flinging it down to him. 'Now, good-bye.'

'Good-bye.'

He walked slowly away, turning and turning again to look at her till he was out of sight. During the retreat

she said to herself, almost involuntarily, and still conscious of that morning's triumph—

'I like Dick, and I love him; but how plain and sorry
a man looks in the rain, with no umbrella, and wet
through!'

--Thomas Hardy

36 d
correcting the manuscript

If a reading of your final draft shows the need of
further alterations or revisions, make them unmistakably clear.

It is not necessary to recopy an entire page for the sake of one
or two insertions or corrections. Copying is necessary only
when there are so many corrections as to make the page difficult to read or messy in appearance.

Words to be inserted should be written above the line, and
their proper position should be indicated by a caret ($_\wedge$) placed
below the line. Words so inserted should not be enclosed in
parentheses or brackets unless these marks would be required
if the words were written on the line. To transfer a group of
words to another place in a sentence, do not encircle them and
try to indicate by lines and arrows the new position. Rather,
cancel the words, and insert them in the proper place. Cancel
words by drawing a line through them. Parentheses or brackets
should never be used for this purpose.

**36
d**

37
capital letters

The general principle is that proper nouns are capitalized; common nouns are not capitalized. A proper noun is the name of a particular person, place, or thing: *Hammarskjold, Alaska, New Orleans, the Capitol, the United States Senate, Colorado River.* A common noun is a more general term which can be used as a name for a number of persons, places, or things: *engineer, doctor, county, town, court house, legislative body, harbor.*

Note that the same word may be used as both a proper and a common noun.

37

CORRECT   Of all the peaks in the Rocky Mountains, Pike's Peak is the one I would like to climb.

CORRECT   Our history class studied legislative work, its part in foreign affairs, and the role our representatives play. Then our American History 27 class visited the Legislative Committee hearing in which the Representative from Ohio expressed his views on the Alliance for Progress.

Abbreviations are capitalized when the words they stand for would be capitalized: USN, ROTC, NBC.

37 a
proper nouns

Capitalize proper nouns and adjectives derived from them.

Proper nouns include the following types:
1. Days of the week, and months
2. Organizations such as political parties, governmental bodies and departments, societies, institutions, clubs, churches, and corporations

CORRECT   the Socialist Party, the Senate, the Department of the Interior, the American Cancer Society, the Boy's Republic, the Optimists' Club, the J. E. Caldwell Company

3. Members of such organizations: Republicans, Lions, Presbyterians, Catholics
4. Historical events and periods: the Battle of Hastings, the Medieval Age, the Baroque Era
5. Geographic areas: the East, the Midwest, the Northwest
6. Race and language names: Japanese, English, Indian, Negro, Caucasian
7. Many words of religious significance: the Lord, the Son of God, the Trinity
8. Names of members of the family when used in place of proper names: a call from Mother telling about my father's new position
9. In biological nomenclature, the names of genera but not of species: *Homo sapiens, Salmo irideus, Equus caballus, Equus,* but not *spaniel*
10. Stars, constellations, and planets, but not the earth, sun, or moon unless used as astronomical names

37 b

37 b
titles of persons

Capitalize titles of persons when they precede proper names.

Cap

When used without proper names, titles of officers of high rank should be capitalized; other titles should not.

CORRECT   Senator Marsh, Professor Bond, Admiral Byrd, Uncle Paul. Both the Governor and the Attorney General endorsed the candidacy of our representative. The postmaster of our town appealed to the Postmaster General.

37 c
other titles

Capitalize the first word and the important words of the titles of books, plays, articles, musical compositions, pictures, and other literary or artistic works.

The unimportant words are the articles *a, an,* and *the;* conjunctions, and prepositions.

CORRECT   *I, Claudius; Summer in Williamsburg; Friar Felix at Large; Childhood and Society; Measure for Measure;* Beethoven's *Third Symphony;* Brancusi's "Bird in Flight."

37 d
to open sentences and
quotations

Capitalize the first word of every sentence and of every direct quotation.

Note that a capital is not used for the part of a quotation that follows an interpolated expression like "he said" unless that part is a new sentence.

CORRECT   "Mow the lawn diagonally," said Mrs. Grant, "and go over it twice."
CORRECT   "Mow the lawn twice diagonally," said Mrs. Grant. "It will be even smoother if the second mowing crosses over the first one."
CORRECT   Mrs. Grant said, "Mow the lawn twice."

A series of short questions or sentences following a colon need not be capitalized, but the first may be.

CORRECT   The first aid questions were dull but important: What are the first signs of shock in an accident victim? should he be kept warm? should he eat? should he drink?

The first word of an unquoted sentence following a colon is capitalized only when the sentence is long or independent in meaning.

CORRECT   Debate on an honor system shrinks each year: Students trust themselves to work or to take exams without supervision, but do not quite trust each other (or themselves) to report dishonorable colleagues.
CORRECT   Students object to his tests: they invite cheating.

37 e
lines of poetry

Capitalize the first word of every line of poetry except when the poem itself does not use a capital.

CORRECT   . . . and vile it were
For some three suns to store and hoard myself.
And this grey spirit yearning in desire
To follow knowledge like a sinking star,
Beyond the utmost bound of human thought.
—Tennyson

37 f
letters

In the salutation, capitalize the first word and any titles or names of the person addressed.

WRONG   Dear sir,   Dear president Johnson,
CORRECT   Dear Sir,   Dear President Johnson,
My dear Sir,   Dear Mr. President,

Cap

In the complimentary close, capitalize the first word only (see section 44a-5).

WRONG Yours Sincerely,   With Best Regards,
CORRECT Very truly yours,   Yours sincerely,

EXERCISES

What words in the following sentences should be capitalized? Why?

1. A canary-colored buick convertible was driving north on fountain avenue.
2. Although the wife of doctor gibbs was a southerner, the doctor himself came from new england.
3. Although many of the natives can speak spanish, they prefer their own indian dialect.
4. A novel experiment in american education was announced on monday by the yale school of law and the harvard school of business administration.
5. "I'm going out to the country club," said marty; "want to come along?"
6. Although technically a veteran, he had served in the coast guard for only two weeks toward the end of the second world war.
7. It was spring; in fact, it was the beginning of may.
8. the douglas fir, often sold under the name oregon pine, is neither a fir nor a pine.
9. He makes these regional divisions: the east, the old south, the middle west, and the far west.
10. When I left high school I intended to major in economics, but in college I became interested in science and graduated as a biology major.
11. Buddhists, christians, jews, and moslems attended the conference, which was held at ankara, the capital of turkey.
12. Both the rotarians and the lions meet in the private dining room of the piedmont inn.

37

38
writing numbers

Numbers appearing in tabular form are always represented by figures, but numbers used as part of an ordinary sentence are sometimes spelled out and sometimes written as figures. There is some variation in usage among publishers, but the following rules are generally accepted. For consistency, all related numbers in one context should be treated similarly. Do not use figures for some and words for others.

38 a
spelling out numbers

Numbers that can be expressed in one or two words should be spelled out. Other numbers are usually expressed in figures.

CORRECT   Like Jack Benny, she is thirty-nine.
CORRECT   The trip north required two station wagons to carry supplies for the twenty-five cyclists.
CORRECT   The prom was planned for 135 couples.

Spell out numbers that begin a sentence, even though they would ordinarily be represented by figures. If such a number is awkwardly long, recast the sentence so that the number does not come first.

CORRECT   Four hundred sixty dollars was the commission.
CORRECT   One hundred Harvard Avenue is the address of the book store.

38
a

Num

AWKWARD Nineteen hundred sixty may mark a new era in social history.

IMPROVED The year 1960 may mark a new era in social history.

38 b
figures for dates and addresses

The day of the month and the year should be expressed in figures, except at the beginning of a sentence and in very formal social notes.

If the year is omitted, the day of the month may be spelled out or written in figures. House numbers are normally written in figures. Street numbers may be written as figures or spelled out.

CORRECT On November 4, 1965, I lived at 117 East 7th Street (or East Seventh Street).

CORRECT Our vacation begins on the 1st of September (or the first of September).

Note that the letters *st, nd, rd* and *th* are regularly used with figures representing street numbers, but need not be added to figures following the name of the month.

CORRECT He works on 84th Street.

CORRECT The 12th of April was stormy.

CORRECT Easter fell on April 12 that year.

38 c
conventional uses

Use figures for long numbers, page and chapter numbers, time expressed by *A.M.* and *P.M.*, percentages, decimals, and technical numbers.

CORRECT The tank truck capacity was 1,275 gallons.

CORRECT Outline Chapter 14, which begins on page 372.

CORRECT My library hours are from 11 A.M. to 2 P.M.

CORRECT My library hours are from eleven in the morning until two in the afternoon.

CORRECT Total rainfall for the year was 7.31 inches.

CORRECT His father loaned him money for 3 per cent interest.

CORRECT The 38th parallel. Longitude 62° 12′ W. A 40-watt bulb.

38 d
sums of money

After a dollar sign ($), always use figures.

If a number is short it may be spelled out and followed by *dollars* or *cents*. When a series of sums is listed, use figures and abbreviations.

CORRECT My share of the job paid $132.75.

CORRECT I paid five dollars for a dinner reservation.

CORRECT These were my expenses: motel, $12.50; meals, $8.00; fare, $5.20; and tips, $2.00.

Be consistent. Write *$6.15*, not *$6 and fifteen cents*.

In sums of money from one to ten dollars, ciphers are used when there are no fractional amounts. For sums above ten dollars, the ciphers should be omitted.

CORRECT These were the prices: $7.00, $8.00, and $10.00.

CORRECT We bought the desk for $95 and sold it a week later for $125.

EXERCISES

In the following sentences, the numbers are all represented by figures. Which of them should be spelled out? Give reasons.

1. 30 years ago the population was approximately 3,000.
2. The frame was supported on 3 posts, each of 7½ inches in diameter.
3. If our expenses can be reduced 10 per cent, we should save about 2,500 dollars.
4. At 10 o'clock we were still waiting at 8th Avenue.

38 d

39
abbreviations

In ordinary, nontechnical writing, abbreviations should be avoided. Spell out Christian names, the words in addresses (*Street, Avenue, New York,* etc.), the months and days of the week, units of measurement (*ounces, pounds, feet, hour, gallon,* etc.). References to volumes, chapters, and pages should be spelled out in the text, but abbreviated in footnotes, parenthetical citations, and bibliographies.

CORRECT Eliott Brodie of 372 West 27th Avenue, Kenosha, moved on December 16, 1966.
CORRECT The quotation is on page 267 of the third edition.
CORRECT For further information on proper terms for addressing dignitaries, consult the appropriate section in the latest Webster unabridged dictionary (**e.g.,** "Forms of Address," **pp.** 51a -54a).

39

39 a
standard abbreviations

Know the standard abbreviations.

A few standard abbreviations are in general use in all kinds of writing: *i.e.* (that is), *e.g.* (for example), *etc.* (and so forth), *vs.* (versus), *A.D., B.C., A.M., P.M.,* (or *a.m., p.m.*), Washington,

D.C.. Names of some organizations and of many government agencies are commonly represented by their initials: DAR, GOP, NATO, CAA, TVA, etc. Dictionaries vary in their preferences for using periods with these abbreviations.

Some abbreviations require periods (*Ph.D., N.Y., Col., oz.*), but others are regularly written without periods (*FBI, Na, ROTC*). The correct form of standard abbreviations can be found in your dictionary, usually in regular alphabetical order, sometimes in a separate appendix.

39 b
titles

Spell out all civil, religious, and military titles except the following ones.

1. Preceding names: *Mr., Messrs., Mrs., Dr., St.* (for *Saint*). (*The*) *Rev.* and (*The*) *Hon.* are used only when the surname is preceded by a Christian name: *Rev. Henry Mitchell,* (or *Mr. Mitchell* or *Father Mitchell*), not *Rev. Mitchell.*
2. Following names: *Esq., M.D., Sr., Jr., Ph.D., M.A., LL.D.,* etc. Do not duplicate a title before and after a name.

WRONG Dr. Rinard Z. Hart, M.D.; Mr. Henry Smith, Esq.
CORRECT Dr. Rinard Z. Hart, or Rinard Z. Hart, M.D.

For the correct forms of titles used in addressing officials of church and state, consult a current almanac.

39 c
technical terms

In technical writing, directions, recipes, and the like, terms of measurement are often abbreviated when used with figures.

CORRECT 32°F.; 1,500 rpm; 25 mph; ½ tsp. salt and 2 tbs. sugar; 12 ft. 9 in.; 5 cc.; 2 lb. 4 oz.

39 c

Ab

Abbreviations like *Co., Inc., Bros.,* should be used only when business organizations use them in their official titles. The ampersand (&) is used only when the company uses the symbol in its letterhead and signature.

> **WRONG**   D. C. Heath & Co., D. C. Heath and Co., Harper and Bros.
>
> **CORRECT**   D. C. Heath and Company, Harper & Brothers, McGraw-Hill Book Company, Inc., Brock & Co.

EXERCISES

Correct any errors in abbreviations in the following sentences.

1. Dr. Geo. C. Fryer lives on Sandy Blvd. near Walnut St.
2. I have worked for the Shell Oil Co. since Oct., '57.
3. Col. House was a personal friend of Pres. Wilson.
4. We expected to go to N.Y. for Xmas.
5. The date is b.c., not a.d.
6. The Acme Corp. ships mail-order goods C.O.D.
7. I was in Wash., D.C., on Aug. 10, 1950.
8. Mt. Whitney, which is 14,495 ft. high, is located in SE California.
9. Rev. Davis will read the psalm on p. 187.
10. The drive to Lexington, Ky., took us 3 hrs., 17 min.
11. I invested $200 dollars in American Tel. and Tel. stock.
12. A temperature of 32°F. is equivalent to zero on the cent. scale.
13. He bought three fl. oz. of aromatic spirits of amm.
14. Turn back to the 1st page of Ch. 3 and read pp. 18 -22.
15. The standard of living in the UAR is different from that in the U.S.

39
c

40
use of italics

Italics are used for titles, unnaturalized foreign words, and words used as such. To italicize a word in a manuscript, draw one straight line below it, or use the special underlining key on the typewriter, thus: King Lear.

40 a
in titles

Italicize all words, including an initial *the, a* or *an*, in the titles of separate publications, such as books, monographs, and pamphlets, but do not italicize the author's name.

Titles of musical works are italicized, but titles of paintings and works of art are enclosed in quotation marks.

In the titles of newspapers, magazines, and periodicals only the distinctive words are italicized. Preceding articles and the name of the city in which a newspaper is published are usually printed in regular type.

**40
a**

CORRECT   *The Blithedale Romance.* Edmund Wilson's *The Shock of Recognition. Of Stars and Men. Dictionary of Foreign Terms.* The *Atlantic Monthly.* The *Christian Science Monitor.* The *Southern Review.* The New York *Times.*

Ital

Titles of parts of published works and articles in magazines are enclosed in quotation marks.

CORRECT The assignment is "Despondency" from William Wordsworth's long narrative poem, *The Excursion.*

CORRECT I always read filler material in The *New Yorker* entitled "Letters We Never Finished Reading."

CORRECT He hoped to publish his story entitled "Nobody Lives Here" in a magazine like *Harper's.*

40 b
proper names

Italicize the names of ships, trains, and aircraft, but not the names of the companies that own them.

CORRECT The cruiser *S. S. Constitution* goes to the Mediterranean Sea.

CORRECT He went east on the Santa Fe *Golden State* and returned on one of United Air Lines' *Mainliner* flights.

40 c
foreign words and phrases

Italicize foreign words which have not yet become accepted in the English language.

If you are not certain whether a foreign word has become naturalized, consult a dictionary. Be sure to check the Explanatory Notes to see how foreign words are indicated. Latin abbreviations used in footnotes and scientific names for plants and animals are italicized.

40
a

CORRECT The dancer unties a knot with her feet in the Mexican *reboza.*

CORRECT *Ibid., circa., op. cit., passim, sic.*

CORRECT The technical name of the Steller's jay is *Cyanocitta stelleri.*

40 d
words and letters as such

When words, letters, or figures are spoken of as such, they are usually italicized.

When a word is quoted, it is usually enclosed in quotation marks.

CORRECT   The misuse of *cool* and *real* is a common fault.
CORRECT   "Fascinating" is now her favorite word.
CORRECT   The letter e and the figure *2* on my typewriter are worn.

40 e
for emphasis

Words which require special stress in a sentence may be italicized.

Overuse of italics should be avoided. Do not italicize for the purpose of calling attention to humor or irony.

CORRECT   I perceive that we inhabitants of New England live this mean life that we do because our vision does not penetrate the surface of things. We think that that *is* which *appears* to be. If a man should walk through this town and see only the reality, where, think you, would the 'Mill-dam' go to?   —Thoreau

EXERCISES

Underline words that should be italicized in the following sentences. If quotation marks are necessary, supply them.

1. Julia played the part of Portia in The Merchant of Venice.
2. He quoted an editorial from the New York Times.
3. The Isle de France was a beautiful ship.
4. Have you read Anthony Powell's Agents and Patients?
5. Our word liberty comes from the Latin libertas.
6. This little projection is called a lug.

40 e

41
syllabication

Dividing a word at the end of a line is mainly a printer's problem. In manuscripts it is not necessary to keep the right-hand margin absolutely even, and so it is seldom necessary to divide a word at the end of a line. If such a division is essential, observe the following principles, and mark the division with a hyphen (-) at the end of the line.

41 a
division between syllables

Divide words only between syllables—that is, between the normal sound-divisions of a word.

When in doubt as to where the division between syllables comes, consult a dictionary. One-syllable words, like *through* or *strength,* cannot be divided. Syllables of one letter should not be divided from the rest of the word. A division should never be made between two letters that indicate a single sound. For example, never divide *th* as in *brother, sh* as in *fashion, ck* as in *Kentucky, oa* as in *reproaching, ai* as in *maintain.* Such combinations of letters may be divided if they indicate two distinct sounds: *post-haste, dis-hon-or, co-auth-or,* etc.

41

WRONG li-mit, sinec-ure, burg-lar-ize, ver-y, a-dult
CORRECT lim-it, sine-cure, bur-glar-ize, very, adult, co-or-din-a-tion

41 b
other rules for division of words

The following rules should be followed when they do not distort the normal pronunciation of a word.

1. The division comes at the point where a prefix or suffix joins the root word, if pronunciation permits.

CORRECT   be-half, sub-way, anti-dote, con-vene, de-tract
CORRECT   lik-able (or like-able), like-ly, place-ment, prepar-ed, Flem-ish, enforce-ment, tall-er, tall-est

EXCEPTIONS BECAUSE OF PRONUNCIATION   prel-ate, pred-e-cessor, extraor-dinary, res-ti-tu-tion, bus-tling, prej-u-dice, twink-ling, jog-gled

2. When two consonants come between vowels (me*mb*er), the division is between the consonants if pronunciation permits (*mem-ber*). If the consonant is doubled before a suffix, the second consonant goes with the suffix.

CORRECT   remem-ber, pas-sage, fas-ten, disman-tle, symmet-rical (*but* symme-try), prompt-er (*but* promp-ti-tude), impor-tant, clas-sic, rum-mage, as-surance, oc-cident, at-tend, nar-ration, of-fi-cial-ly, com-pen-di-um, fit-ting, tel-ling.
BUT NOTE   knowl-edge

3. The division comes after a vowel if pronunciation permits.

CORRECT   modi-fier, oscilla-tor, ora-torical, devi-ate.

**41
b**

REVIEW EXERCISES

Correct in the following sentences any errors in abbreviations, numbers, capitals, and italics.

    1. He made a survey of Athletics in the Universities and Colleges in the U.S.

2. When grandmother was a girl, she lived in Lincoln, Nebr.
3. She always adds a P.S. to her letters.
4. He was traveling in the East last Winter.
5. I spent fifty cents for a pattern, $6.80 for my material, and a dollar and ten cents for trimming; so you see that my dress will cost only $8.40.
6. A 10-ton truck was loaded with #1 *common pine* 2 x 4's, 20 ft. long.
7. 1959 brought us good fortune.
8. "You will surely decide to go," he said, "For you will never have such a chance as this again."
9. After each war we resolve "That these dead shall not have died in vain."
10. Our country entered the second world war in nineteen hundred and forty-one.
11. You have a hard road ahead: There will be tedious hours of work with no one to guide you, perhaps in unpleasant surroundings, and there will be little pay and less honor.
12. The use of the word like as a conjunction is a very common error.
13. My Chemistry and Math. grades were high, and my grade point average was 3.2.
14. Roosevelt was elected president for a 2nd term by an Overwhelming Majority.
15. They discussed the eighteenth amendment and the methods of repealing an amendment to the constitution.
16. The president of the United States rose to greet the president of our university.
17. Queen Elizabeth I tried to preserve the status quo.
18. Ask if either Santa Fe Railroad's city of Los Angeles or Pennsylvania railroad's jeffersonian is still running.

41

42
the library

The library is the heart of a college or university, and all students should learn to use it effectively. Since the amount of knowledge one can carry in his head is small compared with the vast amount stored in books, a vital part of one's college education is learning to find, quickly and efficiently, needed information on any subject. The process of digging out information is called research, and research of an elementary sort is required every time a student works on a term paper. To do this research efficiently, one must be able to use the card catalogue, be familiar with important reference books, and know how to find and use bibliographies and periodical indexes.

42 a
the card catalogue

The card catalogue is the index of the library. Every book and bound periodical in the library is listed on 3 x 5 cards, which are filed alphabetically in drawers accessible to users of the library. A book is usually listed three times: by author's name, by its title, and by its general subject. In some large libraries there are separate catalogues for the author cards, for the title cards, and for the subject cards, but often they are combined in a single alphabetical listing.

Catalogue cards for most books copyrighted in the United States are printed by the Library of Congress, so that they will be the same throughout the country, and the heading of each is the author's surname. Libraries add their own call numbers

Lib

to these cards, and they further convert the basic card for use either in a subject or title card catalogue, as explained later. With the exception of these added changes, the cards for a given work in a particular library are usually identical in every respect.

Author cards, with the addition of the library's call number, are ready for use just as printed by the Library of Congress.

SAMPLE AUTHOR CARD

call number   *book title*   *place of publication & publisher*

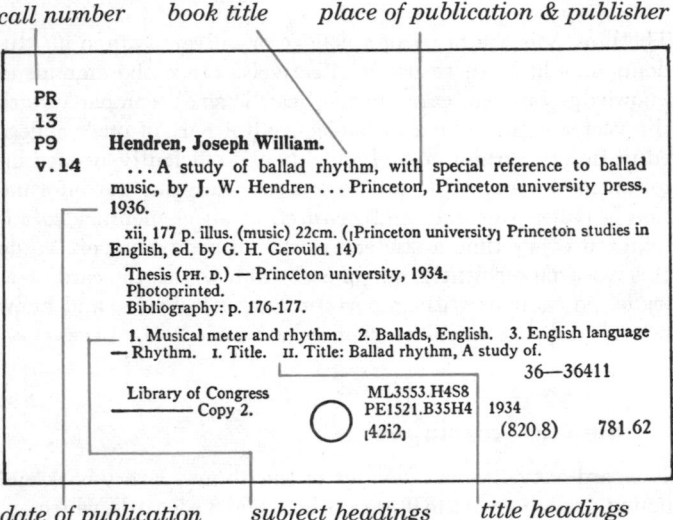

PR
13
P9   **Hendren, Joseph William.**
v.14   ... A study of ballad rhythm, with special reference to ballad music, by J. W. Hendren ... Princeton, Princeton university press, 1936.

xii, 177 p. illus. (music) 22cm. (₍Princeton university₎ Princeton studies in English, ed. by G. H. Gerould. 14)

Thesis (PH. D.) — Princeton university, 1934.
Photoprinted.
Bibliography: p. 176-177.

1. Musical meter and rhythm.   2. Ballads, English.   3. English language — Rhythm.   I. Title.   II. Title: Ballad rhythm, A study of.

36—36411

Library of Congress   ML3553.H4S8   1934
—————— Copy 2.   PE1521.B35H4
                               ₍42i2₎   (820.8)   781.62

date of publication   *subject headings*   *title headings*

In the upper left-hand corner is typed or printed the *call number,* which indicates where the book can be found on the library shelves. Next comes the *author's name,* last name first. On the lines below appear the *title of the book,* the *author's name* as he signs it, the *place of publication,* the *publisher,* and the *date of publication.* The lines that follow explain that the book contains 12 introductory pages (indicated by the small Roman numerals) plus 177 pages of text and illustrations, and that the bound book is 22 centimeters high. Although an independent

**42
a**

book, it is also listed as volume 14 in the *Princeton Studies in English* edited by G. H. Gerould. In 1934 it was accepted as a Ph.D. thesis at Princeton. This edition is photoprinted from typed manuscript. It contains a bibliography on pages 176-177.

This book may be catalogued under three *subject headings:* "Musical Meter and Rhythm"; "Ballads, English"; or "English Language—Rhythm." In a title catalogue it should appear as *A Study of Ballad Rhythm,* and perhaps also as *Ballad Rhythm, a Study of.* The library is not restricted to the title variations or the subjects printed on the card, but may add further entries in either category as it sees fit. The rest of the information on the card is of special interest to librarians.

A *title card* for a book is the same as its author card, except that in addition to the call number, the library adds a form of the title (e.g., *A Study of Ballad Rhythm*) as a heading. Title cards are filed alphabetically according to the first im-

SAMPLE TITLE CARD

chosen title heading

PR	A study of ballad rhythm.
13	
P9	**Hendren, Joseph William.**
v.14	...A study of ballad rhythm, with special reference to ballad music, by J. W. Hendren ... Princeton, Princeton university press, 1936.

xii, 177 p. illus. (music) 22cm. ([Princeton university] Princeton studies in English, ed. by G. H. Gerould. 14)

Thesis (PH. D.) — Princeton university, 1934.
Photoprinted.
Bibliography: p. 176-177.

1. Musical meter and rhythm. 2. Ballads, English. 3. English language — Rhythm. I. Title. II. Title: Ballad rhythm, A study of.

36—36411

Library of Congress
——— Copy 2.

M1.3553.H4S8
PE1521.B35H4   1934
[42i2]   (820.8)   781.62

suggested title heading

42
a

portant word in the title; if the title contains several important words, a card may be made listing another key word first, e.g., "Ballad rhythm, A study of." (The articles *a, an,* and *the* at the beginning of a title are ignored in alphabetizing.) Bound periodicals are listed in the catalogue only by their titles.

Subject cards are intended to help a reader find books on a particular topic *when he does not know the authors or titles.* They are usually the regular Library of Congress cards, with a subject heading typed in red. Note that the same book may be listed under several subject headings.

SAMPLE SUBJECT CARD

chosen subject heading

PR
13
P9
v.14
	Ballads, English.
	
	Hendren, Joseph William.
	...A study of ballad rhythm, with special reference to ballad music, by J. W. Hendren... Princeton, Princeton university press, 1936.
	
	xii, 177 p. illus. (music) 22cm. (₁Princeton university₁ Princeton studies in English, ed. by G. H. Gerould. 14)
	
	Thesis (PH. D.) — Princeton university, 1934.
	Photoprinted.
	Bibliography: p. 176-177.
	
	1. Musical meter and rhythm. 2. Ballads, English. 3. English language — Rhythm. I. Title. II. Title: Ballad rhythm, A study of.
	
	                                 36—36411
	
	Library of Congress ML3553.H4S8
	————— Copy 2. PE1521.B35H4 1934
	               ₁42i2₁ (820.8) 781.62

suggested subject heading

EXERCISES

42
a

a. By consulting the author cards, see if your library has the following books. If so, list the place of publication, the publisher, and the date of publication.

    1. *The Triple Thinkers,* by Edmund Wilson

2. *The Social Insects, Their Origin and Evolution,* by William Morton Wheeler
3. *The Culture of Cities,* by Lewis Mumford
4. *Language,* by Edward Sapir
5. *Henderson the Rain King,* by Saul Bellow
6. *Animals as Social Beings,* by Adolf Portmann

b. Find a title card for each work of nonfiction and note any differences from the author card.

c. Select five of the books which are nonfiction and obtain the following information on each:
    1. What subject headings is each book catalogued under?
    2. What are at least two other books—call number, author, and title—under *one* of the same general subject headings?

d. List all the nonfiction that your library contains by any two of the authors listed above.

42 b
standard reference books
and bibliographies

If a search of the subject headings in the card catalogue fails to produce any books on the subject you are investigating, do not assume that there is no material available. A great deal of information is probably hidden in books and periodicals to which you must be directed by special bibliographies and indexes. Most of these guidebooks will be in the Reference Room of your library, and it pays to get acquainted with the standard reference books early in your college career.

The lists which follow include reference books, bibliographies, and special indexes which should help you find material on almost any subject. (Since these are standard works, full bibliographic entries are not given. For the correct forms in a formal bibliography, see sections 43d and 43j.) Of these works, perhaps the most important are the guides to reference books.

**42
b**

Lib

GUIDES TO REFERENCE BOOKS

GATES, JEAN KEY. *Guide to the Use of Books and Libraries.* 1962.

MURPHEY, ROBERT W. *How and Where to Look It Up: A Guide to Standard Sources of Information.* 1958.

RUSSELL, H. G., R. H. SHOVE, and B. E. MOEN. *The Use of Books and Libraries.* 9th ed., 1958.

WINCHELL, CONSTANCE M. *Guide to Reference Books.* 7th ed. Supplements, 1950–52, 1953–55, 1956–58, 1959–62.

GENERAL ENCYCLOPEDIAS

Collier's Encyclopedia.
Columbia Encyclopedia.
Encyclopedia Americana.
Encyclopaedia Britannica.
New International Encyclopedia.

GAZETTEERS AND ATLASES

Hammond's New Supreme World Atlas. Rev. ed., 1963.
Rand McNally New Cosmopolitan World Atlas. Rev. ed. 1962.
SELTZER, L. E., ed. *Columbia-Lippincott Gazetteer of the World.* 1962.
SHEPHERD, WILLIAM R. *Historical Atlas.* 9th ed. 1964.
Webster's Geographical Dictionary. Rev. ed. 1955.

QUOTATIONS

Bartlett's Familiar Quotations.
STEVENSON, BURTON, ed. *The Home Book of Bible Quotations.* 1949.

STEVENSON, BURTON, ed. *The Home Book of Quotations.* 9th rev. ed. 1959.

REFERENCE BOOKS FOR SPECIAL SUBJECTS
Art and Architecture

BRYAN, MICHAEL. *Bryan's Dictionary of Painters and Engravers.* 5 vols. Rev. ed. by George C. Williamson, 1964.
Encyclopedia of World Art. Vols. 1–9 published 1959–64; vol. 10 in preparation.

**42
b**

GARDNER, HELEN. *Art Through the Ages.*

HAGGAR, REGINALD C. *Dictionary of Art Terms.* 1962.

HAMLIN, T. F. *Architecture through the Ages.* Rev. ed. 1953.

MYERS, BERNARD S., ed. *Encyclopedia of Painting.* 1955.

ROBB, DAVID M., and J. J. GARRISON. *Art in the Western World.* 4th ed. 1963.

ZBOINSKI, A. and L. TYSZYNSKI. *Dictionary of Architecture and Building Trades.* 1963.

Biography

CATTELL, JACQUES, ed. *American Men of Science.* 5 vols. 10th ed. 1961.

Current Biography. Monthly since 1940, with an annual cumulative index.

Dictionary of American Biography. 22 vols. and index. 1928–58.

Dictionary of National Biography. 22 vols. and supplements.

Directory of American Scholars. 4 vols. 4th ed. 1964.

National Cyclopaedia of American Biography. 1898–.

Webster's Biographical Dictionary.

Who's Who, Who's Who in America, International Who's Who, etc. Separate books containing brief accounts of living men and women. Issued more or less regularly.

World Biography. 5th ed. 1954.

Classics

AVERY, C. B., ed. *New Century Classical Handbook.* 1962.

CARY, M., and others. *Oxford Classical Dictionary.*

HARVEY, PAUL, ed. *Oxford Companion to Classical Studies.* 2nd ed. 1937.

SANDYS, JOHN E. *Companion to Latin Studies.* 3rd ed. 1938.

WHIBLEY, LEONARD. *Companion to Greek Studies.* 4th ed. 1931

Current Events

American Annual. 1923–. An annual supplement to the *Encyclopedia Americana.*

Britannica Book of the Year. 1938–. An annual supplement to the *Encyclopaedia Britannica.*

42
b

Lib

Statesman's Year Book. 1864—. A statistical and historical annual giving current information about the countries of the world.

World Almanac. 1868—.

Economics and Commerce

COMAN, E. T. *Sources of Business Information.* Rev. ed. 1964.

Encyclopedia of the Social Sciences. 15 vols. 1930–35.

DEWHURST, J. F., and others. *Europe's Needs and Resources.* 1961.

HAUSER, P. M., and W. R. LEONARD. *Government Statistics for Business Use.* 2nd ed. 1956.

Historical Statistics of the United States: 1789–1945. 1949.

International Bibliography of Economics. 1952—.

Moody's Manual of Investments. 1909–54. This series has been superseded by *Moody's Bank and Finance Manual,* 1955—; *Moody's Industrial Manual,* 1954—; and *Moody's Municipal and Government Manual,* 1955—.

MUNN, G. G. *Encyclopedia of Banking and Finance.* 6th ed. 1962.

Statistical Abstract of the United States. 1879—.

Education

GOOD, CARTER V., ed. *Dictionary of Education.* 2nd ed. 1959.

HARRIS, CHESTER W., ed. *Encyclopedia of Educational Research.* 3rd ed. 1960.

MONROE, PAUL, ed. *Cyclopedia of Education.* 5 vols. 1925.

World Survey of Education. 3 vols. 1951.

History

ADAMS, J. T., ed. *Dictionary of American History.* 7 vols. 1940. Supplement, 1961.

BURY, J. B., and others. *Cambridge Ancient History.* 12 vols. 1923–39.

BURY, J. B., and others. *Cambridge Mediaeval History.* 8 vols. 1911–36.

HANDLIN, OSCAR, and others. *Harvard Guide to American History.* 1954.

**42
b**

LANGER, W. L., ed. *Encyclopedia of World History*. 3rd rev. ed. 1956.

SARTON, GEORGE. *Introduction to the History of Science*. 3 vols. 1948.

WARD, A. W., and others. *Cambridge Modern History*. 13 vols. 1934.

Literature and Drama
A. AMERICAN

CUNLIFFE, MARCUS. *The Literature of the United States*. 1954.

HART, J. D. *Oxford Companion to American Literature*. 3rd ed. 1956.

KAZIN, ALFRED. *On Native Grounds*. 1942.

KUNITZ, S. J., and H. HAYCRAFT. *Twentieth Century Authors*. 1942. First supplement, 1955.

MATTHIESSEN, F. O. *American Renaissance*. 1941.

PARRINGTON, V. L. *Main Currents in American Thought*. 3 vols. 1927–30.

SPILLER, ROBERT E., and others. *Literary History of the United States*. 1948. 3rd edition, 1964. Rev. bibliography supplement, 1964, ed. Richard M. Ludwig. This set includes extensive working bibliographies of major American writers.

B. BRITISH

BATESON, F. W., ed. *Cambridge Bibliography of English Literature*. 4 vols. 1941. Vol. V, Supplement, ed. George Watson, 1957.

BAUGH, A. C., and others. *A Literary History of England*. 1948.

CRAIG, HARDIN, and others. *A History of English Literature*. 1950.

FORD, BORIS, ed. *Pelican Guide to English Literature*. 7 vols. 1954–62.

HARVEY, PAUL, ed. *Oxford Companion to English Literature*. 3rd ed. 1946.

WILSON, F. P., and BONAMY DOBRÉE, eds. *Oxford History of English Literature*. Begun in 1945, this major series of reference works will eventually include fourteen volumes.

42
b

Lib

C. CONTINENTAL AND GENERAL

Granger's Index to Poetry and Recitations.

LEACH, MARIA, and JEROME FRIED, eds. *Funk & Wagnalls Standard Dictionary of Folklore, Mythology, and Legend.* 2 vols. 1949–50.

MAC CULLOCH, JOHN A., and others. *Mythology of All Races.* 13 vols. 1964.

PREMINGER, ALEX, F. J. WARNKE, and O. B. HARDISON, eds. *Encyclopedia of Poetry and Poetics.* 1965.

SHIPLEY, JOSEPH T. *Dictionary of World Literature.* 1959.

SMITH, HORATIO, ed. *Columbia Dictionary of Modern European Literature.* 1947.

STEINBERG, S. H., ed. *Cassell's Encyclopedia of Literature.* 2 vols. 1953.

WELLEK, RENÉ, and AUSTIN WARREN. *Theory of Literature.* 1949.

WIMSATT, W. K., JR., and CLEANTH BROOKS. *Literary Criticism: A Short History.* 1957.

D. DRAMA

GASSNER, JOHN, and R. G. ALLEN. *Drama in the Making.* 1964.

HARTNELL, PHYLLIS, ed. *Oxford Companion to the Theatre.* 2nd ed. 1957.

NICOLL, ALLARDYCE. *The Development of the Theatre.* 4th rev. ed. 1958.

Music and Dance

APEL, W. *Harvard Dictionary of Music.* 1944.

GADAN, FRANCIS, and others. *Dictionary of Modern Ballet.* 1959.

Grove's Dictionary of Music and Musicians. 9 vols. 5th ed. 1954; vol. 10, Supplement, 1961.

MARTIN, JOHN. *Modern Dance.*

SACHS, CURT. *World History of the Dance.* 1937.

SCHOLES, P. A. *Oxford Companion to Music.* 9th ed. 1955.

THOMPSON, O. *International Cyclopedia of Music and Musicians.* 9th ed. 1964.

42 b

Philosophy

BOAS, GEORGE. *Dominant Themes of Modern Philosophy.* 1957.
COPLESTON, FREDERICK. *A History of Philosophy.* 6 vols. 1946.
RUSSELL, BERTRAND, *History of Western Philosophy.* 1945.
URMSON, J. O., ed. *The Concise Encyclopedia of Western Philosophy and Philosophers.* 1960.

Political Science

BEMIS, SAMUEL F. *Diplomatic History of the United States.* 5th ed. 1965.
DE GRAZIA, ALFRED. *Politics and Government: The Elements of Political Science.* Rev. ed., 1962.
Encyclopedia of the Social Sciences. 15 vols. 1930–35.
FRANKEL, JOSEPH. *The Making of Foreign Policy: An Analysis of Decision-Making.* 1963.
Political Handbook of the World. 1927–.
SMITH, EDWARD C., and A. J. ZURCHER, eds. *Dictionary of American Politics.* 1955.
WRIGHT, QUINCY. *The Study of International Relations.* 1955.

Psychology

DREVER, JAMES. *Dictionary of Psychology.* Rev. ed. by H. Wallerstein, 1964.
ENGLISH, HORACE B., and A. C. ENGLISH. *Comprehensive Dictionary of Psychology and Psychoanalytic Terms.* 1958.
GOULD, JULIUS, and WILLIAM L. KOLB, eds. *A Dictionary of the Social Sciences.* 1964.
HARRIMAN, PHILIP L., ed. *Encyclopedia of Psychology.* 1946.
HINSIE, LELAND E. and ROBERT J. CAMPBELL. *Psychiatric Dictionary.* 3rd ed. 1960.

Religion

BUTTRICK, G. A., and others. *Interpreter's Dictionary of the Bible: An Illustrated Encyclopedia.* 4 vols. 1962.
CROSS, F. L., ed. *Oxford Dictionary of the Christian Church.* 1957.
FERM, VERGILIUS. *Encyclopedia of Religion.* 1945.

42 b

HASTING, JAMES. *Dictionary of the Bible*. 5 vols. 1898–1904.
Rev. ed. by Frederick C. Grant and H. H. Rowley, 1963.

HEBERMANN, CHARLES G., and others. *Catholic Encyclopedia*.
17 vols. 1907–22.

JACKSON, S. M., and others. *New Schaff-Herzog Encyclopedia
of Religious Knowledge*. 12 vols. and index. 1908–14. Supplements, 1955.

LATOURETTE, KENNETH S. *History of Christianity*. 1953.

Universal Jewish Encyclopedia. 10 vols. 1939–43.

Science

GRAY, PETER, ed. *Encyclopedia of the Biological Sciences*.
1961.

HAWKINS, R. R., ed. *Scientific, Medical, and Technical Books
Published in the United States*. 2nd ed. 1958.

JAMES, GLENN, and R. C. JAMES, eds. *Mathematics Dictionary*.
2nd ed. 1959.

*Larousse Encyclopedia of the Earth: Geology, Paleontology,
and Prehistory*. 1961.

LE GALLEY, DONALD P., and A. ROSEN, eds. *Space Physics*. 1964.

McGraw-Hill Encyclopedia of Science and Tehnology. 15 vols.
1960. See *McGraw-Hill Yearbook of Science and Technology* supplements to *Encyclopedia,* 1962–.

NEWMAN, JAMES R., and others. *Harper Encyclopedia of
Science*. 4 vols. 1963.

Space Encyclopedia. 1957. Rev. ed. by H. S. Jones and others,
1959.

THEWLIS, J., and others. *Encyclopaedic Dictionary of Physics*.
9 vols. 1961–64.

Van Nostrand's Scientific Encyclopedia. 3rd ed. 1958.

Van Nostrand's International Encyclopedia of Chemical Science. 1964.

Sociology and Anthropology

**42
b**

Encyclopedia of the Social Sciences. 15 vols. 1930–35.

GOULD, JULIUS, and WILLIAM L. KOLB, eds. *A Dictionary of the
Social Sciences*. 1964.

KROEBER, A. L., ed. *Anthropology Today: An Encyclopedic Inventory.* 1953. Extensive bibliographies for work up to 1952.

Social Work Year Book. 1929—.

ZADROZNY, J. T. *Dictionary of Social Science.* 1959.

42 c
finding information in periodicals

For subjects of current interest, magazines are the principal sources of information. For recent theories and discoveries in the social and natural sciences, technical periodicals are the main sources of information.

To find material in magazines and technical periodicals, you must use one or several of the periodic indexes. These list alphabetically every important article in all major periodicals, by author or subject, and generally both, and sometimes also by title. Most of the indexes appear monthly and are cumulated at frequent intervals; that is, all the items listed in the separate numbers are combined into one volume in a single alphabetical order. It may be necessary for you to look through a number of volumes—for those years during which your subject is most likely to have been discussed. The most widely used periodical indexes are:

Readers' Guide to Periodical Literature. 1900—. Alphabetical list under author, title, and subject.

International Index to Periodicals. 1907—. Devoted chiefly to the humanities and the social sciences.

Poole's Index to Periodical Literature. 1802–1881; 1882–1906. Useful for earlier periodicals.

Book Review Digest. 1905—.

Essay and General Literature Index. 1900—. Contains author and subject index to collections of essays and articles.

New York Times Index. 1913—.

Monthly Catalogue (to U.S. Government Publications). 1895—.

Ulrich's Periodical Directory. Classifies periodicals by the subjects they treat, giving a broad view of the magazine in the field.

Lib

Here are two sample entries from the *Readers' Guide,* the first a subject entry, the second an author entry.

FOLK songs, American
Country music; hillbilly music. E. Waldron. Reporter
   12 : 35–7 My 19; 39–42 Je 2 '55

IVES, Burl
American folk songs. por Mus Am 71:20+F '51

Notice that these entries are not in the form you will use in your own bibliography. An explanation is given on the first pages of each volume of the *Guide.* The first reference given above is to an article by E. Waldron entitled "Country Music; Hillbilly Music." It appeared in Volume 12 of the *Reporter* [*Reporter* 12] and extended over two issues: the first part appeared on pages 35–37 of the May 19 issue, and the article was concluded on pages 39–42 of the June 2 issue in 1955 [35–7 My 19; 39–42 Je 2 '55].

The second reference is to an article by Burl Ives entitled "American Folk Songs." It appeared in the February 1951, issue of Musical America, Volume 71 [American folk songs. por Mus Am 71]. The article, which includes a portrait [por], begins on page 20 and is continued elsewhere in the magazine [20+F '51].

42 d
special periodical indexes

General periodical indexes like the *Readers' Guide* index magazines of fairly wide circulation. If you are investigating a technical subject, you may need to get information from the scientific and learned journals. To find relevant articles in these, use the following specialized indexes.

Abstracts of English Studies. 1958–. Devoted primarily
   to research in and criticism of English and American
   literature.
Agricultural Index. 1916–.
Art Index. 1929–.
Bibliographic Index. 1938–.
Biography Index. 1946–.

Biological Abstracts. 1926—.

Business Periodicals Index. 1958—.

Chemical Abstracts. 1907—. See "Annual Subject Index."

Current Anthropology. 1960—.

Economic Abstracts. 1953—.

Education Index. 1929—.

Engineering Index. 1884—.

Historical Abstracts. 1955—.

Index to Book Reviews in the Humanities. 1960—.

Index to Legal Periodicals. 1926—.

Industrial Arts Index. 1913–57. In 1957, this index was divided into two parts: *Applied Science and Technology Index* and *Business Periodicals Index.*

Music Index. 1949—.

PMLA (Publication of the Modern Language Association of America). See "Annual Bibliography," 1921—. Previous to the issue for 1956, the bibliography included books and articles on English, American, French, Spanish, Italian, and German language and literature by American scholars only. Since 1956, the annual bibliography has been far more inclusive.

Psychological Abstracts. 1927—.

Public Affairs Information Service. 1915—. Indexes materials on political affairs, economics, and government.

Quarterly Cumulative Index Medicus. 1927—. Indexes medical literature.

Science Abstracts. 1898—. A. Physics Abstracts B. Electrical Engineering Abstracts.

Sociological Abstracts. 1953—.

United States Government Publications: Monthly Catalog. 1895—. Lists publications by various branches of the government.

Zoological Record. 1864—.

EXERCISES

a. To familiarize yourself with Constance M. Winchell's *Guide to Reference Books,* pick one of the following questions and run down the answer. Consult the *Guide* and its various supplements for likely sources; then check the sources themselves; finally, record on a 3 x 5 card the question, the answer(s), and the sources which were most helpful. Use complete bibliographic form for sources (see sections 43d and 43j).

1. What recent bibliography lists books and articles dealing with the musical works of John Cage, Pierre Boulez, and others?
2. If you were a professional author, what manual might you consult frequently about the legal and business aspects of your work?
3. If you wanted to trace your family tree, what book might give you preliminary assistance?
4. Where would you find a very comprehensive and recent treatment of "Allah"?
5. What is the most recent and comprehensive source of information on Mennonite history?
6. Where would you find a comprehensive list of writings about symbolism in dreams?
7. What is a slightly dated but very complete guide to studies on the Hanseatic League?
8. What literary treatments, in English, might you find of the belief that the murderer's victim—the corpse—bleeds again when the murderer touches it?
9. With what special aid was a recent Biblical concordance compiled?
10. If you saw a Renaissance painting of a young lady wearing a halo and holding a stem on which grew, instead of buds, a pair of eyes, you could be practically certain of identifying her. How?

b. The purpose of the following exercise is to acquaint you with heretofore unfamiliar and specialized reference works, beyond the *Readers' Guide to Periodical Literature* and general encyclopedias. Pick any *three* questions, each one a different topic, and observe the following procedure:

42

(1) Read each question carefully to discover whether it concerns a quotation, title, slang term, place name, person, or idea.
(2) Attack the problem systematically (use a dictionary to clarify any terms you don't understand) by beginning with a refer-

ence guide such as Constance M. Winchell's *Guide to Reference Books* and its supplements or one of the appropriate specialized works listed under 43b of this chapter. The subject cards of the card catalogue may also be helpful.

(3) Once you have found likely sources, consult them, keeping a careful record on a 3 x 5 card of the information gained from each source; the author or editor, title, publisher, edition, and date of each source; and the page reference for the source.

(4) For each question, turn in a 3 x 5 card containing the question, the answer(s), and full bibliographical information on the most helpful sources, including page references and call number.

1. Who ran for governor and in what year on the E.P.I.C. platform, and what was the platform?
2. What did James Starley invent?
3. If, in the eighteenth century, you had been convicted of "pradprigging," what would have been your crime and, in all probability, your punishment?
4. What Mexican hero-god carried a cross and what did it symbolize?
5. How does a Junkers diesel engine differ from a conventional diesel engine?
6. In what decade did the population of the United States shift from a predominantly rural to a predominantly urban one?
7. What device is supposed to have ornamented the tomb of Archimedes and why was it appropriate?
8. What is the title of Hemingway's last book and what is it about?
9. Why might a librarian view with alarm a type of book introduced in 1769 by James Granger?
10. What eight elements are most abundant in the minerals that compose rocks, and of these eight which two occur in the greatest amounts?
11. What famous compatriot of Stalin's died within a few hours of him?
12. By what states and territories was Lithuania bounded, c. 1360?

42

13. Why are brushes made of camel hair and when did the practice begin?

14. What is the "Turner thesis" about the American character and what is at least one major criticism that has been made of it?

15. What biographer of Johann Sebastian Bach has also written books on Jesus and Paul?

16. Who caused Ino's and Athamas' madness and why?

17. When were the first chess-playing machines invented and who are among the well-known writers and scientists to have analyzed the possibilities of machines?

18. "Great Stone Face," "The Great Nullifier," and the "Great Compromiser" formed the "Great Triumvirate": who was each of these nineteenth century U.S. Senators and why was he so nicknamed?

c. Each of the following topics is too broad for a research paper of 1,500 to 2,000 words, but each has several possible, more restricted subjects within it. By using the card catalogue and appropriate reference works, locate at least three books and three articles on a specialized aspect of one general topic. Then compose a thesis, a short outline, and a working bibliography for a research paper of 1,500 to 2,000 words.

1. American cartoon strips
2. African influences on jazz
3. Atomic energy as fuel
4. Ballads of the west
5. Book censorship
6. Chemical basis of heredity
7. Civil rights
8. Conscientious objectors
9. Discotheque
10. Dramatics in psychotherapy
11. Einstein's influence
12. Electronic computers
13. Existentialism in literature
14. France under De Gaulle
15. German foreign policy since 1945

42

43
the research paper

In many college courses you will be required to write long papers, usually of several thousand words, based upon material that you will gather from various sources in the library. Such a paper ought to be an informed analysis on a sharply defined topic. Before you can write at all, you will need to inform yourself adequately, if not fully, on the subject. Then you must do something of your own with the material you have found. A mere collection of quotations and paraphrases will not be satisfactory. You must organize the material into a *pattern* of your own; you must write it up in your own words. In many cases, especially on controversial topics, you will come to some conclusion of your own. If you have informed yourself thoroughly, your opinion is significant and worth setting down. Do not let a false modesty keep you from expressing your own opinion.

The principal steps in the process of writing the paper will be the following:

choosing and limiting the subject
making a working bibliography
tentative plan
taking notes
writing the paper
documenting the research paper
making the final bibliography

43

Lib

43 a
choosing a subject

Choose a subject that interests you.

If you have doubts about a subject's appropriateness, check with your instructor. Most subjects become interesting when you have gotten into them far enough, but for a term paper assignment you will do better to pick a field in which your interest is already aroused. It is probably your best bet because you are willing to learn more about it in detail. You will be spending a good many hours in reading on one subject. What would you like to know more about?

Your choice may be somewhat limited by the resources of your library. A small college library is not likely to have much material on recent developments in medicine, for example. Even a large library may not afford much detailed information on the most recent events or discoveries. There is inevitably a lag between an event and printed accounts of it, and good books and thorough articles take time to write. If the librarian or your instructor tells you that your library is inadequate for a subject you have proposed, choose another subject.

43 b
limiting the topic

Limit the topic so that it can be treated fully in the space assigned.

A term paper should be more than a mere skimming of obvious sources; it should represent a real effort at research, and it should be narrow and deep rather than broad and shallow. See chapter 1 for a discussion of topic limitation. If you start with an interest in a large subject—say, folklore—read a general article in an encyclopedia to acquaint yourself with the ramifications of the field. One encyclopedia lists three main headings under folklore: Beliefs and Customs, Narratives and Sayings, and Art. One subdivision of the last is Folk Music, and this is further divided into Folk Songs and Ballads.

Suppose you decide to write on folk ballads. This narrowing of the topic is a step in the right direction, but as you begin to read you will find it necessary to limit your topic further. One student who wrote an excellent paper finally limited herself to the English ballad "Barbara Allen" as it is found in this country. But she began reading about ballads in general, and she probably made her final limitation only after she had discovered how much material was available on the more general topic.

Here are some other examples of how a subject may be narrowed. One student was interested in President Kennedy's career. After doing some preliminary reading, he narrowed his topic down to two possibilities—the West Virginia presidential primary of 1960, and the confrontation between Russia and the United States over Cuba in 1962. He chose the latter topic because he felt the recent books by Kennedy's advisors gave him more information about the President to work with. Another student, from Oklahoma, was interested in the Indians of the former Indian Territory. It was soon clear that this was too large a subject to be handled, and she decided to limit her investigation to one tribe, the Cherokees. Even this proved too large, and she eventually limited herself to one episode, the forced removal of the Cherokees from Tennessee to Oklahoma. This topic was small enough to permit a good deal of digging into eye-witness accounts and other original documents.

43 c
the working bibliography

The first step in informing yourself on a given subject is to make a working bibliography—a list of books, pamphlets, and articles which you will want to examine or read.

In preparing a long paper, you should not limit yourself to one or two sources for your material. To insure adequate coverage of the topic, you should consult as many sources as your library and your time permit.

43
c

Lib

Here are some suggestions for beginning your working bibliography:

(a) Start with an encyclopedia, reference book, or standard textbook in the general field you are investigating. These will contain selected lists of books and articles.

(b) Consult a specialized bibliography and one or more of the periodical indexes listed under the various headings in sections 42c and 42d.

(c) Use the card catalogue of your library (see section 42a). Listed under subject headings, you will find many books in your field. At the end of the file on your subject you will often find a "see also" card, listing related subject headings that may lead you to additional books. Subject headings listed at the bottom of library cards may guide you to additional material. Sometimes under a subject heading you will find a subdivision devoted to bibliographic cards; that is, cards listing books that are themselves lists of books on the subject.

For some topics, especially those which are recent, you will find relatively few references. Note *all* of these, since your library may not have all the books and periodicals referred to and you will need to use all the sources you can find. Ordinarily, however, you will find more articles than you can look up. In such cases, consult an encyclopedia or selected bibliography to find out the standard authoritative works on the subject, and select any others which seem particularly relevant. Ten or twenty sources should be adequate for a freshman research paper, but be sure that you have covered the several sides of controversial topics.

43 d
bibliography cards

43 c

As soon as you find a reference to a book or article that you think will help you, make a note of it. Write down all the information you will need if you should use the book in your final bibliography.

Each reference should be written down on a separate card or slip of paper (3 x 5 inches), so that you may quickly arrange your bibliography in alphabetical order and discard items that prove useless. This will save time and trouble in the long run. As a rule, the following information should be included:

(a) Name of the author in full, surname first

(b) Title of book or article

(1) For a book: edition, if other than the first; number of volumes, if more than one; place of publication; publisher; date of publication; volume number; page number(s).

(2) For an article: name of periodical; volume number; issue number or name; date of issue (year, preceded by month, if needed); page number(s).

BIBLIOGRAPHY CARD FOR A BOOK

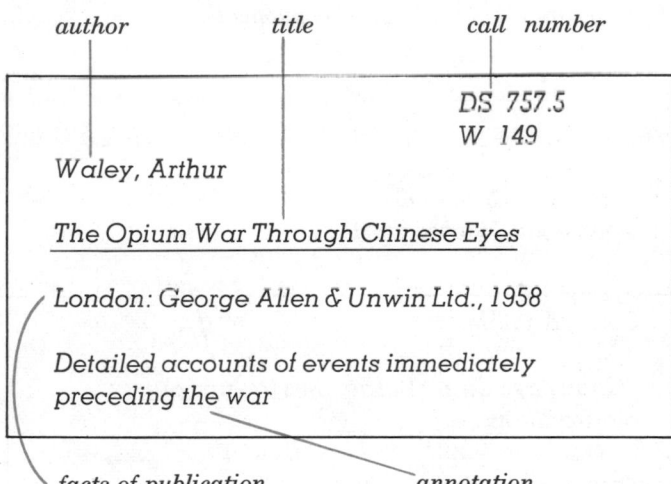

Additional information, not to be included in the final bibliography, may be noted on the card: library call number, scope of the book, bibliography included in the book, source of the reference, etc.

**43
d**

Lib

author   *title*

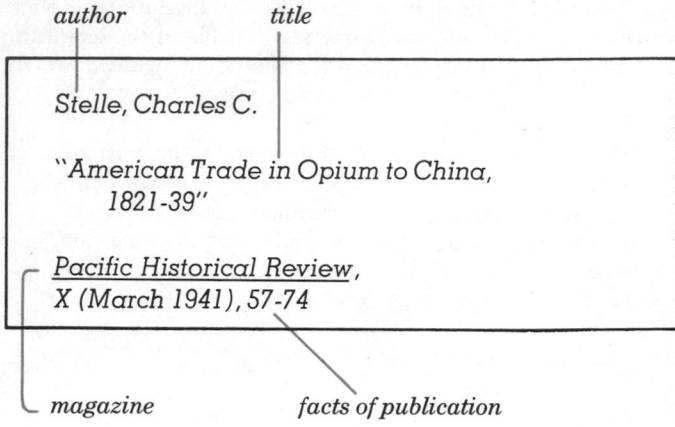

Stelle, Charles C.

"American Trade in Opium to China, 1821-39"

<u>Pacific Historical Review</u>, X (March 1941), 57-74

magazine   *facts of publication*

author (if no byline on story, begin with headline)   *headline*

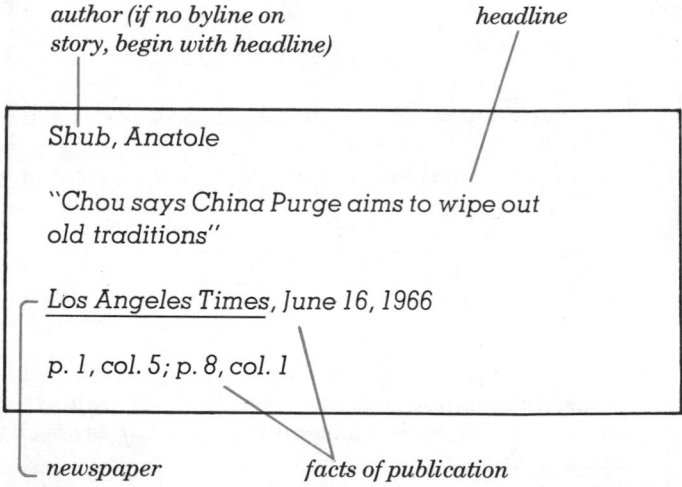

Shub, Anatole

"Chou says China Purge aims to wipe out old traditions"

<u>Los Angeles Times</u>, June 16, 1966

p. 1, col. 5; p. 8, col. 1

newspaper   *facts of publication*

43 d

43 e
choice of source material

After you have made your tentative bibliography, you are ready to examine the books and periodicals themselves. You will probably not have time to read all of them.

Learn, (a) how to find out quickly if a book contains material you want, and (b) how to pick out the best of several books with relevant information.

(a) *To find out the scope and contents of a book,* look first at the Preface, which will usually indicate the author's intention and point of view, and the Table of Contents, which will list the chapter headings and may include a detailed analysis of the chapters. Many works contain introductory chapters which give a general survey of the subject. The Index at the end of a work is an alphabetical list of topics, persons, places, events, etc., appearing in the book. *From the Index you can quickly find out whether a particular subject is treated in the work; from the Table of Contents you will get an outline of the whole book.*

(b) As an aid in choosing between several books as sources consider the following questions:

(1) *Is the book of recent date?* (The date usually appears on the title page; if it is not there, look on the copyright page.) In many subjects, particularly the sciences, the value of the material depends directly upon the date. You should also note, in examining the card catalogue, whether there is a "revised edition" or an "enlarged edition" of the book.

(2) *Can the accuracy of the statements in the book be depended upon?* Is it a popularization or a serious, scholarly work? (A popularization, aimed at entertaining the widest possible audience, seldom indicates the sources on which it is based. A scholarly work is always documented.) Does the writer show signs of bias—political, religious, or na-

43
e

tional? Is the writer an authority on the subject? (If the title page indicates that the author is on the staff of a reputable college, university, or other institution, you can probably trust his work. Similarly, the imprint of a good publisher indicates that the editors and the experts in the field who have read the manuscript have confidence in the book. Additional information about the author may be found in biographical dictionaries, like *Who's Who*.) Chapter 3, "Logic," discusses in more detail the problem of evaluating authorities, as well as other relevant topics such as the difference between fact and judgment.

43 f
the tentative plan

Begin by reading some of the more general accounts of your subject, such as those found in encyclopedias and textbooks. Then go on to more specialized works. When you think you know the general outlines of the subject, make a *tentative plan* or outline of the points you want to cover.

This planning process is somewhat like taking an aerial photograph at 20,000 feet and then dropping down to 2,000 feet for more detailed pictures of limited scope. Remember the word *tentative;* you will probably change the plan several times as you read further in the subject. The advantage of making some kind of plan at an early stage is that you can *read more selectively,* using only those sources that are relevant to your purpose. But *be ready to change* the plan whenever you find abundant material that interests you, or when you find an absence or scarcity of material. It is still not too late to limit your subject further, if that seems desirable. No one can tell in advance what kind of material he will find, or what will interest him most. *The plan of the paper should develop as your reading fills out or modifies your original ideas on the subject.*

**43
e**

43 g
taking notes: quotation,
summary, and précis

As you read, note information that seems relevant or significant. If you are uncertain whether a bit of information is relevant, take it down anyway. It is easier to discard an unnecessary note than to relocate information you remember having read "somewhere."

The notes may in the form of a direct quotation, a paraphrase, a summary or a précis in your own words. Write your notes on cards at least 4 x 6 inches, or on half sheets of theme paper. *Put each point upon a separate card or sheet.* This is very important. You cannot readily organize your material for writing unless it is broken down into small units on separate cards. If more than one card is needed for one point, use the back, or note the subject and name of the book on a new card and continue. Number the cards and clip them together.

The following suggestions on the form of notes may be helpful:

(a) State the topic in the upper left-hand corner, and state on each card the exact source, noting the author, the work, and the page. It is not necessary to write the place of publication and the date on each card since your bibliography cards and the bibliography at the end of the paper will give fuller information regarding the source.

(b) Put quotation marks around material that is exactly quoted. Always quote exactly, even to the punctuation marks and the spelling. Do not use quotation marks for paraphrases or summaries (see also section 30d).

(c) If parts of a quotation are omitted, ellipsis marks (. . .) should be used where the omission occurs, three periods to indicate an ellipsis within a sentence and four periods (or three added to end punctuation) to indicate an ellipsis at the end of a sentence. *Be sure that you do not distort the writer's view by omitting an important qualification or exception that he has made.* Brackets should enclose

**43
g**

words which are not part of the quotation but which you have inserted within the quotation marks for clarity or accuracy. If, for example, there is an obvious error in the text, insert after it the word *sic* in brackets, which indicates that the quotation is exact even though not correct. (See chapters 27, 30, and 34 for discussion of the use of end punctuation, quotation marks, and parentheses and brackets.)

(d) In a summarizing note it may be convenient to omit the articles, copulas, and connectives. Once you are well into your research, you will probably want to rely mainly on summarizing notes, although when you first begin you may wish to take rather full notes and quote occasionally. If you use abbreviations in your notes, be consistent.

Exact quotations, if the passages are not too long, can be very useful in your notes, provided the words of the source are not distorted or "half-quoted" and provided you are prepared to paraphrase, condense, or summarize them later in the process of writing the paper.

Be very careful in your notes to *enclose the exact words of your quoted source in quotation marks.* Otherwise, you may allow borrowed phrases to appear in the paper as your own, or you may carelessly mix your own phrases with those of the source to produce a distorted misquotation.

Remember that whether you are summarizing or quoting someone else's material, you must give credit to the author in footnotes or direct acknowledgment. In the final written paper, quotation should be used sparingly—usually only when the exact words are important, or when the point is very aptly phrased in your source.

The summarizing note, especially the type called a *précis,* is the most useful and versatile way to record your reading. The précis is a brief, accurate condensation which preserves only the main ideas of the material summarized. It omits digressions, rhetorical flourishes, illustrative details or anecdotes, and stylistic niceties in the original and prunes it down by about two-thirds. The précis writer does not, however, string together excerpts from the original or jot down disconnected

43 g

notes. Rather, he tries to record in his own words the ideas which he understands to be the basic ones. He may use a few key phrases from the original, provided he carefully distinguishes them by quotation marks, but his main purpose is to master the original, find its core of meaning, and state this in his own words (see also paragraph outlines, 2b-1).

Often, in taking notes for a term paper, you may wish to make a précis of a long paragraph, or several. To do this, read the paragraph carefully, noting its topic sentence and the sequence in which the basic ideas are taken up. Then read it again, this time making sure you have omitted no major qualifications or connections. Then write a brief, fair summary of these basic ideas and compare your summary with the original, making necessary changes. Précis writing requires practice, but once learned, it is an excellent way of mastering and preserving material—for papers or reviewing. In the following examples, notice that the original of 229 words has been reduced to 68 words, then 59. The one key phrase retained from the original in both summaries is "moral equivalent of war."

ORIGINAL SOURCE MATERIAL   These words are of course literally true. The immediate aim of the soldier's life is, as Moltke said, destruction and nothing but destruction; and whatever constructions wars result in are remote and non-military. Consequently the soldier cannot train himself to be too feelingless to all those usual sympathies and respects, whether for persons or for things, that make for conservation. Yet the fact remains that war is a school of strenuous life and heroism; and, being in the line of aboriginal instinct, is the only school that as yet is universally available. But when we gravely ask ourselves whether this wholesale organization of irrationality and crime be our only bulwark against effeminacy, we stand aghast at the thought, and think more kindly of ascetic religion. One hears of the mechanical equivalent of heat. What we now need to discover in the social realm is the moral equivalent of war: something heroic that will speak to men as universally as war does, and yet will be as compatible with their spiritual selves as war has proved itself to be incompatible. I have often thought that in the old monkish poverty-worship, in spite of the pedantry which infested it, there

43
g

Lib

might be something like the moral equivalent of war which we are seeking. May not voluntarily accepted poverty be "the strenuous life," without the need of crushing weaker people?

—William James

FIRST SUMMARIZING NOTE

A soldier's purpose is destruction and he must therefore harden himself completely. Yet war does train men in heroism and is the only such training now generally available. What is needed to prevent softness is a "moral equivalent of war" whose heroism has war's universal appeal but which lacks war's destructive and brutalizing effects. Perhaps the monk's vow of voluntary poverty is an analogue of this needed equivalent.

FINAL PRÉCIS

Although war demands soldiers who can harden themselves to destroy unfeelingly, it does train men in heroism and is the only such training now generally available. The world needs a "moral equivalent of war" with war's universal appeal but without its destructive and brutalizing effects. Perhaps the monk's voluntary vow of poverty is an analogue of this needed equivalent.

DIRECT QUOTATION

> Chinese trade balance
>
> ". . . prior to the year 1828 large quantities of silver . . . were brought into China, yielding a balance of trade always in favor of China. In 1829 the imports for the first time exceeded the exports. Silver was now required to be exported in payment of the excess of the imports. The reversal of the situation, evidently caused by the rapid expansion of opium trade, lead the Chinese to allege that opium was draining off the wealth of the country."
>
> P. C. Kuo, *A Critical Study of the First Anglo-Chinese War*, p. 50

43 g

PARAPHRASE AND DIRECT QUOTATION

> Chinese trade balance
> According to Kuo, before 1828 China always had a favorable trade balance, thanks to "large quantities of silver" brought into the country. In 1829, though, imports exceeded exports and silver had to be sent abroad for payments. The unfavorable balance, "evidently caused by the rapid expansion of opium trade," led Chinese to blame opium for loss of wealth.
>
> P. C. Kuo, <u>A Critical Study of the First Anglo-Chinese War</u>, p. 50

Note that the usefulness of paraphrase with direct quotation depends on unusual care in separating your interpretive note from the phrases carefully chosen for exact quotation. This method can combine compact efficiency with precision on points of controversy, provided you are careful to avoid mixing your words with those of the source. See also section 30d.

SUMMARY

> Chinese trade balance
> Before 1828, foreign silver brought into China always yielded her a favorable trade balance. In 1829, her imports exceeded exports—silver sent out in payments. Growth of opium trade apparent cause. Chinese blamed opium for loss of wealth.
>
> P. C. Kuo, <u>A Critical Study of the First Anglo-Chinese War</u>, p. 50

**43
g**

Lib

writing the paper

By the time you have completed your reading and note-taking, you should have a pretty clear idea of the plan of your paper.

Make an outline, or revise your tentative plan into final form, and sort and arrange your note cards accordingly. Use the topic headings in the left-hand corner of each card as guides in this organizing process.

Your paper will be written largely from your note cards, but it should be more than a collection of notes glued together with transitional phrases. Your own contribution to the subject you are working on will be the assimilation and synthesizing of many separate sources.

The writing must also be your own. It is permissible to use exact quotations from your sources only if they are enclosed in quotation marks and identified by a footnote reference. But you will seldom need to quote exactly: the bulk of the paper will be your own interpretation of what you have read, and it must be in your own words.

Plagiarism, which may get professional writers into legal difficulties and students into difficulties with the Dean, means trying to pass off someone else's work as your own. There is an important distinction between the use of another investigator's results, properly acknowledged, and the unacknowledged borrowing of his words and phrasing. *To change a word here and there in another writer's sentence or paragraph is to invite trouble. Since it is not an exact quotation, you cannot put such a sentence in quotation marks, but your trivial changes have not made it your own sentence.* Here are two useful suggestions:

(a) Be sure that your notes indicate by exact quotation marks the passages which have been taken verbatim from your sources.

(b) When you have read a note card, turn it over and write up the information in your own words, referring to the card only if you need specific facts (dates, figures, etc.) which you don't remember.

43 i
documenting the paper

Since most of your material will be derived from books and articles, you must indicate the sources of your information in footnotes.

> Footnote references serve four purposes: they give credit to the original authors, they enable the reader to check your use of source material, they indicate the authorities on whom you are relying, and they aid investigators working on related topics.

Whether you quote exactly, or whether you paraphrase or summarize in your own words, you must indicate the source of all direct quotations and of facts for which you personally are not a sufficient authority. It is not necessary to acknowledge the sources of proverbial expressions or familiar quotations, nor of facts and ideas that are common knowledge to those in the field and about which there would be no difference of opinion. (For example, the student who wrote the sample term paper in section 43k did not have to footnote the fact that the Chinese regarded foreigners as "barbarians." No one even casually familiar with Chinese history disputes the fact that over the centuries China had come to regard herself as culturally superior to those not choosing the Chinese way of life.) But any important fact which might be questioned or argued about should be documented. If all the information contained in one of your paragraphs is taken from one book, you can indicate the source by a footnote at the end of the paragraph.

Footnotes may be inserted in the manuscript in one of three ways:

1. At the bottom of each page, as they would appear if the paper were printed. The advantage of this method is that

the reader can see the reference at a glance, without having to turn pages. It takes a little practice, however, to estimate the space the footnotes will require at the bottom of the page.
2. On a separate sheet at the end of the paper, double-spaced.
3. Between ruled lines as the footnote occurs in the text.

FOOTNOTE AT POINT OF OCCURRENCE

had gained a legal monopoly over the opium trade.[1] By

[1]Harley Farnsworth MacNair, Modern Chinese History: Selected Readings (Shanghai, 1923), p. 66

1834, however, the British East India Company's charter

Although this form has the advantage of keeping the footnote close to the index number, some students and instructors dislike the way it interrupts the text.

To indicate the reference of the footnote, use numbers. The index number should be placed at the end of the quotation, sentence, or paragraph to which the footnote refers and then repeated at the beginning of the footnote. Number the footnotes consecutively throughout the manuscript.

content and form of footnotes

Despite minor variations in punctuation and style, most handbooks and journals agree on the following sequence and content for footnotes:

1. *The author's name, in normal order*
2. *The title of the book underlined to indicate italic type*   But if the reference is to an article in a periodical (or in a book), the author's name is followed by the title of the article, in quotation marks, and this is followed by the name of the periodical (or book) underlined.
3. *Information regarding the place and date of publication*   For books, this consists of the city in which the volume was published and the date in parentheses; for articles in periodicals, volume number and (in parentheses) the date.

43
i

4. *The page number*

The form used in the following examples of footnotes is that recommended by *The MLA Style Sheet,* revised edition. It is assumed that a research paper will include a bibliography of works consulted, that the first reference to a book or article will be a full footnote, and that subsequent references to the same book or article will be abbreviated. Normally, an abbreviated footnote reference consists of the author's surname and a page number, but if several books by the same author are referred to, it will be necessary to use a short title in addition to the author's name. The abbreviation *ibid.* (short for Latin *ibidem,* "in the same place") is used to refer to the work cited in the immediately preceding footnote. It is usually followed by a new page number. Note that *ibid.* is italicized since it comes from a Latin word; that it is followed by a period since it is an abbreviation; and that it is capitalized when it is the first word in the footnote.

FOOTNOTE REFERENCE TO A BOOK

¹J. K. Fairbank, The United States and China, rev. ed. (Cambridge, Mass., 1958), p. 27.

FOOTNOTE REFERENCE TO A PERIODICAL

²Charles C. Stelle, "American Trade in Opium to China, 1821-39," Pacific Historical Review, X (March 1941), p. 59.

FOOTNOTE REFERENCE TO ANOTHER BOOK

³J. K. Fairbank, Trade and Diplomacy on the China Coast (Cambridge, Mass., 1953), II, p. 37-41.

⁴Stelle, p. 62.

⁵Fairbank, United States and China, p. 34.

⁶Ibid., p. 36.

Notice that the author's first name or initial is given first. (Bibliographies, which are arranged in alphabetical order, put the author's last name first.) If the author is unknown, the first item in a footnote is the title of the book or article. Commas are used between items, instead of the periods used in a bibliography. If you wish to include the name of the publisher, it is separated from the place of publication by a colon—"Boston: D. C. Heath and Company, 1966."

Volume numbers, for books of more than one volume and for periodicals, are in Roman numerals; page numbers are in Arabic numerals. When the page number stands alone, use *p.* for "page" and *pp.* for "pages." The abbreviations for page numbers may be omitted if the page reference is indicated by a volume number given as a Roman numeral: XIV (July 1965), 119.

As a general rule, reference information given in the *text of the paper* need not be repeated in the footnote. For example, if you say "T. S. Eliot maintains that . . .," the footnote would begin with the title of the book, instead of the author's name. If you write "In his *Notes towards the Definition of Culture,* T. S. Eliot maintains that . . .," the footnote would begin "(New York, 1949). . . ." By occasionally inserting the author's name, or the author's name and his work, into the text and placing the footnote number at the end of the appropriate sentence, you can shorten the length of some of your footnotes.

The following list illustrates the major footnote forms used in the first reference:

BOOK BY ONE AUTHOR

[1]Ralph Ellison, Shadow and Act (New York, 1964), p. 141.

BOOK BY ONE AUTHOR, REVISED OR LATER EDITION

[2]S. I. Hayakawa, Language in Thought and Action, 2nd ed. (New York, 1964), pp. 19-21.

43
i

BOOK BY ONE AUTHOR, TRANSLATED

[3]Curt Sachs, World History of the Dance, trans. Bessie Schonberg (New York, 1937), p. 91.

BOOK BY TWO AUTHORS

[4]John Butt and H. V. D. Dyson, Augustans and Romantics (London, 1940), p. 109.

AN EDITED TEXT

[5]William Wordsworth, The Prelude, ed. Ernest de Sélincourt (Oxford, 1926), pp. 89-90.

[6]Louise Pound, ed. American Ballads and Songs (New York, 1922), p. 5.

SIGNED ESSAY IN A BOOK BY SEVERAL CONTRIBUTORS

[7]John Holloway, "Hardy's Major Fiction," in From Jane Austen to Joseph Conrad, eds. Robert C. Rathburn and Martin Steinmann, Jr. (Minneapolis, 1958), pp. 235-236.

MAGAZINE ARTICLE

[8]Tom Kahn, "The Problem of the New Left," Commentary, XLII (July 1966), 30.

ANONYMOUS MAGAZINE ARTICLE

[9]"Notes and Comment," The New Yorker (July 2, 1966), p. 17.

ENCYCLOPEDIA ARTICLE, SIGNED

[10]G. D. H. Cole, "Socialism," The Encyclopaedia Britannica (Chicago, 1954), XX, 877.

ANONYMOUS NEWSPAPER ARTICLE

[11]"Fantastic Growth Imperils State, Expert Declares," Los Angeles Times, LXXXV (June 19, 1966), 1.

ANONYMOUS ENCYCLOPEDIA ARTICLE

[12]"Sovereignty," The Encyclopedia Americana (New York, 1963), XXV, 317.

43
i

Lib

The following additional words and abbreviations are sometimes used in footnotes, bibliographies, and references:

c. or ca. (circa)	at or near a given date
cf. (confer)	compare or consult
ed.	edition, editor, or edited by
f., plural ff.	page(s) following
id. or idem	the same; usually the same author
l., plural ll.	line(s)
loc. cit. (loco citato)	in the place already cited
ms., plural mss.	manuscript(s)
n., plural nn.	note(s)
op. cit. (opere citato)	in the work cited

This abbreviation must be used with the author's name, to identify which work is being cited. If two works by the same author have been referred to, this abbreviation cannot be used. The general tendency today is to avoid such abbreviations altogether, and to use the author's name, plus a short title if one is needed. See footnote 5 under sample footnotes on page 567.

passim	here and there, throughout
sic	so, thus
v., plural vv.	verse(s)

43 j
the final bibliography

At the end of the research paper, add an alphabetized list of all the works you have consulted. Include in it all the books and articles you have referred to in your footnotes, plus any other books and articles which have furnished background material.

Do not include books which you have glanced at and discarded. If the author's name is not known, the article or book is placed alphabetically.

The form of a bibliographic entry differs slightly from that of a footnote reference. Authors are listed with surname first, to make alphabetizing easy. The items of an entry (see section 43d) are separated by periods instead of commas. *The MLA Style Sheet,* widely followed in the humanities, does not require the inclusion of the publisher's name in the final bibliography. Some other manuals do, and some instructors may prefer the inclusion. In any case you have the publisher's name on your bibliography card, should you wish to include this information in the final bibliography.

SAMPLE BIBLIOGRAPHY

Baugh, Albert C. A History of the English Language. 2nd ed. New York, 1957.

If it should be desirable to list the publisher, the form would be "A History of the English Language. 2nd ed. New York: Appleton-Century-Crofts, Inc., 1957."

Graves, Robert, and Alan Hodge. The Reader over Your Shoulder: A Handbook for Writers of English Prose. New York, 1943.

Kennedy, John G. "Semantics in Logic," The Encyclopaedia Britannica, 1966, XX, 313C-313G.

Pooley, Robert C. Teaching English Usage. NCTE Monograph No. 16. New York, 1946.

Rubin, Louis D., Jr. "H. L. Mencken and the National Letters," The Sewanee Review, LXXIV (Summer 1966), 723-739.

"Semantics," Encyclopedia Americana, 1963, XXIV, 546.

Warshow, Robert. The Immediate Experience. Anchor Book, New York, 1964.

Whorf, Benjamin Lee. "The Relation of Habitual Thought and Behavior to Language," Language, Maturity, and Meaning, ed. S. I. Hayakawa. New York, 1953.

43
i

Lib

Wood, Paul Spencer, ed. <u>Masters of English Literature</u>.
2 vols. New York, 1946.

Woolf, Virginia. <u>The Captain's Death Bed and Other
Essays</u>. New York, 1950.

——————. <u>The Moment and Other Essays</u>. New York,
1948.

*The long dash followed by a period indicates that Virginia
Woolf is the author of the last entry. If the bibliography includes several books by one author, alphabetize them and use
this form.*

43 k
sample research paper

The following paper written by John Bruns, together with a
brief commentary, will illustrate the methods of documenta-
tion just described. Title page, table of contents, and outline
have been omitted, since individual instructors will want to
specify their own requirements.

Cultural Conflict and the Chinese Opium War

Writing in the early months of the Chinese Opium
War, an anonymous English commentator spoke pro-
phetically of its meaning. He foresaw "the fabric of an
empire" staggering "under the first shock from without" and breaking into pieces to be "parceled out
among the ravenous competitors for the spoil."[1] More

[1]"War with China, and the Opium Question,"
<u>Blackwood's Edinburgh Magazine</u>, XLVII (March 1840),
368.

commentary

Note 1: The quoted phrases woven into the text are taken
from a sentence of 103 words, far too long to cite in its
entirety in the opening paragraphs of such a research

43
i

than a hundred years later, a Chinese historian writing of the same war has concluded, "Whether Chinese or Western, radical or conservative, scholars have invariably taken it as a starting point in the study of modern China."[2] What began with Chinese efforts at greater control of the foreign population ultimately resulted in China's defeat and, through the Treaty of Nanking in 1842, even greater commercial and political freedom for Westerners. For it was this treaty which ceded Hong Kong to England; opened five ports to free British trade and manufacturing; curtailed China's right to set tariffs; and opened China to the unsettling impact of the West.[3]

To the anonymous English commentator, the events leading up to the war composed "the circumstantial narrative of Chinese aggression and British supineness."[4] To Commissioner Lin Tse-hsu, sent by the Emperor to Canton to suppress the opium trade, nearly the opposite was true. From the moment the British had begun to import opium, Lin argued in a long letter to the Emperor, they had had hostile intentions, and, he continued, the opium question should have been settled twenty or thirty years earlier, before it had become the cancer it now was.[5] In fact, though the war was fought over a

[2]Hsin-pao Chang, Commissioner Lin and the Opium War (Cambridge, Mass., 1964), p. ix.

[3]Li Chien-nung, The Political History of China: 1820-1928, trans. S. Y. Teng and Jeremy Ingalls (Princeton, N. J., 1956), p. 9; p. 42.

[4]"War with China," Blackwood's, 384.

[5]A letter summarized by Arthur Waley in The Opium War Through Chinese Eyes (London, 1958), p. 119.

paper. By skillful selection of key phrases, however, a writer can catch the tone and the main idea of the original. Note that the footnote begins with the title of the article, since the author is anonymous.

43 k

very tangible commodity, opium, it had more than just an economic meaning. It is a classic example of the effects that cultural differences can have on the relations between two countries.

In a broad sense, the main issue of the Opium War was the amount of control which China could exercise over foreigners on its soil. The superiority which China had exercised over its neighbors for centuries argued for a high degree of control, while at the same time aggressive Western mercantilism demanded a greater degree of freedom. What is striking about the Opium War—more striking, perhaps, than the events before and during the war—is the lack of understanding each side exhibited toward the other, the blindness with which each pursued its own course of action.

Opium had been used by the Chinese mainly for medicinal purposes years before it was imported. But

Paragraph three, in which Mr. Bruns spells out most fully the two conflicting cultural traditions he believes to be found in the Opium War, requires no notes. The writer is giving a full statement of the viewpoint to be supported by his specific sources and his evidence.

(*The footnotes discussed in commentary below appear on p. 573.*)

Note 2: The conclusion of an historian who has conducted a very recent survey of scholarly opinion about the importance of the Opium War is cited. Citation of a recent authoritative summary of scholarly opinion is often a good point of departure.

Note 3: Note that when two separate pages not in sequence are used as sources, the form requires a semicolon: "p. 9; p. 42." If the form mistakenly had been "pp. 9–42," the reader would have been misled into thinking that pages nine *through* forty-two had been consulted.

Note 4: Note that an abbreviated form is used here, since the first citation has given full information. The title of the article and of the magazine are shortened.

**43
k**

it did not gain the status of a vice until the seventeenth century. By the time the Emperor issued a proclamation against opium smoking in 1729, it was being imported from the West.[6] By 1773 the British East India

[6]Hsin-pao Chang, Commissioner Lin and the Opium War (Cambridge, Mass., 1964), pp. 16-18.

Note 5: As both the text and the footnote make clear, the letter is too long to quote. In general, when several translated eyewitness accounts or journals are available, try to get one done by an experienced and reputable translator, as is Arthur Waley.

Note 6: Here are the three cards which went into the footnote.

Early uses of opium
Introduced into China late 7th, early 8th Cent. by Turks & Arabs. Described in poems as a medicine. Swallowed raw.
Chang, Commissioner Lin & Opium War, p. 16

Early uses of opium
First mixed and smoked with tobacco in 1620's by Formosans. Practice spread to China in 1660's. Chinese burned opium extract and inhaled fumes through pipe.
Chang, Commissioner Lin & Opium War, pp. 16-17

Early uses of opium
First duties collected on imported opium in 1589. First importers Portuguese. First proclamation by Emperor against smoking in 1729.
Chang, Commissioner Lin & Opium War, pp. 17-18

43
k

Lib

Company, which controlled the fertile land where most opium was produced, had gained a legal monopoly over the opium trade to China. By 1796, when the importation of opium was prohibited, close to 4,000 chests were being imported annually.[7]

Despite the fact that it had been outlawed in 1796 and again in 1800, the opium trade prospered. In 1816-17, 3,210 chests of opium were imported into China. In 1825-26, 9,261 chests were imported, and by 1833-34, 19,786 chests were being imported—and these figures exclude unknown quantities smuggled in on the eastern and northern coast.[8] In 1793, the Ch'ien Lung Emperor had written to King George III, "As your Ambassador can see for himself, we possess all things. I set no value on objects strange and ingenious, and have no use for your country's manufacturers."[9] This was true, in part. The English had some difficulty in finding Western products that the Chinese wanted.[10] But opium, while

[7]Mu Fu-sheng, The Wilting of the Hundred Flowers (New York, 1963), p. 6.

[8]Chang, pp. 222-23.

[9]Harley Farnsworth MacNair, Modern Chinese History: Selected Readings (Shanghai, 1923), p. 4.

[10]P. C. Kuo, A Critical Study of the First Anglo-Chinese War (Shanghai, 1935), pp. 2-3.

Note 8: Here, as throughout the paper, the shortened form is used for a book when there is no chance of confusion. Note that this form consists of the author's last name and the page reference.

Note 9: Normally a quotation of several lines is set off by indentations and single-spacing, and without quotation marks unless they are in the original. Here, however, the writer has gracefully made the quotation part of his own text; and because the quoted material is only two short sentences, he may use this form.

not officially tolerated, was nevertheless in great demand in China. The popularity of opium created a peculiar state of affairs in which the Chinese government detested opium, discouraged its use, and yet was disinclined to take any positive action to do away with it.

What the Chinese government did do, however, was to stay as aloof as possible from the foreign "barbarians." As early as 1720 it had licensed a group of merchants, the Cohong, to trade with foreigners, to represent them in the imperial court, and to convey to them any necessary messages.[11] The government-created monopoly was potentially a very profitable business venture for the merchants. Profits were cut, though, by a continuous succession of extortion payments to various officials, which was necessary if the Cohong was to keep its position as the only legitimate outlet for Western imports in China. The Cohong, despite its privileged commercial status, was never officially connected with the government.[19]

In the years immediately prior to the Opium War, it was recognized that something concrete had to be done concerning the importation of opium. There had always been moral condemnation of the opium trade, but this was not enough to bring about definite action. Officials who publicly proclaimed the evils of opium as a matter of state policy privately helped to smuggle it.[13] In the 1830's, though, there arose the question of the economic harm which the opium trade could do to China. The rapid growth of the opium trade had shifted China's balance of trade, so that by 1829 her imports were exceeding her exports, and silver was being shipped out of China in exchange for opium, whereas

[11]MacNair, pp. 25-26.
[12]Kuo, p. 8.
[13]Chang, p. 47.

43
k

in previous years it had been paid for mainly with Chinese products.[14]

In 1836 Heu-Naetse, a court official, sent a memorial to the Emperor in which he advised that the importation of opium be legalized. He argued that the most advantageous course of action open to China was . . .

> to permit the barbarian merchants to import opium paying duty thereon as a medicine, and to require that, after having passed the Custom House, it shall be delivered to the Hong merchants only in exchange for merchandise, and that no money be paid for it. The barbarians finding that the amount of dues to be paid on it is less than what is now spent in bribes will also gladly comply therein.[15]

He opposed curtailing or abolishing foreign trade on the grounds that a large number of Chinese depended on foreign trade for a livelihood.[16]

In October, 1836, shortly after the Heu-Naetse memorial was sent, another memorial was sent to the Emperor, this time by Chu-Tsun, another court official. Chu-Tsun advocated complete prohibition of opium, including both importation and production inside China. "As to the proposition to give tea in exchange, and entirely to prohibit the exportation of even foreign silver," he said, "I apprehend that, if the tea should not be sufficient, money will still be given in exchange for the drug."[17] But, while morally an admirable course of action, it left something to be desired in regard to the practical problem of enforcement. Chu-Tsun had said in the memorial that

**43
k**

[14]Kuo, p. 50; p. 52.
[15]MacNair, p. 97.
[16]Ibid., p. 95.
[17]Ibid., p. 100.

. . . if the great officials in charge of the provinces do in truth show an example to their civil and military subordinates, and if these do in sincerity search for the drug, and faithfully seize it when found, apprehending the most criminal, and inflicting upon them severe punishment, it is, in this case, not impossible to attain the desired end.[18]

[18]*Ibid.*, 99.

Note 12: Here are the cards which went into footnote 12.

> Cohong
> *Monopolies bought at high price, kept by paying bribes and extortion to officials. Profits cut by systematic squeezes.*
> *Kuo, Critical Study of First Anglo-Chinese War,*
> *p. 8*

> Cohong
> *Napier's complaint in 1834 that Cohong "exercise no official powers whatever" a long-standing one. Cohong unconnected with government and law.*
> *Kuo, Critical Study of First Anglo-Chinese War,*
> *p. 8*

Note 15: Here the indented block form of quotation is used for a longer passage (see section 36c). Note that the writer has made a smooth transition from his own sentence to the cited passage and correctly used three dots of ellipsis to indicate omitted material at the beginning.

Note 16: Ibid. is used accurately here to indicate MacNair. Note that it is underlined, followed by a period, and completed with a page reference. If the footnote read only "*Ibid.*", the reader would understand this to mean "Mac-Nair, p. 97." See section 43i.

**43
k**

Lib

This hopeful statement seems rather naive in view of the previous willingness of Chinese officials to overlook opium smuggling. But anti-opium support grew, aided considerably by another memorial, sent to the Emperor in November, 1836, by Yuan Yu-lin, a censor, who was strongly opposed to the legalization of the opium trade.[19] The anti-opium group gained the support of the Emperor, and in 1838 Lin Tse-hsu, Governor-General of Hupeh and Hunan, was appointed High Commissioner and ordered to go to Canton to investigate the opium traffic, and to take what action he thought necessary to abolish it.[20]

This strong anti-opium policy can be looked at in at least two ways. Opium smoking can hardly be interpreted as anything but detrimental to the welfare of the Chinese. From this point of view, complete prohibition was much needed. On the other hand, the legalization of the opium trade might have proved itself a shrewd move in terms of China's relations with the West.

Before the importation of opium was outlawed in 1800, Sino-British trade, was, for the most part, a stable process. The great majority of the trade was conducted between two monopolies, the Cohong and the British East India Company. Because it had almost a complete monopoly over the opium trade, the British East India Company could afford to cater to what demands the Chinese made upon it, and was usually inclined to do so rather than endanger its position. After the importation of opium was outlawed, however, the Company was forced to compete with other British interests in smuggling, and, though technically it still had a monopoly over British trade with China, in actuality its share of the China trade was decreasing. This is hinted at

43 k

[19]Kuo, pp. 56-57.
[20]Waley, pp. 12-14.

by the fact that, while in 1830-31 the Company exported $1,910,936 out of a total $6,595,306 in silver bullion which left China, in 1833-34 it exported only $155,030 out of a total of $6,217,820 in silver.[21] In 1834 the British East India Company's charter expired, and Parliament, considering it ". . . expedient for the objects of trade, and amicable intercourse with the dominions of the Emperor of China . . .", opened China trade to all British subjects, under the supervision of the Superintendents of British Trade in China, headed by Lord William John Napier.[22]

The presence of individual British traders in China had several implications. First it meant competition. Private traders, because they were in competition with each other, could not afford to be as acquiescent to Chinese wishes as the British East India Company had been. Second, the British policy toward trade with China could not be as uniform and as well-defined as it had been before. Third, the British government became obligated, to some extent, to protect its subjects in China, though they might have violated Chinese customs or laws. All of these contributed to the tensions which resulted in the Opium War. Had the opium trade been legalized, though, it might well have been "expedient for the objects of trade" for Parliament to reestablish the monopoly, and consequently the relative stability of the Company-Cohong relationship. In addition, if it could be made profitable to obey the Chinese import laws, the Chinese government could at least keep a close watch on the trade, if not completely control it.

But the monopoly was not reestablished, and the above-board trade was not encouraged. On March 18, 1839, Lin Tse-hsu ordered the complete surrender of the

43
k

[21]Kuo, p. 36.
[22]Ibid., pp. 15-16.

Lib

opium held by traders at Canton. Initially, 1,037 chests were offered. But this was a relatively small part of the opium held in Canton by the merchants, and did not satisfy Lin. The following day he asked that Lancelot Dent, one of the more prominent British opium traders, come with him into the city of Canton to serve as a hostage until the surrender of the opium had been made in full. The British merchants refused to surrender him. Meanwhile, the British Trade Superintendent, Captain Charles Elliot, came to Canton from Macao to give Dent official protection. Lin charged that Elliot had failed to regulate the British merchants properly, and ordered troops to surround the foreign compound, completely cutting off communication between Chinese and Westerners. The isolation was enforced until Captain Elliot eventually promised to surrender 20,283 chests of opium to the Chinese. After it had been surrendered, the opium was destroyed and washed out to sea.[23]

British feeling was very strong against the Chinese actions, especially Lin's. One account of life in China at the time of the Opium War begins, "The harsh and unwarrantable measures of the Chinese Commissioner Lin, the imprisonment of Her Majesty's Plenipotentiary and all other English subjects, and his [Lin's] wild career of uncontrolled violence, called imperatively on our part for stronger measures than had yet been resorted to. . . ."[24] This tension was increased because of the

[23]Ibid., pp. 103-110.
[24]W. D. Bernard, and W. H. Hall, The Nemesis in China, 3rd ed. (London, 1846), p. 1.

43
k

Note 23: This footnote, coming at the end of the paragraph, indicates that all the information for the paragraph has come from Kuo, pp. 103-110.

Note 24: The four dots of ellipsis here indicate omitted material at the end of the sentence. The omitted material con-

murder of a Chinese villager, Lin Wei-hsi, by a group of drunken British and American sailors on July 7, 1839. To placate the Chinese, who demanded the murderer and wished to punish him by their laws, Elliot held a trial; suspects were tried and given various sentences, but they were set free in England on the grounds that Elliot had exceeded his authority. Other violent incidents occurred, and Lin, suspecting that the British had designs on the Portuguese island of Macao, had at about this time ordered all British subjects to leave Macao. The evacuation was carried out and Lin refused to allow the British return until the murderer of Lin Wei-hsi was delivered to the Chinese and the British consented to an inspection of all merchant ships.[25]

At this time, though, the British warship Volage arrived from India. Shortly after the arrival of the Volage, the first shot of the Opium War was fired on September 4, 1839.[26]

Over the years, each side believed its course of action was just and that the other side was wrong. China was hurt because of its ignorance of the British. MacNair says, "Although the Chinese could not cope with the English, as had been proven time and again, they were nevertheless unceasingly hostile. Overweening pride in the past blinded them to their present weakness."[27] It was this pride, this refusal to see that the Middle Kingdom was not the only civilized country,

[25]Chang, pp. 196-201.
[26]Ibid., p. 202.
[27]MacNair, p. 147.

cerns the resolution of the East India Company and the British government to protect British citizens and obtain reparation for damages. But since the writer's purpose is to convey the intensity of British feeling against Lin, the latter part of the sentence is unnecessary.

43
k

Lib

that led to much of the conflict between the Chinese and the West. The Emperor's refusal to deal with foreigners on a direct basis led to a naive idea of the British. Chu-Tsun, in his memorial to the Emperor, had said of the British that "In introducing opium into this country, their purpose has been to weaken and enfeeble the Central Empire."[28] Even Lin, who later came to inform himself far more about the English than most of his educated countrymen did, began by reminding the English that it was special kindness on China's part to allow any trade, since China was entirely self-sufficient whereas foreigners could not survive without Chinese tea and rhubarb.[29]

In addition to creating a naive attitude on the part of the Chinese, the policy of isolation served to irritate the British. They were confined in one section of Canton. Their only contact with the Chinese was through the Hong merchants. Any attempt which they made to establish lasting diplomatic contact was thwarted. They failed to understand the Chinese tribute system—the ritual of going to the Chinese court to pay tribute to the Emperor and to acknowledge his benevolence in allowing the benefits of Chinese culture to be shared by the barbarians.[30] Unaccustomed to the Chinese tribute system and bent on expanding markets and profit, the British persisted in their efforts to gain direct diplomatic representation in the Chinese court, though it might well have been to their advantage at the time to abide by the customs of the tribute system. In his instructions to Lord Napier in 1834, Lord Palmerston, the British Foreign Secretary, said that Napier's duty was the "protecting and fostering the trade of His Majesty's subjects with

[28]Ibid., p. 101.
[29]Waley, p. 33.
[30]John K. Fairbank, The United States and China, rev. ed. (Cambridge, Mass., 1958), pp. 116-117.

the port of Canton" and that "the establishment of direct communications with the imperial court at Peking would be desirable. . . ."[31] Hosea Ballou Morse, a well-known scholar, has pointed out.

The chief superintendent was instructed that every effort was to be made to conform to all Chinese regulations and to consider all Chinese prejudices, and yet he was required to adopt a course which would convert him from a mere superintendent of trade into a royal envoy, and would break every Chinese regulation and offend every Chinese prejudice.[32]

Western exploration for new markets and Western commitment to free trade collided with a huge land whose history and philosophy had never made it aware of the meaning of the word "competition." Like the writer for Blackwood's, the English came to believe that if commerce with the Chinese is to be carried on, "it must be, it can only be, upon covenants fresh drawn, consented, signed, and sealed, and lastly ratified with salvoes of British thunder."[33] But, as one historian concludes, "Unfortunately for the repute of private enterprise in the Orient, it reached the China coast at this time chiefly in the form of the opium trade conducted by private traders. This historical circumstance has poisoned Sino-Western relations ever since."[34] The cultural conflict which led to the Opium War and opened China to the West has not yet ended.

[31]MacNair, p. 68.
[32]Ibid.
[33]"War with China," 384.
[34]Fairbank, pp. 118-119.

Note 34: The paper might have ended with the quotation from Fairbank, but it is stronger for ending with the writer's own summary.

Lib

List of Works Consulted

Bernard, W. D., and W. H. Hall. The Nemesis in China. 3rd ed. London, 1846.

Chang, Hsin-pao. Commissioner Lin and the Opium War. Harvard East Asian Series, 18. Cambridge, Mass., 1964.

Fairbank, John K. The United States and China. Rev. ed. Cambridge, Mass., 1958.

———, and S. Y. Têng. "On the Ch'ing Tributary System," Harvard Journal of Asiatic Studies, VI (June 1941), 135-247.

Kuo, P. C. A Critical Study of the First Anglo-Chinese War. Shanghai, 1935.

Li Chien-nung. The Political History of China: 1820-1928, trans. S. Y. Teng and Jeremy Ingalls. Princeton, N.J. 1956.

MacNair, Harley Farnsworth. Modern Chinese History: Selected Readings. Shanghai, 1923.

Michie, Alexander. The Englishman in China. Vol. 1. Edinburgh., 1900.

Mu Fu-sheng. The Wilting of the Hundred Flowers. New York, 1963.

Stelle, Charles C. "American Trade in Opium to China, 1821-39," Pacific Historical Review, X (March 1941), 57-75.

Waley, Arthur. The Opium War Through Chinese Eyes. London, 1958.

"War with China, and the Opium Question," Blackwood's Edinburgh Magazine, XLVII (March 1840), 368-384.

**43
k**

44
correspondence

A letter is equivalent to paying a call in person. Just as in a personal interview, your dress, manners, and attitude speak for you and make an impression, so in a letter, the appearance, form and tone speak for you and make an impression. No matter how persuasive and forcible the content of your letter may be, a poor first impression caused by carelessness in form, mechanics, or pompousness of tone will be hard to overcome.

Attention to form, style, and tone is particularly important in a business letter. Personal letters—those written to friends and intimates—should be easy and natural. No hard and fast rules for personal letters can be prescribed beyond those that are applicable to every kind of good writing. Business letters, on the other hand, should follow strictly conventional forms. They should be courteous and direct in tone, without being stiff or abrupt. Conspicuous familiarity or jocularity is as much out of place as back-slapping or elbow-nudging would be in a personal call. Business letters should be concise and to the point. Wordiness in such a letter is just as annoying as long-windedness in conversation.

44 a
business letters

Business letters should be written on one side only of bond paper, 8½ x 11 inches in size, and of good quality. If possible, they should be typewritten, single-spaced, with double-spacing between paragraphs.

The sample letters which follow illustrate correct block style business forms, chosen because of efficiency and ease for both writer and receiver. (Indented style is described in 44a-1.)

date	April 4, 1965
heading	Hal Levering 336 San Jose Avenue Claremont, California 91711
inside address	Allied Radio Corporation 100 North Western Avenue Chicago, Illinois 60680
salutation	Dear Sirs:
body	I would like to build a Hi-Fi-stereo amplifier. Do you stock any kits which are easily assembled? I am not experienced and cannot spend more than fifty dollars. Please send information regarding specifications and prices. I am also interested to know how such kits compare in quality and price to ready-made amplifiers and will appreciate your help.
close	Sincerely yours,
signature	/s/ Hal Levering Hal Levering

44
a

*printed
letterhead*

ALLIED ELECTRONICS CORPORATION
100 North Western Avenue   Chicago, Illinois 60680

date

April 14, 1965

*inside
address*

Mr. Hal Levering
336 San Jose Avenue
Claremont, California 91711

salutation

Dear Mr. Levering:

body

We do stock several stereo Hi-Fi amplifier kits. A simple one for less than $50 is a Knight KG-250. It costs $39.95 plus $4.95 for a metal case, or $9.95 for a case of oiled walnut. Here are some of its specifications:

Rated Output Power: 24 watts IHF, 48 watts
Response: —db. 30-15,000 cps
Distortion: below 15%

The kit includes equalized preamps for magnetic cartridges and separate bass and treble controls.

There are several other kits and a number of factory assembled amplifiers you may wish to compare in price and quality. A catalogue has been mailed to you from our Pasadena, California outlet.

close

Sincerely,

signature

/s/Ted Starr
EDWARD L. STARR

*initials
(signer
and typist)*

Sales Department

ELS:ade

44

a

44 a-1
the heading

The heading gives the date and full address of the writer, in that order. Avoid abbreviations. On the first page, type the date at the left, flush with the margin. Drop three or four lines. Then type the heading on the left side, flush with the margin of the page. Indented style, with date and address in reverse order at center or right, is passing out of business writing, since the block style is easier to read and to type.

BLOCK STYLE HEADING: June 23, 1966
[3 or 4 lines]
117 East Seventh Street
Claremont, California 91711

Notice that the date is punctuated in the usual manner. In the address, city and state are divided by a comma. The zip code number is separated from the state by two spaces.

44 a-2
the inside address

The inside address should contain the name and the full postal address of the person written to. It should be placed at the left-hand side of the page, flush with the margin and at least three or four lines below the heading. Avoid the use of abbreviations; the names of firms, however, should be written exactly as they appear on the letterhead of the firm. The zip code follows the state. Abbreviate only the following titles: Mr., Esq., Messrs., Mrs., Mmes., Dr., Rev., Hon. The proper titles to be used in addressing high officials and dignitaries may be found in a current almanac.

CORRECT   Gaertner Scientific Corporation
1201 Wrightwood Avenue
Chicago, Illinois 60614

CORRECT Dr. E. A. Herman
     415 Cobb Building
     Seattle, Washington 98105

CORRECT Mr. Allen Workman
     D. C. Heath and Company
     285 Columbus Avenue
     Boston 16, Massachusetts 02116

44 a-3
the salutation

The salutation should be written flush with the left-hand margin, two spaces below the inside address. In formal business letters it is followed by a colon. The following salutations are used when the name of the person addressed is not known, or when a personal tone is not appropriate. Many dictionaries have a section listing proper forms of address for officials and dignitaries (see also section 37f).

CORRECT Dear Sir:
"My dear Sir" is more formal; "Sir" is extremely formal.
     Gentlemen:
     Ladies:
"Mesdames" is correct, but old fashioned.

When a person is addressed by name, the following salutations are used:

CORRECT Dear Mr. (or Mrs.) Ball:
     Dear Dr. Kraft:
     Dear Professor Hogarth:

When the sex of the person addressed is not known, the masculine salutation is conventional. When the marital status of a woman addressed is not known, use Dear Miss ———— (see section 44a-6).

44
a-3

44 a-4
the body

The body of the letter begins two lines below the salutation. Paragraphing may follow either the block style (see sample letter, 44a, pg. 588) or the indented block style (see sample letter, 44a, pg. 589). Typewritten letters are usually single-spaced, with doublespacing between paragraphs. The length of the letter determines the width of the margins, and may also determine how you space breaks between date, heading, and inside address. Try to center the letter attractively on the page. In a short letter, use double-spacing if necessary.

Say what you mean in ordinary, idiomatic English. Insure clarity by using short direct sentences whenever a lump of detail or explanation would cause confusion. Do not omit pronouns, articles, or prepositions, and avoid trite formulas:

POMPOUS AND OLD-FASHIONED   Yours of the 17th at hand, and in reply would beg to state. . . . Will try to carry out instructions in same. . . . Please find enclosed check for three dollars.

IMPROVED   I thank you for your letter of April 17th. . . . I will try to carry out your instructions. . . . A check for three dollars is enclosed.

44 a-5
the complimentary close

The complimentary close should be written two lines below the last line of the body of the letter. It should begin flush with the left-hand margin and should be followed by a comma. Only the first word is capitalized.

The complimentary close, like the salutation, should be appropriate to the person or persons addressed and to the tone of the letter.

44
a-4

IMPERSONAL	Sincerely yours, Sincerely,
	Yours truly,
	Very truly yours,
	Yours very truly,
FORMAL	Very respectfully yours,
	Yours respectfully,
	Respectfully yours,
	Used in letters to persons of superior rank
INFORMAL	Sincerely yours, Sincerely,
	Cordially yours, Cordially,
	Yours sincerely,

44 a-6
the signature

The signature is placed below the complimentary close. It is always written by hand. In a typewritten letter, the writer's name should be typed underneath the written signature. When typing, allow four lines for the written signature between the closing and the typed name. Type the full name entirely in capital letters, or in capital and lower case letters. Begin flush with the left margin. (This allows the writer to sign less formally without blurring his identity.)

A married woman should sign, not her husband's name preceded by *Mrs.*, but her own married name. To aid correct reply, it is current convention to sign the writer's name preceded by Mrs. or Miss without using parentheses. When the writer's full name with Mrs. or Miss is typed, the handwritten signature may be less formal.

CORRECT	Sincerely,
	/s/ Mrs. Mary W. Hoffman or
	/s/ Mary Hoffman
	(Mrs.) Mary Williams Hoffman
CORRECT	Very truly yours,
	/s/ Mary Williams Hoffman
	(Mrs.) John R. Hoffman

**44
a-6**

44 b
mechanical directions

Envelopes should match the paper in color and quality, and should hold the paper easily when it is properly folded. For a business letter written on sheets of full commercial size (approximately 8½ x 11 inches) use either of the following:

1. *an envelope of commercial size (approximately 3½ x 6½ inches)*

Fold the letter so that the result is about ⅓ inch less than an exact half. The horizontal crease will be ⅓ inch below the center. Then fold the half-sheet into nearly three equal sections. (If a letter is folded exactly, it may be difficult to open.)

2. *an envelope of official size (approximately 4 x 10 inches)*

Fold the letter from bottom and top into three sections, almost equal.

44 c
addressing the envelope

The form of the address on the envelope may be exactly the same as that of the inside address. The Postal Department requests that the state *not* be abbreviated unless the zip code is on the envelope. Though the Postal Service is satisfied with city, state, and zip code all on one line, postal workers who sort the mail find it quicker if the zip code (and state) are each on separate lines.

The complete return address should be placed on the front of the envelope in the upper left-hand corner.

44
b

index

For a listing of diction problems with certain individual words and expressions not indexed here, consult chapter 14, Glossary of Words Commonly Misused.

singular pronoun with, 412

Apostrophe, **31:** 471–473; ex. 474
in contractions, 471, **31b:** 473
misused with personal pronouns, 472
in plural of letters and numerals, **31c:** 473
in plural of a word considered *as a word,* 473
with possessive case, **31a:** 471–473

Appear, as linking verb, 352, 388

Apposition, 383

Appositive phrase, **17c:** 357
correction of, 368

Appositives
abbreviated titles or degrees as, 451
in compound constructions, 417
dashes with, 478
defined, 383
intensive pronouns as, 392, 397
nonrestrictive, punctuation of, 450, 478
with *or,* punctuation of, 451
restrictive, commas omitted with, 450–451

Archaic words, defined, 263

Argument(s)
analogies in, 74–76
analysis of structure of, **3c:** 53–57
assumptions, 54–56, 58–59, 63
evidence, 53–57
fact and judgment, 59–64
faulty reasoning, **3b-3:** 66–73; ex. 77–79
final conclusion, 54–57
generalization, 54, 66–71
inference, 53–58
key assumptions, **3b-1:** 58; ex. 58–59
premise, 53–57
validity of, **3b:** 57–79

Articles
defined, 383
repetition of, for parallelism, 191
in titles, 527

As, case of pronoun following, **24d:** 420–421
in comparisons, incorrect omission of, 226

As if or *as though,* subjunctive after, 436

As well as, and agreement of verb and subject, 404

Assertive function of sentence ele-

ment, 345–346, 348

Assumptions, in argument, 54–58, 63
defending, 58
key, **3b-1:** 58; ex. 58–59, 86–88

Astronomical names, capitalization of, 515

Atlases and gazetteers (list), 538

Author, form for citing
in bibliographies, 570–571
in footnotes, 566–568

Author cards, in library file, 533–534

Auxiliary verb
defined, 121, 383
incorrect omission of, 224–225
position of subject with, 349

Avoiding the question, in argument, 76–77
ad hominem argument, 76–77
begging the question, 76
straw man, 77

Awkward repetition, **13e:** 291–292. *See also* Repetition.

Awkward split constructions, **8d-4:** 213–214

Bad, badly, 425–426

Balanced sentences, 234–235

Basic principle of good usage, 262

Be, as linking verb, 352, 388
nominative case with forms of, 419
objective case with infinitive, 420

Become, as linking verb, 352, 388

Begging the question, in argument, 76

Beginning the paper, 24–26

Besides, conjunctive adverb, 378
punctuation with, 378

Biblical references, colon in, 476

Bibliographies
abbreviations in, 522
cards for, **43d:** 554–556
form for, 570–572
information to be included in, 554–556
preparation of final, **43:** 570–572
preparation of working, 553–554
punctuation of, 476, 567–569
sample entries for, 568–569
specialized, 554

Block style for letters, 588, 590, 592

Body of letters, **44a-4:** 592
faults to avoid in, 587, 592

Both . . . and, 388
parallelism with, 191–192

acknowledgments

Grateful acknowledgment is made to authors and publishers of the following works for permission to use these selections as illustrative material:

FREDERICK LEWIS ALLEN, from *Only Yesterday,* pp. 134–135 (Perennial Ed., Harper & Row, 1964). Copyright 1931 by Frederick Lewis Allen. Reprinted by permission of the publishers.

NELS ANDERSON, from *The Hobo,* a Phoenix Book. Copyright 1923 by the University of Chicago Press. Reprinted by permission of the publisher.

E. N. DA C. ANDRADE, from *An Approach to Modern Physics.* Copyright © 1956 by E. N. da C. Andrade. Originally published in England by G. Bell & Sons, Ltd. Reprinted by permission of Doubleday & Company, Inc. and G. Bell & Sons, Ltd.

LINCOLN BARNETT, from *The Universe and Dr. Einstein.* Copyright 1948 by Harper & Brothers, and copyright 1948 by Lincoln Barnett. Reprinted by permission of William Sloan Associates and Victor Gollancz, Ltd.

CARL L. BECKER, from *The Heavenly City of the Eighteenth Century Philosophers.* Copyright 1932 by Yale University Press. Reprinted by permission of the publisher.

SYBILLE BEDFORD, from *The Faces of Justice.* Copyright 1961 by Sybille Bedford. Reprinted by permission of Simon and Schuster, Inc. and William Collins Sons & Company Ltd., publishers.

RANDOLPH BOURNE, from *History of a Literary Radical.* Copyright 1920 by B. W. Huebsch, Inc., 1948 by The Viking Press, Inc. Reprinted by permission of The Viking Press, Inc.

RACHEL L. CARSON, from *The Sea Around Us.* Copyright 1951 by Rachel L. Carson. Reprinted by permission of Oxford University Press.

RACHEL L. CARSON, from *Silent Spring.* Copyright 1962 by Rachel L. Carson. Reprinted by permission of Houghton Mifflin Company.

ELEANOR CLARK, from *The Oysters of Locmariaguer.* Copyright 1964 by Eleanor Clark. Reprinted by permission of Pantheon Books, a Division of Random House, Inc.

WALTER VAN TILBURG CLARK, from *The Ox-Bow Incident,* pp. 51–52. Copyright 1940 by Walter Van Tilburg Clark. Reprinted by permission of Random House, Inc. and Associated Book Publishers Ltd.

AARON COPELAND, from *What To Listen For In Music* by Aaron Copeland. Rev. Ed., Copyright © 1957 by McGraw-Hill, Inc. Used by permission of McGraw-Hill Book Company.

RENÉ DUBOS, from *The Dreams of Reason,* pp. 72–73. Copyright 1961 by Columbia University Press, New York. Reprinted by permission of the publisher.

E. M. FORSTER, from *Aspects of the Novel.* Copyright 1931 by Harcourt Brace & Company. Reprinted by permission of Harcourt, Brace & World, Inc. and Edward Arnold Ltd., publishers.

FUNK & WAGNALLS, from *Funk & Wagnalls Standard ® College Dictionary.* Copyright 1966 by Funk & Wagnalls, A Division of Reader's Digest Books, Inc.

PAUL GOODMAN, from *Growing Up Absurd,* Copyright 1960 by Random House, Inc.

Ab	incorrect **abbreviation** 39
Adj	wrong form of **adjective** 25a, c
Adv	wrong form of **adverb** 25b
Agr	error in **agreement** 23
'/apos	improper use of **apostrophe** 31
Ca	error in **case** 24
Cap	faulty **capitalization** 37
:/colon	improper use of **colon** 32
,/com	improper use of, or missing, **comma** 28
Const	**incomplete construction**; see Scoh 8g
CS	**comma splice** or **fused sentence** error 21
D	faulty **diction**; see Dict, Use, exD, Id, efD, Fig, Rep, gl 10-1⁴
—/dash	improper use of **dash** 33
Def	see *definitions of grammatical terms* 22
Dev	faulty **paragraph development**: check methods; revis⁴ see ¶ Dev 6
Dict	consult the **dictionary**; learn its proper use; see D 10
Dng	**dangling modifier**; see Scoh 8c
efD	use more **effective diction**: avoid clichés, technical term⁴ pretentiousness 13
exD	use more **exact diction**: avoid abstractions, jargon, vagu⁴ and inappropriate words 12
Fig	revise mixed **figures** of speech; replace worn allusions; s⁴ efD 13d
Frag	correct **sentence fragments** 20
gl	see *glossary of words commonly misused* 14
Id	improper use of **idiom**; see exD 12e
K	**awkward**; recast the sentence, phrase, or clause
Log	faulty **logic**: check structure and validity of argument 3
Mix	revise **mixed construction**; see Scoh 8f
MM	**misplaced modifier**; see Scoh 8d
Ms	improper **manuscript** preparation 36
Num	write **number**; spell out number; inconsistent use of nu⁴ bers 38

1c	re-organize your material; see Plan	**Org**
27-34	punctuation error	**P**
27	end punctuation error	**P/./?/!**
27a	improper use of period	**P/.**
27b	improper use of question mark	**P/?**
27c	improper use of exclamation	**P/!**
5	faulty paragraph coherence	**¶ Coh**
6	poor paragraph development	**¶ Dev**
4	faulty paragraph unity	**¶ U**
1	rethink the purpose and plan of your writing project	**Plan**
30	improper use of quotation marks	**''/quot**
8b	faulty reference of pronouns; see Scoh	**Ref**
13e	awkward repetition; see D/efD	**Rep**
7-9,	poor sentence structure; see SU, Sub, Scoh, ||, Ref,	**S**
16-22	Dng, MM, Shift, Mix, Const, Emp, w, Frag, CS, Def	
8	poor sentence coherence	**Scoh**
29	improper use of semicolon	**;/semi**
9	poor sentence emphasis	**S/Emp**
8e	confusing shift of voice, subject, person, number, mood, tense; see Scoh	**Shift**
35, 41	spelling error	**Sp**
7	faulty sentence unity	**SU**
7b	faulty or excessive subordination; illogical coordination	**Sub**
41	syllabication error	**Syl**
26	wrong tense or mode of verb	**T**
4b	weak or missing topic sentence; see ¶ U	**topic S**
4, 7	faulty paragraph or sentence unity	**U**
1-14	wrong level of usage; see glossary of words commonly misused	**Use**
9b, c	wordy sentence or construction; see S/Emp	**w**
10-14	wrong word; see D	**WW**
8a	error in parallelism; see Scoh	**||**
34	improper use of parentheses or brackets	**()/[ ]**
	word omission	**∧**

27
Sept 69

Robert
Yannaccone
601 a 204

rm 6 4 3 - mom.